THIS IS THE PLATE

THIS IS THE PLATE

UTAH FOOD TRADITIONS

EDITED BY

CAROL A. EDISON • ERIC A. ELIASON • LYNNE S. MCNEILL

THE UNIVERSITY OF UTAH PRESS
SALT LAKE CITY

The publisher gratefully acknowledges the following organizations for their generous support of *This Is the Plate*:

The Charles Redd Center for Western Studies at Brigham Young University, 2020 Publication Grant

The Utah State Historical Society

 The Defiance House Man colophon is a registered trademark of the University of Utah Press. It is based on a four-foot-tall Ancient Puebloan pictograph (late PIII) near Glen Canyon, Utah.

Library of Congress Cataloging-in-Publication Data
Names: Edison, Carol A., editor. | Eliason, Eric A.
  editor. | McNeill, Lynne S., editor.
Title: This is the plate : Utah food traditions / edited by Carol A.
  Edison, Eric A.Eliason, Lynne S. McNeill.
Description: Salt Lake City : University of Utah Press, [2020] | Includes
  bibliographical references and index. |
Identifiers: LCCN 2019040631 (print) | LCCN 2019040632 (ebook) | ISBN
  9781607817406 (paperback) | ISBN 9781607817413 (ebook)
Subjects: LCSH: Food habits--Utah. | Food--Religious aspects--Church of
  Jesus Christ of Latter-day Saints.
Classification: LCC GT2853.U5 T47 2020 (print) | LCC GT2853.U5 (ebook) |
  DDC 394.1/209792--dc23
LC record available at https://lccn.loc.gov/2019040631
LC ebook record available at https://lccn.loc.gov/2019040632

Cover photo by Shannon Hall.

Frontispiece: Salt water taffy puller in the window of Druehl and Franklin Druggists, Salt Lake City, 1910. Shipler Commercial Photographers Collection. Used by permission, Utah State Historical Society. All rights reserved.

Errata and further information on this and other titles are available online at UofUpress.com

Printed and bound in the United States of America.

DEDICATION

*This book is dedicated to William A. "Bert" Wilson
who, with kindness, respect, and generosity of spirit, nurtured unequaled
camaraderie among Utah's academic and public-sector folklorists.*

CONTENTS

ACKNOWLEDGMENTS

The editors wish to thank John Alley and Glenda Cotter, our editors at University of Utah Press. John caught the vision of this project from the beginning and expertly shepherded it toward publication before his retirement. Glenda saw the project to completion with keen insight into issues we might face and how to address them. We also wish to thank the BYU Faculty Editing Service for invaluable help in organizing and formatting our manuscript for publication—Suzy Bills and her student editors, Hayley Brooks Cousin, Emily Strong, Nicole Umphress, Kaitlyn Brown, and Heather Randall.

INTRODUCTION: EAT, DRINK, AND BE MERRY, FOR TOMORROW YOU MAY BE IN UTAH

The Unlikely Foodways of the Beehive State

LYNNE S. MCNEILL

EXPECTATIONS VS. REALITY

Utah is not a place many outsiders associate with fine cuisine—or with any cuisine at all. When it comes to drafting a culinary map of the United States, the regional cuisines that stand out to nonlocals are quite well known: cheesesteaks in Philly, wings in Buffalo, barbecue in the South, lobster in Maine, chowder in New England, chilis in New Mexico, and so on. What food does the country associate with Utah? When the eyes of the world turned to Utah for the 2002 Winter Olympics in Salt Lake City, visitors and viewers were treated to a crash course in local foodways, learning about such staples as fry sauce, funeral potatoes, and, of course, green Jell-O, the importance of which cannot be overstated in a discussion of Utah food culture. In fact, many of the Olympic pins available throughout the event depicted these and other iconic Utah foods.

Scarlett Lindeman, writing for *The Atlantic*, explains that when she first moved to Utah as a high-school student, she quickly learned about the local love of Jell-O:

> Home economics was my first class. My teacher, who had an incredible ability to hide and forget multiple pencils in her stiff purple bouffant, stood in front of the class, introduced herself, and with a wide smile began the semester with this question: "Now, how many of your mothers have more than five recipes for Jell-O?" Almost everyone in the class raised their hands. "Now," she said, "tell me, how many of your mothers have more than 10 recipes for

A popular Utah souvenir, on display in Bryce Canyon, Utah. Photo by Lynne S. McNeill, 2018.

inspired by its pioneer history, its diverse ethnic and cultural history, and its varied landscape and climate, Utah is a hive (pun definitely intended) of edible wonders waiting to be discovered. This book you have in your hands is intended to educate, inform, and inspire both locals and visitors alike to delve deeper into the unexpectedly rich history and culture of food in the Beehive State.

FOODWAYS AS AN ASPECT OF REGIONAL CULTURE

Understanding a place through its food is a wonderful (and tasty) endeavor. Everyone knows that people in different places eat different things, and the tie between location and food is so strong that we sometimes find ourselves defining others by their dominant food cultures (in both complimentary and insulting ways). Discovering culinary diversity through travel is an end in itself, for the simple enjoyment of new dishes and flavors, but there are also deeper things to be understood through the cultural study of food. "Foodways" is the term scholars use to designate the culture of food, acknowledging that food culture goes far beyond the physical manifestation of the food itself. The symbolic weight of procuring (whether from nature or from a megastore), preparing (whether from scratch or from a box), serving (whether in a restaurant or at home), and consuming (whether alone or with others, one's own cooking or another's, in a formal setting or on the fly) an intentional construction of material, texture, flavor, temperature, color, aroma, and taste cannot be overstated. As M. F. K. Fisher put it, "Our three basic needs, for food and security and love, are

Jell-O?" I could hear the soft scrape of rising fabric behind me. Many of my classmates kept their hands high. Her excitement increased. "How many of your mothers have more than 15 recipes for Jell-O?" Her eyes gleamed and her smile widened at the response. "Twenty?" I turned around, and at least six or seven classmates with Jell-O–obsessed mothers beamed back.[1]

Add to this the common reputation that Utah is also entirely nonalcoholic and decaffeinated, and you've got a recipe for a foodie desert (hence the popular slogan featured at the beginning that adorns souvenirs in tourist shops).

The reality behind the reputation, however, couldn't be more different. Bringing together foods so mixed and mingled and entwined that we cannot straightly think of one without the others."[2] Food *is* security; food *is* love. The need for sustenance is a primal drive, but the diverse ways different people in different places have developed to meet that need reveal much about the people themselves as well as their relationships to their environment and to each other. Eating may not seem like such a big deal— we do it every day—but the fact that the substances we put into our bodies are often realized through a combination of social, environmental, geographical, economic, and even emotional factors means that food is one predominant way we embody our cultural contexts.

The contributors to this book represent diverse backgrounds, occupations, and interests, but the main thread of shared disciplinary focus is Folklore Studies. Like many other kinds of scholars, folklorists study people and their cultures, but with a unique focus on everyday life—the things so common, so familiar, that they are often overlooked by other disciplines that are more interested in broad systems of governance, kinship, demographics, or economy. Folklorists prefer a smaller scale, a microlevel cultural analysis that considers seriously the experiences and understandings of everyday people. When it comes to food, every culture and region has various institutional levels of influence: imports and exports, restrictions and guidelines, supermarkets and warehouses, farms and factories. But there is also the daily, lived experience of eating, which is stunningly rich with cultural processes and meanings, even when the food involved is as basic as a cheeseburger. It's tempting to think of "traditional" or "culturally representative" foods as old, exotic, or rare,

but the folklorist's perspective reminds us that much of our most robust cultural engagement happens in mundane, familiar settings. Whether we're making a Sunday dinner roast the way our great-grandparents did or ordering a thick shake at Arctic Circle before heading to the lake, we're behaving within a complex set of cultural expectations and beliefs. As folklorist Roger Abrahams explains, it is on the small-scale level of ongoing personal choice that we bring our cultural expectations to bear on our food:

> A central feature of this process is the dynamic of making choices, especially as such decisions draw upon symbolically—rather than nutritionally—coded edibles. Here I refer not only to what foodstuffs are chosen and how they are prepared, but also how many distinct foods are served and in what combinations and quantity; under what conditions they are eaten, with whom, and on what occasion; and what is the received way of bringing the food to the mouth, the etiquette of eating under those circumstances. An analysis of Americans eating at this level would be concerned with, for instance, the distinction between "meal" and "snack," the number and size of "courses," "dishes" within each course, and "helpings" of those dishes.[3]

Not many of us pause to consider when we learned the "right way" to bring food to our mouths, nor the difference between a "snack" and a "meal," but these are shared cultural norms that reflect our expectations and highlight cultural differences when we travel or share food with people from different backgrounds. We could easily, at any moment,

3

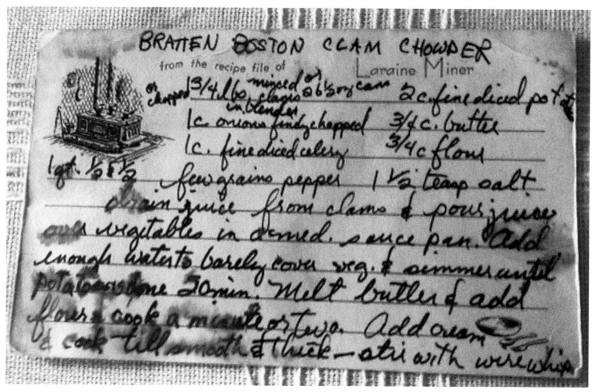

A well-loved family recipe card for Bratten's Clam Chowder. Courtesy Laraine Miner, 2015.

choose to cook and eat differently, and yet many of us tend to stay with the patterns our cultures present for us, even as we explore other options and arenas. Barbara and James Shortridge point out the ease with which we can inject innovation into our eating patterns:

> You can experiment in public by ordering a new item off a restaurant menu. In the privacy of your own home, you can add unfamiliar ingredients to familiar soups or casseroles or put together an Ethiopian dinner from a new recipe book. By temporarily changing diets in such ways and trying out varied tastes, new dishes eventually come into our personal foods inventory. Modern Americans have no lifelong commitment to a cuisine comparable to that which may bind us to a given religion or language.[4]

And yet regional cultural patterns persist, and they persist for a reason. Traditional patterns allow individuals to innovate within a framework that is recognizable and acceptable to their peers. For instance, putting your own twist on funeral potatoes is a way to both adhere to communal expectations of what the "right" food to bring to an event is (surprisingly not often a funeral, in the case of funeral potatoes) and to express your own creativity and culinary ability.

Part of this creative ability is the constant exchange that exists between people and the restaurants they regularly visit. Talking about food as culture, especially as everyday culture, doesn't exclude the experiences of dining out; the two modes of eating are often inextricable. Many "local" recipes are adapted from established restaurants in the area. For example, in Utah, many families have their own Bratten's clam chowder recipe, a favorite dish from Bratten's Grotto, a popular Salt Lake City fish restaurant that closed in the 1980s. Rather than treating the restaurant's original recipe as the "right" way to make the chowder, we see the power of individual tastes and creativities influencing the dish. Bratten's clam chowder recipes are included in many family recipe books, appearing right alongside the recipes passed down from grandparents and great-grandparents.

This fusion of mass-marketed culture and folk culture isn't new. The commodification (or rather, the *de*-commodification) of commercial food products is a common practice, paralleling the adoption of local foodways by many local restaurants and highlighting the fusion of community and individual food experiences into a coherent, albeit diverse, sense of regional foodways.

EDITORS AND CONTRIBUTORS

This volume began its life in the foodie haven that is the Black Sheep Café in Provo, Utah, a contemporary southwestern Native American restaurant.

While enjoying artfully reimagined local dishes like green chile frites and gourmet Navajo tacos, folklorist Eric Eliason sought collaborators for a project he envisioned as a reader for students on the subject of Utah foodways. Folklorists Carol Edison and Lynne McNeill accepted the challenge, and a challenge it indeed turned out to be. The initial idea of an academic reader quickly expanded—the editors realized that a true introduction to Utah food culture would mean various sections on a number of topics that might not be included in a traditional collection of academic essays: regional specialties like Dixie Salad and Sanpete Turkey, noncommercial foods like those acquired through foraging or gardening, and the small-in-numbers but big-in-impact presence of ethnic groups from around the world. And how could we leave out the recipes? Readers learning about these wonderful Utah foods should have the opportunity to make and sample them as well! The project grew into the book you have in your hands: a mix of academic writing, journalism, and memoir—along with a few great recipes—that we feel truly reflects the diversity and scope of foodways in Utah.

As editors, Eric, Carol, and Lynne represent a varied portrait of contemporary Utah culture. Eric grew up Mormon, but outside Utah, as an Air Force brat. He's lived the latter half of his life, however, in the most Mormon part of the world, Utah County, where he has raised his children and works as a professor at BYU. He says he has "always loved Utah with the kind of insider/outsider curiosity of a born Mormon but a zealous convert Utahn." As a respected scholar of Mormon studies as well as folklore, Eric is well positioned to see Utah culture from both emic and etic perspectives. He describes one of his first encounters with Utah foodways:

When I was a freshman at BYU in 1986, I had my first exposure to that icon of Utah culture—fry sauce. This was a godsend since I don't much like ketchup, but I do like sauce for my fries. It did not occur to me that fry sauce was a local specialty. Perhaps in my obliviousness, I did not imagine Utah capable of such a thing. I assumed fry sauce was a new nationwide trend that just so happened to hit Utah at about the time I went to college. So, when I went to visit my parents in Denver—which is hardly far away from a continental perspective—I asked an unsuspecting burger joint cashier for fry sauce. With a confused look on her face, she asked, "Do you mean ketchup?" I was puzzled by her ignorance and repeated what I wanted: "No, I mean fry sauce." She stood there dumbfounded, failing to provide fry sauce, so I asked for some mayonnaise, which the cashier thought was odd (but which was foreshadowed by my LDS missionary experience in the Netherlands and Belgium, where mayonnaise is exactly what people put on fries). Thus began my realization and appreciation of Utah's unique cultural developments, especially its food. Later in graduate school, I was studying in the University of Texas library and was approached by a timid fellow student, seemingly from another country by her accent, who apparently had an assignment to conduct some interviews for a sociology class or something like that. With no introduction or context provided, she asked if there was any food I ate

because of my religious identity. I thought for a second then answered, "Green Jell-O salad with shredded carrots." Maybe thinking I was teasing her or not taking her project seriously, she said thank you and hurried away without asking any follow-up questions or giving me the chance to elaborate. This book, in a way, is that long-over-due elaboration. I hope she is out there some-where and finds it.[5]

Carol grew up in Utah during the 1950s and 1960s, in a Mormon family that has handcart pioneer ancestors on both sides. As such, she grew up eating many traditional Utah foods and engaging in food-related customs like having Sunday roast beef dinners, bottling fruit and chili sauce every fall, and, of course, eating Jell-O. Carol's insider status allows her to both see and comprehend the nuances of Utah foodways as only a native can, observing trends and customs over time. Though she is currently retired, her work as the director of the Folk Arts Program for the Utah Arts Council has enhanced her ability to turn a critical eye to the everyday culture of food in her home state, highlighting how distinctive foods are necessary to the cultural survival of families, tribes, religious groups, occupational groups, and ethnic groups. As she explains,

Sometime in the '80s, after I began working as a public-sector folklorist, I started hearing about something called "funeral potatoes." When a colleague made them for a staff party, they seemed much more tasty than the scalloped potatoes I'd eaten with ham many times at post-funeral Relief Society luncheons. I guess that making those potatoes really "yummy" (as one circulating recipe called them) was one of the benefits of the growing self-awareness and pride among Utah Mormons of their own cultural markers. My own awareness grew when a colleague in the folklore world told me that she had grown to love fry sauce while doing field work in Utah and was sorry it wasn't available elsewhere. What a shock! It had never occurred to me that the dipping sauce we made by blending catsup and mayo with a packet of special seasonings, at my first paying job at the neighborhood Arctic Circle, wasn't something found everywhere.

My adventures in Utah foodways continued throughout my career as the state folklorist; I had the opportunity to interview wonderful craftspeople, performers, storytellers, local historians, and cooks from every cultural community. I learned about traditions, both large and small, from Grouse Creek chili sauce and Dixie salad to pit-roasted lamb and Dutch-oven cooking. It was more than a pleasure to watch talented cooks make Navajo fry bread, Greek baklava (using homemade filo dough so fine that it had to be draped over pillows to dry), or Tex-Mex style breakfast burritos filled with bacon, eggs, potatoes, and a dash of hot sauce. Prickly pear jelly, parched corn, and molasses (sorghum) candy were featured at the Southern Utah Folklife Festival, my very first public-sector project, while my last project, the Living Traditions Festival, featured an explosion of local ethnic foods including Tongan otai, Vietnamese egg rolls, Salvadoran pupusas, and Bosnian cevapi—to name just a few—all made by ethnic clubs in Salt Lake City as a way of sharing their rich heritage with other Utahns. Hopefully this publication reinforces the importance of both those traditions we share as Utahns and those we maintain as part of various folk groups—the mix of culinary magic that will always help define us as a people.[6]

Lynne, like Eric, moved to Utah for school, to earn an MA in folklore at Utah State University. Not being Mormon, she approached the dominant religious culture of Utah with a folklorist's curiosity, grateful to friends and colleagues who could explain the unique customs and terminologies that locals found so familiar. A native of northern California, Lynne initially brought with her some of the various prejudices that Californians tend to have about all other places in the country (prejudices that have led more than one Utahn to sport a bumper sticker stating, "Don't Californicate Utah!"). As she explains,

In my first year of living in Utah, a friend from home visited and we went out to a local Italian restaurant. When she admired the floridly described menu offering of cannelloni but commented only, "If I weren't in Utah, I'd order it!" I nodded sagely in dispirited camaraderie. I just assumed that I was now in the land of flyover cuisine, doomed to subpar meals out and discouraging wine lists. Luckily, I've changed a lot since then (and so has Utah, for that matter). I've moved to Utah three times now—I just can't seem to stay away—and it's now as much my home as California. I scoff appropriately at restaurants that don't serve fry sauce, I spend my autumns canning fruits and vegetables from my home garden, I carry meals over to new neighbors and new parents, and I prefer my funeral potatoes with corn flakes on top, thank you very much. I also enjoy the thriving beer and wine scene that's been galloping ahead ever since the Olympics came to town and gave the imbibers of Utah their first taste of in-state beer advertising—the first time that many non-LDS Utahns felt their interests (not to mention their buying power) were being acknowledged by the state.

It wasn't until I moved to Utah that food (and the related subjects of gardening and canning) became a passion for me. I grew up in a family that "prepared food" more than "cooked," and I always viewed true cooking with a mixture of awe and suspicion—it was something others did, from which I benefited, to be sure, but which appeared to require an innate skillset that I didn't possess. Slowly but surely, however, Utah's genial emphasis on agriculture, food security, locavorism, and a growing appreciation for the gourmet and inventive have swayed me. When I call home to tell my mom about my latest adventures in wood-fired pizza making or preserving, she asks what's become of me. I'll have to give her this book to explain it all.[7]

As your guides through the deep waters of Utah food culture, we hope that our assorted perspectives will help bring out the multivalent nature of eating, cooking, and sharing food and drink. Of course, we're not your only guides in this volume. This book also, wonderfully, brings together an incredible team of folklorists, historians, writers, journalists, students, teachers, arts coordinators, and foodies to help us encompass and describe the diverse nature of Utah foodways.

ORGANIZATION

This book is organized into five sections: official and iconic state foods, heritage, Mormon influence, local specialties, and contemporary foodways. The entries you'll read are as diverse as the contributors. Some will be extremely short, perhaps no more than a captioned photo and a paragraph or two explaining a particular Utah food, such as Hotel Utah hard rolls or Casper's ice cream. Some entries will be longer, scholarly considerations of certain aspects of regional foodways, such as Randy Williams's piece on food storage or Brock Cheney's essay on pioneer foods. Some will be personal reflections on family traditions or personal experiences, like Jean Irwin's artful description of the Nikkei Senior Center luncheons; some will be informative reports on the state of various foods and production methods, such as Lisa Duskin-Goede's exploration of fishing for sport and sustenance, or Sally Rampe's description of salt production. Some will be analytical or interpretive essays, considering things like the cultural impact of certain ethnic groups on state cuisine, while others will be more descriptive, informing readers of the history of various foods and foodways. The goal of this varied formatting is to offer readers both a crash course in the basics of local foods (you can't read a whole book on Utah foodways and come away without knowing what fry sauce is!) and a deeper, more analytical consideration of some of the implications and meanings of these foods and foodways (you probably don't need a fifteen-page analysis of fry sauce, but other topics may merit that depth).

It is, of course, impossible to discuss Utah culture without touching on the influence of the Church of Jesus Christ of Latter-day Saints (Mormons), and this book definitely reflects that dominant cultural presence, though readers will discover a wide range of other influences as well. Utah is at the center of the Mormon Corridor, the stretch of the western United States in which Mormon pioneers settled and established communities (also known as the Jell-O Belt). All cultures need their vices, and while the LDS religion eschews alcohol and many forms of caffeine (though you'll find chapters on both in this volume, indicating they're not as absent as might be expected), there's at least one "bad" food that's decidedly oh-so-good to most Utahns: sugar. The importance of sweetness in Utah—whether in mixed sodas, locally made ice creams, homemade preserves, or fresh honey—is undeniable. Sugar indulgence has shaped the palate of the state, encouraging a slightly different dominant flavor-profile than in other areas. The bitterness of beer and coffee, which shapes so many adult palates, is less familiar in Utah; bitter foods have similarly been slow to be embraced, and while foodies are working hard to popularize a more varied range of tastes, it's common to find sweet ingredients added to dishes that are savory in other regions (marshmallow fluff in chicken salad is one example that stands out).

Mormon families are also typically large, and thus Utah cooking has long been assumed to have a quantity-over-quality focus. As this volume makes clear, however, the cultural scene of Utah foodways is not that simple. Both in spite of and because of its predominant religious influence, Utah has a surprisingly varied food culture, driven by Mormon and non-Mormon forces alike. Much of Utah's commercial and homebrew alcohol production, for example, exists in response to the Mormon Church's restrictions on alcohol consumption, but it often manifests as an appropriation of that very restrictive culture rather than as a rejection of it. In contrast, the Soda Wars, a statewide conflict between purveyors of mixed soda-based beverages, highlights the proprietary sense that many Utahns have about their own appropriation of non-Mormon beverage culture: The vernacular terminology of cocktail mixing and espresso bars is applied in "mocktail" concoctions like the "Dirty Dr. Pepper" (a Dr. Pepper with a shot of coconut syrup), which several competing businesses have attempted to trademark.

When Brigham Young arrived in Utah with the first Mormon pioneers, he declared, "This is the place." We hope that your culinary adventures in the state lead you to a similar conclusion; Utah is most definitely the place for some of the most creative and tasty gastronomic experiences you can have. It is our hope that you find this book an enjoyable collection of information, anecdotes, history, and culture. Whether you're a native Utahn or a visitor to our ski slopes, waterways, and national parks, a student of Utah history and culture or simply interested in the history of fry sauce, this volume has something for you. We hope you enjoy this taste of Utah.

NOTES

1. Scarlett Lindeman, "Jell-O Love: A Guide to Mormon Cuisine," *The Atlantic*, March 24, 2010.

2. M. F. K. Fisher, *The Gastronomical Me* (New York: MacMillan, 1989 [1943]), ix.

3. Roger Abrahams, "Equal Opportunity Eating: A Structural Excursus on Things of the Mouth," in *Ethnic and Regional Foodways in the United States: The Performance of Group Identity*, ed. Linda Keller Brown and Kay Mussell (Knoxville: University of Tennessee Press, 1984), 20.

4. Barbara G. Shortridge and James R. Shortridge, "Food and American Culture," in *The Taste of American Place: A Reader on Regional and Ethnic Foods*, ed. Barbara G. Shortridge and James R. Shortridge (New York: Rowman & Littlefield, 1999), 3.

5. Eric Eliason, in discussion with the author, January 2017.

6. Carol Edison, in discussion with the author, January 2017.

7. Lynne McNeill, in discussion with co-editors, January 2017.

PART I OFFICIAL FOODS / ICONS

2

UTAH'S ICONIC FOODS

ERIC A. ELIASON

Utah has an identity problem.

Many states have rich and unique histories. So does Utah—arguably the most unique of any of the fifty states. This is not the problem. In other states, these histories are relatively accessible by any citizen regardless of religious persuasion or lack thereof. But in Utah, unless one identifies as a believer in the Church of Jesus Christ of Latter-day Saints, state history with its heroic handcart pioneers, dominant founder Brigham Young, and insular Kingdom-of-God-building, can seem "definitely not me" to the large minority of multigenerational Utahns whose "gentile" ancestors have been here just as long as Mormons. Likewise, most active Latter-day Saints, proud Utahns though they might be, likely see their Mormon identity—part of a worldwide religious community—as much more important to them than their Utah identity. Also, many Mormons, maybe even especially active Mormons, are uncomfortable with what historians call the "Utah period" of Mormon history, with its still-popular pioneering settlers, but also patriarchal polygamy, government-run theocratic economics, and extreme state of tension with the rest of America.

What is poor Utah to do? Eat food, that's what. With common historical touchstones in short supply and many cultural and social mores as dividers rather than unifiers, food is emerging as our common ground. It doesn't matter whether you are ultra-, jack-, non-, or even anti-Mormon. By eating fry sauce and Jell-O (or any of the other iconic Utah foods this section addresses), you can participate in Utah's shared identity. Heck, you don't even need to *like* fry sauce or Jell-O, just agree that these are—love 'em or hate 'em—nondenominational symbols of Utahness. In this we are unified. Take religion off the table and put some food on it.

The need for shared identity touchstones may explain why so many Utah foods are just that: Utahn. There are regional foods around the country: southwestern Hispanic-influenced burritos and enchiladas; New England clam chowder; Southern catfish, collard greens, and grits. These food traditions span many states. Certain cities also have well-established identity foods: San Francisco's sourdough bread, Boston's baked beans and cream pies, Philadelphia's cheesesteak sandwiches. Don't get a New Yorker and a Chicagoan arguing about the correct way to prepare a hot dog or make pizza! And these are just famous big-city examples. In a few counties in northern Indiana, fast-food joints will offer a chili-like sauce called "Spanish" for hot dogs, or a "dog with Spanish" instead of a chilidog.[1] Hundreds of similar examples could be given from numerous localities across the country.

There are, of course, a few widely familiar state foods, such as Maine lobster and Idaho potatoes. However, these tend to be singular, and we usually think of them in terms of production rather than consumption. For consumption, Idaho has the "Idaho Spud" candy bar and Maine has the Moxie[2] brand soft drink. If you have never heard of these, you probably aren't an Idahoan or a Mainiac (that's not a rude epithet for "Mainer," just a common optional local term). In these states, potatoes and lobsters are often seen as iconic food designations made by outsiders. A few states, like Louisiana and New Mexico, have whole cuisines—interconnected sets of dishes and ingredients that are distinct from those used in other states. It probably goes too far to say that Utah's multiple iconic food items form a cuisine, but, for sheer number and distinctiveness, Utah's iconic foods are pretty impressive and do credit to the culinary creativity of our state. The following section presents essays on specific Utah iconic food items. They are arranged roughly in order of how well known they are.

Liquor may be a surprising first chapter, but it is appropriate on a number of levels. We are not a dry state, as the rumor often goes among would-be visitors. There are dry counties throughout the United

The ultimate Utah foods meal, including a pastrami burger, fries with two different kinds of fry sauce, scones with honey butter, and an over-the-top jumbleberry shake, as created by the artists at Barry's Parkview Drive Inn in Spanish Fork, Utah. Photo by Eric A. Eliason, 2018.

States, but notably none in Utah. However, no state has a statewide liquor control regime as pervasive and restrictive as Utah's. It has led to such distinctive and ironic institutions as the "state liquor store," where the very government that wants to restrict your hard spirits intake has made itself their only legal purveyor. "Since we don't believe in it, we'll be the only ones to sell it, thank you very much." You can buy beer at supermarkets throughout the state, except for on Sunday, a recent change in a few counties. The details may be fuzzy in people's minds, but the general gist of Utah's alcohol distinctiveness is better known throughout the country than even our Jell-O and fry sauce.

Alcohol is not only noteworthy by its relative absence in Utah, but also because of a brewery and winery tradition that goes back to pioneer days when Mormons took the Word of Wisdom, the dietary

A sign inside Hires Big H Drive-In in Salt Lake City proclaims fry sauce "a Utah tradition," while their website says that their house-made sauce "sets the standard with a delicious blend of secret ingredients." Photo by Carol A. Edison, 2017.

code LDS Church members follow, more according to its original delivery—"not by commandment or constraint"[3]—rather than its later temperance-era teetotalling interpretation. Today Utah is home to a disproportionate number of award-winning microbreweries that seem unable to resist the temptation to reference the dominant state culture in their brand marketing. How about Wasatch Brewery's "Polygamy Porter" or Squatter's Craft Beers' "Outer Darkness" Russian Imperial Stout (named after an LDS sobriquet for hell)?

Ask Utahns about iconic state foods, and Jell-O and fry sauce will most likely stand out as answers; funeral potatoes follow close behind. Some items, like pastrami burgers, may have a dubious claim to Utah uniqueness or origins. Perhaps they are really a Rocky Mountain or even a nationwide phenomenon. But it is the perception and belief that makes something an identity icon. While it is perhaps not as high profile, or with as solid of a uniqueness claim, as fry sauce or even scones, the pastrami burger may be an emergent, or contender, icon. In the case of "Utah thick shakes," many, if not most, Utahns are not even aware yet that these are distinctive. The awareness resides most with visitors or one-time residents who've moved away. Some icons like salt and honey (from the beehive state!) seem like they would be obvious Utah food icons, but they are less developed in our state consciousness than one might think; they are, however, developed enough to be worth mentioning here. Saltwater taffy is the highest-profile common Utah food item to reference the state's most famous ingredient.

Most of the icons in this section are both commercial and traditional. You're likely to encounter them at a restaurant and supermarket, as well as find Utahns making them at home according to traditional family recipes and their own culinary creativity. Perhaps the most concentrated convergence of Utah iconic foods can be found at locally owned and operated burger joints. For example, Barry's Parkview Drive Inn in Spanish Fork serves thick shakes, pastrami burgers, hot buttered scones with powdered sugar, and two varieties of fry sauce, traditional pink and Barry's own special white sauce.[4]

It may surprise many readers that fry sauce is not just a Utah burger joint thing but is also a traditional sauce made at home. Google "fry sauce" and the myriad of blogs, recipes, and personal reminiscences about making one's own fry sauce will attest to this, as will the variety of homebrewed fry sauces that appears at Utah food competitions like the one held at Thanksgiving Point in Lehi. Conversely, funeral potatoes and scones may seem the quintessential homemade Utah dishes for family and church functions, but they can sometimes be found on the menu of Utah homestyle restaurants.

Another surprise when considering all the icons together is the Midwest connection to several of them. Variants of funeral potatoes, usually known by other names, exist throughout the church potluck culture of many states—especially the Midwest. Utah's thick shakes seem to have their origin in technological developments and menu item ideas that began in Illinois—but more than one hundred years after Mormons left Nauvoo.

Utah is the world center for Dutch-oven cooking with much manufacturing located in the state. With the highest percentage of its population participating, whether as scouts or as leaders, in Boy Scouts of any state, Dutch-oven cooking is the quintessential Utah "guy food." Its roots go back to pioneer cooking and is often part of Mormons' "trek" tradition—where young men and women reenact crossing the plains in handcarts. Perhaps this is why, in 1997, Utah designated the cast-iron Dutch oven as the "State Cooking Pot."[5]

Top-down official foods and bottom-up popular cuisine may often be different things but sometimes overlap considerably. Utah's "State Historic Vegetable,"[6] the sugar beet, was historically important as an export crop, but has little if any presence in Utah grocery stores and on Utah tables. Jell-O was and remains popular both before and after the state legislature decreed it a "favorite snack of Utah."[7]

Indicators of what makes a place distinctive are often not found so much at its most developed heart but are set in relief in the stark contrasts found at its edges. There are many things that the Utah/Nevada border divides. There may be no more dramatic line between legal permissiveness and prohibition regarding prostitution, gambling, and alcohol anywhere else in the country. But according to legend, one burger-joint owner on the Nevada side of the twin border town of Wendover had some other shibboleth in mind when he posted a large sign in his window saying: "THIS IS NEVADA! NO, WE DON'T HAVE FRY SAUCE!" So sad for a state to define itself by what it lacks. Better to be in Utah.

NOTES

1. Becky Mercuri, *The Great American Hot Dog Book: Recipes and Side Dishes from Across America* (Layton, UT: Gibbs Smith, 2007), 94; Luke Leger, "B&K

Spanish Sauce," *latent chestnut* (blog), July 16, 2010, http://latentchestnut.blogspot.com/2010/07/b-spanish-sauce.html.

2. Peter Muise, "Moxie, Maine, and Moxie Flavored Cupcakes," *New England Folklore* (blog), July 27, 2014, http://newenglandfolklore.blogspot.com/2014/07/moxie-maine-and-moxie-flavored-cupcakes.html.

3. Doctrine and Covenants 89:2.

4. http://www.barrysdriveinn.com/.

5. "State Cooking Pot, H.B. 203," http://www.le.state.ut.us/~1997/bills/hbillint/HB0203.htm.

6. "State Vegetable and Historic State Vegetable, H.B. 136," http://le.utah.gov/~2002/bills/static/SB0136.html.

7. "Resolution Urging Jell-O© Recognition, S.R. 5," http://www.le.state.ut.us/~2001/bills/sbillenr/sr0005.htm.

3

NO HAPPY HOUR FOR HAPPY VALLEY

The Push and Pull of Alcohol in the Beehive State

LYNNE S. MCNEILL

They [the Mormons] have fought a terrible battle for temperance in Utah, forsooth! The Legislature of Utah has been unanimously Mormon since it first convened, a third of a century ago. There never was a day when it was in session upon which it could not have passed a prohibitory liquor law.
—O. J. Hollister, 1884

Travelers and superficial observers have frequently asserted the existence among the Mormon people of a great abhorrence to the liquor traffic, and that Mormon communities were without saloons, until brought in by gentiles. So often have such mis-statements been repeated, that they have, in some quarters, almost come to be accepted as established facts.
—Theodore Schroeder, 1908

As residents of Utah look longingly at the new freedoms of Eastern Europeans, we are reminded of the ever-suffocating bonds of state control over Utah's liquor industry, with its ever-increasing list of do's and don'ts and exceptions to this or that . . . its "only if the moon is full and the Great Salt Lake is at low tide can you sell that kind of liquor during daylight savings time."
—Tom Barberi, 1990

For some reason, it is a common misperception that Utah is a "dry" (alcohol forbidden) state. This is simply not true.
—TripAdvisor, 2012[1]

Photograph of Becker Brewing employees sitting outside the main office, Ogden, Utah. The brewery opened there in 1892. Courtesy Special Collections & Archives, Merrill-Cazier Library, Utah State University.

HISTORY

The more things change, the more they stay the same. From 1884 until as recently as 2012, there has been a misconception that you can't get a drink in Utah. The history of Utah is full of misunderstandings, hearsay, and general confusion about the nature of alcoholic beverage production and consumption in the state. Visitors to Utah—from before the birth of the state to the present day—have often heard through rumor, legend, or the personal experiences of previous visitors about the trials and tribulations of imbibers in the Beehive State. There is a pervasive popular perception in our national folk culture that Utah is the driest state in the nation, totally

prohibiting alcohol, or, when it emerges more mildly, that the drinks that are available in Utah are either depressingly weak or almost impossible to obtain. The fact that the reality is quite divergent from this perception makes the longstanding popularity of this rumor an interesting cultural study; a major part of Utah's state identity is forged through its contentious relationship with alcohol.

Despite popular assumption, at no point in Utah's history (aside from the period of federal prohibition and Utah's state prohibition which began two years prior) has alcohol ever been outlawed. Breweries, distilleries, and wineries, both publicly and privately operated, were common in the late 1800s, beginning during the initial settlement of the state by Mormon pioneers. This, of course, is the source of most people's confusion. The Church of Jesus Christ of Latter-day Saints, the church of the majority of Utah's early settlers and politicians, explicitly forbids the consumption of alcohol. It strikes many people as logical that alcohol would have been forbidden in a Mormon-run state, but the reality is more complex.

The first commercial brewery in Utah, the California Brewery, was opened by a German immigrant in 1864. As the railroad grew toward its east-west meeting point at Promontory Point, bringing in more non-Mormon settlers, small-scale production grew quickly. The LDS Church even got in on the action: The Mormon-owned Utah Brewery opened in 1871 and thrived for almost fifty years, right up until Prohibition.

The state even had its own proprietary whiskey, the purportedly powerful Valley Tan (a.k.a. leopard sweat, liquid strychnine, and tarantula juice),[2] which caught Mark Twain's attention in 1872. He described it as a "Mormon invention...made of (imported) fire and brimstone." (He also described Salt Lake City as "a land of enchantment, and goblins, and awful mystery," though he did later note how pleasant it was to have "no visible drunkards" on the streets.)[3] Should contemporary visitors feel nostalgic for this heyday of Mormon liquor production, Park City's High West distillery has brought Valley Tan back—reviewers at *The Whiskey Jug* describe it as "fruity with notes of blueberries and apricots followed by notes of vanilla, grains, spice, Juicy Fruit gum and saw dust. Not wickedly complex but nice in its own weird way."[4] (Some might say that last part could apply to Utah as a whole.)

Far from being an underground operation among a religious population of teetotalers, the liquor trade was a thriving component of the business of the Utah Territory among Mormons and non-Mormons alike. In 1873 the territorial legislature actually granted Brigham Young, LDS Church president and leader of the Mormon pioneers, the exclusive rights to the manufacturing and distribution of hard liquor in Utah. While Young himself didn't approve of the consumption of alcohol (his own son-in-law described him as hating "intemperance and its evils" and wishing "that all the whiskey that the Gentiles brought had been so filled with poison as to have killed all who drank it"),[5] he did have solid business sense. Sale and taxation of alcohol drew in huge revenues for the new territory.

By 1875, German immigrant Jacob Moritz's Salt Lake City Brewery was one of the largest breweries in the West and was shortly joined by Fisher and Becker breweries. In 1890 the population of Salt Lake City had grown so large that the bottling laws were amended to allow breweries to bottle their beer in separate buildings for the sake of increasing production.

Making beer was clearly a popular and desirable business; in Manti, Utah, home of the third completed Mormon temple in the state, the local newspaper wrote in 1893 that

> the Manti Brewery is a sign that should adorn a large building near this city.... It would bring more people, more money, and more trade to this city. It would cause more land to be more thoroughly cultivated and would be of more benefit to Manti than any manufacturing plant that could now be established. We hope to soon see some enterprising men at work on this project.[6]

Right up through the drafting of Utah's state constitution, the production and consumption of alcohol was common and protected; the LDS Church president at the time even argued *against* some of his fellow Mormons that Utah must not become a dry state, as the goal was not to create a theocracy. Of course, as the nationwide temperance movement grew in power, Utah was an easy state to sway. In 1911, eight years before federal Prohibition, several cities in Utah had gone dry, and in 1917, the Twelfth Session of the Utah legislature voted to make Utah a completely dry state. The nation followed suit two years later.

Interestingly, two of the bigger breweries in the state, Salt Lake City Brewing and Becker Brewing, attempted to stay open by changing their names and brewing nonalcoholic beverages. Nearing the end of

Prohibition, voters in Utah, by a 2-1 majority in a special off-year election, chose to allow the sale of 3.2 (percentage of alcohol by weight) beer, now known in Utah and elsewhere as "near beer." Again, the nation followed and the Twenty-First Amendment, repealing Prohibition, passed just months later.

Unfortunately, the repeal of Prohibition kicked off a downturn for Utah's alcohol industry. Breweries began closing down, and for almost two decades no beer was bottled in the state. It wasn't until the late 1980s that the scene began to pick up again.

Today, there are over twenty breweries, wineries, and distilleries in the state. The push and pull between alcohol production and consumption in Utah hasn't changed, and today's issues highlight both the similarities and the differences in Utah's alcohol culture of the past and the present.

THE MORMON QUESTION

As is probably clear by now, it's impossible to talk about alcohol in Utah without talking about the Mormon Church, and this is often at the heart of complaints and confusion about drinking in Utah. The connection goes beyond politics and religion, however; the dominant religion of Utah has an enormous influence on the culture of the state, regardless of individual religious affiliation. There is sometimes a perception of Mormon hypocrisy among drinkers in the state—Mormons don't drink but are largely in control of how alcohol is sold, distributed, and consumed. The state-run liquor stores, managed by a committee mostly made up of nondrinkers, are the only outlets for any alcoholic beverage other than "near beer." Nondrinkers' assumptions about the nature of

drinking culture rankle imbibers, and drinkers can easily feel targeted by people they perceive to be morally judging them (people who, many point out, don't have an understanding or appreciation of the product they're controlling). This perception is aptly summed up by journalist and historian Will Bagley, who describes the members of Utah's Department of Alcoholic Beverage Control as "a hardy band of mostly teetotaling busybodies determining what, where, how and when sinners can get a drink."[7]

This question of moral judgment is complicated by the fact that strict adherence to the Word of Wisdom, the section of the Mormon Doctrine & Covenants that details restrictions on food and drink, wasn't required until 1921. Earlier, it seems that it was drunkenness, not moderate imbibing, that was discouraged. Beer isn't mentioned at all—only wine (approved, if homemade, for sacramental use) and "strong drink"—and there are several other proscriptions that are not held to (nor written into state law) with the same ferocity (such as avoiding meat except in times of cold or famine). Add to this ambiguity the reality of Mormon-owned distilleries and saloons from the inception of the state. Stories of Joseph Smith running a saloon remain as popular today as they were in 1848. Add also the prominent ads for alcoholic beverages in early editions of the LDS-owned *Deseret News*, while local beer merchants in more recent times were forbidden to advertise their products, resulting in some clever ads, such as one SLC convenience store that advertised its "COLD BEE?" (displayed on the storefront). Given this historical perspective, the moral judgment many drinkers in the Beehive State feel from their nondrinking peers starts to seem overdone.

But just how overdone *are* Utah's liquor restrictions? It's true that there are many states with restrictive liquor laws, some even more restrictive than Utah's. But Utah's restrictive liquor laws seem to be unique in some ways, as they are regularly a popular subject for news features. As Fox News reported in 2013:

> Utah is by no means the nation's only place with strict regulations of getting a drink. Dry counties scatter the country and the US Department of Treasury categorizes 18 states as "control" states, meaning in places like West Virginia, for instance, when you buy a bottle of liquor, the state is the wholesaler. But no state seems to take alcohol control to the level that Utah does. Some business owners, residents and politicians in Utah agree with visitors who say it's downright weird.[8]

That seems to be the word for it: "weird." More than excessive or negative, the emphasis is usually on the perceived illogic of many of the regulations. While there are definitely many untrue rumors about the extremity of Utah's alcohol restrictions (the most common being that the state simply bans all alcohol), the actual regulations are in fact intriguingly specific, and impact visitors and residents alike:

> I was waiting in a hotel lobby near the SLC airport, and I thought I'd just get a beer while I waited. The poor woman working behind the counter explained to me (like she had no doubt explained to hundreds of out-of-staters) that I had to purchase some food with my alcohol. Me:

Moshen Asgari, right, supervises the removal of the "Zion curtain" from the bar at his Vuda Bar and Winery in Draper. A bill was introduced in the 2017 legislative session that would get rid of the barriers and make other changes to Utah's liquor law. Photo by Paul Fraughton. Courtesy *Salt Lake Tribune*.

> "But I just ate....I don't want any more food." Woman: "*sigh* The least expensive item on our menu is a cupcake. Would you like that?" Me: "Okay....I'll order a cupcake with my beer." Woman: "Would you like the cupcake to go?"[9]

The above scenario demonstrates the rule that in a restaurant (which has a specific type of liquor license) alcohol can't be ordered without food. Some establishments will say that a first drink can't be ordered without the *intent* to dine (so that one might order a drink, decide nothing looks good on the food menu, and then leave, but they would be denied a second drink until ordering food).[10] The explanation above also illustrates one of the common realities of this rule—that getting around it is both easy and pointless. Minimal food can be sold, and that food can even be packaged to go, so that the regulation can be met without the patron being required to eat the food on site.[11]

But that's not the only quirky rule concerning alcohol served in restaurants.

At the [restaurant], we were sitting at the bar and ordered some drinks. The bartender made our drinks right in front of us, but instead of handing them to us, she had to walk around the bar to our side to give them to us. She explained that Utah law forbade her to slide the drinks over the bar, since we were in a "restaurant," and not a "bar."[12]

This is one manifestation of the infamous "Zion Curtain"—the conceptual or physical barrier between the making of drinks and the people ordering them. Typically, a restaurant with a bar is required to hide bottles of alcohol and the mixing of drinks from diners so that diners aren't tempted (nor children intrigued) by the creation of drinks. Things get tricky when the various types of licenses get into the mix. Taverns and restaurants that sell only 3.2 beer aren't required to have a divider, and many old restaurants were grandfathered in without one. Perhaps more significant than the awkwardness of the barrier is the implication for drinkers that nondrinkers need to be shielded from their chosen beverages and the scandalous act of making them. A proposed bill to eliminate the Zion Curtain, supported by the Utah legislature, was voted down in the senate in 2013, highlighting

that these ideas aren't simply archaic holdovers from a bygone era. The curtain finally fell in 2017.

But the challenge is still present. It's still not smooth sailing for drinkers in Utah. Here are two more examples.

We ordered a pitcher of half and half to have with our pizza. The server didn't know what it was. We told her just make the pitcher half light beer and half dark beer. She proudly brought out two pitchers: one half full of dark beer and the other half full of light beer.[13]

I ask my server for a mimosa. He looks at me quizzically and asks me what that is. I describe it and he gets visibly upset and says he's got to get the manager. Manager comes out and chews me out for ordering an alcoholic beverage before noon.[14]

Stories like these don't so much target a specific rule as highlight a pervasive theme in the vernacular representation of Utah's alcohol culture. The perception is that the people serving drinks in Utah are both uninformed and judgmental about the alcoholic beverages and the people who order them. Additional common tropes are that servers don't know which wines or beers to recommend with food (having never tasted them), and don't know how quickly a given patron might become inebriated (many stories circulate about well-meaning but patronizing servers asking diners if they need to have a cab called after just one drink).

Cultural perceptions go the other way, too, and

many Mormons play with drinking culture the same way that non-Mormons play with Mormon culture. One popular LDS custom is the hosting of dressy "mocktail" parties that put nonalcoholic mixed drinks in fancy glasses. On a more questionable note, some young Utahns will host "white trash" parties, where guests drink root beer out of bottles that look like beer bottles. At these events young women will often dress immodestly and emphasize (real or fake) pregnancies while drinking their "beer," and men will wear wife-beaters (cotton tank-top–style under-shirts) and cut their hair into mullets. It's a display that supports the exoteric way many drinkers in the state suspect that nondrinkers perceive them. Not all engagement with alcohol is playful, either. Many ex-Mormons see their first alcoholic drinks as a serious rite of passage, an act that visibly and socially confirms a shift in status.[15]

It's not all strife and conflict, of course. "Weird" can easily be positively spun into "quirky," and it seems like the opportunity for a unique cultural relationship to alcohol is appealing to many drinkers and producers in the state. The folk culture of Utah's drinkers, from slang to customary celebrations to homebrew, revels in the appropriation of Mormon culture. Terms like "near beer" and "Zion Curtain" quickly become familiar to visitors who frequent bars and restaurants, but more local traditions, like the annual "Pie and Beer Day" (a play on the Mormon "Pioneer Day" celebration of July 24) are well known among locals. Many restaurants that typically take a proalcohol stance for sales and gustatory purposes will host Pie and Beer Day celebrations, serving everything from traditional fruit pies to pizza pies with their favorite brews.

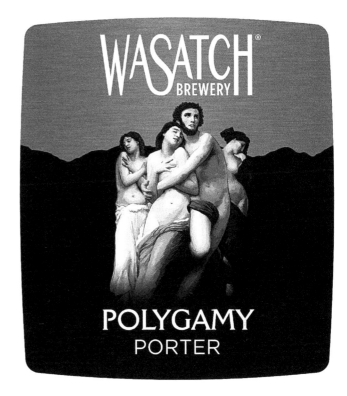

Wasatch Brewery's most recent label for their famous Polygamy Porter. Other label designs have featured the tag lines "Bring some home for the wives!" and "Why have just one?" Courtesy Wasatch Brewery.

Many of Utah's most popular commercial beers have names that play with Mormon ideas and concepts. Squatters' "Outer Darkness," an Imperial Stout, is a reference to the LDS version of Hell, while Wasatch Brewery's "Polygamy Porter" suggests that patrons "take some home to the wives." More general references to more liberal themes, in opposition to the predominantly conservative Mormon population, are also common. The label of Wasatch Brewery's pale ale "Live and Let Live" supports same-sex marriage by featuring an ambiguously gendered couple riding a chairlift together.[16] The beer features a blend of two different malts and two different hops, and as the makers explain,

> We realize this beer is not for everyone, and we will not force it on those who prefer more traditional brew styles. These pairings are not the norm in Utah right now and we expect resistance from many. However, we are confident that in the near future Utah will look back and wonder why they didn't embrace and celebrate *Live and Let Live's* natural combinations. They will also realize that *Live and Let Live* is not a threat to traditional beers.[17]

And it's not all politics and religion, either. Many of the state-produced alcohols reference other aspects of Utah culture such as the incredible natural landscapes and outdoor activities the state offers (such as Uinta Brewing's Cutthroat pale ale, a reference to a local trout, and their Yardsale winter lager, a reference to spectacular falls on the slopes), or the history and monuments of the state (two being Uinta's Golden Spike Hefeweizen and Epic Brewing's Spiral Jetty). Given that a recent report reveals that a majority of Utahns support the privatization of liquor sales in the state, perhaps the emphasis on the great drinking divide is itself becoming something of a traditional trope more than the reality.

CONCLUSION

While it would be easy to write off alcohol culture in Utah as simply reactionary, it seems more accurate to describe it as an embrace of the other. Drinkers in Utah are a distinct counterculture, a population that seeks ways to distinguish itself from the dominant culture of the state. But that distinction often takes the form of appropriation and transformation; non-Mormons find a way to make the dominant culture of Utah a part of their own culture as well, but with a twist. The strange rules and regulations, the contradiction inherent in who makes the laws and who is bound by them, the perplexing history that seems to fly in the face of common perceptions of Utah—all these things give alcohol culture in Utah its own unique identity. It turns out that drinkers in Utah share more than expected with the Mormon pioneers who settled the territory in 1847: surviving in inhospitable climes, proud of their minority status, and creating a vibrant food and drink scene in the barren desert. Utahns are Utahns, it seems, whichever path they choose.

NOTES

1. For these quotes, please see the following: http://utahgentiles.com/gentiles/Hollister/Hollister-news1.htm; "Mormonism and Intoxicants," *American Historical Magazine* 3 (1908): 240; Tom Barberi, *Legalizing Adulthood in Utah* (Salt Lake City: Aspen West Publishing, 1991); and "Utah: Only in Utah," TripAdvisor, https://www.tripadvisor.com/Travel-g28965-c62071/Utah:United-States:Only.In.Utah.html.
2. Win Blevins, *Dictionary of the American West* (Kingston, Ontario: WordWorx Publishing, 2015), 189.
3. Mark Twain, *Roughing It* (Hartford: American Publishing, 1872), 108–9.
4. Josh Peters, "High West Valley Tan Review," last modified January 12, 2015, http://thewhiskeyjug.com/oat-whiskey/high-west-valley-tan-review/.

5. Del Vance, *Beer in the Beehive*, 2nd ed. (Salt Lake: Dream Garden Press, 2008), 28.

6. Ibid., 31.

7. Will Bagley, "Early Utah Saw No Evil in Liquor Ads," *Salt Lake Tribune*, November 4, 2009.

8. Alicia Acuna, "Booze Blues: Utah's Laws Make It Tricky to Get a Drink," last modified January 31, 2013, http://www.foxnews.com/us/2013/01/31/booze-blues-utah-laws-make-it-tricky-to-get-drink/.

9. Anonymous, in discussion with the author, October 2015.

10. This lack of clarity (which I once experienced with a restaurant manager after her explanation of the rule was different from the explanation I'd previously received there) emphasizes how confusing rules like this can be.

11. The assumed intent of the rule is to ensure that alcohol will be consumed with food, which slows the absorption of alcohol in the body and thus slows down inebriation. Serving food "to go" defeats this purpose.

12. Anonymous, in discussion with the author, October 2015.

13. Anonymous, in discussion with the author, November 2015.

14. Anonymous, in discussion with the author, November 2015.

15. Raven Haymond has written about this rite of passage among former Mormons: "Tasting the Forbidden Fruit as Rite of Passage: Former Mormons Reflect on Their First Sips of Alcohol and Coffee," *Western Folklore*, 77, nos. 3–4 (2018): 313–46.

16. Utah was the eighteenth state in the United States to legalize same-sex marriage ahead of the federal mandate.

17. Mary Brown Malouf, "Utah Beer Comes Out in Support of Gay Union," *Salt Lake Magazine*, February 13, 2009.

Award-winning first-place Jell-O at the 2017 Thanksgiving Point "Utah Foods Cook-Off." Food prepared and photographed by Aimee Eliason.

4

GREEN JELL-O

Becoming an Iconic Utah Symbol

JACQUELINE S. THURSBY

Jell-O has been a popular food item in American homes since the early 1900s, but in recent decades it has become publicly associated with Utah culture. Around 1986, Kraft Foods' sales of Jell-O were lagging, so the company created state Jell-O competitions to increase sales. In 2000, Iowa won the number one spot for Jell-O consumption, and Utah finished second. Challenged, up for energetic competition, and having created the slogan "Take Back the Title," many Utahns, along with students at Brigham Young University, created a campaign to reclaim the first-place title. A petition to make Jell-O the official state snack of Utah circulated and gathered over fourteen thousand signatures. "By 2001 the resolution had overwhelming support in the state legislature as well, receiving only two dissenting votes."[1] The 2002 Olympics were held in Salt Lake City the next year, and a green Jell-O cloisonné pin became one of the most popular souvenir items available. The green-specific Jell-O identity was to be celebrated, and since 2002, the popularity and variety of Jell-O competitions throughout the state have become sources of entertainment and family fun. There is an assortment of options to meet the interest of everyone in Utah who loves to celebrate this iconic food.

Any consideration of Jell-O's historical and cultural importance, in America in general and Utah in particular, is incomplete without mention of now-disgraced comedian Bill Cosby, who during the 1970s was seen as America's fun and wholesome dad. Jell-O historian Louis Weber explains that, in 1974, "Bill Cosby became the spokesman for Jell-O–brand pudding. His vibrant, upbeat personality was perfect to project the idea that Jell-O is a fun food for kids. He began with a 'Kids Love Pudding' campaign....After thirteen years promoting pudding, Bill Cosby was so successful in appealing to young moms and kids that he became the spokesperson for Jell-O gelatin as well."[2]

THE MAKING OF UTAH JELL-O ICONOGRAPHY

In 2001, lawmakers in Salt Lake City were making decisions about what should be named Utah's state snack. Though some lawmakers preferred to choose ice cream, Jell-O won the competition. The decision by Utah's lawmakers went international. The BBC News reported on February 6, 2001, that Utah's choice was "not just any snack, but jelly—known in the United States by the commercial name of Jell-O. This is not a joke.... Apparently the state's capital, Salt Lake City, has earned the dubious distinction of having the highest per capita consumption of Jell-O not only in the U.S., but in the whole world."[3] Katty Kay of the BBC also reported that there would be an official Jell-O week (activities undefined), and that the reason ice cream was not chosen as the state snack was due to the perspectives of some leaders: "'Ice cream is not sexy,' said Senator Gene Davis, 'it's not wiggly and jiggly.'"[4] The stage was thus set for the popularity of the green Jell-O pin at the 2002 Olympics held in Salt Lake City. According to an article in the *Deseret News*, during the Olympics that year there was even "a temporary Jell-O exhibit in the downtown ZCMI Center."[5] From there, the folklore of Mormons and Jell-O was literally carried all over the world. For eight years, the *Salt Lake Tribune* has sponsored a Jell-O haiku contest with entry categories for adults, elementary school children, and secondary school students. There are first-, second-, third-place, and honorary mention awards; the winning haiku poems are printed in the paper. The 2014 contest had entries that "poked fun at all sorts of events and current topics: air pollution, booze, mudslides, polygamy, gay marriage, and the attorney general scandal." There were "nearly 250 entries.... [A]ll were judged by members of the Utah State Poetry Society and *Tribune* staffers."[6] First place in the adult entries was by Kelly Grover:

Proud Mormon Staple.
Add a shot of devil's brew,
Conflicted Jell-O.

First place in the secondary school entries was by Mikayla Wise:

Build upon Jell-O,
things are sure to fall down.
North Salt Lake Landslide.

First place in the elementary entries was by Gunner Schram:

I have a pillow
Made of Jell-O, midnight snack
or breakfast in bed.

In midsummer, Thanksgiving Point (Lehi) sponsors a family day called "Jiggle Fest."[7] The day

Official Snack of Utah souvenir pin, 2002 Salt Lake Winter Olympics. Used by permission, Utah State Historical Society. All rights reserved.

is dedicated to Jell-O but also includes what are called lovely cousins: fry sauce, funeral potatoes, and Dutch-oven fare. Hourly Jell-O fights are scheduled, sprinklers are turned on at the top of every hour, there is a cook-off competition of favorite family recipes with substantial prizes, and an outdoor movie is shown at dusk.

At the 2014 Utah State Fair, adventurous foodies could try deep-fried green Jell-O. Ordinary Jell-O (actually of a variety of flavors) is made, set, cut into strips or balls, frozen, rolled in crumbs similar to Panko, and then deep fried; it is better tasting than it may sound. It was served piping hot and surprisingly seemed a little addictive after the first few bites. It was different but appealing.

There is no doubt that Jell-O has been a staple and a very popular American dessert for decades. In 1992, Sarah E. Newton, a folklorist then at Chico State University in California, wrote an article published in *Western Folklore* called "'The Jell-O Syndrome': Investigating Popular Culture/Foodways."[8] In it, she suggested that the study of many foods popular in America had been neglected and gave examples of varied uses of Jell-O over the twentieth century ranging from table anecdotes, food play, desserts, and salads to jokes and radio ads.[9] She concluded her article by stating,

> Such connections as these presented above between foodways, folklore, and popular culture, illustrated through a study of Jell-O, suggest some of the complex cultural responses the American folk have had to this one national commercial food product. Although some of those responses are more deliberately contrived,

An example of "seven-layer Jell-O" (in this case ten-layer!), often regarded as the ultimate test of Jell-O making skills. Courtesy Mark Fickett.

even literary, the fact remains that the people have responded to as well as created and perpetuated a great body of lore about this particular food. Numerous foodway scholars have shown how the study of particular family celebrations or food events or ethnic dishes can give insight into the values, gender roles and sense of identity of the participants.[10]

Since the 2002 Olympics and the cloisonné Jell-O charm available there, green Jell-O does seem to have become a national marker for Utah foodways. Eric Eliason and Tom Mould recently published a text on Mormon folklore studies, and when Eliason shared a description of their project with an LDS member of the Burlington First Ward in

North Carolina, the woman chuckled and said that she looked forward to "reading about green Jell-O, funeral potatoes, and 'all those wild stories about wacky Mormons.'"[11] The book these serious scholars assembled is a probing and erudite study of the expressive cultural forms of Mormonism over time and place, but they acknowledged that Jell-O has a recognized presence in the folkloric LDS paradigm.

There are several aspects of the fairly recent national lore about Utah and green Jell-O, as mentioned above, that might need a little clarification. To begin with, the Utah/green Jell-O association may not be as ubiquitous as some may think. A few months ago, my husband and I entertained a couple who were natives of Utah but presently living in Oregon. They were passing through Provo, so I prepared dinner for them. The menu included a "Layered Pear Cream Cheese Mold," a recipe published by Kraft Foods and prepared with green Jell-O. That was a deliberate choice—we were in Utah after all. The salad was good, but the couple said they had never heard of green Jell-O associated specifically with Utah—so much for my attempt at regional humor.

ORIGINS AND PROGRESS OF AMERICA'S JELL-O

The origin of Jell-O as we know it winds back to Peter Cooper of Le Roy, New York, an industrialist, inventor, and philanthropist who obtained the first patent for a gelatin dessert in 1845. Though packaged in appealing little boxes, the product was difficult to use. "Home cooks still relied on sheets of prepared gelatin" which had many steps and ultimately had to be "dripped through a jelly bag before they could be turned into shimmering molds."[12] Over time other versions of gelatin for home use became available, including Knox, but none were easy to use. In 1897 Pearle Wait, another resident of Le Roy, New York, a patent medicine inventor and skilled carpenter, created a fruit-flavored gelatin and added coloring. His wife, May Davis Wait, named it Jell-O, probably after a cereal-based coffee substitute product named Grain-O. (See Elaine Clark's Postum article in this collection.) In 1899 Wait sold the formula to another Le Roy company, Woodward's Genesee Pure Food Company, which also manufactured and sold Grain-O.[13] According to Phillips, that company was ultimately sold to the Postum Cereal Company which later became Kraft/General Foods.

There are old folk beliefs about Jell-O and the gelatin origins concerning renderings "from the hides and bones of animals, typically pork skins, pork, horses, cattle bones, and split cattle hides."[14] Further, "popular belief has it that gelatin comes from horses' and cows' hooves. . . . Kraft, the maker of Jell-O, asserts that hooves do not contain the necessary collagen and therefore are not used in the production of its Jell-O brand gelatin product."[15] Except for the very strict vegans, most vegetarians do not exclude Jell-O from their diets.

The current generation of Jell-O users most often thinks of Jell-O as a dessert, but the history of the product has changed as time has passed. When refrigeration was very expensive, the gelatin products were a treat for the rich. Once a molding for meat, it became a salad ingredient and then a dessert with blurred boundaries along the way. Some people of the dessert-only generation comment on the "weirdness" of vegetables or meat in Jell-O, but the old variations can be found in Grandma's recipe collections and were considered perfectly normal at the time.

The small burg of Le Roy, in New York's Finger Lakes region, is located only a few miles from Palmyra which was the early home of Joseph Smith, the LDS church founder and first president of the Church of Jesus Christ of Latter-day Saints. Many Mormons traveling to visit the prophet's early homestead and the Hill Cumorah Pageant stop to see Le Roy's Jell-O Gallery. The gallery is a small museum sponsored by the Le Roy Historical Society, and visitors may submit a vote there for their favorite flavor. Museum curator Lynne J. Belluscio stated: "I can always tell when that pageant is going on, because the votes for lime always go up."[16] The gallery provides a walk through the twentieth century with Jell-O artifacts reflecting efforts of the Jell-O manufacturers to keep abreast of the times. Beginning in the 1930s, radio entertainers Jack Benny, Mary Livingston, and Don Wilson brought the J-E-L-L-O song into homes all over America every Sunday evening. The song can be heard at the museum, and there are twentieth-century advertisements, examples of packaging over time, and other artifacts and souvenirs relating to Jell-O, the wiggly dessert.

Lime Jell-O, declared to be the contemporary favorite, was introduced in 1930. Congealed salads became very popular at that time and, according to Kraft, "almost one third of the salad recipes in the average cookbook [were] gelatin based."[17] Lime flavor complemented salads, appetizers, relishes, and entrees, so it became very popular. The company continued to develop flavors, pudding mixes, and eventually Jell-O pudding treats.

MOLDED GRAPE SALAD
(SERVES 6)

1 small package of lime Jell-O
1 package cream cheese, or try a mixture of cream cheese and yogurt
Fruit for mixture below
Grapes and fresh mint for garnish

Dissolve the lime Jell-O in 1 3/4 c. boiling water, set aside.

Fruit mixture:
1 c. crushed pineapple, drained
3 Tbsp. lemon juice
2 c. of any type grapes, sliced and seeds removed
1/4 c. chopped walnuts or pecans

In a 6-cup mold or dish, pour half of the dissolved Jell-O and add the fruit mixture. Chill until partially set. In another bowl, blend the cream cheese and the rest of the dissolved Jell-O and spoon onto the first partially set layer. Chill until firm and garnish with the grapes and fresh mint.

UTAH AND JELL-O

For many home cooks, Jell-O and its many iterations are still popular. The fruit-flavored gelatin became a well-known dessert early in the twentieth century primarily because of aggressive magazine and media advertisements. It was easy to prepare, refrigeration was available in nearly every home, most families liked it, and sales were good throughout the States. In time, however, more women were working outside the home and cooking less, and Kraft Foods decided to promote Jell-O as a family dish prepared at home. The recipes for "Jigglers" (Jell-O prepared as a finger food) was revived in the 1980s and advertised.

We can only guess why green was chosen as the color for the collectible Olympic pin. It is true that lime Jell-O salads show up frequently at church social gatherings (often with shredded carrot in the green Jell-O), but other colors, flavors, fruits, vegetables, nuts, marshmallows, and even hard-cooked eggs are found in Jell-O recipes.

Jell-O itself is an inexpensive item, and Latter-day Saints are encouraged to have ample food storage in case of emergencies. The product keeps well and is easy to rotate. That too may be influencing its continued popularity. Wikipedia suggests that perhaps the Jell-O stereotype developed when Gordon B. Hinckley was president of the church. He was comfortable with the press and gave many interviews to reporters, candidly answering questions. Some people seemed to associate this simple food with the so-called strange beliefs of the LDS people. Ultimately, the Mormons have embraced rather than rejected the Jell-O stereotype, but it is a tongue-in-cheek cultural practice, an adapted folkloric identity with no scriptural or doctrinal basis.

Folklorist William Bascom suggested that folklore functions in four ways. Reductively explained, those are: (1) repeated cultural elements serve as a buttress against societal repressions; (2) they serve to reinforce or validate group behavior; (3) they contribute to education and acculturation; and (4) "[folklore] . . . fulfills the important but often overlooked function of maintaining conformity to the accepted patterns of behavior."[18] Jell-O is harmless, and playing with the stereotype is simply another way to enjoy or disparage LDS culture. Good-humored Utahns play with the stereotype.

Utah senator Mike Lee cheerfully invites visitors

CRANBERRY SALAD
(SERVES 8–10)

Dissolve 1 small package of raspberry Jell-O in 1 cup boiling water.
  Stir in 1 16-oz. can of whole cranberry sauce and chill until partially set.
  Add 1/2 cup chopped celery and chill again until partially set.

Meanwhile:
In a small saucepan soften 1 Knox gelatin packet in 1/2 cup cold water over low heat.
  Beat in 1/2 cup mayonnaise, 2/3 cup canned milk, and 1 tablespoon lemon juice.
  Chill this mixture, then whip it and add 1 cup miniature marshmallows.
  Spoon this mixture over the first cranberry layer of Jell-O and continue to chill until firm.
  Cut into individual squares and place on a lettuce leaf to serve.

to meet with him in his office in Washington, DC, any Wednesday at 3:30 pm for "Green Jell-O with the Senator." His address is 315 Hart Building, and everyone is welcome. To be certain that he is in town, he suggests following @SenMikeLee on Twitter for updates. It won't win a culinary prize, but it is fun at five dollars a serving.[19]

Folklorist Lisa Duskin-Goode shared a story about an annual neighborhood barbecue held at the local LDS church in northern Utah. She said it was a large gathering of neighbors, church members and nonmembers alike. There was a lot of good food, and the tables were laden with steak and chicken for the adults and hot dogs and hamburgers for the kids. "But the best part was the twenty or so beautiful

THE JELL-O MATRIX

Added Ingredients	Lemon	Lime	Strawberry	Raspberry	Orange
carrots & celery	picnic with the in-laws	Relief Society brunch; teen grounding	Summer wedding buffet	Thanksgiving; hospital siege	any buffet or angelic visitation
cottage cheese	funeral or missionary reunion	anytime, anywhere	Swiss Days; Valentine dance	Christmas Eve dinner	revelation or Halloween (add black jelly beans)
mini marshmallows	grand-parents' birthday (add prunes)	Polynesian baby blessing	Fourth of July picnic	Pioneer Day picnic	Temple dedication; mall opening
pineapple, coconut, banana	senior citizen luau	Tongan ward dedication	Ward banquet or missionary farewell	Christmas brunch; Marion Stand-off	Samoan ward dedication
Fruit cocktail	Dinner on Monday	Dinner on Tuesday	Dinner on Wednesday	Dinner on Thursday	Dinner on Friday

Source: Roger B. Salazar and Michael G. Wightman, *No Man Knows My Pastries: The Secret (Not Sacred) Recipes of Sister Enid Christensen* (Salt Lake City: Signature Books, 1992).

Jell-O salads. Some green, some red, some orange or yellow—all were a different array of color and flavor."[20] She wrote: "I sometimes tire of the super sweetened artificial colored stuff, but it suddenly hit me that here was a showing of love."[21] This chapter features three of Duskin-Goode's favorite Jell-O recipes.

In conversation about this paper topic with Cassy Budd, a BYU professor and one of my LDS neighbors, I was told that her family owns a fine antique crystal bowl that once belonged to the great-grandmother of one of her family members. For as long as she can remember only Jell-O has been served in that bowl, and it has been passed down through the generations. Her sister, who has it now,

is a reluctant cook but she makes great Jell-O, and the family has created a holiday Jell-O game. The sister mixes different flavors of Jell-O and gels it in the beautiful bowl. At holiday celebrations, the family game is to guess what flavors are in the bowl. At Christmas this year the mix was cherry, orange, and pineapple, and one of the younger children guessed it.[22] My mother, who is not LDS but Missouri Baptist, used to make cherry Jell-O, let it barely set, and then beat in a pint of softened vanilla ice cream until the mixture was smooth. It was scooped up and served in pretty dishes and was always a family favorite.

A recent development in the world of Jell-O creativity is a Keurig machine that produces instant

PEACHES 'N' CREAM GELATIN DESSERT

(SERVES 12–15)

1 1/3 c. graham cracker crumbs (about 22 squares)
1/4 c. sugar
1/3 c. butter, melted
Topping:
1 package (8 oz.) cream cheese, softened
1/4 c. sugar
1/4 c. milk
1 carton (8 oz.) frozen whipped topping, thawed
1 can (15 1/4 oz.) sliced peaches, drained
1 package (3 oz.) peach or orange gelatin
3/4 c. boiling water
1 1/4 c. cold water

In a small bowl, combine the crumbs, sugar, and butter. Press into a 9-by-13-inch dish. In a large bowl, beat cream cheese and sugar until smooth; gradually add the milk. Fold in the whipped topping. Spread over crust.

Cut peach slices in half lengthwise; arrange over top. In a small bowl, dissolve the gelatin in boiling water; stir in the cold water. Refrigerate for 1 1/2 hours or until slightly thickened.

Gently spoon gelatin over peaches; chill until set. Cut into squares.

Jell-O shots. On GrubStreet.com is a blurb about a machine Keurig invented "which can crank out 20 Jell-O shots in about ten minutes, using proprietary, K-cup–style pods."[23] It suggests that this machine can be put to many good uses such as for patients who have difficulty swallowing pills, or possibly for people who just want Jell-O immediately.[24]

The Jell-O Matrix was first published in *No Man Knows My Pastries: The Secret (Not Sacred) Recipes of Sister Enid Christensen*, a 1992 spoof on Mormon cuisine. It is based on stereotypical cultural food

combinations and is created primarily to entertain. Even so, some of the suggestions sound appealing if you are at a loss for variety. When it comes down to it, the reality is that Jell-O is an unassuming family sweet with multiple cultural attributes. Iconic or not, it will likely be around for a long time.

NOTES

1. "Why Mormons Love Green Jell-O," Mormon Culture, 2014, accessed January 26, 2015, http://mormonculture.org./2014/05/27/why-mormons-liove-green-Jell-o/.
2. Louis Weber, *Celebrating 100 Years of JELL-O* (Lincolnwood, IL: Publications International, 1997), 4.
3. Katty Kay, "Utah loves Jell-O: Official," BBC News Homepage, February 6, 2001, http://news.bbvc.co.uk/2/hi/americas/1156021.stm.
4. Ibid.
5. Valerie Phillips, "Unmolding History: N.Y. Museum Chronicles Jell-O's Success," *Deseret News*, June 28, 2006.
6. Kathy Stephenson, "We're Over the Rainbow for Jell-O Haiku," *Salt Lake Tribune*, 2014, http://www.sltrib.com/home/1846447-155/were-over-the-rainbow-for-Jell-O-haiku/.
7. "Jigglefest, "Thanksgiving Point Institute, Inc.,'" July 19, 2014, https://www.thanksgivingpoint.org/events/jigglefest/.
8. Sarah E. Newton, "'The Jell-O Syndrome:' Investigating Popular Culture/Foodways," *Western Folklore* 51, nos. 3–4 (July–October 1992): 249–68.
9. Jell-O has certainly been a part of American food culture and is a common presence in cafeteria lines, at dinner tables, church and family celebrations, and at post-funerary dinners for more than a century. Though Newton's essay focused on Midwest Jell-O customs, the presence of Jell-O in Utah is an old tradition as well. For instance, in a 1996 *Relief Society Manual*, assembled for use in the Provo (Utah) Oak Hills Stake, there are three menus listed for use at post-funeral luncheons. The first is a buffet and

lists sliced ham, potato casserole, green beans or other seasonal vegetables, Jell-O salad, rolls, butter, and cake. The second menu is for a light lunch of sandwiches, and the third is a box lunch for the road. A reminder included in the manual suggests that a set menu under short notice has its advantages, but certainly exceptions can be made. Of interest here is the specific listing of a Jell-O salad. One of the women in my own ward congregation said that if the proper dinner were not served to her family after her funeral, including Jell-O and funeral potatoes, she would return and haunt us all. On the other hand, there are many Utah residents who seldom use Jell-O. So, like most foods, it varies according to taste, context, and tradition. (Silja Allen et al., *Relief Society Action Manual* [Provo: Provo Utah Oak Hills Stake, 1996]).

10. Newton, "'The Jell-O Syndrome,'" 266.
11. Eric Eliason and Tom Mould, eds., *Latter-Day Lore: Mormon Folklore Studies* (Salt Lake City: University of Utah Press, 2013), 6.
12. Weber, *Celebrating 100 Years*, 4.
13. Phillips, "Unmolding History," 2.
14. "JELL-O Dolly," Snopes, 2007, accessed April 1, 2015, http//www/snopes.com/food/ingredient/ jello.asp.
15. Ibid.
16. Phillips, "Unmolding History," 1.
17. Weber, *Celebrating 100 Years*, 6.
18. William Bascom, "Four Functions of Folklore," *Journal of American Folklore* 67, no. 266 (October–December 1954): 333–49.
19. https://www.lee.senate.gov/public/index.cfm/ jell-o-with-the-senator.
20. Lisa Duskin-Goode, "Love Is Twenty Jell-O Salads" (unpublished manuscript, 2000), 1.
21. Ibid.
22. Cassy Budd, conversation with author, April 25, 2014.
23. Clint Rainey, "Ultimate Bro Invents a Keurig Machine for Instant Jell-O Shots," GrubStreet. com, March 26, 2015.
24. https://getjevo.com/.

5

UTAH'S FRY SAUCE

MICHAEL P. CHRISTENSEN

In the good old USA, everything is hyperbolic. American citizens both succeed and suffer due to capitalism. We are hardworking but driven by materialism and consumption. Bigger, of course, is always better, and we should always want more, never settling for less. It is, after all, the American way! Stereotyped or not, an honest look in the mirror reflects an excessive, gluttonous lot. This is certainly true when inspecting American cuisine. After all, we are the country that invented the meat-within-meat-within-meat "Turducken." Americans love their gravies, dressings, dips, and sauces, too. And when it comes to dipping, dunking, or drenching foods, Utahns are A-1. Whether it's mashed potatoes drowning in homemade gravy, vanilla bean ice cream drizzled with caramel, or ranch dressing mixed with iceberg salad greens, all have a place at Utah's kitchen table. However, none of these matches the distinction of Utah's own fry sauce.

The creamy, pink dipping sauce, made primarily of a combination of ketchup and mayonnaise, is possibly the most iconic food at Utah's buffet table. There are other, more traditional condiments used for dipping (ketchup, cocktail sauce, or barbecue sauce, for example), but by serving fry sauce, Utahns have shared something clearly their own. This culinary gesture, however, is more than simply taste and texture. Instead, serving Utah's own fry sauce subtly reveals Utah's long and storied history of independence and its pioneering spirit. Like other Utahn characteristics, especially Mormonism, fry sauce reveals a community rooted in industry and entrepreneurship. Early Mormon settlers came to the Utah territory seeking a way of life free from religious persecution. Mormon settlers wanted to live differently and to find a better way in all things. In creating this utopia, Utah's LDS Church leaders implemented "new" and "better" ways, some that have endured and others that have failed. Brigham Young invented the Deseret Alphabet, a coded, secret way of communicating. City and town streets were laid out in precise grid patterns, something that had not often been used before. That Utah also has its own distinctive dipping sauce is no surprise.

Although *possibly* linked to Utah's pioneering spirit, independence, and Mormon settlement, fry sauce is not a divisive creation. Rather, the creamy condiment builds bridges between

Mormons and non-Mormons, both groups readily identifying with something that is universal: food. Fry sauce is a Utah institution. Love it or hate it, it links Utah and Utahns of all ilk.

ORIGINS

Fry sauce origin stories are varied, but nearly all follow a similar pattern: *Someone*, at *some* burger joint that is *somehow* or *somewhat* related to the Arctic Circle restaurant chain, thought it would be a good idea to mix some mayonnaise and ketchup and use it as a dipping sauce. One popular version claims the iconic sauce was invented in Provo, Utah, at Stan's Drive-In, in 1955. At Stan's (then a franchise of Arctic Circle), "one winter evening in 1955 two high school students, Ron Taylor and Max Peay, developed the original Fry Sauce recipe while working the night shift together. They liked what they mixed together for themselves and began sharing it with their friends as an alternative to ketchup."[1] In Taylor's own words,

> Back in 1954 when I was a sophomore [in high school], I was hired by Bob Peay who was running a new Arctic Circle on 9th East in Provo. One evening Max Peay, Bob's younger brother, and I were working together. When we weren't busy we would often try making ourselves new things that weren't on the menu when we got hungry. We deep fried bananas, we made Strawberry Short Cakes using Twinkies, and all sorts of other things. One night Max and I decided to try to find something to go with our French fries

besides ketchup. We ended up mixing a bit of mayonnaise with the ketchup and liked it a lot. We started sharing it with our friends when they came and asking them to try it and see if they liked it. They did. And it wasn't long until a lot of our customers were asking for that "French fry sauce stuff" instead of ketchup. In time we started serving it instead of ketchup unless they asked us to do otherwise, which wasn't often.[2]

Two years later, Ron's father, Stan Taylor, had bought the Arctic Circle from the Peays. Later that fall, a sales representative from Arctic Circle came to the popular drive-in, asking for permission to take the fry sauce recipe to the Arctic Circle headquarters in Salt Lake City to test corporate interest in using it in franchise outlets because it was such a hit. "Well, neither Dad [n]or I fully understood what that would eventually mean," Taylor reflects, "but we told him yes, that was fine with us. Obviously, they liked the idea and were soon using it at all their stores."[3] The rest, as they say, is history.[4]

Others claim that the sauce was invented even earlier, around 1941. At the time, Don Carlos Edwards, owner and operator of Don Carlos Barbecue, was the genius who blended ketchup and mayonnaise, forever changing the cultural identity of Utah. Edwards's sauce, called "pink sauce," was used on both burgers and fries, and was

37

said to have other ingredients in the original recipe. Of course, that recipe is kept top secret by Arctic Circle, the quick in-and-out burger joint Edwards would open in 1950 (and later franchise) just a block away from his original barbecue restaurant.[5] To this, Taylor responds by claiming that Arctic Circle's "corporate memory has changed somewhat as to how and when Don Carlos 'developed' their fry sauce."[6] It seems that along with the commercialization of the formula came the formalization of the fry sauce narrative.

When Salt Lake City hosted the Olympic Winter Games in 2002, fry sauce became forever memorialized with its own collectable pin, part of a larger food-themed set. "It wasn't until the Olympics...that [Arctic Circle] really promoted it as much as they did. I called them once," explains Taylor, "to ask if they would like to know the real story, but the lady hung up on me. I guess I don't blame them. I'm sure they thought I was some kind of kook."[7]

American Fork, Utah, resident Lee Parker has also been theorized to be the originator of fry sauce. In 1953, Parker, who was managing (you guessed it) the local Arctic Circle at the time, opened Parker's Drive In.[8] Others say it was "the Arctic Circle in Midvale, Utah, that created this delicious little wonder...during my ten-year stint there, I drank this sauce like it was mother's milk. We even made salad dressing out of it."[9]

There are some who suggest the origin of fry sauce is only *connected* to the Utah-based Arctic Circle chain, but it was popularized *outside* Utah borders. "It was popularized initially...in southern Idaho" recalls another who commented on the allrecipes.com website.[10] "I know because it was my job to make it...long, long ago in southeast Idaho." Whether inside or outside Utah's borders, the conservative element in these origin stories is, once again, Arctic Circle.

Of course some claim that fry sauce wasn't invented at an Arctic Circle—or at Stan's Drive-In, or Don Carlos Barbecue, or Parker's Drive In, or by any of the aforementioned. In fact, Shar Wassenberg claims Utah's iconic sauce wasn't even created in the state of Utah (*gasp!*). According to Wassenberg, it migrated from the Midwest and was invented by her daughter. "[Fry sauce] wasn't invented in my years as a Utahn, but my daughter, who worked at Burger King when we lived in Iowa, made up the sauce, suggesting it to friends, which became asked for when people would come in to eat—long before the actual Utah 'Fry Sauce' came to be. Could it be possible that a Utah entrepreneur had driven through and received such a concoction at that Burger King to take back to present to the world of culinary cuisine in Utah? Maybe not, but it is an interesting concept," she reflects.[11] Another doubter, Miss Molly, even claims that "the sauce has nothing to do with Utah."[12] If not, Utah has certainly felt a responsibility to carry on the tradition.

However you choose to look at it, fry sauce is deeply rooted in the history of Arctic Circle, whether the restaurant was truly associated with its invention or not. Stan's, Parker's, and Don Carlos's all have a link to Arctic Circle, now with seventy-three company franchises in seven states (over 50 percent in Utah).[13] Over the past sixty years, Arctic Circle has certainly promoted this aspect of its history, as shown in the company's advertising and marketing campaigns. In fact, a customer can buy a bottle of the "original" fry sauce from the Arctic Circle website, ensuring that one has indeed purchased the "most imitated, and also the least duplicated."[14]

But fry sauce wasn't officially and formally embraced by Arctic Circle management, at least not in the beginning, and not in 1970s Vernal, Utah. Fawn D'Anza, whose mother, Lorraine Christensen, made the fry sauce for the chain, explains: "Arctic Circle would 'fine' [owner] Jerry [Morris] because [our restaurant] would serve [fry sauce] to the customers instead of ketchup. It took Arctic Circle awhile to implement the fry sauce, but people in the Basin raved about it long before it was 'ok'd' by Arctic Circle and they began to package it."[15] What was once not formally recognized as part of the franchise has now become the norm in this folk food tradition. Whether teenage ingenuity or corporate creation, fry sauce was here to stay.

And many would follow Arctic Circle's lead. Other burger-focused restaurants in Utah serve the sauce, including (among numerous others) the popular Crown Burger, Apollo Burger, and Astro Burger, all owned by the descendants and friends of Greek immigrants who originally started the chain back in 1978.[16] Since these early days, other commercial versions of fry sauce have been created, bottled, and sold by local restaurants and entrepreneurs. Hires Big H Fry Sauce, Stephen's Gourmet Fry Sauce, Some Dude's Fry Sauce, and Arctic Circle's Original Fry Sauce all compete for fry sauce supremacy. In late 2012, twenty staff members of the *Salt Lake Tribune* got together to have a taste test with these four offerings. Perhaps validating the idea that Arctic Circle is the impetus behind this thing called fry sauce, their

Original Fry Sauce came in first place, with an average score of seven out of ten, followed by Hires Big H, Stephen's Gourmet, and Some Dude's.[17]

HOMEMADE VARIANTS

But fry sauce is not limited to commercial enterprise, and of course there are also plenty of homemade recipes. In July 2014, Thanksgiving Point, a multiuse events facility in Lehi, Utah, hosted the first-ever "Utah Foods Cook-Off." Citizen contestants were invited to participate in four categories: funeral potatoes, Dutch ovens, Jell-O, and fry sauce. In the fry sauce category, plenty of homemade versions were presented, some quite exotically. According to one juror, the fry sauce taking "3rd place had plums in it and another excellent entry had mint!"[18] Another entry allowed the taster to "play" with the food by "combin[ing] and then double dip[ping] in bacon bits…yum!"[19] It seems there is a larger subculture of experimental Utah foodies when it comes to fry sauce. Perhaps, again, this reflects the ingenuity and creativity of Utah's pioneering spirit.

Other homemade versions of fry sauce aren't quite as exotic as these examples but still provide a look at a well-established, dynamic, regional folk food tradition. An online internet search for "homemade fry sauce" yields a number of results (and a number of "correct" versions, of course). The varying recipes come from around the country, with most referencing "Utah" or "western states" origin. Here are a few samples of homemade versions from Utahns. Note that the first three examples come from small businesses.[20] This indicates fry sauce exists in a normative as well as a folk and/or elite context,

Photo by Shannon Hall.

somewhere in between corporate and personal kitchens.

- "I use Mayo, Ketchup, Worcestershire and sugar." —Jeremy Erkkila, Director of Food & Beverage, The Ridge & Stonebridge Golf Clubs
- "Ketchup, Mayo, garlic powder, worchestire [*sic*] sauce, salt and pepper (and of course a couple other secret ingredients)." —Kyle Moore, former owner Kyle's Grill and Café
- "very simple, ketchup, mayonnaise, salad dressing, and dill pickle juice. DANG I wish I had written them all down when we closed the last location." —Craig Thomas, whose family owned and operated three Frostop burger places
- "I'm not a fry sauce expert but we have made it many times; usually [with] kids. Normally [we] made with just mayo and catsup, but I've also made it with BBQ sauce/mayo, Homemade (an actual brand name) chili sauce/mayo, as well as a spicier version with Buffalo wing sauce/mayo a couple of times. I would probably consider the catsup and mayo version the most "correct." —Teresa Tate
- "I'm a fry sauce purist, so just ketchup and mayo. I'm open to a bit of variation with fry sauce (adding bbq sauce or hot sauce, perhaps) but I draw a line when relish is introduced (there's no room for chunks in fry sauce!)." —Jamie Gregersen

As you can see, the essential elements here are mayonnaise and ketchup, with a few dynamic variants added in. And, like many recipes, legends abound about "secret ingredients" and the "correct versions" of fry sauce. Arctic Circle may lay claim to being the inventor of fry sauce, but similar concoctions exist and contain many variants. Other ingredients found in fry sauce include barbecue sauce (made popular at Utah's Training Table restaurant), dill pickle juice, mustard, hot sauce, garlic, lemon, chopped onion, liquid smoke, horseradish, buttermilk, vinegar, sugar, paprika, Worcestershire sauce, red wine vinegar, onion powder, salt, cayenne pepper, chili sauce, Tabasco, tomato soup, and egg whites.

But for purists, "authentic" fry sauce doesn't rely on these additions. In a February 14, 2012, allrecipes.com discussion thread, Mrs. Michael O. states plainly that real Utah fry sauce will have none of these tricks.

> Here's my advice. Go fifty/fifty on the mayo to ketchup ratio. Mix & taste, then figure out which you prefer more of and go from there in a larger batch. Usually it's more mayonnaise than ketchup. You CAN also add a drop of liquid smoke & have it taste exactly like major restaurant chains but that's NOT what REAL Utah Fry Sauce is about. If it ain't broke folks...Sometimes simplicity is its own perfection.[21]

Besides variants in ingredients, the basics of fry sauce are known by other names. Of course, food fans from across the country have told of golf sauce, country club sauce, Mississippi comeback sauce, bingo sauce, "metchup,"[22] and, my personal favorite, steak finger sauce, sold at the Del Mar Restaurant and Club in Logan, Utah, in the 1970s.[23] Whatever

the name, at least one individual maintains that the original Utah fry sauce is such a part of Utah culture, the actual recipe is "embedded in the Word of Wisdom..." solidifying its connection to place and identity.[24]

NOSTALGIA, IDENTITY, AND COMMUNITY

Utah's fry sauce is for more than just dipping. For many, it is a symbol of youth, implying fond memories and nostalgic notions. Sheri Candland fondly recalls the fry sauce of her youth: "[Fry sauce] brings back memories of when I was really young and my mom would buy me a burger from Arctic Circle with fries and a lime rickey. Simple, easy, lovely times."[25] In 2014 the author conducted an informal online survey asking, "When do you first remember eating fry sauce?" Over 50 percent of survey respondents recalled "in childhood" or "as a kid." Others couldn't remember the time specifically because fry sauce has simply always been there. "I can't. [Fry sauce] has always been around," said one participant. Another replied, "[Fry sauce has been around] my whole life," and "[has] just always been there."[26] These sentiments reflect not only the nostalgic, good feelings fry sauce elicits, but also the significance of *where* fry sauce could be found. At the time, national chains were not carrying fry sauce. Instead, those reflecting on which restaurants served fry sauce specifically mentioned homegrown, locally owned burger joints. In addition to Arctic Circle and Greek offerings, respondents listed JCW, A&W, Purple Turtle, Chubby's, the Hi Spot, Maddox, and others.

Stan, Sarah, and Ron outside Stan's Drive-In in Provo around the time fry sauce took off. Courtesy Ron Taylor.

One of these home-grown hamburger places was the Frostop Drive In. Craig Thomas reflects fondly when asked about fry sauce:

> As someone who literally grew up inside a Frostop Drive In, I love fry sauce. My mother owned and operated the two Frostop locations in Granger and my aunt had the location in Kearns. People used to joke that my family bled fry sauce. So, yes, I have made fry sauce. In fact, many more gallons of the lovely sauce than I can imagine.

It has been many years since I have made the Frostop recipe, and since my mom's passing, I think we have lost most of the Frostop recipes. I have always considered my family's version the CORRECT version because it was the Frostop version. Making fresh Fry Sauce was part of our daily routine for over 30 years. My family NEVER ate at any other drive in/burger restaurants growing up. I remember the first time eating at another burger place in town and having strange green pickle chunks in the fry sauce, and all I could think of at the time was, *what a lame copy!* Our recipe was later copied by other businesses like Scot's Drive In and Ab's Drive In [which were] started by the families of former Frostop employees.[27]

With nostalgia comes identity, and fry sauce certainly functions as a cultural identifier for Utahns. Fry sauce is a potent symbol, delineating insiders from outsiders, an indication of Utah's cultural divide as well. While some native Utahns or longtime residents perceive fry sauce as distinctly Utah's own—something to be revered and celebrated—others find it unsophisticated or downright plebeian. As one former Utah resident, Mike Varilone, put it, "I can't stand it. It's just awful... and lends itself to poor taste. Those who eat it don't want to taste their food."[28] Debbie Welder agrees, simply stating, "Not appealing," and, "I find it flavorless."[29] She further suggests she doesn't eat fry sauce (or other sauces for that matter) for both taste and general health concerns. "I don't like ketchup or mayo. In fact I don't eat any condiments or dressings," she explains.[30]

Beyond taste and/or health reasons, there are others who suggest fry sauce functions as a symbol for status, identity, and membership. These folks may in fact enjoy the taste of fry sauce but draw the line when it is associated with larger cultural implications. Sheri Candland (referencing the 1978 Jonestown Massacre) says, "I am eating the fry sauce, not drinking the Kool Aid."[31] I asked my sister-in-law, a lifetime Utah resident and avid fry sauce fan, why some people would actually hate something that tastes good to so many. Her answer:

To spite it. To avoid being labeled a fry-sauce-loving Utahn. When I bartended...I met...many people who were embarrassed to be from Utah. So many people who buy into the idea that Utah, and everything uniquely Utahn, is lame. It's a weird thing. I think it's a Mormon thing that becomes a Utah thing, because people assume that all things Utah are influenced by Mormons. Utah beer sucks, liquor laws make us look backward, too many chain restaurants...we're cheap...[and] I don't know anyone from [other states who are] not proud of where they're from.[32]

Another conversation (with a young woman requesting anonymity) went like this: "Fry sauce tastes good. It's...a Utah staple [and] reminds me of being a kid. [But] I associate Utah with Mormons. And I don't want to be associated with Mormons."[33] Finally, "[R]umor has it that a truck stop in Wendover, Nevada, has a sign that [reads] 'NO, WE DON'T HAVE FRY SAUCE. THIS AIN'T UTAH."[34] Clearly, fry sauce's connection to Utah

and possibly Mormonism, real or perceived, also indicates a cultural divide.

EVOLUTION?

It was the earlier, ma-and-pa, local burger chains that embraced fry sauce, making it the clear choice for most customers. Responding to competition, eventually national chains would take notice, and soon McDonald's, Carl's Jr., Burger King, and Sonic were offering fry sauce with meals. At least, the chains located in Utah were. Local palates manipulating nationally chained restaurants is quite remarkable, and the culinary impact of Utah's fry sauce continues to spread.

Unfortunately for some Utah expatriates, fry sauce has not spread far enough. Many former Utahns lament their loss online: "My hometown is Salt Lake City and I currently reside in Ohio....One thing we do find that we miss is the fry sauce!" Another midwesterner is simply astonished that those outside of Zion have not fully embraced fry sauce. "I moved from Utah to Iowa about 7 years ago," writes Tara Wellman. "When I realized no one knew what 'fry sauce' was, I was shocked!" And moving farther southeast we find Amanda Lusby in mourning: "When I moved to Florida I was devastated that I could not find fry sauce anywhere. It's been nearly 4 years since I have had any."[35] For these unfortunates I leave the *real, authentic, original-original* Utah fry sauce recipe:
    1/2 c. ketchup
    1/4 c. mayonnaise
    1 spoonful mustard
    And, of course, the secret ingredient.

NOTES

1. "Fry Sauce—a Provo Original," Utah Diners Guide, last modified March 9, 2011, http://www.utahdinersguide.com/wordpress/?cat=6.
2. Ron Taylor, e-mail to Eric Eliason, June 20, 2014.
3. Ibid.
4. Commemorative plaque on display at Stan's Drive-In, Provo, Utah.
5. Lee Benson, "About Utah: Fry Sauce and Arctic Circle Hit Big 6-0," *Deseret News* (Salt Lake City), March 8, 2010.
6. Taylor to Eliason, June 20, 2014.
7. Ibid.
8. Sam Penrod, "End of an Era: Parker's in American Fork Closes after 58 Years in Business," *Deseret News*, December 30, 2011.
9. Mrs. Michael O, allrecipes.com comment, February 14, 2012.
10. allrecipes.com discussion with author, February 18, 2014.
11. Shar Wassenberg, e-mail message to Eric Eliason, June 21, 2014.
12. allrecipies.com discussion, November 12, 2010.
13. "Franchise Opportunities," Arctic Circle, http://acburger.com/franchise-opportunities.html.
14. "Original Fry Sauce," Arctic Circle, http://acburger.com/menu/fry-sauce.html.
15. Fawn D'Anza, e-mail message to Eric Eliason, July 21, 2014.
16. Ted McDonough, "Greeks Bearing Burgers," *City Weekly* (Salt Lake City), June 11, 2007.
17. Kathy Stephenson, "Utah Fry Sauce Showdown: Which Bottle Blasts the Competition?" *Salt Lake Tribune*, November 6, 2012.
18. Juror, e-mail message to Eric Eliason, July 19, 2014.
19. Ibid.
20. Jeremy Erkkila, Kyle Moore, Craig Thomas, Teresa Tate, and Jamie Gregersen, e-mail message to the author, February 18, 2015.
21. Mrs. Michael O., allrecipes.com comment, February 14, 2002.
22. danisaur, allrecipes.com comment, March 7, 2011.
23. As a child, one of my first favorite memories of fry sauce included dipping and eating the battered and deep-fried steak fingers my parents would bring home.
24. "Fry Sauce Survey" on Survey Monkey, June 17, 2014.
25. Sheri Candland, Facebook message to author, June 4, 2015.
26. "Fry Sauce Survey."
27. Craig Thomas, email message to author, February 18, 2015.
28. Mike Varilone, phone conversation with author, June 4, 2015.
29. Debbie Welder, Facebook message to author, June 4, 2015.
30. Ibid.
31. Candland, Facebook message.
32. Mindy Christensen, Facebook message to author, June 4, 2015.
33. Anonymous, Facebook message to author, June 4, 2015.
34. Dan Eliason, email message to Eric Eliason, July 2, 2014.
35. Jillee, "Authentic Utah Fry Sauce! Dipping Heaven!" One Good Thing by Jillee, http://www.onegoodthingbyjillee.com/2012/02/make-your-skirt-fly-up-authentic-utah.html.

6

FUNERAL POTATOES IN UTAH

JACQUELINE S. THURSBY

State fairs often offer unique regional examples of interest, but Utah's fair offers one autumn competition that is particularly appropriate and has only been included for the last few years. On September 12, 2014, the fourth annual "Utah's Own[1] Funeral Potato Contest," sponsored by the Utah State Fair and "Utah's Own," was held in the Salt Lake City Fairground's Zion Building. Eight entries, each using at least five of "Utah's Own" products in their home-prepared casseroles, were reheated and arranged on a counter under bright lights for the three judges to taste and evaluate. All professional tasters, one of the judges was the deputy commissioner of the Utah Department of Agriculture. Besides requiring five brand-identified local products, the judges looked for overall presentation and tasted the entries for consistency, creaminess, and suitable texture. Careful samplers of the entries, between tastes the judges cleansed their palates with crackers and grapes. The anxious entrants and a couple dozen observers waited and watched. Tension was high until at last the first-, second-, and third-place winners were declared. They were ceremoniously awarded ribbons and Harmon's $150, $100, and $50 gift cards, respectively. Pictures were taken, hands were shaken, and it was good fun.

Funeral potatoes are so common in Utah that the name of the contest is the only point in the official guidelines that "funeral potatoes" were mentioned. Most people in the state just know what they are by way of cultural practice and common lore. In my Provo, Utah, home, there is a bookshelf with a collection of spiral-bound community cookbooks from various regions in the United States. These are often produced as fundraisers by church groups, clubs, botanical garden or symphony clubs, and Junior League chapters from varied corners of the country. There is now a series of colorful state cookbooks containing recipe collections from Florida to Alaska, and nearly every one of those cookbooks has a few recipes for casseroled potatoes and cheese. The ingredients are similar and include potatoes, cream soup, sour cream,

Funeral potatoes souvenir pin, 2002 Salt Lake Winter Olympics. Used by permission, Utah State Historical Society. All rights reserved.

Courtesy 12 Tomatoes, http://12tomatoes.com/
cheesy-funeral-potatoes-video/.

butter or margarine, onions, cheddar cheese, and
a common topping of cornflakes or breadcrumbs
tossed with melted butter. I found one community
cookbook from Iowa where the recipe was actually
called "Funeral Potatoes,"[2] but most recipes were
labeled "Cheesy Potatoes," "Yummy Potatoes," "Disappearing Potatoes," or, if the sour cream was omitted in the ingredient list, they were sometimes called
"Potatoes Au Gratin." The recipe hype is common,
but the title "funeral potatoes" has become a popular
regional marker, particularly in northern Utah.

Representative cookbooks reflect social bonds
that occur around communities of individuals with
common interests, and the frequent presence of the
cheese-and-potato recipe in the cookbooks of America attests to its popularity both in private family

gatherings and at the all-American covered-dish
church supper tradition. If you have an opportunity
to read about some of the food history of the United
States over the centuries since the 1600s, it is interesting to note that creamed or cheese potatoes, often
with a toasted bread-crumb topping, have been lovingly served since the early colonial days.[3]

Many people living in Utah now are descendants of Latter-day Saint converts from the eastern
and southern states who made the long trek to Utah
in the mid-1800s from their settlement in Nauvoo,
Illinois. It is clear that foodways and common food
preferences traveled with them, and as the crops
flourished in Utah and southern Idaho over time,
many of those traditional foods were preserved—
even to today. Then and now, homemakers and
cooks have exchanged recipes, and the humble but
substantial cheese-potato dish was carried on, shared,
and continued to comfort the hardy settlers of the
Intermountain West as well as their contemporary
progeny.

In 2000, Margaret Brady, Utah folklorist, wrote
a book called *Mormon Healer and Folk Poet: Mary
Susannah Fowler's Life of "Unselfish Usefulness."*[4]
Using Fowler's diary manuscript as a base, Brady tells
the story of this woman's life as wife, mother, and
active Latter-day Saint in the communal settlement
of Orderville, Utah, and then as a long-time resident
of Huntington. In Mary Susannah's continual redef-
inition of herself and her motivations in relation to
connections in a particular kind of community, one
where shared beliefs and service were the community
ethos, the reader is given a glimpse into the comfortable interconnectedness of close, supportive survival.
Teaching one another how to live, how to cook with

For several years a state-sponsored program known as "Utah's Own" held competitions at the state fair to encourage the use of Utah-made products. Funeral Potatoes Competition, Utah State Fair 2014. Photo by Carol A. Edison.

a minimal supply of food, how to heal, and how to live peaceably, we observe the undergirding of today's often village-like LDS wards (congregations), especially in much of Utah. Victor Turner called these groups by the Latin term *communitas* rather than "community," to suggest that the communitas was a modality of social relationship rather than simply a regional group.[5] I am not from Utah though I have been here nearly twenty years, and it was the women of my neighborhood ward who took gentle interest in my uninformed ways and taught me to make absolutely delicious funeral potatoes.

These social relationships share comforting and familiar commonalities. Presently in Utah, this delicious commonality has emerged and become internationally well known in part because of the 2002 Olympic pin. A centuries-old, very simple comfort food of creamed potatoes with cheese and some kind of crisp topping is a dish almost everyone enjoys. Locally, if one is really hungry for funeral potatoes and can't make them, they need only to pop over to Draper, Utah, to the Whole Foods Market and purchase a freshly made bowl of this warmly satisfying sustenance.

Traditionally, after church, synagogue, or mosque funerals in the United States, it is customary for family and friends to gather at the church or hall for a light luncheon usually provided by women of

Auguston Farms is one of several Utah companies offering dehydrated foods that Mormon faithful purchase to store in preparation for future needs. The addition of funeral potatoes to their offerings was undoubtedly a big hit. Photo by Carol A. Edison, 2018.

the church or a community of friends. In Utah, the Relief Society sisters (women of the congregation) prepare the meal and the iconic funeral potatoes are often, though not always, present. The standard meal in many LDS (Latter-day Saint or Mormon) congregations is baked ham (usually plain); a version of the scalloped or casseroled, cheese-flavored "funeral potatoes"; a tossed green salad; a Jell-O salad (green if served by culturally savvy sisters aware of Mormon kitsch); rolls; and cookies, brownies, pie, or cake.

Throughout Intermountain Mormondom, particularly in Utah County, just south of Salt Lake City,

the menu has become so entrenched in some congregations (including mine), that one of the women in my own ward said that if we didn't serve the traditional meal, "the proper meal," when it was her turn to be in the casket, she would come back and haunt us all.[6] For many of the Latter-day Saints in this region, the menu, including funeral potatoes, has become a serious tradition. It has become "conceived as everyday cultural behavior," Simon Bronner reminds us in a discussion of traditions in the United States.[7]

The Provo, Utah, Oak Hills Stake has a guideline booklet called the *Relief Society Action Manual*,[8] designed to assist Relief Society sisters in giving consistent service at the after-funeral banquet. I interviewed several women from various wards and stakes in Utah County and the menus described in the manual are typical of post-funeral meals served over the last two decades. The main menu is as described above; the second ("nice for spring or summer") is made up of ham sandwiches, varied salads, baked beans or vegetables, and cake; and the third is used if the interment is far away or if people have to leave immediately after the service. The lunch contains ham sandwiches, cut-up raw vegetables, potato chips, a cookie or brownie, a carton of milk or juice, and a napkin. Besides the expected use of funeral potatoes to comfort bereaved family and friends, the recipe is sometimes served at other times. One creative family decided to call them "baptism" potatoes because with Mormons' typically large families, there are far more baptisms than funerals (most LDS children are baptized at eight), so the popular casserole has become part of post-baptism celebrations as well.[9]

In the last twenty years or so, several articles have appeared in local Utah newspapers and

COOK'S COUNTY FUNERAL POTATOES

3 Tbsp. unsalted butter
2 onions, chopped fine
1/4 c. all-purpose flour
1 1/2 c. half-and-half
1 3/4 tsp. salt
1/2 tsp. dried thyme
1/4 tsp. pepper
2 c. shredded sharp cheddar cheese
9 c. (1 30-oz. bag) frozen shredded hash-brown
  potatoes
1/2 c. sour cream
4 c. sour-cream-and-onion potato chips, crushed

Adjust oven rack to middle position and heat oven to 350 degrees. Melt butter in a Dutch oven (or pot) over medium-high heat. Add onion and cook until softened, about 5 minutes. Add flour and cook, stirring constantly, until golden, about 1 minute. Slowly whisk in half-and-half, salt, thyme, and pepper and bring it to a boil. Reduce heat to medium-low and simmer, stirring occasionally, until slightly thickened, 3–5 minutes. Off heat, whisk in cheddar until smooth. Stir potatoes into sauce, cover, and cook, stirring occasionally, over low heat until thawed, about 10 minutes. Take off heat, stir in sour cream until combined. Scrape mixture into a 13-by-9-inch baking dish and top with potato chips. Bake until golden brown, 45–50 minutes. Let cool 10 minutes. Serves 8–10. Make ahead: potato mixture can be refrigerated in baking dish, covered with aluminum foil, for up to 2 days. Bake potatoes 20 minutes, then uncover and top with potato chips. Bake an additional 45–50 minutes.

GUNN'S ANTI-FUNERAL SHREDDED POTATO CASSEROLE

Nancy Gunn, a part-time member of the Brigham Young University English department faculty and long-time Utah resident, created a low-fat recipe called the Anti-Funeral Shredded Potato Casserole, "which allows you to enjoy a potato casserole without causing a funeral." Gunn's recipe and others are included in her article "Funeral Potatoes: A Utah Tradition."[10]

1 (26-oz.) bag frozen shredded potatoes
8 slices diced fat-free cheese slices
1/3 c. chopped onion (optional)
1 can low-fat cream of chicken or cream of
  mushroom soup
1 c. light sour cream plus 1 Tbsp. cornstarch
1 tsp. salt (optional)
1/4 tsp. pepper
3/4 c. Butter Buds liquid, divided
1 3/4 c. crushed cornflakes, divided
Cooking spray

Coat a large baking dish with cooking spray. Mix 1/4 cup cornflakes, 1/2 cup Butter Buds, and remaining ingredients together; place in dish. Mix remaining 1 1/2 cups cornflakes and 1/4 cup Butter Buds. Sprinkle over top of casserole and bake at 350 degrees for 35–40 minutes.

magazines describing healthy and not-so-healthy variants of funeral potatoes. In the May 2011 issue of the nationally published *Cook's Country Magazine*, the LDS religion is credited with giving this popular dish its name. Since I found the same name in an Iowa cookbook, I am not so sure, but according to Valerie Phillips's *Cook's County* article, "Mormons call it 'Funeral' or 'Ward Party' potatoes. In the South it's 'hash brown casserole,' but I've heard it called 'neighborhood potatoes' in Massachusetts and 'cheesy potatoes' in Washington."[11] Phillips included the *Cook's County* version in her article.

AUTHENTIC
MORMON FUNERAL POTATOES
(IF THERE IS SUCH A THING)

This article would be remiss if an authentic Latter-day Saint basic recipe for funeral potatoes were not included. The *Relief Society Action Manual*, includes a simple version of this popular and filling side dish. The recipe is as follows:

10 large potatoes boiled in their skins until firm. Peel and grate or chop.
2 cans of cream of chicken soup
1 c. sour cream
Several chopped green onions
1 c. grated cheddar cheese

Combine. Bake at 350 degrees till lightly browned and bubbly, about 40 minutes. One 9-by-13-inch baking dish yields about 10-12 servings. The dish can be prepared ahead. Reheating takes about 40 minutes.

Another variant is Penny Bird's Lazy Woman's Fake Funeral Potatoes which produces two batches instead of one. Bird, a retired English professor, explained to me that "it saves time if there are two funerals in the ward instead of one, or if you would simply like to enjoy the dish with your family without the hassle of a funeral."[12]

it encodes will be found in the pattern of social relations being expressed."[13] The 2002 Olympic charm helped to spread the fame of Utah's simple casserole, but regardless of the version, Utah's unpretentious funeral potatoes send a communiqué of untroubled warmth and comfort—a welcome message.

NOTES

1. Utah's Own is a state program sponsored by the Utah Department of Agriculture and Food designed to help consumers find quality, locally made products, protect the environment, and strengthen Utah's economy.
2. Dorie Gruetzmacher et al., *Cooking in Muscatine: Sponsored by the Master Gardeners of Muscatine County* (Muscatine, IA: Muscatine County Extension Service, 2002), 319.
3. Cookbooks ranging from *The Williamsburg Art of Cookery* (1742), to *Civil War Recipes: Receipts from the Pages of Godey's Lady's Books* (mid-1800s), to the *1896 Boston Cooking-School Cookbook*, and on to the *1904 World's Fair Souvenir Cook Book*—and forward through the twentieth century, include recipes for potatoes prepared a variety of ways, including what came to be called "Delmonico Hashed" in the 1920s which is similar to what we call "Funeral Potatoes" today.
4. Margaret K. Brady, *Mormon Healer & Folk Poet: Mary Susannah Fowler's Life of "Unselfish Usefulness"* (Logan: Utah State University Press, 2000).
5. Victor W. Turner, *The Ritual Process: Structure and Anti-Structure* (Chicago: Aldine Publishing, 1969), 96.
6. Jacqueline Thursby, "Funeral Potatoes, Other Foods, and Funeral Rituals among the Mormons of Utah," *The Mid-Atlantic Almanac: The Journal of the Mid-Atlantic Popular and* [as per their website] *American Culture Association* 14 (2005): 1–16.
7. Simon Bronner, *Following Tradition: Folklore in the Discourse of American Culture* (Logan: Utah State University Press, 1998), 13.
8. Sandra Covey et al., *The Relief Society Action Manual* (Provo, UT: Oak Hills Stake, 1993, 1996).

This uncomplicated comfort food has become known well beyond Utah borders as a symbol of family togetherness, warmth, and plenty. Many local people smile when funeral potatoes are mentioned. Anthropologist Mary Douglas suggests that food preferences often reveal codes. She states that food can carry "a general set of possibilities for sending messages. If food is treated as a code, the messages

9. Kristi Young Bell, interview with author, January 24, 2004.

10. Nancy Reynard Gunn, "Funeral Potatoes: A Utah Tradition," *This People Exploring LDS Issues and Personalities* 19, no. 3 (1998): 102.

11. Valerie Phillips, "Magazine Turns the Spotlight on Funeral Staple," *Deseret News* (Salt Lake City), April 26, 2011.

12. Penny Bird, conversation with author, January 2005.

13. Mary Douglas, "Deciphering a Meal," reprinted in *Food and Culture: A Reader*, ed. Carol Counihan and Penny Van Esterick (New York: Routledge, 1997), 37.

7

UTAH SCONES

ERIC A. ELIASON

To most of the world, scones (with jam and clotted cream) are an iconic feature of the English teatime meal. They are lightly sweetened, single-serving, dry, heavy cakes similar to American biscuits, made with various grains, leavened with baking powder, and cut into triangles or rounds and baked in especially shaped sheet pans. In recent decades they have become sweeter and more likely to contain bits of fruit or chocolate. In Utah a scone is something quite different—plain, flat, wheat-flour dough, deep or griddle fried to a light, puffy, golden brown in oil or lard. They more resemble *sopapillas*—a traditional pastry served with honey and powdered sugar, known for over three hundred years by many names and variations throughout the Spanish-influenced world.

In the American West, such bread is also often cooked in larger sizes for a meal, as are sopapillas stuffed with taco and enchilada-like filling in New Mexican cuisine. Navajo fry bread with chili on top is an iconic staple among the Diné that has spread to other tribes[1] and gained popularity among non-Natives, especially at fairs and powwows. Utah scones are eaten in all these ways but can also be shaped and cut as sandwich bread, as is done at the only-in-Utah location of The Sconecutter restaurant in Sandy. They highlight their signature items' versatility with the motto "everything tastes better on a scone," and they bill themselves as "home of Utah's homegrown scone."[2]

And homegrown it is, as "scone" refers to this kind of bread only in Utah. David Eddington, BYU linguist and specialist in Utah regionalisms, calls "scone" the only truly unique Utah word.[3] Recipes can vary somewhat from their Hispanic and Native counterparts. Fair vendors who travel the Intermountain West often have separate marquees for Utah and outside of Utah, saying "scones" or "fry bread," respectively. Online recipes for "Utah scones" and less commonly "Mormon scones" or "elephant ears" are more likely to suggest syrup and jams as toppings than sopapilla recipes are, and more often contain eggs and buttermilk than fry bread recipes do.

Scones are a heritage comfort food with an "old-timey" connotation, often eaten at family gatherings as a special indulgent treat, rather than as an everyday food as they might have been in a past with fewer options and less influenced by health-food marketing.[4] At least one non-LDS online recipe contributor has remarked that preparing and eating scones is a way to settle in as a true Utahn.[5] With so much of Utah's predominant culture defined by Mormonism, food items such as scones, thick shakes, and fry sauce serve as bridge-building, non-denominational shared identity markers.

But why "scones" and not "Mormon fry bread" or "Utah sopapillas"? Definitively explaining this peculiar usage may not be possible, but several facts can help piece together some plausibilities.

Courtesy Taylor Thurston.

- Utah has the highest percentage of English ancestry of any U.S. state.[6] The Mormon Church's earliest members came from the predominantly English New England states and from western New York where New Englanders had moved. Also, England was by far the most successful nineteenth-century Mormon mission field. For much of the mid-1800s, England had more Mormons than Utah, but most eventually came here.

- Before the twentieth century, English scones were more often fried on a griddle and had not yet begun to employ special cutters or pans. One variety, drop-scones, are still made by dropping a portion of batter on a griddle.[7] When Mormon pioneers came to the Great Salt Lake Valley in 1847, they were technically in Mexico. Many original settlers served in the Mexican-American War (1846 to 1848) during this formative time, coming in contact with Hispanic culture in the Spanish mission towns of Santa Fe, Tucson, San Diego, Los Angeles, and Sacramento.[8]

- For theological reasons, Mormon pioneers sought, at times, to befriend and teach Indians more often than was common in the West.[9]

- In 1864, the U.S. government attempted to force the Navajo out of the Four Corners region to a reservation in eastern New Mexico. According to Navajo tradition it was during this "Long Walk" that the government gave them rations of wheat flour, sugar, and lard, and Navajo fry bread was born.[10]

- When English settlers came to North America they gave the name "robin" to a genetically quite distinct indigenous species of thrush that reminded them of the smaller yet also red-orange breasted flycatcher-related "robin" of their homeland. Today these birds are known to birders as the "American Robin" and the "European Robin" respectively but just "robins" to those who live near them. (Similarly, LDS apologists suggest Book of Mormon references to cattle and sheep may refer to llamas and alpacas.)

- In the United States, "scone" is pronounced like "cone." In England, this pronunciation is known but can be seen as "posh" or affected. "Sconn" as in "John" is much more common.[11] According to the Oxford English Dictionary, today's more conservative American pronunciation was also the nineteenth-century British pronunciation.[12] "Sconn" moved from London northward, likely from the working class upward. The new pronunciation never got to Ireland. The following anonymous traditional poem perhaps hails from the moment when the pronunciation shift had reached its presumably working-class maid but not its more refined implied author:

> I asked the maid in dulcet tone
> To order me a buttered scone;
> The silly girl has been and gone
> And ordered me a buttered scone ["sconn"].

By the time this pronunciation shift made it to the heart of British Mormonism in England's northeast, the Mormons, who tended to be skilled professionals, were long gone to Utah.

With these data in mind, the name and nature of Utah scones might be explained by imagining predominantly English Mormon Utah settlers encountering a local foodway that was, at the time, somewhat similar to one of their own. Utah scones probably have *both* a continuous tradition back to England *and* have been significantly shaped by ongoing contact with Spanish and Native peoples. To the extent that Utah scones were adopted rather than imported, their naming may be an example of the process that "robin" underwent. Utahns today pronounce "scone" the same way other Americans and their English ancestors would have, but not in the manner of most modern Britons.

The influence of sopapillas on Utah scones could have begun the moment the Mormons arrived in 1847, but Navajo influence would wait until at least 1864. Mormons possibly influenced Navajos as they tried to make something to eat with their federal food. Contact between Mormons and Navajos was extensive at this time, but much of it hostile due to significant Navajo participation in Utah's 1865 to 1872 Blackhawk War.[13] Perhaps counterintuitively, conflict often accelerates cultural interchange.

But for Mormons, Navajos, and Mexicans alike, vectors of cultural influence may have played only a small role. In a shared hardscrabble frontier environment, with nothing but a campfire, a skillet, and a limited set of long-lasting portable staples like wheat flour, lard, yeast, and sugar, what else can be done but to make something that looks a lot like sopapillas, or fry bread, or scones? Other American pioneers along the Oregon Trail prepared similar fare, calling it "dough gods,"[14] a term perhaps a little too much like taking the Lord's name in vain for Mormon tastes and hence not popular in Utah today. But whatever the circumstances of their origin, scones are a living part of Utah's cultural fabric that comes in unbroken succession from the very formative pioneer experiences that created not just scones, but the whole state of Utah.

NOTES

1. Linda Stradley, *I'll Have What They're Having: Legendary Local Cuisine* (Dallas: Three Forks, Press 2002).
2. Facebook.com/Stonecutter.
3. Other words Utahns sometimes may think are unique are actually used elsewhere. But nowhere else is "scone" used to mean what it does in Utah. Doug Fabrizio, David Eddington, and Ben Zimmer, "Speaking American, Speaking Utahn," June 17, 2014, produced by *Radio West*, podcast, MP3 audio, http://radiowest.kuer.org/post/speaking-american-speaking-utahn.
4. Jeni Potter Scott, "Homemade Utah Scones," *Bakerette* (blog), accessed May 13, 2014, http://bakerette.com/homemade-utah-scones/.
5. Annalise, "Utah Scones with Cinnamon Honey Butter," *Completely Delicious* (blog), accessed September 11, 2011, http://www.completelydelicious.com/2011/09/utah-scones-with-cinnamon-honey-butter.html.
6. US Census Bureau, "Census 2000 Brief," http://www.census.gov/prod/2004pubs/c2kbr-35.pdf. See also, "English Ancestry Maps," Epodunk, http://www.epodunk.com/ancestry/English.html.
7. Leslie Wiener and Barbara Albright, *Simply Scones: Quick and Easy Recipes for More Than 70 Delicious Scones and Spreads* (New York: St. Martin's, 1988), 3.
8. Norma Baldwin Ricketts, *The Mormon Battalion: U.S. Army of the American West, 1846–48* (Logan: Utah State University Press, 1997).
9. Howard A. Christy, "Open Hand and Mailed Fist: Mormon-Indian Relations in Utah, 1847–52," *Utah Historical Quarterly* 46, (Summer 1978).
10. Jen Miller, "Frybread: This Seemingly Simple Food Is a Complicated Symbol of Navajo Culture," *Smithsonian Magazine*, July 2008.
11. British Library, "Map Your Voice Project," http://www.bl.uk/evolvingenglish/mapabout.html.
12. *Oxford English Dictionary*, 2nd ed., *s.v.* "scone."
13. John Alton Peterson, *Utah's Blackhawk War* (Salt Lake City: University of Utah Press, 1998).
14. Kathy Stephenson, "Utahns Enter the Scone Zone," *Salt Lake Tribune*, May 3, 2006.

8

DUTCH-OVEN COOKING

BOB KING

It happens every spring in Utah: the World Championship Dutch Oven Cook-Off. Over several days, dozens of teams like "Ma and Pa Kettle" and the "South Rim Rednecks" compete with stews and desserts, biscuits and breakfasts. Many can be seen sporting t-shirts and hoodies emblazoned with "IDOS," for the International Dutch Oven Society, headquartered in Logan, Utah.[1]

All the hullabaloo over cooking with the cast-iron kettle would puzzle the Utah pioneers, mountain men, and miners for whom the Dutch oven made common sense—a versatile, durable kitchen tool that could braise, fry, roast, or bake over a campfire. But it's the connection to Utah's pioneer past that likely fuels the modern interest, the challenges and contingencies of cooking outdoors trumping the convenience of a propane Coleman stove. It is no surprise that in Utah, with its Pioneer Day holiday, the Dutch oven was, in 1997, declared the official state cooking pot by the Utah state legislature.[2]

"Dutch" usually has a pejorative sense—a Dutch date isn't quite a date in the traditional sense; a Dutch door is a bifurcated portal; a Dutch oven is a heavy-duty pot rather than any sort of conventional oven. Proper seasoning of the cast iron, tending the hot coals and regulating the cooking temperature, and proper cleaning and storage of the kettle adds to the challenges, but also to the appeal of Dutch-oven cooking. Practicing the pioneer craft and cooking outdoors makes those sourdough biscuits taste even better.

One can find enameled, cast aluminum, or ceramic Dutch ovens suitable for indoor cooking with a stove or oven—you can invest in a Le Creuset for about $300. The traditional Dutch oven is heavy, cast iron, and has a lipped, tight-fitting lid that allows the strategic placing of hot coals atop, making for more even heating on the inside. The craft comes in maintaining a steady, desired temperature; longer cooking efforts require a steady supply of new coals and fuel for the banked fire. A long-handled lid remover

Dutch oven souvenir pin, 2002 Salt Lake Winter Olympics. Used by permission, Utah State Historical Society. All rights reserved.

or long-handled pliers is a necessary tool for the committed Dutch-oven chef. The IDOS hoodie is optional.

When you make the effort to cook over a campfire with a Dutch oven, you are making more than a perfunctory meal. The Dutch-oven chef is feeding friends and family in a pioneer tradition, outdoors in the American West, where food always tastes better.

BURNT OFFERINGS

"Lodge Only" is the motto of Larry Davis of Boulder, Utah, where he served for decades at the Anasazi State Park Museum. He retired from the government but keeps on cooking—he and his spouse, Judi Davis, have a loyal regional following and always draw a crowd for their slow-cooked pork ribs, boneless chicken breasts, and double chocolate cake with pudding inside.

Chef Larry wasn't always this capable, and he tells the tale of his first efforts with the Dutch oven, a tale of "burnt offerings." Sometime last century, he dug a pit, filled a Dutch oven with carrots, pork steaks, and onions, buried it in the coals, then headed into the woods for an outdoor seminar with a crowd of young men, who returned quite hungry. Lifting the lid with great expectations, Larry found a steaming black mass of carbonized protein and charred black vegetable matter, with one small gleam of orange from a carrot slice.

He has since progressed on the ancient Greek trajectory from Information to Knowledge to Wisdom, and has much to say about charcoal (Kingsford), aluminum gear (use cast iron), the art of seasoning and cleaning Dutch ovens, and the deeper

Lynn Sanders, who learned to cook in a Dutch oven while working with his dad as a hunting guide, always prepared Dutch-oven potatoes at the Southern Utah Folklife Festival. Photo by Carol A. Edison, 1987. Courtesy Utah Folklife Archives.

Dutch ovens (don't). For the standard ten-inch Dutch oven and an even temperature of 325 degrees, he invokes the "three up, three down" rule: instead of an even ten briquettes above and below, move to thirteen up and seven down, and a quarter turn of the pot every fifteen minutes.[3]

A parks colleague and longtime friend of Davis, Norm Forbush of Cedar City, Utah, owns thirty Dutch ovens and knows how to use them. He retired after decades with Utah State Parks; at the Iron Mission State Park he orchestrated staff and volunteers for an annual Dutch-oven dinner every November to celebrate Iron Mission Days, with at times a hundred Dutch ovens simmering for a thousand guests.[4] He is coauthor of a folksy, quirky cookbook, *Going Dutch with Flash*.[5]

BUFFALO BOB'S DUTCH-OVEN GAME HENS

If it tastes good at home, it will taste even better camped out in the red rock desert or the Uintah Mountains. Thirty years ago, camped on the west side of the Henry Mountains, this relatively straightforward effort helped secure my reputation. For hearty appetites, allow one game hen per person. In a cooler or ice chest, they will need two to three days to thaw, but will help keep things cold. As usual, take care handling raw poultry. The standard 12-inch Dutch oven can readily handle up to three game hens; four or more might call for the 14-inch model.

3 Tbsp. vegetable oil
3 to 4 game hens, thawed
One onion, quartered
One lemon, quartered
Salt, pepper, and cumin to taste
Butter, flour, and perhaps wine for a pan sauce

1. For the campfire, briquettes or a mix of firewood and briquettes will work; have about a dozen glowing briquettes ready to place on the lid.
2. As the fire settles, rub the skin with oil and season the skin and insides of the game hens with salt, pepper, and cumin. Place a quarter onion and lemon inside each bird, and space them evenly in the Dutch oven.
3. When the fire dies down, bank the coals and nestle the Dutch oven. I prefer to cook poultry hotter than the norm, i.e., at 400 degrees rather than 350.
4. After about 25 minutes, quickly check the birds and turn the Dutch oven 180 degrees to ensure even cooking.
5. After another 25 minutes, check for doneness. Given the unscientific nature of campfire cooking, an instant-read thermometer is a good tool. Look for a reading of 150 degrees at a minimum (165 degrees and higher is often recommended but tends to dry out the bird). The game-hen leg should move easily and the juices run clear. If they are done, remove them from the Dutch oven and let them sit for five minutes, topped with aluminum foil, while you rustle up a pan gravy with the butter, flour, game-hen bits and juices, adding liquid if necessary (wine, stock, whiskey, etc.).
6. With the cooking over, build up the fire for the evening and enjoy the game hens. Outdoors you may use your fingers and hands for dining.

For both Norm and Larry, Dutch ovens are popular in Utah because "the food tastes better." Utah has more Dutch ovens per capita than any other state, and it's an enduring part of Boy Scout jamborees and family reunions. A well-seasoned Dutch oven that's been in the family for many a camping trip or outdoor venture, that's tucked into many a campfire's glowing bed of coals, becomes a talisman of the West, luminous, nestled in the glowing coals at twilight.

NOTES
1. "IDOS," International Dutch Oven Society, http://www.idos.com/.
2. Susan Haws, "Dutch Oven Cooking," Utah State University Extension, https://digitalcommons.usu.edu/cgi/viewcontent.cgi?article=1019&context=extension_curall.
3. Larry Davis (Dutch-oven caterer), phone interview with the author, November 12, 2015.
4. Norm Forbush (Dutch-oven caterer), phone interview with the author, November 17, 2015.
5. Norm Forbush, *Goin' Dutch with Flash* (self-published, 2000).

9

THE SHORT SWEET HISTORY OF THICK SHAKES

DENNIS CUTCHINS

In order to understand the nature of Utah milkshakes we must first know a little bit about milkshake history and terminology. The bad news is that milkshake history is, by its very nature, extremely ephemeral. Most of it has been preserved only in memory, and most of that has been forgotten. But we do know a few things. Iced or crushed ice drinks have been around for a long time. The term "frappé" has long referred to the kind of iced drinks now typically known as "smoothies": crushed ice mixed with fruit or other flavorings. In Boston and in other places on the Eastern Seaboard, however, "frap" has become a generic term that includes any cold, thickish drink, including those made with ice cream. But milkshakes are younger than frappés. The Oxford English Dictionary lists the first use of the word "milkshake" in an ad for Beermann's Palace Soda Stand in Atlanta in 1886.[1] We don't have samples of what Beermann was serving, but it was likely chocolate milk or chocolate malted milk—not something we would now call a "milkshake" since it probably lacked ice cream.

The creation of the modern milkshake was the result of two happy coincidences. The first was the invention of the Cyclone drink mixer by the Hamilton Beach Company in 1911. That first drink mixer is one that many of us would still recognize. It had a round or teardrop-shaped motor housing with a long, thin mixing spindle protruding from the bottom. Hamilton Beach hasn't changed the design much over the years, and thousands of this style of mixer are still in use. A metal cup with ingredients is held under the rotating spindle and manipulated by hand. After its introduction, the Hamilton Beach mixer quickly became a common feature at soda fountains across the country, and it was typically used to make crushed-ice drinks and chocolate milk.

And that brings us to the second happy event. Charles R. Walgreen Sr. began his drugstore chain in Chicago in 1901; by 1919 there were twenty Walgreens drugstores in and around Chicago, many of which had soda fountains.[2] These were snack bars that typically served sandwiches,

Photo by Katherine Neish.

cold drinks, candies, and ice cream. But Walgreen was not satisfied with the ice cream that was commercially available at the time. It was really ice milk, relatively thin when thawed, and not very rich. So, in 1919, in the basement of one of their Chicago stores, Walgreens began making their own richer brand of ice cream with added butter.[3] The result, at least in retrospect, seems inevitable.

The item that most of us would recognize as a milkshake was probably invented in the summer of 1922 in a Chicago Walgreens by a man named Ivar "Pop" Colson.[4] Colson simply added two scoops of Walgreens ice cream to a typical chocolate malt (milk, chocolate syrup, and malted power) and mixed it with his Hamilton Beach drink mixer. He charged twenty cents for the drink, which quickly became immensely popular. Walgreens folklore suggests that Al Capone may have even been one of the first satisfied customers.[5]

The next innovation in milkshake history also took place in Illinois when an ice cream company named Prince Castle, famous for its distinctive white cinderblock buildings, began selling "multimixers," more powerful drink mixers that allowed up to six drinks to be mixed at the same time.[6] One of their multimixer salesmen, a fellow named Ray Kroc, used his connections in the industry and his knowledge of mixers to start his own restaurant chain.[7] Kroc's desire for product consistency at his McDonald's restaurants eventually led him to pioneer the milkshake machine, an ice cream freezer and mixer in one.[8] The milkshake machine, like the soft-serve ice cream machine it's modeled on, stirs the ice cream/milkshake constantly to create a smooth consistency while it simultaneously freezes it. These machines mean that basic shake flavors like chocolate and vanilla can be made without a drink mixer. More complicated flavors, ones that require flavored syrup, fruit, or added candy bits, still require a drink mixer, even at McDonald's.

WHAT MAKES A SHAKE?

All of this history can help us define the three basic types of milkshakes. The first and oldest style of milkshake is made with hard-serve ice cream mixed by hand with milk in a drink mixer. Other ingredients, like flavored syrup or fruit, may be added during the mixing process. Few restaurants, however, make these hard-serve ice cream shakes anymore. The second style of milkshake, and probably the most popular today, is made in basically the same way, but instead of hard-serve ice cream with added milk it uses soft-serve ice cream. For flavors other than chocolate or vanilla, however, these shakes are still blended by hand in a drink mixer. The final style of modern milkshake is really a matter of degree (literally) rather than process or ingredients. If the temperature on a soft-serve ice cream machine is turned up slightly then the product that is dispensed is a partially frozen, drinkable mixture that may be, like the other styles of shakes, then mixed with other ingredients in a drink mixer. The differences in most shakes are thus the result of three variables: the mix that is used in the soft-serve or milkshake machine (these are kept secret by most restaurants); the ingredients that are mixed in by hand with a drink mixer; and the temperature of the ice cream. The temperature is important, since it dictates not only the thickness of the shake, but also the "extra" ingredients that may be added. Thin shakes won't suspend candy bits, for instance, or heavy pieces of fruit.

UTAH MILKSHAKES

And that brings us to Utah. Nearly all of these creations have one thing in common: Outside of the Intermountain West they are almost always "drinkable" (we'll come back to that "almost" bit in a minute). In Utah, however, most soft-serve machines

are set to 18 degrees Fahrenheit—cold enough to make shakes thick. And that's unusual. Folks who grew up in the Intermountain West may not readily recognize anything special about Utah shakes, but for people who grew up elsewhere—Illinois, in my case—Utah shakes are definitely different. "Thick shakes" or "over-the-top" shakes are rare outside of Utah, Arizona, and Idaho. For most of the country, a shake is something you can drink through a straw. I recently interviewed Reed Reinholt, the CEO of Iceberg, a small chain of restaurants famous in Utah for its "concretes," shakes so thick that the server hands them to customers upside-down. Reed notes that Sorensen's Iceberg recently acquired the franchise rights for the "Iceberg" name and concept and is in the process of expanding.[9] They now have sixteen locations in Utah, Arizona, and California. He notes that the five stores in California, however, sometimes receive complaints from customers about the thickness of the shakes. Brad Kimball, owner of the Taylor Freezer Company of Utah, echoes this idea. He explains that the corporate offices of the Taylor Company are located in Illinois, and that executives there are always somewhat surprised by the success of "thick shakes" in Utah.

The regional popularity of thick shakes may be clear, but their origin is less clear. One candidate for bringing thick shakes to Utah is Iceberg. Reinholt believes that they may have originated with Hap Vitale, a soft-serve ice cream machine salesman who worked for the Taylor Freezer Company of Utah in the 1950s and 1960s. Vitale realized that the new Taylor soft-serve ice cream machines (which sometimes doubled as milkshake machines) could be set colder and thus produce a much thicker product

Photo by Shannon Hall.

than earlier models.[10] He also tested new drink mixers that could handle this thicker ice cream. Vitale came up with the Iceberg name and concept and sold the idea to several of his customers, including Lamar Sorensen. Sorensen's original Iceberg, which opened its doors on April 12, 1960, is still located at the corner of 3900 South and 900 East in Salt Lake City. Brent Matthews, a former partner at the Taylor Freezer Company, isn't so sure that Iceberg originated the thick shake. He thinks Arctic Circle,

another Utah-based company, is an equally likely candidate.[11] Either way, he believes that thick shakes started to become popular in the early 1960s. That ballpark date jibes well with what Stan Taylor, the original owner of Stan's Drive-In in Provo, said in an interview in 2014. Stan, who died in 2016, was around to experience much of this fast-food history. He purchased an Arctic Circle franchise in Provo in 1957 while he was still an employee of Geneva Steel. In 1961 he became frustrated with the management at Arctic Circle and bought the restaurant outright. When I asked him if he served "over the top" or thick shakes in those early days, he scoffed. That, he said, would have been a waste of money.[12] My dad agrees with this estimate. His family moved to Utah in 1959, and he says that he doesn't remember anyone serving thick shakes then. But by the fall of 1964 they were around, though they were not the norm.[13]

Most of the folks I interviewed agreed more or less on the early 1960s date for the thick shake innovation, but no one was able to identify a place. Several locations in the Bear Lake area, with their iconic seasonal raspberry shakes, are a possibility, but not a strong likelihood. Brad Kimball believes that the Dairy Keen restaurant in Heber City, owned and operated by the Mawhinney family for nearly seventy years, may have been the source of the original thick shake.[14] But this is not likely, either. Jan Mawhinney, one of the owners of Dairy Keen and the daughter of the original owner, believes that they started serving thick shakes between 1968 and 1972.[15] Kimball did add that Dairy Keen sells more shakes than any other single restaurant in Utah, and Mawhinney agrees. She told me that the restaurant served more than three thousand shakes per day over the 2014 Labor

Day weekend. That's a stunning number in anyone's book. David Mawhinney, Jan's nephew, gave me a "behind the counter" tour in the fall of 2014. On busy days, he explained, the store at that time had about thirty people working, and fifteen to twenty of them were doing nothing but making shakes in an impressive assembly line.[16] It takes a little less than two minutes to make a shake when all the cylinders are firing, and I can vouch for the quality. When you visit Heber remember that they'll custom-mix flavors, too. I tried strawberry-Oreo a few years ago and it remains one of my favorites.

THE ORIGINS OF THICK

All of this brings us no closer to an answer about origins, but if you've been paying attention then you may have noticed that most milkshake innovations occurred in Illinois. It's quite possible that thick shakes could have started there. I recently spoke with Kent Colberg, a salesman for the H.C. Duke restaurant equipment company in Moline, Illinois. H.C. Duke is the company that originally made the "Electro Freeze Arctic Swirl" drink mixers now widely used to make thick shakes. Colberg explained that H.C. Duke began manufacturing these heavy-duty blenders in 1984 at the specific request of Dairy Queen International.[17] Dairy Queen wanted the blender in order to begin making their "Blizzard" brand of thick shakes. Blizzards are made using thicker soft-serve ice cream and blending in candy and other unusual toppings. Colberg then added that a local restaurant, Whitey's Ice Cream, also located in Moline, had been serving thick shakes for as long as he could remember. I called Whitey's main office and spoke to

Shake menu at Granny's Drive-In in Heber City. Photo by Eric A. Eliason, 2018.

Jon Tunberg, the owner. He explained that Whitey's opened for business in 1933 and that his dad, Bob Tunberg, worked at the restaurant and then bought it in 1953. Jon agreed that Whitey's has always sold

thick shakes, as far as he knows. He said that one of the company's advertising slogans used to be: "The shake's so thick that the straw is just for show."[18] Jon, his dad, and Chester Lindgren, the original "Whitey," even developed their own heavy-duty mixer back in the mid-1960s to handle the thick shakes they were creating.[19] The thick consistency, and the new heavy-duty mixer, allowed for heavier ingredients to be used, and Jon may have been the first person to mix candy into a shake. In 1969, when he was still in high school, he tried blending a Nestle Butterfinger candy bar into a shake. He shared it with some of his friends, and they began requesting the new flavor. Soon it became a regular menu item, and other candy flavors joined it. According to Jon, some H.C. Duke employees, in the restaurant to service other machines, may have noticed these custom-made heavy-duty blenders in the early 1980s, and used them as a model for their own "Arctic Swirl"–style blender.[20] Jon wryly mentioned that he wished he had bought DQ stock in the early 1980s, since he heard that the Blizzard, similar in many ways to the shakes Whitey's had been serving for years, actually saved the company.

The evidence, finally, is inconclusive, but highly suggestive. Thick shakes likely originated in the

Midwest, perhaps at Whitey's Ice Cream in Moline, Illinois, or, as Tunberg speculates, at Tom Drewes Frozen Custard in St. Louis (Tom Drewes, established in 1929, also serves an item known as a "concrete"). But thick shakes have remained a rather isolated item there. I grew up a mere fifty miles from Moline and I can't remember ever being served a thick shake. That's saying something, too. My dad is a certified milk-shake connoisseur. He traveled a good deal for his job, and he knew most of the best shake places within a seventy-mile radius. So thick shakes, while they may have originated in Moline, didn't really spread. In Utah, on the other hand, they have become the norm. Strolling into a Utah restaurant and asking for a shake that you can drink through a straw is likely to be met with stares of confusion and disbelief. One teenaged employee at a local drive-in asked me several times if I was sure that was what I wanted, then had to call her supervisor over to make sure it was okay. My friend's brother, on the other hand, visits Utah once or twice a year and looks forward to the thick shakes. He makes a point to stop at the Purple Turtle in Pleasant Grove and get a thick style of shake that, while it may not be an exclusively Utah food, is certainly hard to find in other parts of the country.

NOTES

1. "Milkshake," *OED Online*, accessed September 19, 2014.
2. "Our Past," Walgreens. com, accessed September 23, 2014.

3. John U. Bacon, *America's Corner Store* (Hoboken, NJ: John Wiley and Sons, 2004), 48.
4. Ibid., 67.
5. Ibid., 68.
6. Chris Stach, "The Land of the Last One-in-a-Million," *Riverside Brookfield Landmark*, rblandmark.com, September 13, 2005.
7. "The Ray Kroc Story," McDonalds.com, accessed September 23, 2014.
8. "A Fair Shake," *Snopes.com*, Snopes, January 26, 2007.
9. Reed Reinholt, telephone interview with the author, July 14, 2014.
10. Ibid.
11. Brent Matthews, telephone interview with the author, July 14, 2014.
12. Stan Taylor, personal interview with the author, June 25, 2014.
13. Lyle William, personal interview with the author, September 19, 2014.
14. Brad Kimball, telephone interview with the author, July 14, 2014.
15. Jan Mawhinney, telephone interview with the author, September 4, 2014.
16. David Mawhinney, personal interview with the author, September 13, 2014.
17. Kent Colberg, telephone interview with the author, September 18, 2014.
18. Jon Tunberg, telephone interview with the author, September 18, 2014.
19. Ibid.
20. Ibid.

UTAH'S PASTRAMI BURGERS

TED MCDONOUGH

Tasked with naming a food to represent each of the fifty states, an Oregon newspaper selected a hamburger topped with pastrami as the most representative Utah dish. Jell-O salad was a mere runner-up in the 2014 *Willamette Week* survey.[1]

Online, recipe blogs give instructions for making an authentic pastrami-topped "Rocky Mountain Burger," giving special attention to preparing a thick "Utah fry sauce" with which to slather the sandwich. The specialty burger—known ubiquitously in Utah as the Crown Burger after the first restaurant to serve the sandwich in the late 1970s—helped Salt Lake City snag the number two spot on *Travel + Leisure Magazine*'s 2011 list of the country's best cities for burgers;[2] it garnered a feature story for itself in the *New York Times*.[3]

The pastrami burger has even caught the fancy of the hipster-foodie town of Portland, Oregon, where Chef Nick Zukin—perhaps the nation's greatest Crown Burger evangelist—once created a version of the sandwich for a Portland Jewish deli. He traveled to Utah to get the formula just right, giving full credit to the state that loves its hamburger patties heaped with warm, red pastrami. Utah is the place that made a 1950s get-'em-in-the-door fast-food gimmick into a staple food group—or, as Zukin put it in his food blog, a "city on a hill where all burgers come with pastrami."

For better or worse, the pastrami burger is linked in the popular imagination with the Beehive State. Not that there is anything inherently Utahn about pastrami—an East Coast Jewish deli meat—or the hamburger, for that matter. Nothing about it is inherently Utahn except perhaps that Utahns continue to gobble up Crown Burgers forty years after their introduction, and except for the tenacity of a group of Utahns that tourists might not think of when they think of the Beehive State: Greeks.

The early 1900s brought thousands of Greek immigrants to Utah's Bingham Canyon copper mine and the coal mines of Carbon County. Many who didn't mine opened restaurants.

The progenitor of the Utah Greek family that would hit on the winning pastrami burger formula arrived in Utah from Crete in 1909 and later earned U.S. citizenship for his service as a

A pastrami burger with fry sauce. Courtesy Katherine Mikkelson.

soldier in World War I. He opened a Greek coffee-house named Anekti Karthia, or Open Heart.

Michael Katsanevas returned to Greece during World War II, later returning to Utah with three of his children, hoping to earn enough money to bring his wife and other children later. When work as a janitor at the Utah Capitol and at Hill Air Force Base didn't bring in enough money, a community fundraiser did, allowing Katsanevas to send for his family in 1954.

Through the 1960s and 1970s, the Katsanevas family operated the Athenian, a legendary restaurant and nightclub on Salt Lake City's 200 South. But some of Katsanevas's children went searching for work in California, which was then experiencing a postwar burger craze. The story of Utah's famous Crown Burger begins near Anaheim, California, where pastrami burgers remain popular today. There, Jim Katsanevas, the eldest of the Katsanevas children, learned to make a pastrami burger, serving the sandwich as the Zorba Burger at his restaurant, Minos.

Jim's sister Rula and her husband, John Katzourakis, took the pastrami burger with them when they returned to Utah and opened the first Crown

Burger in 1978 on Salt Lake City's 200 South with Rula's brother, Nick Katsanevas.

Rula recalled that the pastrami-topped burger was an instant hit, causing lines around the block. Fellow Cretan John Lyhnakis, then operating an Anaheim-area burger restaurant, received a phone call from Salt Lake City. "These guys opened up Crown Burger, and it's booming with what we got going in California," recalled his son Vasili Lyhnakis. His father quickly sold his California restaurant and moved to Utah to help start the first of many Astro Burger restaurants with cousin Angelo Tsoutsounakis.

Soon the Salt Lake Valley was wall-to-wall with Greek-owned burger places: Apollo Burger, Atlas Burger, Atlantis Burger, Olympus Burger, and Palace Burger—each patterned on Crown Burger's winning formula and each prominently featuring an eponymous "char-broiled" pastrami-topped burger.

The restaurants included seven Crown Burgers opened by Katsanevas brothers, sisters, in-laws, and nephews: brothers Steve and Manuel on North Temple; sister Rita and her husband, John Klonizos, in West Valley City; Jim Katsanevas on Highland Drive; Nick Katsanevas at 3300 South; and Manuel's son Chris with his first cousin, Mike Katsanevas, in Sandy. Bill Katsanevas, nephew to the immigrant brothers and sisters, opened a Crown Burger in Layton with John Katzourakis's brother Mike.

Today, the formula at many of the restaurants remains little changed from the first Crown Burger forty years ago, from the small pieces of paper inscribed with numbers handed to waiting customers to the large menu that can feature everything from charbroiled burgers to dolmades, Philly cheesesteak sandwiches, chicken kebabs, and seven-ounce rib-eye-steak sandwiches.

Typically, the entire operation is on display for patrons to watch as their food is prepared to order using revolving spits of meat, a grill, and a controlled inferno where hamburgers cook over the open flame. Conspicuously absent is a heat lamp, as made-to-order food from fresh ingredients is an enduring hallmark of the restaurants.

Greek founders continue to run many of the restaurants, donning aprons, sweeping the floors, and flipping burgers, but the faces at the order counter increasingly belong to more-recent immigrants; a typical ordering experience ends with a Somali-Utahn handing you a burger cooked by a Mexican-Utahn through a window to which is appended a hand-lettered pen-and-notepaper sign imploring "Try Our Baklava."

The original Crown Burger restaurants stand out among the forest of Utah's pastrami-burger places due to interiors designed by Salt Lake City interior designer Ken deCondé. He fitted the restaurants with imported European furnishings to reflect the royalty of the Crown name.

At Crown Burger No. 2 on North Temple, customers dine beneath a chandelier at tables surrounding a brick fireplace bordered by two tall wooden lions and decorated with European tapestry. On the back wall, statues in armor hold plants while wooden gargoyles balance lamps on their heads. Booths are lit by electric candles in brass holders. A stylized forest scene is etched into glass. Habitual staging grounds for prom dates, Crown Burger restaurants have even hosted a wedding reception or two.

Hunting-lodge-meets-King-Arthur's-castle décor

notwithstanding, the pastrami burger remains simple. A patty charbroiled over open flame and topped with a mound of house-cured red pastrami thicker than the burger itself on a sesame-seed bun with lettuce, tomato, American cheese, and Utah's staple ketchup-and-mayo "fry sauce," the Crown Burger is presented half-wrapped in paper for ease of eating and served with a side of fries, onion rings, a salad, or rice pilaf.

The burger has obsessive fans, is dreamed of by Utah expats, and is perhaps the first request of returned LDS missionaries. The demand for a traveling Crown for the airplane is frequent enough that the owners of Crown Burger No. 1 once devised a system of separating out the burger's component parts for later reassembly to avoid sogginess during transport in airplane luggage.

Pastrami on a burger is "like peanut butter and chocolate: two great things on their own, even better when combined," Chef Zukin once explained on his food blog.[4]

The fast-food burger may be on the skids nationwide as Americans turn to allegedly healthier fare, but the pastrami burger shows no sign of slowing. Now a mandatory offering on locally owned fast-food menus throughout Utah, the burger is increasingly seen in surrounding states, popping up on menus in Denver, Mesa, Albuquerque, and Las Vegas. It hasn't yet crossed the Rocky Mountains in a big way, but the pastrami burger seems destined to be Utah's culinary gift to the world.[5]

NOTES

1. https://www.wweek.com/portland/blog-32043-utah-pastrami-burger-the-mt-olympus-of-the-beehive-state.html.
2. https://www.travelandleisure.com/slideshows/americas-best-burger-cities-2011?slide=100782#100782.
3. John T. Edge, "Pastrami Meets the Patty in Utah," *New York Times*, https://www.nytimes.com/2009/07/29/dining/29united.html.
4. http://supersizedmeals.com/food/article.php/20060130132059143.
5. A version of this selection originally appeared in the *Salt Lake City Weekly*, June 11, 2007.

Brigham Young admired bees because they are collaborative, purposeful, focused, and industrious. He initially named the region "Deseret," the Book of Mormon word for honeybee. Fifty years later when the territory became the State of Utah, the beloved symbol of the bee was transformed into the state motto—"Industry." Photo by Carol A. Edison, 2019.

11

BEES AND HONEY IN THE BEEHIVE STATE

KRISTI A. BELL

At the time of their epic pioneering trek westward, Brigham Young, the leader of the Church of Jesus Christ of Latter-day Saints, admired the attributes of bees. They are collaborative, purposeful, focused, and industrious—characteristics he wanted to foster in his people. He was firm enough in this opinion that he called the land he and his people settled "Deseret"—the word for honeybee in the religion's founding scripture, the Book of Mormon.[1] Though the federal government did not accept this name, opting for "Utah" after the indigenous Ute Indian tribe, the beehive figures prominently in the state seal and flag, the word "Industry" is the state motto, and the honeybee and the beehive have become well-loved symbols that are still in abundant use by religious, governmental, and commercial ventures after more than a century and a half.[2]

While bees and their hives are used symbolically in Utah, bees and the honey they produce are also part of the state's agricultural heritage and economy. Honey is produced in Cache Valley; along the Wasatch Front; in the Uintah Basin; midstate in Millard, Garfield, and Iron Counties, as well as in the St. George area, Utah's arid southwest corner. As they gather nectar from alfalfa, sweet clover, and other blossoms, bees transfer pollen, fertilizing fruit and other crops. Sometimes beekeepers encourage this process by moving hives seasonally to access early nectar from mountain flowers or placing bees where they can easily pollinate orchards.[3]

The largest and perhaps the best-known Utah honey company is Miller's Honey, started in 1894 by Nephi Miller in Providence, Utah. Today Miller's Honey sells pure raw honey, creamed honey, honey butter, honey vinegar, honey and sea salt rub, and a variety of lotions, soaps, and cleansers containing honey. Known for being strained—not filtered or cooked, Miller's honey is also known for its high-quality taste. The company focuses on clover honey, but also sells a limited number of wildflower honey products that are darker in color. The darker the color of the honey, the more robust the taste; the lighter in color, the sweeter.[4]

While Miller's remains the largest, there are many other beekeepers who sell their product at stores, farmers markets, fruit stands, and online. They range from commercial producers like Cache Valley's Cox Honeyland, another century-old family business,[5] and central Utah's

Wayne N. Smart working in his bee yard, c. 1960. Courtesy Dean R. Smart.

Knight Family Honey, who twenty years ago revived a tradition of beekeeping from their pioneer ancestors,[6] to numerous small batch producers. Beekeeping has become one of the most popular hobbies in the country and small producers are responsible for about 40 percent of the honey produced each year.[7]

Many beekeepers make money from their hives as well as from their honey. Byron Anderson started with one hive in 1980, buying two more over the next few years and stocking them with inexpensive queen bees. Today he has around three hundred hives. While he kept his first hive in his backyard, none of his current swarms are located on his own property. He finds farmers growing alfalfa and exchanges honey for the privilege of putting some of his hives on their land. He also rents his swarms out as pollinators. During summers he rents them to local orchard growers, and in the winter he takes

them to California where they are used to pollinate almond trees.[8]

During the last few decades, beekeepers everywhere have faced growing challenges in maintaining the healthy bee population necessary for basic agricultural production. Luckily concerns over the Africanization of the honeybee were calmed over time as the gentle European honey bee that Utahns have managed since frontier times has been interbreeding with the invasive Africanized honey bee, diluting their aggressiveness.[9]

In other good news researchers have discovered that one out of every four bee species in the country lives in Utah, making the state home to more bee species than most states. About half of those species dwell within the original boundaries of the Grand Staircase–Escalante National Monument where 87 percent of Utah's flowering plant species also live, contributing to the rich diversity of pollinators.[10]

But the future health of bee populations is always a concern. Throughout history bee populations have fluctuated when for unknown reasons worker bees have left the hive to search for food, then not returned. In 2006, when the number of disappearances rose dramatically in North America, this syndrome was named Colony Collapse Disorder.[11] Though the cause of this phenomenon is still not completely understood, it appears that

Beehive souvenir pin, 2002 Salt Lake Winter Olympics. Used by permission, Utah State Historical Society. All rights reserved.

parasitic mites and the growing use of insecticides may be culprits. Global awareness of the problems is resulting in bans on some offending chemicals.[12]

As beekeeper Lee Knight explains, "The honeybee is just like a canary," the bird coal miners used to detect the presence of poisonous gases or lack of oxygen. "The fact that we're seeing so many of them dwindling is a definite sign we as a planet need to change. People think they're saving the bees by becoming beekeepers, but that's not necessarily true," he adds. "It's a good thing to tend to these wonderful creatures, but if the human race wants to truly save them, the best thing we can do is stop using toxic chemicals to treat our crops and re-forest the flowers and other plants the bees need to make this wonderful honey."[13]

NOTES

1. The story is told in the Book of Mormon (Ether 2:3) of the Jaredites, who lived at the time of the Old Testament's Tower of Babel. The Jaredites are said to have made a 344-day voyage across the ocean to North America bringing along the "deseret," which means "honey bee" in the language of the Book of Mormon.

2. For an examination of the significance and use of the beehive symbol in Utah, see the exhibition catalogue for a 1980 exhibit of the same name. Hal Cannon, *The Grand Beehive* (Salt Lake City: University of Utah Press, 1980).

3. W. P. Nye, *Beekeeping in Utah* (Logan, UT: Biology and Systematics Laboratory, 1976), available online at https://digitalcommons.usu.edu/cgi/viewcontent.cgi?article=1284&context=piru_pubs.

4. https://www.millerhoney.com/.

5. https://www.coxhoney.com/.

6. https://www.knightfamilyhoney.com/about-us.

7. "Beekeeping Is Buzzing in Utah," https://bascousa.com/blog/beekeeping-is-buzzing-in-utah.html.

8. Byron Anderson in discussion with the author, fall 2015.

9. https://ag.utah.gov/documents/AHB-FAQ.pdf.

10. "Utah's Grand Staircase–Escalante National Monument Home to Rich Bee Diversity," https://www.sciencedaily.com/releases/2018/11/181107082457.html.

11. https://www.apiservices.biz/en/articles/sort-by-popularity/492-colony-collapse-disorder-ccd.

12. Kimberly Amadeo, "Colony Collapse Disorder and Its Impact on the Economy: What Happens If We Don't Save the Bees in Time?" https://www.thebalance.com/bee-colony-collapse-disorder-facts-and-economic-impact-3305815.

13. Ibid., https://bascousa.com/blog/beekeeping-is-buzzing-in-utah.html.

12

SALT

SALLY HAUETER RAMPE

Utahns know their salt, and settling on the banks of "America's Dead Sea" was no coincidence. Thanks to reports from fur trappers and Capt. John C. Fremont, the Mormon pioneer leaders knew their destination was the valley of the Great Salt Lake before they left Nauvoo, Illinois. It would be naïve to believe the enterprising leaders of the Mormon Church were not aware of salt's power in the world economy, and historical documents show that "soon after their arrival in the valley a group of men were sent to the lake to extract salt from the lake shore. They reported that they 'prepared 125 bushels of coarse white salt, and boiled down four barrels of salt water to one barrel of fine white table salt.'"[1]

Currently the state of Utah owns the Great Salt Lake and all mineral rights and, according to the Utah Department of Wildlife, mineral extraction on the lake "makes close to $300 million dollars a year!" Food-grade salt, better known as "table salt," is no longer harvested from the lake because of the costly process to make it safe for consumption, but a great deal of salt is still extracted for use in detergents, paper-making, plastic, vinyl, glass and ceramics, road salts, and mining extraction.

Reports of individuals extracting salt for their own table-salt use are scarce; however, many Utahns have stories of "floating" on the water near the historic Salt Palace or at Antelope Island State Park. In fact, "floating" on the lake was part of Utah's tourism campaign during the 1920s and 1930s. If you want to take a dip, you only need to search recommendations on where to do it and many past doers will give their opinion. Currently there are several groups of open-water swimmers who "dip into this lake and swim from 400 yards to six miles" once a week.[2] Just like all accounts of swimming or floating in the lake, the regular swimmers recommend that you don't swallow the water or you might find yourself gagging and choking on a combination of brine shrimp, flies, and salt.

Souvenir pin honoring the salt industry, 2002 Salt Lake Winter Olympics. Used by permission, Utah State Historical Society. All rights reserved.

The high percentage of salt in the Great Salt Lake allows visitors to float, not swim, and has long been a signature way of marketing the state to tourists. Image is in the public domain.

Past are the days of using salt from the Great Salt Lake on the dinner table, but that doesn't mean that Utahns aren't using local salt to flavor their dishes. Just two hours south of Salt Lake City on Highway 89 in the town of Redmond, Utah, there is an ancient sea-salt deposit. Here the Redmond Trading Company mines 12,000 tons of salt a week. This salt, touted to contain "more than 60 natural trace minerals including iodine,"[3] is a "Utah's Own Product" and can be found in homes and five-star kitchens throughout Utah, as well as in health food stores across the world. The salt is believed to heal ailments and cure illnesses because of the sediments found in

it. The company website has testimonials from consumers of the healing powers of Real Salt, including claims such as reducing high blood pressure so drastically that they no longer have heart conditions. There is great pride in serving Real Salt on the dinner table and Utah families who use the Real Salt blue-lidded saltshaker aren't offended when asked, "Is Your Salt Real?"[4]

NOTES

1. Linda Thatcher, "The Great Salt Lake Mineral Industry," *Beehive History* 16 (1990): 31–32.
2. Howard Berkes, "Salt, Flies, Pickled Tongues: A

Cargill is one of several national companies that extract industrial salt from the Great Salt Lake. Photo by Carol A. Edison, 2018.

Perfect Great Salt Lake Swim," NPR, last modified June 7, 2013, http://www.npr.org/templates/transcript/transcript.php?storyid=188901981.

3. Redmond Trading Company, "Real Salt® FAQ," accessed June 6, 2014, http://www.redmondtrading.com/pdfs/RealSalt_FAQ.pdf.

4. Additional sources: Great Salt Lake Ecosystem Program, "Industries," accessed June 6, 2014, http://wildlife.utah.gov/gsl/industries/index.php; "Great Salt Lake Open Water Marathon Swim," accessed June 6, 2014, http://www.greatsaltlakeopenwater.com; Visit the Great Salt Lake, "An All-Encompassing Resource to Help You Plan Your Journey in, around and above Great Salt Lake," accessed June 5, 2014, http://www.visitthegreatsaltlake.com; Alex Cabrero, "Central Utah Town Boasts 'Greatest Salt on Earth,'" KSL, November 20, 2012, http://www.ksl.com/?sid=23056752; Richard H. Jackson, "Great Salt Lake," Utah History to Go, accessed June 6, 2014, http://historytogo.utah.gov/utah_chapters/the_land/greatsaltlake.html.

13

SALT WATER TAFFY

BARBARA LLOYD

Salt Lake City gained its name and its claim to salt water taffy by being situated near a large, inland body of salt water. Originally produced on the Atlantic Seaboard in the late 1800s, salt water taffy became an instant hit with tourists on the East Coast, and most likely some entrepreneur decided his own version of taffy might benefit from the Great Salt Lake connection.

Anyone living in Salt Lake City during the 1950s and 1960s will remember going downtown to watch salt water taffy being stretched by a machine in the window of Richard's Candies. It was mesmerizing to watch the confection being pulled almost to the point of falling off the stainless-steel hook, only to be picked up by a second hook and drawn again. As this process was repeated, the lush pastel ribbon would become lighter and lose its shine as air was breathed into it through the pulling process, and the rhythm of the machine mimicked the ebb and flow of the ocean itself.

In spite of the name, the candy contains no salt water,[1] but the idea became a successful marketing tool and was a popular treat. Visitors to Utah could return to their home state or country with a candy gift that seemed almost indigenous to the Intermountain West, and a few customers actually believed that the product was made from the waters of the Great Salt Lake.

Hand-wrapped in two-inch squares of waxed paper and sold by the pound or in a gift box, the candy created an enticing palette of pink, green, brown, orange, yellow, gray, and white. The flavors included the standard three of strawberry, vanilla, and chocolate, but also mint, lemon, cinnamon, licorice, root beer, and others; some flavors were available with added walnuts. As I remember, the texture of Salt Lake's salt water taffy was different from the commercial taffies available today, with individual pieces being larger and softer than grocery store varieties. It

Salt water taffy souvenir pin, 2002 Salt Lake Winter Olympics. Used by permission, Utah State Historical Society.

Salt water taffy puller in the window of Druehl and Franklin Druggists, Salt Lake City, 1910. Shipler Commercial Photographers Collection. Used by permission, Utah State Historical Society. All rights reserved.

seemed like a hand-made confection—soft lumps of flavor and sweetness that upon opening could be enjoyed immediately or pulled apart with ease and reshaped by the consumer—typically children.

This old-fashioned treat can still be found in Salt Lake City, but it isn't quite the same. During the 1950s, Salt Lake was one of the headquarters for the U&I (Utah & Idaho) Sugar Corporation, whose product source was sugar beets. My mother maintained that sugar from beets was different from cane sugar—milder and more flavorful—which may have contributed in part to the difference in

Salt Lake's taffy at that time. Few sugar beets are produced in the area today, and the U&I Sugar Corporation, under new ownership and having a new name, divested itself of the sugar beet industry in the 1970s.[2]

Although salt water taffy was a popular commercial product, home taffy-making was enjoyed and often encouraged as a way to remember pioneer heritage. For some, making taffy was a link to ancestors who worked hard for everything they had, including candy. The connection wasn't lost on anyone who ever stretched taffy.

My grandmother and mother would make "vinegar taffy." The candy-maker would create a syrup by combining two cups of sugar, half a cup of white vinegar, a pinch of salt, a pat of butter, and a small amount of either cream of tartar or light corn syrup to keep the mixture from crystallizing as it cooled. The ingredients were put in a pan and placed on medium heat until they reached a soft rolling boil. The syrup would bubble gently until it reached a soft-crack stage. In my family, this meant dipping a spoon in the pan of syrup and then lifting it up and letting the liquid run back into the pan in a very thin thread. When the thread would become a fly-away wisp, the syrup was ready. At that point, the candy—dangerously hot—was poured onto a flat buttered surface, either a plate, a marble candy slab, or—in my grandma's home—on the ceramic-tiled kitchen counter. The candy was left undisturbed to cool a bit. When it was still warm but able to be handled safely, the taffy-maker would butter his or her fingers and begin to knead and stretch the pliable mass. One great aspect about taffy-making is that the stretching activity was one that could be shared, and often

was a social enterprise. My sister recalls our grandmother's taffy:

> It made the kitchen smell like vinegar, but the taste was wonderful. A great combination of sweet and tart, but oh it was so sticky, especially when you first started to pull.[3]

My childhood friend, who grew up in Salt Lake, tells of her grandmother Olive and her great aunt who grew up in Providence, Utah. The girls, along with their ten siblings, made money working hard in sugar-beet fields when they were young. Referring to the taffy, my friend relates that

> I didn't much like it, but do remember my grandmother and her sister, my aunt Vern, making and pulling it. It had a golden shimmery color and was sweet, tart, and salty all at once. . . . I just remember . . . my grandmother and her sister pulling it until it lost its sheen. The taste was nothing like what is sold today. It was rich and intense and a beautiful golden color. I do have a box of my aunt's handwritten recipes. . . . I'll look to see if she has anything written down. And I'll ask mom. But, I think making taffy was just one of the things that was passed down . . . not written down.[4]

Through the pulling process, the candy was transformed from a sticky, hopeless, translucent ball into rich, opaque ropes of taffy. When it reached the right consistency, the rope, roughly one-half to one inch in diameter, was coiled back onto the buttered surface. Scissors were used to cut the candy into pieces that then were individually wrapped in waxed paper squares—rolled up and twisted on both ends to keep the candy secure. Some cooks would add flavoring and color before the pulling process to resemble the salt water taffy found downtown.

Clearly a pastime, taffy-making happens far less often in homes and at social events today. Very few children are now entranced by the motions of salt water taffy being pulled in a store-front window, but those of a certain age will remember seeing the slow dance of a pulling machine and the feel of slick candy ropes slipping through buttered fingers.

NOTES

1. Though both salt and water are ingredients in salt water taffy, actual salt water is not required. http://www.exploratorium.edu/cooking/candy/recipe-taffy.html.
2. https://worldhistory.us/american-history/the-history-of-ui-sugar-a-beet-sugar-powerhouse.php.
3. Name withheld by request (senior-aged native Utahn who grew up in Salt Lake City), discussion with author, November 14, 2014.
4. Name withheld by request (female, senior-aged native Utahn who grew up in Salt Lake City), personal communication with author, November 16, 2014.

14

OFFICIAL FOODS OF UTAH

Symbols of a Shared Identity

CURTIS ASHTON

By the end of fourth grade, most children in American public schools can identify at least a few of the official symbols of their home state. While there is no national mandate requiring state symbols, all fifty states recognize the power of designating official emblems in order to foster a unique identity within the Union.[1] Every state has the prerogative of choosing not only which items to list, but also what categories the list should contain. For example, Utah does not have a state nut, state meal, state pie, state grain, state beverage, or state candy. Other states do. On the other hand, Utah does have a state cooking utensil, state historic vegetable, and state fish. Other states do not.

Utah Code 63G-1-601 lists the thirty-three state symbols of Utah. Beginning with the adoption of Utah's state seal in 1896, the list of symbols has continued to grow and change. (The most recent amendment came in March 2019, when the Gila monster was named the state reptile.) Of the thirty-three official state symbols, this essay explores nine related to food. By tracing the historical and contemporary debates over state food symbols, I hope to show the role foods play in Utah's official political space. As I do so, I also hope to expose some dynamic shifts as official foods reveal diverse interests and identities within the state over time.

Three symbols I identified relate specifically to the Beehive State's iconic beehive. Since this symbol is addressed in other chapters, here I only mention that it serves as a starting point for many later official symbols. The beehive and honeybees point to other trends in Utah's official foods. For example, just as bees make their honey from both cultivated and wild sources, people in Utah celebrate both domestic and wild foods grown or gathered from a harsh landscape. Also, Brigham Young's pioneer metaphor of cooperative industry for the State of Deseret is still reflected in the foods (and other symbols) we celebrate, though the nature of that cooperation is shifting. And like honey, many of our food symbols are on the sweet side.

FOOD FROM THE WILDERNESS

Many of the white settlers who arrived in Utah before the coming of the railroad expected to make a living by farming. However, the climate in the Great Basin was so different from their previous experience that many years of lean harvests went by before these pioneers developed productive farming methods. Utah's official state fruit and vegetables celebrate the triumph of foods introduced into this harsh wilderness that made it to cash-crop status. But official foods also acknowledge, with humility and gratitude, the wild plants and animals that kept people alive through hard times. Putting the two together shows rhetorically the value to Utahns of wilderness as both a thing to be tamed with patience and hard work and as a resource to lean on and not take for granted. Since wild resources come first, in both historical times and in official designations, I will discuss the state flower, fish, animal, and grass before I discuss the state fruit and state vegetables.

After statehood, the first amendment to Utah's state symbols came in 1911, when the sego lily was recognized as the state's official flower. This small desert bloom is not easily cultivated as it needs far less water and sandier soils than other garden flowers. Yet its importance as a food source in the history of Utah is well known. White settlers learned from native inhabitants of the Great Basin that the bulb is edible, and as a result, many people supplemented early meager harvests and staved off starvation by digging wild bulbs.

Along with native plants, fish and game were an important component of pioneer diets. Small wonder that the state fish is a trout and the state animal is an elk—both prized eating. However, the law

In 1911, the well-known story of how sego lily bulbs helped keep early pioneers from starving convinced legislators to name it the official state flower. Courtesy C. Maylett.

designating Utah's state fish and state animal came sixty years after the sego lily's designation. By then, fishing and hunting had changed from subsistence practices to licensed sports. At the same time, the environmental movement of the 1960s and early 1970s contributed to a growing number of states choosing to identify native species as symbols. Thus, these two symbols in particular, while related to the sego lily because of pioneer roots, have additional layers of meaning representing an ongoing relationship with managed, edible wildlife resources.[2]

Just as the Cutthroat trout represents fishing in Utah, the elk represents big-game hunting in the state. It is not surprising, therefore, that these

UTAH'S STATE SYMBOLS

Date	Category	Symbol
1896	Seal	State seal (removed from Code)
1911	Flower	Sego lily
1913	Flag	Flag of Utah (removed from Code)
1955	Bird	Seagull
1959	Emblem	Beehive
1959	Motto	"Industry"
1969	Gem	Topaz
1971	Animal	Elk
1983	Insect	Honeybee
1988	Fossil	Allosaurus
1990	Grass	Indian rice grass
1991	Rock	Coal
1994	Folk Dance	Square dance (includes round, contra, line, etc.)
1994	Mineral	Copper
1996	Astronomical Symbol	Beehive Cluster (constellation of Cancer the Crab)
1996	Star	Dubhe (Big Dipper constellation)
1996	Tartan	Honors first Scots and those of Scottish heritage
1997	Cooking Pot	Dutch oven
1997	Fish	Bonneville cutthroat trout (formerly rainbow trout)
1997	Fruit	Cherry
1998	Railroad Museum	Ogden Union Station
2002	Historic Vegetable	Sugar beet
2002	Vegetable	Spanish sweet onion
2003	Hymn	"Utah We Love Thee" by Evan Stephens
2003	Song	"Utah This Is the Place" by Sam and Gary Francis
2011	Firearm	John M. Browning M1911 pistol
2011	Flag	"Honor and Remember" Flag (emblem of military service and sacrifice)
2012	Winter Sports	Skiing and snowboarding
2014	Tree	Quaking aspen (formerly Colorado blue spruce)
2017	Works of Art	Native American rock art
2017	Work of Land Art	Spiral Jetty
2018	Dinosaur	Utahraptor
2019	Reptile	Gila monster

Source: https://le.utah.gov/xcode/Title63G/Chapter1/63G-1-S601.html.

Sugar beets, Utah's official "historic" vegetable. Courtesy Molly Yeh.

symbols were adopted at the same time.[3] But elk as a source of food and revenue relates to endangered species in a different way than trout. Elk and deer are not threatened in Utah; what are endangered are the apex predators that eat them. Utah has not been a leader in fostering the return of these predators, at least in part because of competition over this particular prey.[4]

Before leaving wild foods, I will touch briefly on the selection of Utah's state bird. While eleven states have official game birds or birds that have historically been used for food, and two chose domestic fowl as state birds, Utah's seagull is not used as a food source. But decades before any official designation, the seagull (officially, the California gull) had already been memorialized in song, story, and visual media for its role in keeping an infestation of "Mormon crickets" at bay. Here is just one famous description of the "miracle of the gulls" rescuing wheat fields from crickets in the summer of 1848:

> When it seemed that nothing could stay the devastation, great flocks of gulls appeared, filling the air with their white wings and plaintive cries, and settled down upon the half-ruined fields. All day long they gorged themselves, and when full, disgorged and feasted again, the white gulls upon the black crickets, like hosts of heaven and hell contending, until the pests were vanquished and the people were saved.[5]

Remembering this story from the pioneer settlers' point of view helps us see the food connection—without the gulls there was no wheat, and without wheat, no flour to survive the winter. Fitting that a bird that might otherwise be seen as a scavenging nuisance can be honored as among the wild things from the mountain wilderness that prop us up when other "staffs of life" may wobble.[6]

Utah chose a state grass in 1990 from four candidates, all native species to the Great Basin. The winning candidate, Indian rice grass, marks a departure from other food symbols. Unlike elk, trout, and even sego lily, white settlers never seriously adopted this native edible plant as a food source. Yet its very name suggests that it has been part of native diets in the area. Including this wild food among our other state symbols expands the canon beyond the pioneer experience.

DOMESTIC FOODS

Guidebooks for travelers on the Transcontinental Railroad in the 1870s encouraged passengers headed to California to spend an extra day and tour Salt Lake City. They invariably pointed out the orchards and garden plots made possible by extensive irrigation using City Creek and other water sources:

Half hidden among a luxuriance of foliage of every shade of green, the houses seem like pleasant cottages and villas in an immense garden, and glittering streams in every street mark with silver lines the length of the broad avenues.[7]

Though it is picturesque to imagine Salt Lake City as "an immense garden," residents understand the real work of keeping things from withering in the high-mountain desert sun.

Utah today has considerably fewer farmers than in the nineteenth and early twentieth centuries, but even then, the amount of land suitable for farming was never large. Today, farmland accounts for approximately 21 percent of Utah's total acreage. About 16,700 farms still operate in the state.[8] Other chapters of this book describe the role of small-scale gardening, food preservation and storage, and celebrating harvests through fairs and festivals. Here I want to describe how Utah came to have state fruits and vegetables, and why these particular foods won symbolic status.

In the same legislative session that introduced an amended state fish and a new state cooking utensil, Representative Fred Hunsaker of Logan, Utah, proposed the cherry be named the new state fruit. His bill was the result of a research report submitted from his constituents at Millville Elementary School. The students' report gave several reasons for their recommendation, including

- Cherries are grown throughout the state, from Box Elder to Washington Counties.
- Although cherry production

Souvenir pin honoring cherry production, 2002 Salt Lake Winter Olympics. Used by permission, Utah State Historical Society. All rights reserved.

accounts for less than 1/8 of 1 percent of agricultural land, Utah still produces billions of cherries and ranks as one of the top five cherry-producing states in the nation.

- Japanese citizens sent cherry trees to Utah following World War II. The trees were planted around the state capitol building and represent peace and friendship between the two places.

Currently Utah is home to four sour cherry varieties and ten varieties of sweet cherries, including the "Utah Giant." Hunsaker's bill received little opposition, and the cherry was adopted as an official state symbol.

Like the state fruit, the state vegetables were recommended by schoolchildren. This time, two high-school classes promoted two different vegetables. The debate raged for two years before a compromise was reached in 2002 to name the sugar beet a historic vegetable and the Spanish sweet onion as the state's contemporary vegetable. Both choices represent foods that were once more important to Utah's economy than they are now, but since commercial beet sugar production moved completely out of the state in the 1930s, a designation as historic seems more appropriate. A closer look at history reveals that onion production, which continues today, in fact began earlier than sugar beets.

Arguments in favor of onions as a symbol of Utah include its historical significance as an easily cultivated garden crop. The heirloom variety "Utah Jumbo" is touted as "great for inexperienced gardeners and those that like low maintenance gardens."[9] When farmers were having trouble growing familiar garden vegetables in Utah's alkaline soil,

ELK ROAST WITH SWEET AND SOUR SAUCE
(SERVES ABOUT 8)[10]

1 Tbsp. vegetable oil
4 lbs. elk roast
2 large Spanish sweet onions, sliced
3 medium carrots, cut into 2-inch pieces
1 lb. red potatoes, cut into 2-inch pieces
(Substitute sego lily bulbs for up to half of the potatoes for an even more authentic Utah experience!)

Sauce
1/4 c. honey
1/4 c. sugar (from sugar beets, if possible)
1/4 c. tart cherry juice
1/2 tsp. grated lemon or orange peel
1/4 tsp. ground cloves
1 tsp. salt
1/2 tsp. freshly ground pepper

In a large Dutch oven, heat oil and brown the elk meat on all sides. Drain. Add onions and sauté till just tender.

In a small measuring bowl, combine ingredients for sweet and sour sauce, then pour over the roast. Cover tightly and roast for 1 hour, basting as needed with pan juices. Add additional vegetables and continue to cook for 1 to 2 hours, or until vegetables are tender.

onions were a trouble-free alternative. They also go nicely with the state's official cooking utensil, the Dutch oven.

In recent years, onions have reappeared in pioneer stories and artwork as Utah residents have commemorated the heroic efforts made to rescue the Martin and Willie handcart companies in the fall of

CUTTHROAT TROUT WITH CHERRY GLAZE

2 large trout, cut into 4 fillets
2 1/2 c. tart cherries, pitted and quartered
1/4 c. unsalted butter
1/3 c. red wine vinegar
2 Tbsp. honey
1 Tbsp. cornstarch
1/3 c. cold water
salt and ground black pepper to taste

Simmer cherries, butter, vinegar, and honey in a saucepan over medium heat about 10 minutes, or until cherries are softened and the mixture has reduced. Whisk the cornstarch and cold water together and then stir into the cherry mixture. Bring back to a simmer, stirring constantly until thickened, about 5 minutes. Remove sauce from heat.

Preheat the oven's broiler and set the oven rack about 6 inches from the heat source. Salt and pepper the fish, then place them skin sides down on a broiling pan.

Broil for 30 seconds, then remove from broiler and spoon the cherry glaze generously over the fillets. Broil 6 to 10 minutes until glaze has baked onto the fish and the meat is no longer translucent. (You may want to reglaze with cherry sauce once or twice during cooking.)

Let stand 1 minute before serving over wild rice with extra cherry sauce.[11]

1856. Among the supplies sent to succor the starving emigrants were bushels upon bushels of onions.

In contrast, sugar beets had a rockier beginning in our state. Early in the territory's history, Brigham Young saw hundreds of dollars bleeding out of the area as settlers paid high prices for imported sugar. In an effort to promote greater self-sufficiency, Young authorized John Taylor, who was serving as a mission president in France, to research and buy equipment for beet-sugar production before coming home from Europe. Provo was an early candidate for the new "sugarhouse" that would supply the territory with cheap sweets. The plan later changed to the Salt Lake Valley. Although today residents in a southeastern section of Salt Lake City know their neighborhood as Sugar House, these initial efforts to establish a viable industry failed. Sugar beets did not come to prominence in the Utah economy until the 1880s when advances in production and distribution technologies led to a fifty-year boom. At its height, Utah employed hundreds of people in seventeen sugar plants across the state. One key to the success of the industry was a partnership between church and state. While some criticize the historic involvement of the LDS Church in Utah's enterprises, the counterargument of the church's interest in lowering unemployment in the state cannot be ignored. As the industry became mechanized over time so that it could no longer be a leading employer, the church also withdrew involvement.

Although there was heated opposition about the appropriateness of sugar as a vegetable (for instance, *Deseret News* ran an editorial in 2000 that compared the sugar beet to a snickers bar for its sugar content), by acknowledging sugar beets as a state symbol, we capture an important moment in our history that might otherwise be forgotten.[12]

CONCLUSION

Official state symbols are meant to endure. They can forge an identity for citizens across the state over many years. As lawmakers have added symbols to our state repertoire, they face the challenge of promoting a positive contemporary image while acknowledging where our roots lie. Some newer symbols, like Utah's official cooking utensil (the Dutch oven) seem overly nostalgic, while others, like the proposed state snack (green Jell-O) can seem too much removed from a weightier past.

Looking at Utah's official foods as a whole, trends still favor a pioneer heritage and cooperative work ethic, though efforts to include nonpioneers are also evident. Sweet foods still win out over non-sweets. Perhaps the contemporary national obesity crisis will prompt rethinking of this trend.

NOTES

1. https://statesymbolsusa.org/.
2. Consider the 1997 Utah Code amendment that replaced rainbow trout with Bonneville cutthroat trout as Utah's state fish. In 1971, when Governor Cal Rampton signed Senate Bill No. 19 in favor of the rainbow, cutthroat trout were thought to have been entirely fished out of Utah. Trout, suckers, and chub were harvested from rivers and lakes so successfully that by the late nineteenth century, people imported fish to take the place of native species. Having the popular but nonnative rainbow as a stand-in could still show the state's commitment to fishing in its history and contemporary economy. But by changing the state fish to a recovering native species, the official position could speak to another of the state's interests, namely, fostering healthy ecosystems. See "First Bill to Reach Rampton's Desk: A Fish Tale with Antlers," *Ogden Standard-Examiner*, January 21, 1971.
3. The elk became the official animal and the rainbow trout became the official state fish of the State of Utah when Governor Rampton signed Senate Bill No. 18 and Senate Bill No. 19 on February 1, 1971. They were the first bills of the 1971 legislative session to reach his desk.
4. In 2010 Utah's wolf management plan adopted a "zero tolerance" approach to establishing viable packs of wild wolves. While the wolf battles in Utah have much to do with ranching and standing up for state's rights, there is also a significant concern that wolves will deplete the big game available in the state. See Sarah Brown, "The Gray Wolf Stalemate: Why Utah's Wolf Management Law Threatens the Gray Wolf's Recovery Throughout Its Historical Range," *Utah Environmental Law Review* 32, no. 1 (2012).
5. Orson F. Whitney, *History of Utah* (Salt Lake City: George Q. Cannon and Sons, 1892).
6. Celebrating the gulls is, of course, from the pioneer point of view. Remembering this story from the native Goshute point of view, the gulls' feasting on crickets represented competition over a vital staple source of protein.
7. Henry L. A. Culmer, *A Tourists' Guide Book to Salt Lake City* (Salt Lake City: J. C. Graham, 1879), 3.
8. The United States Department of Agriculture Economic Research Service (USDA, www.ers.usda.gov) provides the following statistics on farms and farmers:
   - Utah: approximate land area of 52,553,947 acres.
   - Farmland is 11,094,700 acres or 21.1 percent of total land.
   - Organic agriculture accounts for about 73,147 acres.
   - Number of Farms: 16,700.
   - Principle Farm Operators: Men, 14,903; Women, 1,797.
9. "Folia," MyFolia, myfolia.com.
10. Adapted from "Sweet and Sour Elk Pot Roast," *Elk USA*, www.elkusa.com/elk_Pot_Roast.html.
11. Adapted from Cherry-Glazed Salmon at Allrecipes.com.
12. Lee Benson, "Sugar Beets: More Sugar than Beet," February 16, 2000, https://www.deseretnews.com/article/744099/Sugar-beets-more-sugar-than-beet.html.

15

THE UTAH FOODS COOK-OFF AT THANKSGIVING POINT

ERICA BROWN

Utahns have become increasingly self-aware of the distinctive parts of our state's culinary culture. This is possibly a product of having hosted the 2002 Winter Olympic Games when a large number of popular Utah foods were featured on Olympic trading pins as a way of capturing and celebrating Utah culture. In 2014, Thanksgiving Point, a nonprofit farm, garden, and museum complex in Lehi, Utah, developed a new community program—the Utah Foods Cook-Off. The cook-off is held in conjunction with Jiggle Fest, an outdoor Jell-O fight that takes place every year on Pioneer Day weekend in honor of Utah's notable Jell-O consumption.

Each year, cook-off contestants enter dishes in four categories: Jell-O, Dutch oven, funeral potatoes, and fry sauce. In 2019 a new category was added: fry bread. Entries can reflect either traditionality or innovation and are ranked by a panel of judges on both presentation and taste. Winners in each category receive ribbons and gift baskets while the recipe provided by the Best-in-Show awardee is published on the Thanksgiving Point website. The cook-off and the Jiggle Fest bring together people from a cross-section of Utah communities in acknowledgment of their shared culinary heritage.

Courtesy Thanksgiving Point "Utah Foods Cook-Off."

Dutch oven bean soup, winner of the 2014 Dutch oven competition at the Thanksgiving Point Utah Foods Cook-off. Courtesy Thanksgiving Point "Utah Foods Cook-Off."

PART II HERITAGE

16

UTAH'S FOOD HERITAGE

CAROL A. EDISON

Do you remember eating the crusty hard rolls at the old Hotel Utah[1] in Salt Lake City or trying your first shrimp cocktail at Maddox in Brigham City? Did you look forward to Spudnuts[2] or Snellies[3] at church functions, always wishing you could have them at home too? Did your mom ever serve a quickly created meal of Lynn Wilson's tamales topped with canned chili and did she pack Clover Club potato chips in your school lunch? I suspect such experiences were widely shared by those who grew up in Utah in the 1950s and 1960s.

But Utah's food heritage is much larger than the specialties of local restaurants or local products fondly remembered. It is built upon influences originating with all the people who, over time, have made this land their home. Local and imported ingredients, ideas about what is healthy and what tastes good, and the recipes and ways of preparing food that have been handed down all contribute to that heritage.

This section features essays from a diverse group of writers who offer a glimpse into the richness and range of the state's food traditions. Written by folklorists, journalists, and historians who are also members of distinct cultural communities, they chronicle both the history of food in Utah and the specific food traditions that are lovingly perpetuated within folk groups.

There are some wonderful surprises within these chapters. One marvels at the resourcefulness of Utah's Native American tribes in not only gathering and hunting for sustenance, but also purposefully cultivating specific food resources that they returned to year after year. The state's first Anglo settlers, the Mormon pioneers, actually had a much more varied and extravagant diet than many imagine. Myths of piety have overshadowed the fact that many came from robust culinary traditions, both Yankee and Continental, and they strove to cook familiar foods, even when forced to use substitute ingredients. Finnan haddie made from salted Utah Lake fish was not an anomaly![4]

Some culinary traditions born from nineteenth-century lifestyles continue today while others are experiencing somewhat of a revival. Many Utahns still enjoy hunting to provide food for their families, and though most fishers are more interested in sport, a lot of fish is still consumed

Some Utahns go to great lengths to maintain access to the foods that are part of their ethnic heritage. Every fall, Salt Lake's Sifantonakis family covers their precious fig tree (*sikia*) with tarps attached to a wooden structure built specifically for that purpose. They also routinely grow basil, grapes, and other specialties for traditional dishes from their native Crete. Photo by Carol A. Edison, 2016.

From rural ranch communities to urban Polynesian and Southern European groups, cooking meat out-of-doors is a Utah tradition. Spit-roasted lamb was a specialty for twentieth-century Serbian immigrants, pictured above, especially at Easter. Today the general public can still experience this tradition at Salt Lake's annual Greek Festival. Used by permission, Utah State Historical Society. All rights reserved.

around campfires and kitchen tables every year. On the other hand, foraging for wild plants, berries, and seeds, growing herbs and vegetables in backyard gardens, and local breweries—including those in residential basements—have all experienced a revival of interest in recent years. Luckily, root cellars have not been part of the revival, and we continue to enjoy the convenience of modern electrical appliances to keep our foodstuffs cool.

The culinary traditions of Utah's minority communities and families can also be surprising. Who could have guessed that Salt Lake's oldest Japanese ladies meet monthly to create and enjoy a luncheon of traditional Japanese foods, prepared together over many hours using only the finest of ingredients and

Sleshi Tadesse shares his culinary heritage at Mahider Ethiopian Restaurant and Market in Salt Lake City. A colorful array of stewed chicken, beef, and vegetables, served on *injera*, the traditional sourdough flatbread used as both plate and a utensil for scooping up the food, is his signature dish. Photo by Carol A. Edison, 2019.

proper techniques? Who knew that for at least one Utah family, eating ravioli at Thanksgiving is more important than turkey? And what a nice surprise that a family of Spanish Colonial descent passes down and enjoys Grandma's recipe for prune pie—sometimes "forgetting" to call it by its other name, "plum pie," because it tastes too good to share.

And then there are Utah's Italian and Greek communities. Can you believe that two generations ago neighbors routinely pooled resources and imported enough grapes to make table wine for the year? Or that they still care enough about having the

right culinary components to nurture Mediterranean fig trees in Utah's harsh climate? The Italians, known for their cheese and sausage, and the Greeks, known for their lamb, have always raised fresh fruit, garden vegetables, and the herbs that make their cooking unique. Today it seems that the times have caught up with them: The world not only hungers for their traditional food, but also recognizes their cuisine as both healthy and hip.

It's important to note the unusually large contribution of Utah's relatively small Greek community to the state's culinary offerings and distinctive foodways. Greek restaurants—from high-end to family restaurants to a bevy of fast food cafes—dot the urban Utah landscape. Whether purveyors of family-style comfort food, ethnic-inspired gyros and souvlaki, or one of the many hamburger stands that supply Utah's much-loved pastrami burger, the contribution of Greek restaurateurs is significant.

These authors also eloquently remind us that Navajo mutton stew, Chinese chop suey and egg foo young, Tongan backyard pig roasts, and many other dishes of meaning and significance to specific communities are all Utah heritage foods too. Each certainly adds flavor and richness to our state's culinary heritage.

A wide variety of food traditions are alive and well in Utah, and even if they are not easily experienced around a kitchen table, most can be accessed in a restaurant or at one of Utah's many ethnic festivals. Created from recipes passed down and refined over time, they help perpetuate family and community culture and heritage and contribute to the abundance of culinary traditions that compose Utah foodways.

NOTES

1. Until its closing in 1987, Hotel Utah was known for its signature hard rolls—soft inside and hard outside. *Salt Lake Tribune*, February 8, 1998.

2. Spudnuts were glazed donuts made from potatoes, initially marketed by boys, door-to-door, in the 1950s and 1960s. Amy McDonald, "Whatever happened to…Spudnuts?" *Salt Lake Tribune*, September 29, 2015. Salt Lakers Al and Bon Pelton created them in the 1940s and later developed a mix that was franchised, making Spudnuts a nationwide hit for many years. "Pelton's Reports Spudnuts Selling 15 Pct. over 1953," *Deseret News*, July 22, 1954.

3. A product of Salt Lake's Snelgrove Ice Cream Company, Snellies were individual-serving–sized rectangular chunks of vanilla ice cream, without a stick, dipped in a coating of chocolate. Purchased in bulk and stored in dry ice, they were a popular confection for group gatherings in the 1950s and 1960s.

4. Brock Cheney, *Plain but Wholesome: Foodways of Mormon Pioneers* (Salt Lake City: University of Utah Press, 2012), 113.

BERRIES, ROOTS, GREENS, AND SEEDS

Indigenous Cultivation of "Wild" Plants

DANILLE ELISE CHRISTENSEN

Indigenous peoples of Utah—including the Fremont and Ancestral Puebloans long ago and the Navajo (Diné), Goshute (Kutsipiuti), Southern Paiute (Nuwuvi), Ute (Núčiu), and Northwestern Shoshone (So-so-goi) in more recent times—have practiced a variety of agricultural techniques suited to the wide range of climates and soils within the present state boundaries, including irrigation, terracing, crop rotation, installment of windbreaks, and stewardship of so-called wild plants. Like gardening elsewhere in Utah, indigenous cultivation practices have been "embedded in religious ideologies and enforced through social mechanisms," but these webs of values, knowledge, and customs reflect longtime experience with Great Basin environments rather than an imposition of practices and expectations developed in the context of foreign ecosystems.[1]

Historically, Navajo and some Paiute and Ute bands tended crops (e.g., maize, crookneck squash, and field pumpkin) using methods easily recognized by Europeans as agricultural, while other Native peoples in the region emphasized additional modes of resource management.[2] In the fragile environment of the West Desert (e.g., Tooele and Juab Counties), Goshute families gathered berries, roots, greens, and seeds from at least eighty-one plant species, relying especially on grasses and insects—including the periodic swarms of protein-rich orthoptera that Indians of the Basin-Plateau celebrated, but that European-Americans experienced as a plague.[3] Thus, in 1882, one former federal official praised white settlers in Utah Territory for taming a "barren desert" peopled only by "a few naked Indians making a meal from a pint of roasted crickets or dried grasshoppers." A few years later, during a Pioneer Day celebration, Orson F. Whitney (b. 1855, Great Salt Lake City, Utah Territory) began his speech about Utah's vegetative "blossoming" by observing, "Thirty-nine years ago it was a wilderness, a desolation, scorched by the sun, and trodden by the roving red man, whose food consisted in part of wild roots dug from the ground, reptiles that crawled and hissed and rattled among the hot rocks of the plain, and the crickets and grasshoppers that noisily chirped upon the mountain sides."[4]

Characterizing unirrigated Utah as a wasteland and native cultural strategies as "roving" erases the knowledge, labor, and skill involved in less sedentary and more dispersed forms of food cultivation. Hunter-gatherers have often been dismissed as nonmanagers of land and resources—that is, they are portrayed as simply finding and harvesting wild food—when in fact (like other agricultural endeavors) a broad range of indigenous practices have aimed to increase "the quantity or quality of culturally preferred plants."[5] For instance, the bulbs of the blue camas lily (*Camassia quamash*) have been an important food source for many Indians in western regions of North America. The cooked bulbs are sweet—much like a baked pear—and were often served with a dressing of oil or flattened ("like biscuits") and then dried. These bulbs once grew in great numbers on the Big Camas Prairie in what is now southern Idaho, but they can also be found in northern Utah (e.g., Kamas Valley) and have been traded and transplanted by northwest coast tribes as well. Traditional camas cultivation techniques included annual maintenance (controlled burns and manual clearing of stones and weeds), removal of poisonous lookalikes, and replanting or reseeding the beds. Some camas harvesters cut out sections of turf, removed only the biggest bulbs, and replaced the turf so that the smaller bulbs could continue to grow; others would "crush the soil where the bulbs were harvested and place the broken stalks bearing the ripe seed capsules into the holes" before covering

Many native people, including those in northern Utah, regularly monitored and harvested the bulbs of the blue camas lily. Whether eaten fresh or dried, they added a sweet element to the diet. T. Abe Lloyd, *Wild Harvests* (blog), 2012. Photo © 2012 T. Abe Lloyd.

them. Bulb depletion was also minimized by designating specific harvesting sites and times.[6]

However, many white immigrants and settlers refused to acknowledge Indian care and use of camas beds, and in the 1870s, foraging hogs and cattle ranged over the Camas Prairie—an area that had ostensibly been attached to Fort Hall reservation lands and protected by treaty. This disregard for and destruction of the camas fields and other traditional food sources led to malnourishment of the Shoshone and Bannock confined to the reservation, and then to a series of conflicts, raids, and killings that became known as the Bannock War.[7] The same pattern held true in Utah Territory, as Anglo colonists moved south from the Salt Lake Valley into Utah Valley and beyond. The area around Utah Lake, for instance, had been a primary summer camp for the Timpanogos, who met there to hunt, fish, trade, and forage, but new settler gardens, fields, and pastures tended to uproot, exhaust, or block access to these resources and prompted compensatory raids and then cycles of retaliation.[8] Stands and thickets were not randomly apportioned: In northern Utah's Morgan Valley, Mountain Green settler George Higley (b. ~1831, Leeds, Canada) was reportedly sentenced to be whipped after being found guilty of picking serviceberries (*Amelanchier alnifolia*) historically harvested by Little Soldier's band of "Weber Utes" (Cumumba).[9]

Despite intercultural disconnects about what counted as cultivated land, newcomers to the region clearly recognized that many so-called wild plants were closely linked to Native custom and practice. Oak-leaf/skunkbush sumac (*Rhus trilobata*) and wax currant (*Ribes cereum*), for instance, both have alternate vernacular names in English that incorporate the term *squaw*. *Orogenia linearifolia*, a plant in the parsley family whose corm can be eaten in the early spring, has been called "turkey peas" but also "Indian parsnip" or "Indian potato"; a purslane called "miner's lettuce" (*Claytonia perfoliata*) also goes by the name "Indian lettuce."[10]

As with camas fields, these and other food resources were surely not as naturally abundant as they appeared to early nonindigenous observers in Utah. Nineteenth-century white settlers recorded that ground cherries (*Physalis longifolia*) grew "spontaneously" in Utah fields, and that the "whole country was covered with wild berries" that grew "very thick," including huckleberries (*Vaccinium membranaceum*), grouse/whortleberries (*Vaccinium scoparium*), mountain strawberries (*Fragaria vesca*), grayleaf red raspberries (*Rubus idaeus* L. spp. *strigosus*), white bark/black raspberries (*Rubus leucodermis*),

thimbleberry (*Rubus parviflorus*), chokecherry (*Prunus virginiana*), Juneberry/serviceberry, and silver buffaloberry (*Shepherdia argentea*).[11]

But just as Mormon pioneers gladly transplanted wild roses (*Rosa nutkana* or *woodsii*), golden currant (*Ribes aureum*), whitestem/wine gooseberry (*Ribes inerme*), and blue elderberry (*Sambucus nigra* L. ssp. *caerulea*) from the mountains into their home lots, these other apparently spontaneous stands of berries had likely been indigenously encouraged in situ.[12] To the north, for instance, Douglas Deur has documented Klamath strategies for cultivating convenient, dense stands of black huckleberry bushes. Historically, Klamath maintained summer berry camps by respecting the boundaries of neighboring family camps and by observing a first-foods ceremony, in which they scattered the first baskets of berries picked each year. These techniques helped to avoid overpicking and also seeded grounds near the camps with favored genetic material. Periodic prescribed burns were also important: Regular burning is especially beneficial for fruiting shrubs and edible root plants, since it keeps out competing species, enriches the soil, kills insect (e.g., tent caterpillar) populations, and ensures that certain areas will lie fallow.[13]

Similar management strategies have been used by other northwest, plateau, and basin groups: Clover and silverweed patches, yellow pond lily seeds, and epos roots are just some of the foods maintained and increased by burning, weeding, regularly disturbing and aerating soil, cleaning roots at the harvest site, replanting small bulbs, scattering seeds, and picking selectively. As with many cultivated plants, regular and responsible harvesting of these "wild" foods enhances productivity and aesthetic and ethical appeal; Timbisha Shoshone elders, for example, have said that plant habitats should be tended in a way that visibly shows their interrelationship with people. Indians in western regions have also pulled down old cones with whips, pinched back the growth tips of pinyon pine, and cleaned mesquite groves; some have pruned plum trees (*Prunus americana*), willow branches (*Salix exigua*), rose bushes, and sagebrush in order to encourage fruiting, desirable structure, and robust regrowth.[14]

Ute bands, which employed some of these practices, typically stayed small in number to avoid outstripping local yields and periodically rotated or shared habitual territories so that grounds could lie fallow. They moved systematically to gather seeds in July and berries and fruits in August and September in the valleys of central and northern Utah; Jason Cuch (b. 1924, Utah), a White River elder and World War II veteran, remembered his grandparents picking chokecherries and currants in late summer and wild garlic in the spring. In the early 1920s, one Whiterocks resident reported that in earlier days, elderly Ute women would fill willow baskets with mountain berries, dry them, and return them to the baskets to be buried in the ground until needed. Chokecherries were among the berries that could also be mashed with their pits and shaped into cakes, then dried and stored.[15]

Like Ute peoples, other indigenous groups in what is now central and northern Utah also gathered sunflower and grass seeds and ate cactus fruit. Specific foods encouraged and enjoyed by Navajo in the southern part of the state include tulip prickly pear (*Opuntia phaeacantha*), banana yucca (*Yucca baccata*), husk tomato/hairy groundcherry (*Physalis*

pubescens), and pale wolfberry (*Lycium pallidum*). Lutie Tauchin (b. 1876, near the Carrizo Mountains in northeastern Arizona), a member of the Biibitohdnii Clan, recalled that in the days before Navajo removal to Fort Sumner her mother's family traveled widely, "looking for wild seeds and whatever they could get to eat." When they learned that "there were lots of piñon nuts on Gray Mountain," they moved there, alongside many other Navajo "picking nuts, yucca, and other wild foods."[16]

Historically, Indians throughout the Great Basin and Colorado Plateau also ate the greens and seeds of what whites called lambsquarters (*Chenopodium album*) and redroot pigweed (*Amaranthus retroflexus*), among other herbaceous plants.[17] The extent and variety of seeds and grains harvested by Native people are suggested by the many samples John Wesley Powell collected from Paiute bands in the early 1870s, which are now held by the National Museum of Natural History (NMNH). They include screw beans (*Prosopis pubescens*); seeds collected from grapes, purslane, and cattails (*Typha domingensis*); and grains from bulrushes, buckwheat, witch grass (*Panicum capillare*), and love grass (*Eragrostis purshii*). Seeds were gathered in baskets, and some were roasted and ground into flour. Powell's collection includes small sunflower seeds (*Heliomeris multiflora*) used to make bread; the NMNH also holds an 1876 sample of *Helianthus annus*, a nonnative, large-seeded sunflower called Moheack by Paiutes, "after the Pai Ute chief who first planted it," as well as "Native bread" and pine nuts purchased from Utes in 1915.[18]

For all, protein-rich pine nuts (*Pinus edulis* and *monophylla*) have been a major food source; they can

This circa-1960 photo of a Paiute woman cleaning pine nuts captures an activity that still takes place today. After being picked, pine nuts are put into a shallow basket made from sumac called a winnowing tray. Any debris is then cleared away by hand, the nuts are roasted over fire, the shells are cracked with a rock, and the nuts are then tossed upwards so that the wind can help remove the shells. Courtesy Special Collections Department, University of Nevada, Reno, Libraries.

be roasted, cracked, roasted again, and ground into flour. While pinyon jays (or other corvids) are the major planters of these heavy wingless seeds, humans have often kept a sharp eye on pine-nut development in order to predict future crops. Cones take twenty-six months (three growing seasons) to develop mature seeds, and good crops of pine nuts tend to appear in cycles of three to seven years. In addition, cones are vulnerable to climatic shifts and insect depredations

over the course of their growth, so harvesting sites are not reliable from year to year. According to Annie Lowry (b. 1868, Lovelock, Nevada), a Northern Paiute whose life story was recorded in 1936, each year scouts in her region visited pinyon forests within the group's jurisdiction and brought back sample cones. These were tested for "quality and ripeness" by men who assembled for the annual pine-nut powwow each September; they determined whether the group should visit a particular stand and decided when the pine nuts were likely to be ready. Similarly, when Western Shoshone gathered for annual pinyon festivals, they apparently drew on their knowledge of what was happening in the forests to choose the site of the next pine-nut harvest a year in advance. Southern Paiute bands fostered forest productivity and reduced harvest uncertainty by regularly "patch burning" pinyon-juniper habitats, pruning the lower limbs of trees to keep the fire at ground level.[19]

From Native peoples, white colonizers learned to enjoy these foods and to augment flour with roasted crickets, sunflower seeds, and roots and greens that had been dried and grated. Sego lily bulbs (*Calochortus nuttallii*), a favorite among Southern Paiute, became famous as a survival food (and then a nostalgic delicacy) for the first Mormon pioneers, but settlers also recalled learning to eat thistle roots and the inner portion of the arrowleaf balsamroot tuber (*Balsamorhiza sagittata*; "Mormon biscuit"). Emily Stewart Barnes (b. 1846, Bedfordshire, England) ate "two kinds of pigweeds" in 1850s Utah Territory: "one light colored, which Aunt called 'fat hen,' and the other was red."[20] Even after access to other food sources became easier, some of these foodways persisted. For example, wild hops (*Humulus lupulus*)

Note: The leaves, stems, and raw seeds of the chokecherry contain hydrocyanic acid (prussic acid), which is toxic unless neutralized by drying or cooking. Do not eat raw parts of the plant.[21]

CHOKECHERRY PUDDING

(SHOSHONE-BANNOCK)

Lightly wash chokecherries, then add water and bring to a boil. Strain seeds, if desired, then mash boiled berries and add sugar to taste; mix in as much flour as needed for a slightly runny pudding.[22]

CHOKECHERRY JELLY

Wash berries. In a large kettle, cover with water and simmer for 20 minutes, until soft (stir to prevent sticking). Strain through a clean cloth. Chokecherries have little or no pectin, but a jell can be achieved by adding crabapple juice (wash crabapples, cook for 30 minutes with a little water, then strain). Combine equal parts chokecherry and crabapple juice (one pound of chokecherries will give about 2 cups juice), then add an equal amount of sugar (or a bit less). Bring to a boil and stir when necessary. When the jelly clings to a spoon, pour into hot sterilized jars, wipe jar rims, and seal with two-piece lids; process in a boiling water bath for 10 minutes.[23]

grow throughout Utah and much of the United States and have long been used as fermenting and leavening agents in indigenous beverages and breads. Edna Porter Little (b. 1908, Porterville, Utah) recalled that in her youth, she and her siblings would sneak sips from the crock of homemade root beer her mother kept in their Centerville cellar: "She made it with dandelions, hops, sugar, and root beer flavoring."[24]

However, settler foraging practices tended to transgress indigenous norms that moderated both the quantity and frequency with which plants were harvested. As a result, even Utah's native flowers suffered. In May 1926, Dr. Philena Belle Fletcher Homer (b. 1877, Harrison Valley, Pennsylvania), a Cornell-trained botanist and State Conservation Chairman of the Utah Federation of Women's Clubs, noted the environmental consequences of uninformed collecting. With Decoration Day approaching, Homer urged women not to send children to gather "handful after handful" of frail wildflowers from the hillsides. Unsupervised children, she said, pulled Indian paintbrush (Castilleja) up by the roots, took too many flowers, and picked "the last bloom for seeding of some delicate flower" rather than leaving it to replenish itself. "Most of our favorite wild flowers are disappearing," she lamented.[25]

Lack of ecological knowledge on the part of burgeoning nonnative populations and increased density of use among formerly migratory indigenous people contributed to the destruction of traditional food systems. Too little or too much disturbance of foraging areas limits biodiversity, because more competitive plants will eventually take over in either case. And confinement to reservation lands, even when those so constrained practice a sustainable use ethic, can result in unsustainable pressure on plant populations.[26] These social and environmental changes had dire consequences for indigenous peoples' health and sovereignty.[27]

In an attempt to address Native food and community needs, over the last century a number of experiments with subsistence gardening and field-based farming on reservation land have been attempted. More recent efforts have focused on growing traditional foods in the context of reviving and reclaiming broader forms of traditional ecological knowledge, with local environmental expertise considered alongside related management practices, social institutions, and worldviews.[28] Such an approach differs from *foraging* and *wildcrafting*, practices that have recently experienced a surge in general popularity across the United States. These terms are commonly used to describe the ability to identify and gather "found" plants and seeds, but they may not reflect an intention to cultivate these foodstuffs as part of an entire sustainable ecosystem.

NOTES

1. Sandra L. Peacock and Nancy J. Turner, "'Just Like a Garden': Traditional Resource Management and Biodiversity Conservation on the Interior Plateau of British Columbia," in *Biodiversity and Native America*, ed. Paul E. Minnis and Wayne J. Elisens (Norman: University of Oklahoma Press, 2000), 133–79, at 165.

2. For additional, group-specific information about foodways, see the following: Daniel E. Moerman, *Native American Food Plants: An Ethnobotanical Dictionary* (Portland, OR: Timber Press, 2010); "We Shall Remain: Utah Indian Curriculum Project," The Utah American Indian Digital Archive, https://utahindians.org/Curriculum/; "Native American Ethnobotany: A Database of Foods, Drugs, Dyes and Fibers of Native American Peoples, Derived from Plants," The Native American Ethnobotany Database, http://naeb.brit.org/; The Navajo Nation, http://www.navajo-nsn.gov/; Paiute Indian Tribe of Utah, http://www.utahpaiutes.org/; Confederate Tribes of the Goshute Indian Reservation, http://www.goshutetribe.com/; Northwestern Band of the Shoshone Nation, http://www.nwbshoshone.com/; The Ute Indian Tribe of the Uintah and Ouray Reservation, http://www.utetribe.com/; The "Culturally Significant Plants" guides and "related links" prepared by the USDA Natural Resources Conservation Service and found at the PLANTS Database are also useful. USDA: Natural Resources Conservation Service, http://plants.usda.gov/java/.

    On crop irrigation in what is now Utah, see Robert Harry Lowie, "Notes on Shoshonean Ethnography," *Anthropological Papers of the American Museum of Natural History* 20, no. 3 (1924), http://digitallibrary.amnh.org/handle/2246/173. See also Robert C. Euler and Catherine S. Fowler, "Southern Paiute Ethnohistory," *Anthropological Papers* 78 (1996), Department of Anthropology, University of Utah.

3. Lowie, "Notes on Shoshonean Ethnography," 195; Floyd A. O'Neil, "The Utes, Southern Paiutes, and Gosiutes," in *The Peoples of Utah*, ed. Helen Papanikolas (Salt Lake City: Utah State Historical Society, 1976), 27–59; Linda Murray Berzok, *American Indian Food* (Westport, CT: Greenwood Press, 2005), 85.

4. A Gentile, *Utah and Its People: Facts and Statistics Bearing on the "Mormon Problem"* (New York: R. O. Ferrier, 1882), 1, http://lccn.loc.gov/mm75011879; Orson F. Whitney, "Pioneer Day," *The Woman's Exponent*, August 1, 1886.

5. See Douglas Deur, "'A Caretaker Responsibility': Revisiting Klamath and Modoc Traditions of Plant Community Management," *Journal of Ethnobiology* 29, no. 2 (2009): 298, as well as other contributions to that same issue; Kent G. Lightfoot et al., "Rethinking the Study of Landscape Management Practices among Hunter-Gatherers in North America," *American Antiquity* 78, no. 2 (2013): 285–301.

6. Nancy J. Turner and Harriet V. Kuhnlein, "Camas (Camassia Spp.) and Riceroot (Fritillaria Spp.): Two Liliaceous 'Root' Foods of the Northwest Coast Indians," *Ecology of Food and Nutrition* 13, no. 4 (1983): 199–219, at 211; USDA NRCS National Plant Data Center and Corvallis (OR) Plant Materials Center, *Common Camas (Camassia quamash)*, USDA NRCS Plant Guide (Washington, DC: United States Department of Agriculture Natural Resources Conservation Service, May 31, 2006), http://www.plants.usda.gov/plantguide/pdf/cs_caqub2.pdf. For more on indigenous management of bulbs and other

plant populations, communities, and landscapes, see Peacock and Turner, "'Just Like a Garden.'"

7. George Francis Brimlow, *The Bannock Indian War of 1878* (Caldwell, ID: Caxton, 1938), esp. 37–45; Dick D'Easum, *Bannock War at Camas Prairie*, Historical Society Reference Series 474 (Boise: Idaho Commission for Libraries, 1969).

8. David Rich Lewis, *Neither Wolf nor Dog: American Indians, Environment, and Agrarian Change* (New York: Oxford University Press, 1994), 34–38.

9. Muriel Shupe, *Mountain Green the Beautiful* (Logan, UT: Herald Printing, 1985), 136–37.

10. Berniece A. Andersen and Arthur H. Holmgren, *Mountain Plants of Northeastern Utah*, rev. ed. (Logan, UT: Utah State University Extension, 1996), http://extension.usu.edu/htm/publications/file=6260. For Ute (and some Goshute and Shoshone) names for culturally important plants, see Ralph V. Chamberlin, "Some Plant Names of the Ute Indians," *American Anthropologist*, New Series, 11 no. 1 (1909): 27–40.

11. Andersen and Holmgren, *Mountain Plants*; Jill Mulvay Derr, "'I Have Eaten Nearly Everything Imaginable': Pioneer Diet," in *Nearly Everything Imaginable: The Everyday Life of Utah's Mormon Pioneers*, ed. Ronald W. Walker and Doris R. Dant (Provo, UT: Brigham Young University Press, 1999), 228–30; Stanley L. Welsh et al., *A Utah Flora* (Provo, UT: Brigham Young University, 1993).

12. On transplanting mountain berries and currants, see Brock Cheney, *Plain but Wholesome: Foodways of the Mormon Pioneers* (Salt Lake City: University of Utah Press, 2012), 84, 149, and Kate B. Carter, *Pioneer Recipes: Lesson for May, 1950* ([Salt Lake City, Utah]: Daughters of Utah Pioneers, Central Company, 1950), 334. See http://tahoe.lib.usu.edu/record=b1724291.

13. Deur, "'A Caretaker Responsibility'"; Peacock and Turner, "'Just Like a Garden.'"

14. Deur, "'A Caretaker Responsibility'"; Peacock and Turner, "'Just Like a Garden'"; Turner and Kuhnlein, "Camas and Riceroot"; Catherine S. Fowler, "'We Live by Them': Native Knowledge of Biodiversity in the Great Basin of Western North America," in *Biodiversity and Native America*, ed. Paul E. Minnis and Wayne J. Elisens (Norman: University of Oklahoma Press, 2000), 99–132; Jeremy Spoon and Richard Arnold, "Collaborative Research and Co-Learning: Integrating Nuwuvi (Southern Paiute) Ecological Knowledge and Spirituality to Revitalize a Fragmented Land," *Journal for the Study of Religion, Nature and Culture* 6, no. 4 (2012): 477–500. In *Enduring Seeds: Native American Agriculture and Wild Plant Conservation* (Tucson: University of Arizona Press, 2002), Gary Paul Nabhan suggests how other indigenous groups have cultivated agave, wild rice, and sunflowers.

15. On Ute resource management and traditional ecological knowledge, see Lowie, "Notes on Shoshonean Ethnography," 201–2; O'Neil, "The Utes, Southern Paiutes, and Gosiutes"; Lewis, *Neither Wolf nor Dog*; Betsy Chapoose et al., "Planting a Seed: Ute Ethnobotany, a Collaborative Approach in Applied Anthropology," *Applied Anthropologist* 32, no. 1 (2012): 2–11; and Leslie G. Kelen and Eileen Hallet Stone, eds., *Missing Stories: An Oral History of Ethnic and Minority Groups in Utah* (Salt Lake City: University of Utah Press, 1996), 34–35 (full transcript available in "Jason Cuch," Folder 6, Box 1, Ute Indian Oral History Project Collection, Accn0853, Special Collections, J. Willard Marriott Library, University of Utah).

16. Interview with Mrs. Dan Tauchin, December 10, 1960, Doris Duke Oral History Project, Ms 659, Special Collections, J. Willard Marriott Library, University of Utah.

17. Moerman, *Native American Food Plants*; O'Neil, "The Utes, Southern Paiutes, and Gosiutes"; Mae Parry, "The Northwestern Shoshone," *Utah History to Go* (Salt Lake City, UT: State of Utah, [c1999] 2014), http://historytogo.utah.gov/people/ethnic_cultures/the_history_of_utahs_american_indians/chapter2.html.

18. Quote from "Seed Helianthus Introduced Moheack," Catalog no. E21684-0, Smithsonian National Museum of Natural History. To see images of seeds contributed by Powell and others, go to http://collections.si.edu and search for "Utah native plants" (no quotation marks). For more on Powell's survey of Indians "who have not yet been collected on reservations," see G. W. Ingalls and John Wesley

Powell, *Report of Special Commissioners J. W. Powell and G. W. Ingalls on the Condition of the Ute Indians of Utah; the Pai-Utes of Utah, Northern Arizona, Southern Nevada, and Southeastern California; the Go-Si Utes of Utah and Nevada; the Northwestern Shoshones of Idaho and Utah; and the Western Shoshones of Nevada* (Washington, DC: Government Printing Office, 1873), 6, https://catalog.hathitrust.org/Record/009582764. On Shoshonean harvesting and processing of grass seeds, see Lowie, "Notes on Shoshonean Ethnography," 201-5, 215.

19. On pine nut management, see Lalla Scott and Annie Lowry, *A Paiute Narrative* (Reno: University of Nevada Press, 1966), cited in Ronald M. Lanner, *The Piñon Pine: A Natural and Cultural History* (Reno: University of Nevada Press, 1981), 78–81; Ronald K. Miller, "Southwest Woodlands: Cultural Uses of the 'Forgotten Forest,'" *Journal of Forestry* 95, no. 11 (1997): 24–28; and Spoon and Arnold, "Collaborative Research and Co-Learning." Berry and root grounds were monitored in similar ways; see Peacock and Turner, "'Just Like a Garden,'" 157–58. On pine nut harvesting, see Lowie, "Notes on Shoshonean Ethnography," 202–3.

20. Carter, *Pioneer Recipes*, 333; Derr, "Pioneer Diet"; Andersen and Holmgren, *Mountain Plants*, 1996.

21. For more information on the chokecherry (Prunus virginiana) and its cultural uses, see Natural Resources Conservation Service, "Chokecherry Plant Guide," PLANTS Database, United States Department of Agriculture, accessed January 22, 2016, http://plants.usda.gov/plantguide/pdf/cs_ prvi.pdf.

22. Adapted from "(more) Choke Cherry Pudding," *Native Tech: Native American Technology and Art*, accessed January 22, 2016, http://www.nativetech.org/recipes/recipe.php?recipeid=45. George P. Horse Capture (A'aninin, b. 1937, Fort Belknap Indian Reservation, Montana) affirms that grinding the seeds releases the "essence of the fruit that lies in the center of the pit"; "Reservation Foods," *Foods of the Americas: Native Recipes and Traditions*, ed. Fernando and Marlene Divina (Berkeley, CA: Ten Speed Press, in association with Smithsonian National Museum of the American Indian, 2004), 98.

23. Adapted from Shirley B. Paxman, "Elderberry Jelly," in *Homespun: Domestic Arts and Crafts of Mormon Pioneers* (Salt Lake City: Deseret Book, 1976), 6–7; the recipe includes a chokecherry variant that calls for crabapple pectin. See also Manitoba Association of Home Economists, "Crabapple and Chokecherry Jelly," in *Home & Family*, accessed January 22, 2016, http://www.homefamily.net/how-to-use-chokecherries/.

24. Moerman, *Native American Food Plants*; Edna Eliza Porter Little, *My Life Story: Edna Eliza Porter Little, May 29, 1908–May 31, 2000*, Typescript, ed. Douglas R. Little (Ivins, UT, c2008), 2; copy in possession of author. On hops and brewing in Utah, see also Cheney, *Plain but Wholesome*, 63, 76, and Carter, *Pioneer Recipes*, 334.

25. Philena Fletcher Homer, "Garden Flowers for Decoration Day," *Relief Society Magazine* (May 1926): 257.

26. Peacock and Turner, "'Just Like a Garden'"; Fowler, "'We Live by Them.'"

27. See Judy Kopp, "Crosscultural Contacts: Changes in the Diet and Nutrition of the Navajo Indians," *American Indian Culture and Research Journal* 10, no. 4 (1986): 1–30; Diné Policy Institute, *Diné Food Sovereignty: A Report on the Navajo Nation Food System and the Case to Rebuild a Self-Sufficient Food System for the Diné People* (Tsaile, AZ: Diné College, 2014), accessed April 4, 2019, https://www. dinecollege.edu/wp-content/uploads/2018/04/dpifood-sovereignty-report.pdf

28. See, for example, Chapoose et al., "Planting a Seed"; Spoon and Arnold, "Collaborative Research and Co-Learning"; Diné Policy Institute, *Diné Food Sovereignty.*

18

NATIVE AMERICAN FOODWAYS IN UTAH

PATTY TIMBIMBOO-MADSEN

Saa-beesh (long ago/prehistory), as hunters and gatherers, our people moved from area to area during the year to gather food, medicines, and material for tools. During that time period foods were pure and natural. The time to gather began after the Warm Dance (ceremonial dance), which brought in the coming of a new year. What would the Dam Appua (Our Father) bless them with? More snow would definitely bring better food sources. Soon, in the spring, the hunter-gatherers would begin their journey for the first fresh food sources of the year.

Baa (water) was the most important resource for all life. What on earth does not benefit from water? It is life for plants, animals, and humans, and the existence of lakes, streams, oceans, and rivers.

Floral foods, or plant-based foods, were vital to the people's survival. Greens, such as wild onion, arrowroot, watercress, buttercup, squaw cabbage, and dandelion, were all eaten raw or boiled. The wild onion could be dried out and saved. They also gathered roots, bulbs, and tubers, especially thistle, bulrush or tule, cattail, and bitterroot, and they collected various kinds of cactus, most importantly the prickly pear. Mesquite beans, oak acorns, and screwbeans were important as was the pinyon nut, which is high in protein and carried them through many winters.[1]

The hunter-gatherers gathered a variety of berries—the service berry, gooseberry, chokecherry, sumac or squawberry, currant, raspberry, elderberry, buffalo berry or buckberry, coyote berry, and blueberry. The chokecherry grew in greater abundance and was especially important. Harvesting chokecherries involved gathering families together to dry and save the berries for winter. The people celebrated this staple by performing the chokecherry dance.

Seed grasses, including redtop, bluejoint or wheat, wild rye, peppergrass, Indian ricegrass, bluegrass, and arrowgrass, all contributed to their diet. Sagebrush, saltbrush, arrowroot, sunflower, stickseed, pine, wild rose, hystrix, columbariae, chia, tansymustard, and cattail were also important.

Faunal foods, or animal-based foods, were extremely important resources to the indigenous people of the Great Basin. The knowledge of animals and the hunt were passed on from

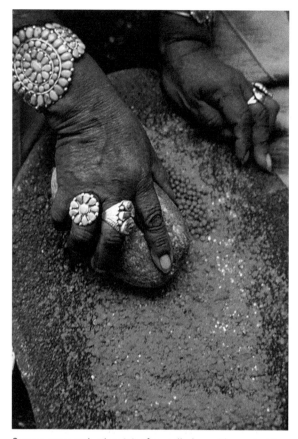

Sumac, or squawbush as it is often called, provides material for making baskets as well as a red berry that is ground and made into a kind of punch. Paiute cook Mary Snow demonstrated how to grind squawbush berries at the 1978 Southern Utah Folklife Festival. Photo by M. J. Keller. Courtesy Utah Folklife Archives.

trappers, and settlers arrived in northern Utah with their horses, bison became easier to kill. By 1834 there were no more bison in northern Utah. Today, Utahns again have access to this historical meat, but as they prepare stew and steaks the meat cooks faster and there is less fat.

Deer provided food, and their hides were used to make clothing, moccasins, and leggings. The meat was easily cut up to eat fresh or to dry. The dried meat would feed them through the winter or on longer trips. Deer fats were used to add flavor to food or as mosquito repellent or paint, or to sooth burns. Deer stomach linings were used for water jugs.

The Newe (The People) also hunted elk that they would eat fresh and then dry what was left for the winter. The elk would be shared with all the people of the family. Elk hides were used for floor coverings and soles for moccasins while the antlers were made into handles.

Mountain sheep, which were smaller than bison but larger than deer, were more difficult to capture because of the mountain terrain where they lived. There were times that the sheep did come down in elevation, and during these times they were hunted. People sometimes worked together in large-scale communal hunts. Antelope were gathered in open areas between hills and valleys, and rabbits, especially jackrabbits and cottontail rabbits, were herded into places where they could not escape.

The indigenous people hunted sage hens and wild turkeys as well as mud hens, ducks, geese, and swans, and gratefully gathered their eggs. Small animals including rock chuck, woodchuck, badger, porcupine, fox, beaver, marmot, and mink, along with rats, prairie dogs, gophers, squirrels, lizards, and

generation to generation. Another life was taken in order for the Newe to survive! Hunters were told to honor the animal with prayer, song, and thankfulness for the life they were about to take!

Bison were all-important not only as a food source but also as a provider of shelter, materials for adornments, and medicine. When explorers, snakes supplemented their diet, as did locusts, grass-hoppers, caterpillars, and ants. Fish, taken from rivers, lakes, marshes, and springs were a special treat.

Today our lifeways are much different than those of our ancestors. Long gone are the days of eating healthy for most Native Americans. We are experiencing sickness from our food sources. The clothing and tools needed for traditional harvesting, hunting, and cooking are also endangered. We are now fighting the battle of chemicals put into the ground. Fish have been poisoned with mercury. The deer are suffering from Mad Cow Disease, impacting our ability to use their hides. Property rights on lands where we traditionally harvest and protections for endangered species affect us. Our treaty rights still afford us the right to hunt and gather, but it is limited to what we can take. Some traditional foods, clothing, and medicines are still used while some are just used for special occasions. When we can identify any traditional resource in abundance, then we are able to teach and demonstrate to our children how to use them. Today we try to continue to make and enjoy foods like pine-nut gravy, ash bread, jerky, buffalo stew, buffalo steaks, and chokecherry porridge. Some of the ingredients have changed as has the manner in which we cook them. Though some of the new ways make it simpler, the family togetherness isn't what it used to be.

Pine nuts and berries have always been so important to native diets that weavers craft special baskets for tasks like gathering, winnowing, and storage. Goshute basket-maker Molley McCurdy made beautiful baskets well into the late 1980s. Photo by Carol A. Edison. Courtesy Utah Folklife Archives.

NOTES

1. Valerie Phillips, "Deseret Smorgasborg: Class Focuses on Native-American Dishes," *Deseret Morning News* (Salt Lake City), March 10, 2004.

Contrary to popular belief, some pioneers did move beyond the culinary deprivations of the trail and frontier subsistence to enjoy diets similar to those found in adjoining western states. Artwork by Francisco Kjolseth, courtesy *Salt Lake Tribune*.

19

LUMPY DICK AND FINNAN HADDIE

Food in Early Mormon Utah

BROCK CHENEY

Utah's first Anglo settlers, the Mormon pioneers, were agrarians, like most of their fellow Americans in the mid-nineteenth century. In those days, farming was either the primary or secondary profession of most Americans. In other words, Mormon pioneers were in the food business. Though there were also mechanics and artisans, farmers made up the bulk of early Deseret's work force. Utah's pioneer story is a story all about food.

This story has been told with varying degrees of detail only a handful of times. The Daughters of Utah Pioneers established some key details in *Heart Throbs of the West* (vol. 11), which has an extensive chapter of recipes and food lore gathered primarily from Mormon pioneer women and their daughters. Jill Mulvay Derr wrote a general overview of the subject in her essay "I Have Eaten Nearly Everything Imaginable," found in the larger anthology *Nearly Everything Imaginable* (1999). And most recently *Plain but Wholesome: Foodways of the Mormon Pioneers* (2012) provides a thorough exposition on the topic. This short essay can only provide a brief appetizer; interested readers should follow up with these and other sources below.

Being a Mormon pioneer meant participating in a cycle of migration and settlement. For most Mormon pioneers, the availability of food was bound directly to this cycle. Originating with conversion to Mormonism, the pioneer then migrated to Utah, either as an American from the eastern states or as an immigrant from Europe. This meant experiencing the foodways systems of the Mormon Pioneer Trail—an experience usually lasting three to four months. Following their arrival in Utah, pioneers found a place to settle, often by assignment from Brigham Young, and then built farms on virgin ground. The process of trail migration and farm building was usually accomplished (by design) in poverty.[1] Only once Mormon converts had settled on newly built farms and plowed virgin ground did they gain access to comfortable, familiar foods. This process took anywhere from five to ten years.

The foodways of the Mormon pioneers are readily divided into these three segments of the pioneer experience: trail foods, settlement privations, and civilized comfort foods. Often, because of the dramatic difference between privation and comfort, we tend to focus on privation as the hallmark of Mormon pioneer foodways. After all, eating weeds and wild animals seems quite dramatic! However, in the broad picture of Mormon settlement, these are just momentary interruptions to otherwise comfortable eating patterns.

The trail experience was usually accomplished in three to four months, with the possible addition of a six-week sea voyage for European converts. Again, while we often focus on the dramatic tragedies of the Martin-Willie handcart disaster of 1856, such mishaps were rare.[2] Most pioneers were well supplied with provisions for the trail which, though not usually as tasty as foods fresh from the farm or market, could readily provide health and comfort. Andrew Jenson, a pioneer of 1866, remembered a comfortable daily ration which included "1 1/2 pounds of flour and one pound of bacon each day for each adult besides sugar, molasses, dried fruit and other eatables."[3] Additionally, beef cattle were slaughtered along the trail from time to time, providing fresh meat. This provision came from the Perpetual Emigration Fund (PEF), which aided immigrants in their journey to Utah.

Many travelers supplemented their initial PEF rations with wild foods gathered along the trail. Caroline Clark, an English immigrant, noted, "At times Roland goes to the river and catches us fish, and sometimes John shoots birds. We get wild currants and gooseberries to make puddings. So, altogether we get along very well."[4] The joyous tone in Caroline's writing conveys optimism as she writes her immigration advice to friends in England.

These trail staples came together to make recipes and menus. For example, one Mormon traveler noted a meal near Fort Laramie in Wyoming composed of "fried beef and bacon, with biscuit."[5] The bacon, beef, and flour have been noted in the daily PEF ration. Making biscuits, however, requires lard, salt, and baking powder beyond those rations. Indeed, Caroline Clark advised her friends in England, "Be sure when you come to bring plenty of flour, suet, lard, currants, raisins, a little tartaric acid, bicarbonate of soda, baking powder…"[6] From here, cookery manuals of the day provide a historical biscuit formula from some of these recommended ingredients:

Cream of Tartar Biscuit

Take a quart of flour, mix into it two tea-spoonsful of cream of tartar, two tea-spoonsful of salt, a table-spoonful of lard; then take a pint of warm water and a tea-spoonful of soda, knead it into the flour, and work it well. Roll it out about half an inch thick, and cut the biscuit with a round cutter, or into square pieces. —*The Great Western Cookbook, 1857*[7]

Such uses for flour provided the primary carbohydrate fuel that moved the Mormon migration across the plains to Utah. Once settled in Utah, Mormon pioneers would make use of flour with yeast or sourdough to make leavened loaves of bread. On the trail and even in early settlement, however, Mormon pioneers often made a thin gruel with wheat flour called "Lumpy Dick." Here, "dick" is a synonym for a form of pudding, also called "duff." Pioneer Johanna N. Lindholm left us this preparation of the dish:

Lumpy Dick
Heat milk scalding hot—in a bowl beat an egg with a fork a few moments then add some sugar, pinch of salt & grated nutmeg, flour enough to use up the egg—rub between your hands till about like rice, then stir into the hot milk. Cook a few moments and serve with milk or cream
—*Kate B. Carter Collection, Daughters of Utah Pioneers Memorial Museum, n.d.*[8]

Once Mormon immigrants reached Utah, they became tools in Brigham Young's plan for settlement. As the Mormons' Great Basin kingdom spread out along the waterways and riparian zones of the Intermountain West, Brigham Young directed new converts in the building of settlements designed to monopolize resources away from other non-Mormon immigrants. For Mormon converts, this required building new farms and breaking new ground, rather than settling on land that had already been improved. For many, this meant that the most productive and desirable ground had already been taken by earlier waves of immigrants. The tasks of clearing rocks, brush, and trees from fields meant that reliable, profitable harvests were still years away.

The settlement process spanned almost half a century as the Mormon colonies spread out from Salt Lake City. But in each new village the same process unfolded as settlements crept farther and farther from the nucleus of Mormonism. Twenty years after the first arrival of settlers in the Salt Lake Valley, older pioneers were eating high on the hog, while

Lumpy dick, a pioneer-era standby, was a pudding made by stirring dry flour into boiling milk and serving it with sweet milk and molasses or sugar. Georgia Drake, *Pioneer Stories* (blog), 2011.

a hundred miles away, new waves of settlers were forced to live lean.

Often this meant settlers were forced to eat weeds until their crops and fields proved themselves. Emily Stewart Barnes remembered the lean year of 1856 in Kaysville, saying, "We did the best we could to not starve to death.... We had to go early in the morning to gather nettles to eat.... We also gathered some sego roots and pulled some wild onions to eat. There were two kinds of pigweeds; one light colored, which Aunt called 'fat hen' and the other was red."[9] In Manti, early settlers saw these weeds as an echo of manna. "The place where the weeds were gathered was down on the south side of the stone quarry," one recalled. "After each day a-gathering, there was none left for the next day. But like the food miraculously supplied to the Israelites in the wilderness, each day, just so the Lord provided for this supply of pig weed each day."[10]

Such weeds were primarily gathered for their roots. The roots and tubers of sego lilies and pigweed provide a starchy carbohydrate, though not nearly as tasty or refined as a potato. Settlers often boiled these roots in milk to break up their fibrous texture.

Other settlers adapted local domestic and wild foods to replicate ethnic dishes from their homeland. One such example comes from Wilhelmina Henrietta Morrison Eriksen, whose parents emigrated from Scotland to Manti during its early settlement in the 1850s. In Scotland they prepared a fish dish called *finnan haddie* which is traditionally made with haddock. The fish would be salted and smoked to preserve it for shipping to inland markets away from the sea. It could then be prepared in a cream sauce or soup.

Wilhelmina's recipe, on the other hand, makes use of Utah's native trout. In the 1850s, as Wilhelmina was growing up, Mormon settlers began to make use of the fisheries of Utah Lake. Trout were caught, salted, and dried on the shores of the lake, and then shipped and sold throughout Utah. Wilhelmina's mother used these salted trout to make an approximation of finnan haddie, using a tomato base rather than cream.

Finnan Haddie with Tomatoes

Freshen fish by pouring boiling water over it & letting it stand till cool. (Remove skin & bones and separate into larger flakes.) About one & one-half pounds of fish should be used. Melt three tablespoonfuls butter in a saucepan. Add one teaspoon minced onion & cook to a pale straw color. Add three tomatoes peeled & cut in slices. Cook over a slow fire till soft. Add one teaspoonful of minced parsley, one-eight teaspoonful pepper & a few gratings nutmeg. Add fish & cook over hot water till the fish is very hot. Arrange boiled rice in a circle on a chef plate and fill center with fish mixture. —*Wilhelmina Henrietta Morrison Eriksen, 1859–1935*[11]

Eventually these new settlements began to yield herds and crops and started to produce output more reminiscent of the civilizations Mormon converts had left behind, whether in New England or Europe. Eating weeds to stave off starvation makes a better story than eating ice cream in the parlor, and so generations of Mormon children have been raised on stories of their ancestors eating weeds. In truth, however, the hardships of the trail and early settlement are just a moment within a much larger story. For every meal of pigweed these settlers thereafter compensated with a hundred meals of roast beef with potatoes and gravy from flourishing farms. Eliza Brockbank Hales remembered her childhood in Spanish Fork in the 1860s, ten years after her parents' immigration. She wrote, "Our food was plain but wholesome. We had milk, home-made bread, vegetables, dried fruit, and meat. Our home-cured hams were tops. We also had a barrel of corned beef and a good root cellar for potatoes, apples, vegetables, and so on."[12]

Likewise, it might go without saying that the higher one sat within the hierarchy of the Mormon Church, the better one ate. In part this may be due to the fact that the church leadership entered the Salt Lake Valley in the earliest companies of pioneers; their luxurious tables may be due in part to having paid their dues early on, and thus were benefitting from years of wealth accumulation ahead of later emigrants. Still, it seems more than coincidental that at the dinner table of Abraham Smoot, a stake president and bank owner in Provo, we find him playing host to Brigham Young, and also Col. Thomas Kane, the Mormons' special envoy to Washington, DC. Here, Kane's wife, Elizabeth, recorded the following dinner menu in 1872:

> What had we to eat? What had we not! Turkey and beef, fresh salmon-trout from the lake, wild duck, chicken-pie, apple fritters, wild-plum, cranberry- and currant-jellies, a profusion of vegetables; and then the mince-pies (drawn from the oven after grace was said!), smoking plum puddings for us, and wholesome plain ones for the children (who preferred the unwholesome!); pears, peaches, apples and grapes, pitchers of cream and scarcely less creamy milk, cakes, preserves and tarts numberless, and tea and coffee.[13]

Although a feast of this magnitude was certainly reserved for special occasions and special guests, run-of-the-mill homes knew similar, if less diverse, comforts once they had proved the test of years. Manuscript collections of Mormon pioneer recipes abound with formulae for cakes, puddings, cookies, and pies of all sorts. Here, the definitions of "Mormon pioneer foodways" require more nuance, as first-glance impressions may seem to vary little from contemporary foodways of the day in Denver or San Francisco.

However, even once Mormon pioneers achieved some stability after settlement, other concrete barriers continued to shape the nature of food in Utah. The distance from Utah to outside markets remained fixed, and the height of the Rocky Mountains imposed limitations on imported goods. Further, Utah's local economy sustained an ongoing trade deficit to the end of the nineteenth century. The Mormons' only exports were agricultural commodities, while their imports were much greater. In terms of foodways this meant that such staples as refined white sugar or coffee came at a dear price.

Newspapers and diary accounts indicate that Mormon pioneers continued to spend their hard-won cash and credit on coffee and tea.[14] These could not be grown in Utah, and Mormons had no choice but to import them. Sugar was a different matter. Though Brigham Young tried nearly from the outset to build a sugar mill capable of sustaining the sweet tooth of the settlements, the effort never found success in his lifetime. Instead, many of Utah's early settlers rendered sap and syrup from sorghum cane or sugar beets which they reduced to black molasses in home-fired evaporation efforts. For example, in 1857 Wilford Woodruff produced more than 100 gallons of molasses syrup, and 250 gallons the following year.[15] Most of this would have supplied his growing polygamous family; some might have been used as barter or exchange.

The confluence of home-produced molasses and imported coffee can be seen in a cake recipe from Mormon pioneer Ruth Mosher Pack. With molasses as its main sweetener, its flavor is reminiscent of gingerbread. It calls for baking soda as leaven, which still requires an acid to activate the chemical reaction. This acid is provided by using a cup of strong-brewed coffee. For more formal occasions, a cup of imported white sugar is added to the cake, though brown sugar would also work.

The problem of imported goods, and primarily

MOLASSES CAKE

1 c. molasses
1 c. brewed coffee (cooled)
1 tsp. soda
1 c. sugar
2/3 c. shortening
3 1/2 c. flour

Beat 2 eggs and add liquids together. Add soda to flour and mix well. Bake in a moderate oven 1 hour.[16]

When the Word of Wisdom was still just good advice and before it became a commandment, territorial Utah produced its share of hard liquor for both export and local consumption. Photo by Danny Clark, 2018.

of sugar, is one hallmark of Mormon pioneer food-ways. A second might be the prevalence of immigrant food on the landscape. Because the Mormon migration originated from missionary converts abroad, much of the early settlement in Utah came from Europe. Danish, Swiss, and English foodways have persisted for years and generations, often maintaining distinct cultural integrity in spite of generations of intermarriage. In nineteenth-century Denver, German and Irish immigrants assimilated to American culture quickly; in Utah, Scandinavian settlements stubbornly maintained food, language, and dress customs for generations after immigration. Dairy cattle in the Heber Valley still wore traditional Swiss head yokes into the 1970s.

A third factor which can be seen in historical Mormon foodways is a reliance on wild-gathered foods. In part this originates with the settlement patterns rooted in poverty. I believe it goes beyond this. The first generation of Mormon pioneers arrived in this landscape without any cultural knowledge of the local plants and animals. Paiute and Shoshone Indians were willing to share this knowledge early on, and Mormon settlers depended on native plants

during the proving period of their farms. Once settled, however, Mormon farmers continued to go to the mountains or streams for food because of the abundance provided there. Settlers brought wild berry bushes to their city lots and continued to hunt deer and elk for meat. This pattern continues today for many Mormon families in Utah.[17]

Strangely, the dimension that does not seem to influence foodways practices for Mormon pioneers is religion. Mormon doctrine originating from Joseph Smith in 1833 indicates that devout Mormons should abstain from "hot drinks" and "strong drink." This admonition, usually called the "Word of Wisdom," was originally given as a piece of good advice, not as a commandment. In the terms of the day, "hot drinks" were understood as coffee and tea; distilled liquor was the "strong drink" in question. Perhaps the socially liberal religion that embraced polygamy was flexible enough to let the health code go as just good advice. In any case, Mormon pioneers drank plenty of tea and coffee. Likewise, they brewed beer, fermented wine, and even distilled whiskey.[18] Some apologists have argued that these latter endeavors were aimed at export rather than local consumption. Historical records show that Mormon pioneers did not feel so restricted as modern generations do when it comes to these beverages.

In the end, drawing a circle around what these thousands of Mormons ate 150 years ago is a task much greater than can be accomplished in these few pages. In truth, they ate everything from crows and wolves to ice cream and fresh oysters on the half shell. Perhaps these few recipes will be enough to start you on your own culinary exploration of what Mormon pioneers ate.

NOTES

1. Brock Cheney, *Plain but Wholesome: Foodways of the Mormon Pioneers* (Salt Lake City: University of Utah Press, 2012), 112.
2. John D. Unruh, *The Plains Across: The Overland Emigrants and the Trans-Mississippi West, 1840–1860* (Chicago: University of Illinois Press, 1979), 408, 516n74; Cheney, *Plain but Wholesome*, 43.
3. Andrew Jenson, *Autobiography of Andrew Jenson* (Salt Lake City: Deseret News Press, 1938), 21.
4. Caroline Hopkins Clark, "Diary of Caroline Hopkins Clark and Letters to England," MSS 114, Box 6, Fd4, Utah State University, Logan.
5. Stella Jaques Bell, *Life History and Writings of John Jaques* (Rexburg, ID: Ricks College Press, 1978), 142.
6. Clark, "Diary," 6.
7. Angelina Maria Collins, *The Great Western Cookbook; or, Table Receipts, Adapted to Western Housewifery* (New York: A. S. Barnes, 1857), 59.
8. Courtesy Kate B. Carter Collection (Salt Lake City: Daughters of Utah Pioneers Memorial Museum). Trail immigrants may not have had access to eggs or cream, but nutmeg was a trail staple.
9. Claude Teancum Barnes, *The Grim Years; or, The Life of Emily Stewart Barnes* (Kaysville, UT: Inland Printing, 1964), 53.
10. Barbara Lee Hargis, "A Folk History of the Manti Temple: A Study of the Folklore and Traditions Connected with the Settlement of Manti, Utah, and the Building of the Temple" (Master's thesis, Brigham Young University, 1968), 25.
11. Mount Pleasant Pioneer Relic Home Blog, accessed July 12, 2009, http://mtpleasantpioneer.blogspot.com. The blog entry contains a photo facsimile of the recipe as written in the hand of Wilhelmina Eriksen.
12. Eliza Brockbanks Hales, "Reminiscences of a Pioneer Childhood" (Logan: Utah State University, Library Special Collections).
13. Elizabeth Kane, *Twelve Mormon Homes Visited in Succession on a Journey through Utah to Arizona* (Salt Lake City: Tanner Trust Fund, University of Utah Library [1974]), 9.
14. Cheney, *Plain but Wholesome*, 156.
15. Scott G. Kenny, ed., *Wilford Woodruff's Journal, 1833–1898* (Salt Lake City: Signature Books, 1983), entry for November 14, 1857.
16. Daughters of Utah Pioneers, *Heart Throbs of the West*, ed. Kate B. Carter (Salt Lake City: International Society Daughters of Utah Pioneers, 1939–1951), 11:357.
17. See Cheney, "Berries, Bulbs and Beasts," in *Plain but Wholesome*, 76.
18. See Cheney, "Wetting the Whistle," in ibid., 153.

Though Hotel Utah no longer exists and their hard rolls are no longer available, a chain of local grocery stores, Harmons, continues this beloved Utah food tradition. Photo courtesy Harmons Neighborhood Grocery.

HOTEL UTAH HARD ROLLS

KYLIE SCHROEDER

On June 9, 1911, Hotel Utah opened its doors in Salt Lake City. Among other tasty treats, the hotel's kitchens were known for their hard rolls (a version of the bolillo roll) which were deliciously crusty on the outside and soft and fluffy on the inside.

Master baker Hans J. Risto brought the recipe for what was a common German roll called *broetchen* or "little buns" from his native Germany. There he had apprenticed under his father, becoming a master baker before immigrating to Utah in 1955. His secret was to double bake the rolls by pulling out the partially baked rolls, sprinkling a little water on them, and then baking them again. The other important element was to bake the rolls in a stone oven—something that wasn't easy to find in most Utah bakeries at the time.[1]

Hotel Utah closed in 1987 before reopening as the Joseph Smith Memorial Building. Though there are now several restaurants in the complex, they no longer serve the legendary hard rolls, only the soft Lion House Dinner Rolls. But with this copycat recipe you can make a version of Hotel Utah rolls at home.

HOTEL UTAH HARD ROLLS

2 Tbsp. yeast
1/2 c. warm water
1/2 c. sugar
1 cube butter, melted (2 Tbsp.)
1 c. cold water
3 eggs, beaten
1 1/2 tsp. salt
5 c. flour

Combine yeast, warm water, and sugar. Let stand until yeast is dissolved. Add melted butter. Add cold water, eggs, salt, and flour. Mix and knead. Let rise twice. Roll out. Cut and place on greased baking sheets. Let rise again. Bake at 325 degrees for 25 minutes or until golden brown.[2]

NOTES
1. "Risto, Baker at Hotel Utah, Dies," *Salt Lake Tribune*, February 8, 1998.
2. Recipe by Rebecca Pace, Faith, Family and Friends Cookbook, https://www.familycookbookproject.com/recipe/1592394/hotel-utah-hot-rolls.html.

IN PRAISE OF IMMIGRANT ITALIAN FOODWAYS IN UTAH

STEVE SIPORIN

Italy is the food capital of the world. And everybody knows it.

Italy has long been recognized for its elegant, satisfying, and nourishing diet as well as for gourmet dishes made with the best ingredients. Appropriately, the World Food Programme—the world's largest humanitarian program dedicated to fighting hunger—is located in Rome, where it was established by the United Nations in 1961. Italy is also home to the Slow Food Movement, which was founded in 1986 in an effort to "oppose the standardization of taste and culture, and the unrestrained power of food industry multinationals and industrial agriculture."[1]

One of the core characteristics of Italian cuisine is the short distance from peasant foodways to those of the elite. Independent of social and economic class, Italians' food aesthetics and taste preferences are the same. But until recently, only the wealthy could afford to eat those foods that everyone desired, especially the high-calorie, high-protein meats and cheeses.[2] As historian Hasia Diner writes concerning Italy during the late nineteenth and early twentieth centuries (the period of mass emigration), "Food was limited, getting it difficult, but knowledge about it was widespread, and its meaning powerful."[3]

In other words, the peasants knew quite well just what they were missing.[4] They were the ones who grew the crops and raised the animals, and some of these laborers worked in the great landowners' kitchens and served at their well-appointed tables. For many peasants, eating meat was a holiday experience limited to two or three times a year. As one immigrant recalled, "Over there, if you had a piece of fat, you was lucky, and boy, it tasted good."[5]

In the rural countryside of Italy, a world dominated by what anthropologists and folklorists call the "image of limited good,"[6] hard work rarely led to improvement in one's economic situation—but it was rumored that in America, the land of "unlimited good," hard work could make a difference. Here in Utah, thanks to wage-labor jobs in the mines, on the railroads, and elsewhere, men could, by living frugally, save money, buy a plot of land, and send home for their families or a "mail-order bride." It might take years. Giovanni Nicolavo, for instance, left his home in San Giovanni in Fiore in southern Italy in 1903, but his wife and daughter didn't follow until 1909.[7] Like other Italian immigrants to Utah, they grew a bountiful garden and raised pigs that they slaughtered and then transformed into sausages, prosciutto, salamis, soppressata, and other preserved meats. Other immigrants made goat, sheep, and cow cheeses. The Nicks—as the Nicolavos came to be called in Price—pooled their cash each year along with their Italian neighbors in order to buy an entire boxcar of grapes from California to make their own wine. They could eat, finally, like the *signori*, the landowners back home—like gourmets.[8] That was a fine thing. As Diner says, "Italian immigrants placed a high premium upon eating certain foods and eating them well."[9]

But the goal never was to become gourmets or to be known as gourmets. The goal was to gain a necessity (nourishment) and to enjoy it sociably, surrounded by family and friends—and thus to survive whole, in body and spirit, with dignity, and to celebrate their survival.

Although Utah offered opportunities that didn't exist in Italy, economic reality in the coal-mining communities of Carbon County was still notoriously difficult. For one thing, the need for miners was seasonal. In the 1930s the United States was not yet the air-conditioned nation it is today, so the energy demand, including the demand for coal, dropped in summer, leading to unemployment. Work was also interrupted by strikes. Most terrible of all were the

Preparing tasty traditional foods for her family was one of the many ways Mary Nick Juliano of Price honored and perpetuated her Italian heritage. Photo by Steve Siporin, 1983. Courtesy Utah Folklife Archives.

mine disasters—which left behind widows with children and no income.

A small but significant way of overcoming these economic difficulties was by planting large gardens that supplied food inexpensively. By bartering what they grew and sharing with each other, immigrants created a community-based self-sufficiency that aided survival. As Edna Romano, of Helper, Utah, told me, "Those that had the farms and the cows and the milk helped the others.... They had huge gardens...and all kinds of animals.... [T]hey all helped each other.... They could stay out on strike and hold up because they really stuck together."[10]

You and I may plant tomatoes because those available in the supermarket, shipped from California, Mexico, and even beyond, are tasteless, odorless, and hard as rock. Immigrants to Utah also appreciated their flavorful homegrown tomatoes as well as oregano raised from the seeds they had brought with them from Italy. A few even planted their own Mediterranean fig trees, seeming to dare the cold Utah winters. Each autumn they dug up the trees, potted them, and kept them dormant but alive in their cellars, replanting them again in the spring. Even today in the Salt Lake Valley, there are descendants of immigrants who leave their fig trees outdoors in place but cover and protect them with ample insulation. All for a few figs?

Clearly the figs themselves are important, but it is easy to see in this process a self-conscious symbol of southern Italian ethnicity and the efforts some immigrants and their descendants were and are willing to make to conserve that valued identity. Besides the pleasures of eating and sharing their own homegrown fruits, vegetables, and herbs, the immigrant generation also had the satisfaction of knowing they had succeeded, thanks to their own efforts, and there would be a future for their children in Utah.

Some immigrants even used their traditional food knowledge from Italy to create new ways of earning a living. One example is the Colosimo family, whose locally produced sausages have become one of the most widely distributed Italian foods in Utah. Ralph Colosimo, an immigrant from Calabria in southern Italy, became the critical link in a living chain of culinary knowledge. He sold homemade Italian sausage (salsiccia) on a small scale in Magna, Utah, beginning in 1923; today his descendants sell his southern Italian and other types of sausage in supermarkets and grocery stores throughout northern Utah.[11]

Rich Colombo also took his family sausage recipe to a successful commercial level. For many years he made and sold his family's version of this flavorful Italian standby in his R and A Market in Helper. Rich was born in Utah; his sausage recipe came from his grandfather Ralph Saccomano, who arrived in Utah, the sausage recipe in his head, along with his two brothers in 1889. They settled in Spring Glen, between Price and Helper. The commercial sausage-making and the grocery store were to come later, but the Saccomano brothers early on used their traditional Italian agricultural skills to make a living. On their 188-acre tract they planted orchards, grew fruits and vegetables, and then peddled them in the nearby mining camps.[12]

Even the traditional know-how required to make Italian cheeses like ricotta and caciovallo survived the dislocating force of immigration and the even more corrosive forces of modernization, standardization, and cultural homogenization. The cheese-making tradition was passed from Luigi Nicoletti, born in southern Italy, to his son Tony, who carried it forward on a ranch in Butterfield Canyon, Utah. It appeared that at this point the knowledge of the process had fizzled out, but one child, Michele Nicoletti, had been quietly paying attention, watching her father make cheese, and in 2009 she revived the family cheese-making craft not just as a personal hobby but as a business, supplying Utah customers once again.[13]

The Italian word *companatico* has no precise, one-word equivalent in English. It means "what you eat with bread" or, to be etymologically closer, "what accompanies bread."[14] In other words, in the historical Italian diet, the fundamental element was bread; other foods merely "accompanied" that fixed, central item: "for it is the bread that counts, and the bit of cheese or salami or handful of olives or home-made pickles are meant to enhance the pleasures of a fresh roll or loaf."[15] Utah historian Philip F. Notarianni underscores this point by citing a southern Italian proverb that also testifies to the importance of bread to the Italian peasant. The proverb comes from the region of Calabria, the original home to many Italian immigrants to Utah. The proverb states, "When in the house there is bread, there is everything. . . . Those without fire live, those without bread die."[16] Can the importance of bread be stated any more clearly? And of course, traditional Italian bread has real substance and is not to be confused with the "soft bread" immigrants first encountered in America.[17]

Not surprisingly, then, it appears that most Italian families in Carbon County baked their own bread. Each week or so, using the domed, brick, outdoor bake-ovens that they had also built, they made enough bread to last for a week to ten days. Memories of this ritualized activity were cherished among members of the first generation born in Utah.[18]

Our awareness of the Calabrian bread proverb and the transplanted custom of baking homemade bread may help us appreciate a remarkable Carbon

During the 1920s and 1930s, the Verdi family used an outdoor cooking oven much like the village ovens found in the old country. Used by permission, Utah State Historical Society. All rights reserved.

County story more deeply than if we heard it without this cultural context. Elizabeth ("Sabella") Felice Marrelli, an immigrant to Helper from Calabria, when faced with a grave crisis, turned to bread for a solution.[19] Twelve years after her arrival in Helper as a picture bride, her husband died. She had no income and no job, nor, given that she had four children all under twelve years of age, did she seem to have a viable way to go forward:

> I was alone. This time I had four mouths to feed. What did I do? I baked my bread. Every morning at five o'clock I kneaded one hundred pounds of flour into many loaves of my good bread. These loaves were baked in an outside oven. It was not easy, but we had each other and

we made the best of life at that time. You do what you have to do and think about it later.[20]

Signora Marelli recognized that there was a need and a market for bread among the single Italian miners, and that she could meet that need and compete in the marketplace. Using her traditional baking skill and unstinting labor, she found a way for her family to survive, and even triumph, over adversity. The miners (and not just Italians) ate that good Italian bread, preferring it to the puzzling "soft bread" of America. They were gourmets, too. Only in later years, when homemade bread went from being a daily necessity to becoming an occasional luxury, would they know it.

NOTES

1. http://www.slowfood.com/international/2/our-philosophy?-session=query_session:43B12008075a232337GQ3220FC75, accessed March 1, 2014. For a folkloristic look at the Slow Food movement, see Jeff Howard, "Rosemary and Time: Slow Food and the Folklore of Taste," *Digest: A Journal of Foodways and Culture* 2, no. 2 (Spring 2014), accessible at http://digest.champlain.edu/index.html.
2. For an eye-opening tour of traditional peasant fantasies about indulging in such foods, see Luisa Del Giudice, "Mountains of Cheese and Rivers of Wine: *Paesi di Cuccagna* and Other Gastronomic Utopias," in *Imagined States: National Identity, Utopia, and Longing in Oral Cultures*, ed. Luisa Del Giudice and Gerald Porter (Logan: Utah State University Press, 2001), 11–63.
3. Hasia R. Diner, *Hungering for America: Italian, Irish, and Jewish Foodways in the Age of Migration* (Cambridge: Harvard University Press, 2001), 34.
4. One of the pieces of evidence for the narrowness of the peasant diet in Italy was the outbreak of a new and deadly disease, pellagra, from at least the early 1700s onward, a result of overdependence on a single crop. That crop was corn, usually eaten in the bread-like form of polenta.

    Even though the poor classes were the victims of a narrow diet, they may have invented some of the classic dishes of Italian cooking. According to a sixteenth-century Venetian source, ravioli were invented by a peasant woman from Lombardy named Libista. (Ortensia Lando, *Commentario delle più notabile e mostruose cose d'Italia e altri luoghi di lingua aramea in italiana tradotto. Con un breve catalogo de gli inventori delle cose che si mangiano e bevono, novamente ritrovato* [G. Salvatore and S. Salvatore: Venice, 1553]. Reprint [Bologna: Pendragon, 1994]. As cited in Albert Capatti and Massimo Montanari, *Italian Cuisine: A Cultural History* [New York: Columbia University Press, 2003]: 63.)
5. Peter Mossini, *In Their Own Words: Ellis Island Interviews* (New York: Checkmark Books, 1997), 44. Perhaps no one needs to be reminded, but historically in most peasant societies around the world, with the major exception of India, meat was a very desirable food.
6. See George M. Foster, "Peasant Society and the Image of Limited Good," *American Anthropologist* 67, no. 2 (1965): 293–315. Foster's idea, which applies cross-culturally to peasant societies everywhere, was that from the peasant's point of view there is a limited amount of the good things in the world—land, food, power, etc.—to go around, and they are always in short supply. There is no way to increase the total amount of arable land, for instance, so if one person gets more, someone else gets less.
7. Steve Siporin, "Our Way of Life Was Very Clear," *Northwest Folklore* 8, no. 2 (Spring 1990): 5. The Nicks went on to raise ten children on their homestead at the edge of Price.
8. For the old-world diet, especially of southern Italians, and their reactions to American abundance, see Diner, *Hungering for America*, particularly chapter 3, "'The Bread is Soft': Italian Foodways, American Abundance."
9. Ibid., 51.
10. Tape-recorded interview by the author with Edna

Romano, Helper, Utah, June 21, 1990, Fife Folklore Archives, Utah State University, "Italian-Americans in the West" Project, IAW-SS-A004.

11. "The Colosimo Story,"Colosimo's, accessed May 12, 2014, http://www.colosimosausage.com/AboutUs.aspx.

12. Tape-recorded interview by the author with Rich Colombo, Helper, Utah, August 6, 1990, Fife Folklore Archives, Utah State University, "Italian-Americans in the West" Project, IAW-SS-A016.

13. Kathy Stephenson, "Italian Cheese in Utah, Just Like Dad Used to Make," *Salt Lake Tribune*, July 7, 2009.

14. Indeed, the word *accompany* means "with bread" (*con pan*).

15. Gillian Riley, *The Oxford Companion to Italian Food* (New York: Oxford University Press, 2007): 137–38.

16. Notarianni cites this proverb, in dialect, in his essay, "Places of Origin: Calabresi in Carbon County, Utah," in *Old Ties, New Attachments: Italian-American Folklife in the West*, ed. David A. Taylor and John Alexander Williams (Washington, DC: Library of Congress, 1992): 67–79.

17. Diner, *Hungering for America*, 48.

18. Tape-recorded interview by the author with Kerry Nick Fister, Price, Utah, January 14, 1983.

19. See Steve Siporin, "Folklife and Survival: The Italian-Americans of Carbon County, Utah," in Taylor and Williams, *Old Ties, New Attachments*, 80–93.

20. "Elizabeth Siletta Felice Marrelli," unpublished typescript, in Siporin, "Folklife and Survival," 87.

22

RAVIOLI FOR THANKSGIVING

NORA ZAMBRENO

The Rauzi family's tradition of ravioli-making began with Pietro Rauzi and Giuseppina Corazza, the first generation of their Italian American family, who emigrated from the northern province of Trento, Italy, to the United States in the early 1900s. They married and eventually settled in West Weber, unincorporated Weber County, where they resumed the agrarian lifestyle of their native homeland.

Today, three generations (third, fourth, and fifth) of Rauzis reside in Davis, Weber, and Cache Counties and continue the custom of ravioli-making preserved and handed down by "Nonna." Ravioli continues to be the heart of the family's Thanksgiving meal.

The recipe transcript that follows is an excerpt from a special Thanksgiving edition of *Access Utah*, a public radio program produced by Utah Public Radio, in November 1998.

NARRATOR: Joanne Rauzi, Nonna's daughter-in-law, is recognized as the family authority on their special ravioli recipe. (Judy and Eileen are Nonna's daughters.)

JOANNE RAUZI: When I was first married to my husband, we would go over to his mother's house where his grandmother would join us and we would all make ravioli. Even his aunt would come over and help. As we watched her make it, she would add about five pounds of flour and a handful of this and a handful of that. After several years of doing this, I asked her if I could measure and keep track of what she added—including the meat—just to figure out how much of everything went into ravioli. Our current recipe is close to the original. But we always test our meat, and if it's not quite right, we add a little more spice if we don't think it has enough flavor.

The filling is eight to ten pounds of hamburger, and we always use extra-lean [meat] so there is no grease inside. We add about two pounds of fresh pork sausage, four tablespoons of salt, one tablespoon of pepper, and two to three medium onions. We blend the onions in a blender with about six stalks of celery and a cup of water. That way you don't get big chunks of onion or big chunks of celery. We add the blended mixture to the meat with six eggs, a cup of parmesan cheese, two cups of breadcrumbs, and half a cup of parsley flakes.

Then it's time to add the spices to the meat. We start out with one tablespoon [each] of allspice, poultry seasoning, Italian seasoning, sage, and thyme. We mix it really well and taste it to see if it has enough spices. We just put drops of it on a saucer and microwave it. If we think we want it more spicy, we just go ahead and add more.

NORA ZAMBRENO: And this recipe—we should probably mention—this is to make nine hundred to a thousand individual ravioli (raviolo).

JOANNE RAUZI: Yes. That's what we make each year—some for Thanksgiving and some to freeze and eat later. But there's still the noodle dough. In the olden days, we always did it by hand. Nonna, my husband's mother, would just start adding ingredients. She would start with five pounds of flour and add what she needed until it was noodle dough. I've kind of learned her recipe and modified it to work in my Bosch mixer. I had to make a size that would fit comfortably. So we use eight cups of flour and twelve eggs. I usually break my eggs in a separate bowl, so I don't get eggshells. Then we add two cups of warm water, a cup of oil, and two teaspoons of salt. We mix that really well in my mixer. When it's mixed well, I start adding flour, one cup at a time. The recipe calls for another four cups of flour, but I just add until it's the right texture and do not fully measure it.

NORA ZAMBRENO: You're about to mix another batch of dough, right? About how many times do

For five generations the Rauzi family of northern Utah has prepared homemade "chickens" (ravioli) for Thanksgiving. Photo by Nora Zambreno, 1998.

you do this? Do you just keep making the dough? You've got all the filling made.

JOANNE RAUZI: I usually stay busy making the dough as others roll and stuff the ravioli. I'll probably make five to six batches. We'll go through at least twenty-five pounds of flour.

NORA ZAMBRENO: Tell me about the device that's being used to form the individual raviolo.

EILEEN RAUZI UDINK: It's simply a ravioli maker. It is a metal tray with a dozen squares on it with holes. We put a long, rolled piece of dough on top of it, and then place some meat filling in each square. We put another piece of rolled dough on top of that and take a rolling pin and roll it together.

JUDY RAUZI COMBE: So now we're getting close to making chickens.

NARRATOR: The Rauzis add a unique feature to their ravioli, which they refer to as "making chickens." After the ravioli are removed from the form and sealed, they're turned on their sides. A finger inserted into the dough causes the ends of the ravioli to rise up.

JUDY RAUZI COMBE: Most of the people who make ravioli leave it in the form of a square. If you go to a restaurant and buy ravioli, you'll see a little square with a mound of meat in it. We go one step further. This is, again, a tradition from my Nonna, and most people don't do this. First, we go around and seal the edges to make sure all the edges are sealed. Then we stand it on its edge and push our finger down the top-middle edge. Nonna used to call these little chickens. She'd say, "This was the head,

and this was the tail." They really ended up looking like chickens. Making chickens is what the little kids love to do as part of their contribution. My Nonna made it up to give them something to do. A "chicken" is a finished ravioli.

When it comes to eating the ravioli, we eat them one of two ways. We either make a tomato-based meat sauce with Italian seasonings in it and lots of parmesan cheese on top. The other Rauzi tradition is to have them with what we call burnt butter. It has to be real butter; it can't be margarine. We brown the butter in a pan. You have to watch it very carefully till it foams up and browns. Once the butter is browned, you pour it over the ravioli and then add a generous amount of parmesan cheese on top of that. People like that almost as much as they do with the sauce. So the Rauzis, for Thanksgiving meals or anytime, we have to actually make both kinds.

23

STELLA'S ROOT CELLAR

MELISSA S. COY

"The root cellar was built with my mother being kind of a specialist in how to handle foods," explains Dr. Floyd O'Neil as we visit in his office at the American West Center at the University of Utah. Born in 1927, Dr. O'Neil lived in Roosevelt, Utah, until he was fifteen years old. Like other isolated farming families in the country, the O'Neils did not have electricity, and it was the Rural Electrification Administration under the New Deal that brought electrical services to the outlying areas of Duchesne County by 1940.[1]

Lacking a refrigerator, the O'Neils relied on their root cellar for the family's food storage, continuing, in this region, the lifestyle of generations of Utahns before them. While building the cellar was a family endeavor, maintaining its contents was the responsibility of Dr. O'Neil's mother.

Stella O'Neil supervised the cellar's construction. At roughly ten feet wide and twenty-eight feet long, the structure was two-thirds underground, its "sloping roof" covered in a layer of roofing felt that was topped with "heavy layers of dirt" containing high amounts of clay. The felt prevented "the dirt from sifting down into the food" and the clay soil prevented leaking. The floor sloped downward from the entrance, where there was "a second door that you opened like the old cellar doors on the outside of buildings, and so that meant that the cold—which is great in the Uintah Basin—couldn't get in." A small opening in the roof, about three inches in diameter, ventilated the cellar. A large beam, made from a tree Stella chose from the nearby Uintah Mountains, ran the length of the room along the ceiling.

O'Neil's father constructed sturdy wooden shelves on one side of the cellar, where his mother stored the tomatoes, peas, corn, and asparagus that she canned. Along the same wall were two barrels. The smaller barrel was for curing pork, while the hogshead barrel held kosher dill pickles. "God knows we didn't eat that many, and I've never been in favor of embalmed cucumbers anyway," says O'Neil, so the extra pickles were sold at Ashton's Grocery Store as "Stella's Pickles." On the opposite wall, bins held dry goods (rice and macaroni) and root vegetables (carrots, turnips, parsnips, beets, and rutabagas). The O'Neils maintained an egg incubator, heated "by a kerosene

Uintah Basin root cellar owners Estella Crapo O'Neil and Vaun Alexander O'Neil. Courtesy Floyd O'Neil.

flame that distributed the heat very carefully," and the children turned over the eggs twice daily. The coolest section of the cellar contained eggs and dairy products. Cabbages wrapped in cheese cloth hung from the large overhead beam so that Stella "didn't have to give up shelf room for canned cabbage." Homemade cheeses, wrapped in cheese cloth, also hung from the center beam.

Dr. O'Neil notes that while the family was not prosperous, "we were never hungry." His mother cooked with fresh herbs, making "highly flavored food that was not heav[ily] spiced" in the French cooking style of her family's heritage. The cellar was an important asset to the family during the Great Depression; Stella O'Neil wasted neither food nor space. From the outside, "it looked like a pit house of the ancient people," O'Neil adds. "Maybe they knew something that we didn't think they knew." Although the family's root cellar drew upon long traditions of food preservation, it is clear that it was quite sophisticated: "So many of us had root cellars, but only a few of them were as elaborate as Mother's. Very few. I never saw another one that elaborate."

NOTES

1. John D. Barton, *A History of Duchesne County* (Salt Lake City: Utah State Historical Society and Duchesne County Commission, 1998), 250–53.

24

JAPANESE NIKKEI SENIOR CENTER LUNCHEONS

JEAN TOKUDA IRWIN

Her words were quiet, firm, and delivered with a soft fierceness that belied the frailness of the gray-haired Japanese American doyenne standing tall at four feet eleven inches. "The orange slices must be uniform!" "NEVER waste a grain! Do not invite famine! Do not disrespect the hard work of farmers," she scolded as we listened to the lone grain of rice rattling in the paper sack. The ubiquitous but firm and pointed finger waved as she lectured us trembling younger cooks. Twenty years later, these admonitions echo still.

Carl Inoway and Dr. Shig Matsukawa initially called upon the Japanese American community to honor *Issei* residing in Salt Lake Valley. In 1970, the Japanese Church of Christ formed the Salt Lake Izsei Center and began the tradition of monthly free luncheons to celebrate first-generation Japanese Americans.[1] A year later, the Buddhist Temple, the Japanese American Citizens' League (JACL), and the United Way joined in the effort. As the Issei population diminished, the Issei Center was renamed the *Nikkei* Senior Center. Today, the center operates under the original charter led by an all-female board. Women from the Japanese Church of Christ, the Salt Lake Buddhist Temple, the *Daiichi* (First) LDS Ward, and two JACL chapters rotate monthly responsibilities.

Yeiko Homma is in her nineties now. She often holds court in the kitchen of the Japanese Church of Christ with grace and aplomb. Younger cooks rely on her opinion for the menu, necessary ingredients, and instruction. Many cultural values are embedded in this work. *Issei*, *nisei*, *sansei*, *yonsei*, and *gosei*, the generations of nikkei diaspora (individuals of Japanese descent living outside of Japan), fuel these gatherings. Honoring elders perpetually abides in the Japanese and Japanese American psyche. "Living Treasures," those celebrated by the Japanese government for preserving and promulgating the traditional arts and crafts, are held in high esteem. Attention to

The monthly Nikkei Senior Lunch at the Salt Lake Japanese Church of Christ, February 2016. Courtesy Jean Irwin, 2016.

Yas Iwamoto preparing maki-zushi. Photo by Jean Irwin, 2016.

the food of the season and the visual appearance of food remain ever central in this culture faithful to the aesthetic.

While all luncheons feature traditional cooking, *yaki-manju*, a traditional pastry featuring sweet bean paste, embodies the artistry and precision of preparation. Yeiko Homma insists lima beans must be purchased from Winco's bulk barrels because packaged bags are inferior. Teams of women wash the beans and soak them overnight. They then peel the cooked beans and strain them in a cloth to remove excess moisture. The next cook rotates a *surikogi* (pestle) in a clay *suribachi* (ridged mortar), mashes the cooked beans until soft, adds sugar to the beans, and then stirs and cooks them again. Several women painstakingly shape small, flat ovals of dough around balls of

cooled *an* (sweetened lima beans). A younger woman brushes the pastry with beaten egg and sprinkles poppy seeds on top. Someone less enchanted with shaping dough supervises the baking. She sets aside overbaked ones—only the best are served. Ten to fifteen women spend approximately twenty hours making 330 yaki-manju, each two and a half inches long, for dessert.

The same meticulous attention governs other dishes' preparation. Those in charge wash rice until the water clears before steaming. Knowledgeable cooks cut ingredients for a winter stew—carrots,

CHIRASHI GOHAN

(SUSHI RICE WITH MIXED INGREDIENTS)
Served at the Nikkei Luncheon at the Japanese Church of Christ on January 26, 2019.
Courtesy Jean Irwin

This is an easy way to eat sushi (vinegared rice) at home that does not involve special equipment, raw fish, or stuffing and rolling. You can use many ingredients and it is a great way to use up leftovers. Chirashi Sushi does not require meat. Other ingredients are by choice. There is no "set" recipe and ingredients vary by individual/family preference and sometimes, in Japan, regionally. Chirashi Gohan is also a visual feast, sort of like rice confetti, supporting the very important Japanese aesthetic to make food that is a feast to the eye as well.

Sushi Rice (An electric rice cooker is recommended.)
4 c. short grain rice (washed and rinsed until water is
     clear then drained)
Add 5 c. water

Soak rice 30 minutes before cooking.
     When rice is done, leave lid on and steam for 10 minutes.
     Fluff the rice with a wooden paddle and, while rice is warm, add the following vinegar mixture; then toss rice with the wooden paddle and fan, toss and fan, toss and fan.

Awase Su (vinegar mixture)
2/3 c. sugar
1 c. white vinegar
1 Tbsp. plus one pinch of salt
1 pinch of *ajinomoto* (Japanese MSG) if desired

Combine and heat to dissolve sugar but DO NOT boil; stir constantly and cool.
     Now that the sushi rice has been seasoned with awase su, add ingredients of your choice, in your preferred amounts, and toss.

1. Seasoned shiitake mushrooms: soak 8 big mushrooms overnight and boil covered in water for 10–15 minutes. Partially drain and slice into 1/4-inch strips. Do not use stems. Add 2 Tbsp. *mirin* (rice wine), 3 Tbsp. sugar, 2 Tbsp. *shoyu* (soy sauce), and 1/2 tsp. salt and simmer until liquid has reduced.
2. 24 in. of *kampyo* (dried gourd strips): wet kampyo and massage with 1/2 tsp. salt, rinse and soak 1/2 hour. Rinse; cover with water. Add: 1 tsp. *dashi* (powdered fish broth stock), 2 tsp. sugar, 2 tsp. shoyu, 1/2 tsp. salt, and 2 Tbsp. mirin. Simmer until tender but NOT falling apart. Dice in 1/2-inch pieces.
3. 1 large seasoned carrot: julienne into 1-inch pieces. Add enough water to cover. Add 1 heaping tsp. dashi, 1 Tbsp. sugar, and 1/4 tsp. salt. Simmer until firm but not crunchy or mushy.
4. *Tamago* (egg omelet): 4 eggs, 1/4 c. prepared dashi stock, 1 Tbsp. white sugar, 1 tsp. mirin, and 1/2 tsp. shoyu. Oil and heat pan and reduce to medium-low. Whisk together and pour into flat pan, lifting edges to allow uncooked egg to spread. Fold once and cook gently, do not brown. Cool and slice into strips 1 inch long by 1/8 inch wide.
5. 2/3 c. blanched and drained snow peas, slivered.
6. 4 *Inarizushi-no-moto* (prepared) tofu pockets: julienne into one-inch pieces.
7. 1/2 c. blanched, fresh green beans: cut into 1/2-inch pieces.
8. 1/4 c. chopped chives or scallions.
9. 2/3 c. Dungeness crab flakes or tiny cooked shrimp.
10. 1/2 c. slivered *kamaboko* (fish cake).
11. 1/2 c. sliced bamboo shoots.
12. *Sakura Denbu* (dried codfish flakes) which are pink, like cherry blossoms; some believe this is a "must have" ingredient.
13. Finish with sprinkles of *Kizami Nori* (slivers of toasted seaweed) on top of the Chirashi Gohan.

Japanese potatoes, shiitake mushrooms, *konnyaku* (jellied potato cake), *kombu* (kelp), chicken, fish cake—into amazingly uniform sizes. Appearance is paramount. Cooks often carve carrots into tiny cherry blossoms to adorn chilled soups.

Similarly, *maki-zushi* requires patient hand work. Cooks julienne and dice vegetables, roast *nori* (seaweed), and fan and toss the vinegar sushi rice in a wooden *hangiri* (flat, round cypress or pine bowl) in order to ensure seasoning coats each grain. *Tamago* (delicate egg omelets) constitute only one among what will total five to seven ingredients for the center of the maki-zushi.[2] A cook pulverizes tiny shrimp in the suribachi and adds sugar and red food coloring before tossing the shrimp in a skillet until flaky; it is ready to be a bright note of color inside the maki-zushi. The maker then pats seasoned rice onto roasted nori. Next, she places the colorful ingredients into the center of the rice and, with the aid of a bamboo mat, rolls and forms the maki-zushi before slicing to serve. Maki-zushi quintessentially exemplifies Japanese attention to careful visual aesthetics and seasoned preparation of many individual ingredients to create a whole dish.

At all luncheons and events where food is served, *gohan* (rice) serves as a metaphor for health and cultural wellbeing.[3] *O-cha* (green tea) completes the meal.

In an additional effort to please the eye, themed centerpieces grace the luncheon tables. For example, the luncheon for Halloween in 2015 featured plastic pumpkins filled with packaged *osembi* (rice crackers)

and seasoned seaweed sprinkles. A holiday lunch delighted lucky door-prize winners with cash folded into complex origami shapes.

Japanese American food traditions flourish in Utah. In addition to Nikkei luncheons, food culture is visible through *Nihon Matsuri* (spring festival of Japan), *Aki Matsuri* (fall festival), various food bazaars, and *Obon* (celebration of departed ancestors). These events with food as cornerstone ensure that future generations understand the importance of celebrating the eye, the stomach, and the soul. *Itadakimasu* and *gochisosama deshita*.[4]

NOTES

1. Salt Lake Issei Center, now Nikkei Senior Center, notes an organizational entity, not a physical location.
2. Seven is auspicious. Buddhists believe in seven reincarnations. The Japanese celebrate the seventh day after a baby's birth and mourn the seventh day and seventh week following a death. Five is better than four. The word four sounds like death. Buildings do not have a fourth floor. Airplanes do not have seat number four. Maki-zushi does not have four ingredients in the center.
3. In World War II, Japanese prisoners of war upon release were asked if they had been fed. When they answered "no," they were given food but not rice. Therefore, symbolically, they were neither well fed nor in good health. In short, for the Japanese, rice is synonymous with food.
4. *Itadakimasu* begins the meal with "I receive this food" and expresses appreciation for nature, the person who prepared the food, and the one who served it. At the meal's end, *Gochisosama deshita* expresses gratitude: "It was quite a feast."

25

KALI OREXI

Greek Food in Utah

ELAINE BAPIS

My mother grew up on a goat ranch in the desert southeast of Price, Utah. Her parents, Ellen and Fotis Konakis, made and sold an array of goat cheeses, cured olives, and garden vegetables. Their desert farm provided a cultural oasis for Greeks who traveled there nearly every Sunday for a taste of Greek cooking, socializing, and the kind of hospitality they knew so well. They met each other with courtesies. "Καλώς ορίσατε" (kalós orísate; welcome), the hosts greeted. "Καλώς σας βρήκαμε" (kalos sas vríkame; good we found you), the guests replied. For a few hours once a week they placed their orders for cheese and olives and then sat at a table full of Greek cuisine, storytelling, song, drink, and dance. With glasses of wine, they toasted: "Καλή όρεξη" (kali orexi; good appetite), some said. "Στην υγειά σας" (stin ygeiá sas; to your health), others answered. It was always that way, and somehow the food tasted better after those words.

Greeks could always expect a full table when visiting Greek households. Such generosity through food meant the family would always have pastries, cheese, olives, bread, liquors, homemade wine, and other culinary amenities on hand. As my mother put it:

> If a visitor leaves without food they will feel like they are unwanted. In my house I've always treated [sic] *just* like my parents did. I knew the Greek people's customs and I knew what was expected of me and I found something—whatever it was.[1]

Cuisine lay at the heart of Greek identity and was served mainly in the home where the promise of hospitality and the dedication to nurturing the family and community through food was always present. Because Greeks understood the need to connect with fellow Greeks, they

In 1923 Gregory and Mary Halles (couple in center, front row) hosted a baptismal dinner for their daughter, Athena. Gathering family and friends to celebrate important occasions with food has always been a fundamental part of Greek culture in Utah. Peoples of Utah Collection. Used by permission, Utah State Historical Society. All rights reserved.

recreated the "old country" fellowship in homes. A day with family and fellow immigrants held their spirit together in the midst of a Utah society very different from theirs. Eventually Utahns embraced Greek culture through food, but it took most of the century to get there.

The early 1900s saw a major migration from Greece to the United States. Largely from the Peloponnesus and Crete, Greek men sought the new country for opportunity since their homeland was still economically devastated from the War of Independence against the Ottoman Empire. The 1900 United States census records indicate the Greek population in Utah to be three. By 1910, there were well over four thousand. Utah Greeks made up a rather large percentage of immigrants in the mining and railroad industry in Carbon County, Bingham, Salt Lake City, and Ogden.[2]

With an eye for making a living in Utah, Greek men eventually became citizens and mail-ordered brides and started families; by the 1920s, Greeks had built churches and cultural centers to solidify their communities. For the rest of the twentieth century, Greeks became prominent participants in Utah society and, by the millennium, census records showed twelve thousand Greeks in Utah. While their population did not skyrocket, their culinary presence did.

Whether from a restaurant, at the Greek festival, or as a guest at a private celebration, Utahns know about Greek food, and it is not because of a large Greek population. Rather, it is the significance of food as a defining feature in Greek culture. In fact, Greek food in the home was synonymous with Greek identity, and that was paramount in keeping the family and community together. Food defined you and if anyone came into your house, food was the way you offered guests a gift from your heart—food, homemade and time consuming, meant you were proud to give, not just a new recipe you came up with, but what was inherited and understood as culturally sanctioned. If you traveled to Greece, you would find the same dishes. In fact, if you traveled anywhere and were invited into a Greek home, you might be served a variation, but the core cuisine was the same. In addition, food meant socializing, something Greeks have perpetuated both here and abroad.

Traditional Greek cuisine means quality food as fresh as possible. It was not hard to transport that heritage to the West with Greeks' passion for gardens. Vegetables were essential to Greek cuisine, and planting them meant satisfying Greeks' discerning palate. If you visited many early Greek households during the Utah summer, you would find rows of tomatoes, bell peppers, lettuce, cucumbers, broad beans, Swiss chard, spinach, carrots, zucchini, eggplants, onions, garlic, and just about every other vegetable available to complete their gastronomic customs.

Even city gardens were like farm gardens with a variety of plants. They were cultivated, planted, hoed, irrigated, weeded, picked, and handed over to the cook. When you looked at each plant on each row, you saw a table full of Greek cuisine: spinach for *spanakopeta*; eggplant for *moussaka*; lettuce, tomatoes, cucumbers, bell peppers, and onions for *horiatiki salata*; zucchini and carrots for lamb stew; broad beans with olive oil and lemon juice and Swiss chard for *horta*; and of course the essential herbs to complete every dish. Put a dab of yogurt (also prepared at home) on *yemista* (stuffed tomatoes, peppers, eggplant, and zucchini), and you couldn't be happier that it was summer.

Next to the garden you would see herbs such as oregano, mint, basil, and dill—most unavailable in local grocery stores in the early years. With their herb gardens, cooks could dry and store a winter supply. What they did not grow they found from roving vendors or from a specialty store that cropped up in Price, Salt Lake City, Ogden, Bingham, and surrounding copper towns.

When guests departed from Greek households, they always left with a bag of fresh garden produce, never mind if they went home to their own crops. Sharing garden produce meant exchanging friendship, hospitality, and gratitude. Produce was essential to the transmission of Greek culture for those who cared to sustain that custom.

When Greek men immigrated to Utah at the turn of the twentieth century, they opened bars and coffee houses. Greeks established businesses as early as 1900 in Salt Lake City. In Carbon County, bars stretched from East Carbon to Wellington, Price, and Helper. On Carbon Avenue in Price, three coffee houses cropped up to serve Greek coffee and a few Greek sweets. Some even cooked Greek food in the back for the bachelors who were regulars. Immigrants opened boarding houses and fed Greeks traditional food.

Once women immigrated, Greeks created the foundation for their Utah future by building churches with fellowship halls. By the 1920s, the Price and Salt Lake communities founded their churches and took their culinary traditions to social events at the fellowship halls. Whether it was observing a religious holiday, a family event, or a fundraising party, celebrations took place in the church hall. Ogden Greeks staged their parties in various fraternal halls or other venues for the same social interaction until 1964 when they built a church and social hall of their own. At these occasions, tables were spread with delectable main dishes and intricate desserts. Greek weddings, baptisms, and funerals could not be called "Greek" without tables filled with traditional dishes and drinks shared with guests.

In Price, restaurants and grocery stores appeared, oftentimes with a section for Greek food items. Bill's Café, owned by Bill Flementakis, became one of the most well-known restaurants in Price. Mr. Flementakis served Greek specialties every day, but the most popular ones were lamb stew and lamb with spaghetti. As one Price resident remembers, everyone knew Bill's café as the place for "the best lamb in town."[3] This café gave Greeks a place to socialize and enjoy their traditional customs.

One "supermarket" in Price began out of a truck. Nick Halamandaris sold food to outlying areas until he had enough business to open his store. He brought in five-gallon cans of feta (from my grandfather's ranch), imported olive oil, stocked herbs, and supplied residents with fish, all by the late 1940s.[4]

In Bingham and Leadmine, Greeks owned grocery stores that supplied a few traditional items such as Greek cheese and olives. The Panhellenic, The Independent, and Bingham Grocery were just a few of the many food and mercantile businesses started by Greeks in the copper-mine area where patrons could get a small selection of ingredients for Greek dishes.[5]

When the copper towns closed, Greeks either moved their businesses or closed them for good. In 1945 Mr. Christ Pappasotiriov relocated his Bingham-Copperfield grocery business to Salt Lake City and opened Sunny Market (later Broadway), a small grocery store that sold Greek items. By 1971 the store became the first pharmacy-grocery in Utah and supplied the surrounding Greek communities with many of the items for Greek cuisine.[6]

By midcentury, Greek food made its way into more local restaurants and nightclubs. At the landmark Lamb's Grill in downtown Salt Lake City, patrons could find lentil soup, braised lamb shank, and feta cheese on its menu. The Stadium Café on Second South served delicious Greek-style dishes such as okra with lamb or chicken. You could even pick out your own food from the kettle on the stove at the Stadium.[7] During the 1960s, Andy Luras's My Wife's Place offered a full Greek menu on Wednesdays only (complete with linen service) where Greek University of Utah law students and others enjoyed such menu items as dolmathes, roast lamb, lamb chops, stuffed calamari, green beans, and oven-roasted potatoes.[8] One popular nightclub in Salt

Lake City, the historic Athenian, brought a vibrant social scene to the public landscape where guests could enjoy Greek food, dance, music, and entertainment. Before you knew it, Utahns soon found rice pilaf offered with their halibut, lamb on skewers served with village salad, and egg-lemon soup complementing their main course. Utah's Greek women helped to develop a public palette for Greek desserts when they took their kitchen art to the streets. Ogdenites made pastries and bread to sell at bake sales in front of J. C. Penney and other businesses on Washington Boulevard.[9] They set up tables full of sweets and found many repeat customers. Soon Greek communities organized the annual "bazaar" held at their church halls. They advertised and watched non-Greeks come year after year to buy the fruits of their hard work. Baklava, kourambiethes, and melomacarona eventually earned their way into the appetites of the non-Greek community for good.

Enthusiasm for traditional fare validated what Greek women already knew: their pastries were unique and delicious. Food outreach added respect to female culinary aesthetics and provided a source of elegance and cultural prominence for Utah's Greek women. At the same time, their culinary art helped fund the building of churches and cultural halls and added to their philanthropic work.

When the cultural revolution of the 1960s and 1970s exposed a multicultural and ethnic America, sharing more culinary heritage made sense. Though Greeks had learned how to be American, it was now more popular to be ethnic. Instead of the familiar nineteenth-century pioneer history, the mantra was becoming the "Peoples" of Utah.[10] What was ordinary in Utah's Greek communities was now exotic and socially relevant to Utahns. And if it took a new label like "ethnic" to jump-start broader public acceptance of their private cultural practices, few minded.

Popularizing ethnicity provided a perfect segue for reputation-building in Greek communities based on culinary heritage. Greek food entered a smattering of restaurants earlier, but who would have guessed that Greeks would be well known for their hamburgers by the mid-1970s? With the introduction of Crown Burger in Utah, the sister of the former owner of The Athenian brought a sort of Greek American fusion burger onto the Salt Lake City landscape. From there, dozens of Greek-owned restaurants opened. Astro, Apollo, Olympus, Yiannis Greek Express, Atlantis, and Greek Souvlaki are among the most popular Greek food establishments in Salt Lake City today.

Those of us who grew up before the multicultural explosion kept our cuisine in its place—at home—but when we saw the outside world endorse such dishes as gyros, souvlaki, dolmathes, pastitsio (pasta casserole), tiropeta (cheese triangles), spanakopeta, calamari, and more at restaurants such as The Other Place, Aristo's, The Hellenic House, and others every day, we said good-bye to our self-consciousness.

Sharing Greek cuisine with the outside world gave a sense of pride and pleasure to entrepreneurs who saw Greek food as a viable livelihood in Utah. Add to that the Greek festivals that made their way onto the popular scene by the late 1970s and 1980s, broadening original bake sales and annual bazaars and converting them into fully integrated festivals. Food enthusiasts visited Price in July, Salt Lake City in early

Renowned Greek cook Bessie K. Markos, the author's mother, with her Easter bread, circa 1990. Courtesy Elaine Bapis.

dances on stage in front of Utah audiences. These great-grandchildren would not know that you had to grow oregano and dry it because most stores did not carry it in pre-midcentury Utah. Nor would they realize that olive oil was not readily available for daily cooking until it became a sensation for foodies.

With the multicultural explosion, the expanding Greek festivals, and the public craving for Greek cuisine, the label "Greek" soon became a trendy marketing tool for yogurt companies, drawing on "cultural authenticity" for its sales and endorsement. It may seem to some that the public now owns so much of Greek food culture that nothing indigenous remains within households, but there are a few food traditions dependent on family dynamics for their cultural life.

Greeks can now find just about everything in the public realm that their grandparents served, except for some of the exclusive items that still remain culturally specific. Holiday bread, for example, is specific to Easter, Christmas, and New Year celebrations; it's recognizable by the ingredients and bread designs. A coin is added to New Year's bread, dyed Easter eggs to Easter bread dough, and nuts and cherries to Christmas loaves.

But the central celebration on the church calendar, Easter, remains the most internal to household culinary tradition because of its intricate connection to Greek Orthodox religious practices. The Lenten period stipulates a special vegetarian diet that culminates in a feast after Easter church services. Greek families celebrate the resurrection with a table full of painstakingly prepared food, featuring lamb on the spit, Easter bread with dyed eggs, magiritsa (soup), pastitsio, and enough dyed eggs for each guest to commemorate the resurrection. Easter brings heritage, religion, and food

September, and Ogden later that same month. Patrons saw members volunteering to give the public what it now wanted—an insider's taste of Greece. Women's groups made pastries and breads, and families ran booths that sold Greek coffee, gyros, tiropeta, and other cultural fare. Youth groups staged traditional dancing while patrons enjoyed specialty dishes. At all three Greek festivals of Utah, food was and is their central feature. It would be no surprise that festivals mimicked food's central role of hospitality and home.

Early immigrants' great-grandchildren grew up with friends whose families opened local restaurants and who were proud to perform Greek folk

BESSIE'S MOUSSAKA

My favorite summer recipe from the garden is the eggplant casserole "Moussaka." My mother, Bessie, would wait for the perfect eggplants to grow; from that point in the summer, we would have our scrumptious delight.

Bessie never followed a recipe, so here is what it was like cooking with her as she created her magical dish.

The Eggplants: Find two medium-sized eggplants from the garden, wash them, and, with a sharp blade, cut the stem off and cut the eggplant into thin, round slices. No need to peel. The skins give the dish its beauty, and they are not tough if they are garden-picked. On a large cookie sheet, pour a few tablespoons of olive oil to cover the pan. Place slices on the olive oil and lightly salt and pepper the slices. Turn them over and repeat. Broil the eggplant slices until golden brown on each side. In a casserole baking pan, drizzle melted butter and breadcrumbs to cover the pan completely. Place a layer of the cooked eggplant slices in the baking dish.

The Meat Sauce: In a frying pan, brown a pound or two of ground beef with oregano, salt and pepper to taste, and a dash of paprika (mother loved to experiment with spices and liked the coloring of paprika; sometimes she would throw in a bit of cinnamon). Once the ground beef is cooked through, add a can of tomato sauce. (Bessie used the homemade tomato sauce we all helped can.) Simmer for a few minutes, then pour the meat sauce over the layer of eggplant in the casserole dish. Place another layer of eggplant slices on top of the meat sauce.

The Béchamel Sauce: Complete the dish with a béchamel sauce made of butter and flour rue and about a quart of whole milk. Stir milk into the rue; when thickened, remove from stove and stir constantly while pouring 6 to 8 beaten eggs into the cream sauce. Sometimes Bessie added grated cheese such as *kefali* (head cheese). Pour the cream sauce over the top layer of eggplant and sprinkle with a dash of paprika and cinnamon. Cook for about an hour at 350 degrees, depending on the size of the casserole container. The top should be golden brown and bubbly. Plan to let it rest for about 45 minutes before serving.

Serve with a village salad: Mix garden tomatoes, cucumbers, green bell peppers, minced onions, fresh parsley, and oregano. Add fresh feta cheese and pitted kalamata olives. Drizzle with good olive oil and white vinegar and toss. Don't forget the homemade bread to dip into the leftover salad juice.

inseparably together. It is one time you know if you are Greek or not.

Yet both the feast, a private, intragroup bonding with ground rules understood through family transmission, and the festival, an intergroup exchange establishing intercultural connections through enterprise, help sustain cultural practice and identity. Utah Greeks both integrated into and broadened Utah culture and society as their cuisine and their festivals became an integral part of local events and their restaurants served varying degrees of Greek menus.

Greeks may not own goat ranches today or travel forty miles on a juniper-laden dirt road to get Greek *fellowship*, but they do know food customs. Greek food in Utah is both a private cultural practice that transmits heritage and a public pleasure transcending the limited integration of the early immigrants. Greek food is a friendly gesture and a source of emotional gratification. Whether in the home, at the Greek festivals, or at a restaurant, it all begins with the old-world spirit of hospitality and the belief that no matter the person, you always treat a guest with a full meal, generously prepared and shared. To be sure, the act of food generosity is a tradition that requires serious attention, for cuisine without hospitality is just food. A greeting at the door is an invitation to the table, deeply engrained with the body and soul of culture. When you enter, you are honored.

Food works dynamically to connect the individual to the group as well as the group to the larger public. Food is a cultural unifier and a source of aesthetic satisfaction and self-presentation. Offering a person something that has an aesthetic attachment and cultural history is more than an act of nourishment. It is a gift encoded with a set of beliefs about who people are, where they came from, and what they value. Now on its fifth generation in Utah, Greek culture thrives as a social outreach, popular livelihood, and personal expression. What once seemed exotic and strange to Utahns has become so much a part of the regional landscape that it appears indigenous now, almost as if it has always been here. *Kali orexi* (good appetite)!

NOTES

1. Bessie Markos, personal interview with the author, October 1986.
2. Pamela S. Perlich, "Utah Minorities: The Story Told by 150 Years of Census Data" (Bureau of Economic and Business Research, David S. Eccles School of Business, University of Utah, October 2002), 12.
3. George Himonas, personal interview with the author, May 4, 2014.
4. Gust Himonas, personal interview with the author, May 4, 2014.
5. Stella Saltas, personal interview with the author, May 8, 2014.
6. Leo Sotiriou, e-mail message to author, May 18, 2014.
7. Nyal Stamoulis, personal interview with the author, May 4, 2014; Frank Karras, personal interview with the author, May 4, 2014.
8. Nick Colessides, e-mail message to author, May 2, 2014.
9. *Ogden Standard Examiner*, March 24, 1966.
10. This reference is from Helen Papanikolas's *Peoples of Utah* (Salt Lake City: Utah State Historical Society, 1977).

26

BREWERIES IN LATE NINETEENTH-CENTURY LOGAN

CHRISTINE COOPER-ROMPATO

Many Mormon pioneers in Utah brewed in their homes.[1] Hops are native to Utah, and the early pioneers, many of European heritage, brought with them their brewing practices and experience. Large-scale breweries opened in Salt Lake City soon after it was founded, and breweries also flourished in Ogden. The situation with brewing in the smaller community of Logan, however, was quite different. In the late nineteenth century, Logan leaders believed that they had the power to legislate and even forbid the sale of alcohol, and their frequent attempts to crack down on alcohol sales led to much controversy among its residents.

The earliest named brewer found in Logan's records is Henry Worley, who arrived in Utah from England in 1869.[2] A. J. Simmonds suggested that Worley was brewing as early as the early 1870s, and that local residents expressed concern about public drunkenness:

> On Valentine's night, 14 February 1873, a number of young men were walking toward a dance being held at Logan Hall. They had been drinking heavily and laughed, jostled, and quarreled as they moved toward the dance. Ten days earlier county coroner Charles O. Card complained to the Logan City Council that brewer Henry Worley was dispensing of his product too freely. The council asked two of its members to see if Card's accusations were true regarding "frequently large drunken crowds." Worley was warned, but nothing more.[3]

Three days later a group of men were gathered outside of Worley's place, on the corner of Second and Thomas (now Center and Third West), when a justice was shot by another man who was probably under the influence of alcohol. The shooter was eventually caught and lynched.[4]

In the middle to late 1870s, Logan passed ordinances that prohibited the sale of liquor; retail and wholesale beer sales also appear to have been included in these ordinances. During this period

In 1897, to commemorate the 1847 arrival of Mormon pioneers in Utah, the Pabst Brewing Company of Milwaukee produced this beer mug that pairs a portrait of Mormon leader and prophet Brigham Young with the state's beehive symbol. Courtesy Utah Folklife Archives.

authorities. Those venders would then be arrested and brought before the judge to pay a fine.[6] Henry Worley appears in Logan court records for liquor infractions on several occasions. He was brought before the judge in April 1881 and fined five dollars for selling liquor, either hard liquor or beer.[7] This particular case attracted some attention from the townspeople and demonstrates how many local community members protested the measures taken by the city to police the antialcohol ordinances.

LOGAN CITY BREWERY

The first evidence of a named brewery in Logan appeared in the May 6, 1885, *Utah Journal*, which announced that Logan City Brewery was formally established under the proprietorship of William Wood Beirdneau.[8] Beirdneau (also spelled Birdno), son of prominent pioneers Nehemia Wood and America Ann Beirdneau, worked as a sawyer on Logan's Main Street.[9] Three days later, the newspaper published an advertisement for the business, which vended wholesale "Keg and Bottled Beer" by the case; for those who wanted to purchase beer by the glass or the bottle, the advertisement proclaimed, "Our Beer Is for Sale on Draught or by Bottle at Edwards & Fry's, Main Street."[10] Advertisements for the brewery appeared regularly throughout 1885, and the ads stated clearly that Beirdneau would accept "ALL KINDS OF Marketable Produce" in exchange.[11] This was typical for many Utah businesses, which were used to working on the cooperative model.[12]

of prohibition, local residents continued to petition the town council for liquor licenses—which were not granted. A January 1880 article titled "Suppressing the Liquor Traffic in Logan" described how rejected petitioners threatened to sue the council. The paper defended the ordinance, claiming that "the city cannot afford to purchase financial wealth [i.e., liquor license fees] by repaying her people with the poverty of vice and corruption."[5]

There were many attempts to catch those selling alcohol illegally. The town hired men to seek out illicit alcohol and report on its whereabouts to the

Less than one year after its initial opening, the Logan City Brewery was for sale, with the proprietors listed as Affleck and Beirdneau; no doubt Affleck was

William's father-in-law or brother-in-law.[13] Several "for sale" notices appeared in the March 1886 Logan papers, and in April the *Salt Lake Herald* picked up the notice as well, reporting that Affleck and Beirdneau were trying to sell out.[14] One week after notice of the sale appeared in the Salt Lake paper, the brewery was reportedly sold to Herman Vogel, a German brewer who had been living (at least until 1884) in Salt Lake City.[15] Vogel took over Beirdneau's advertisement design, adding the cost ($3.50 for keg or case), as well as the note that read "All Kinds of Grains Taken."[16] Several months later Vogel fell afoul of the law, incurring a twenty-five-dollar fine for "disposing of beer on Sunday."[17] The brewery must have been successful, for in 1888 he also advertised that the business was "now connected by Telephone" to facilitate orders.[18] The 1890 Sanborn fire insurance map for Logan shows the brewery on First Street on the east side of Main, just west of the Central Flour Mills.[19]

Logan City Brewery continued to flourish in the 1890s, but the story took a dark turn in March 1898. After about thirteen years of operating the business, Vogel attempted to commit suicide with his shotgun. Newspapers across the state reported on the incident and followed the affair closely.[20] Vogel reportedly survived the initial injury, but his wound became infected and he subsequently died, after which his stepson, F. C. Kidgell, took over the business.[21] Under Kidgell, the business continued; records show that he filed for several liquor licenses and paid fines for various infractions, including selling beer retail under a wholesale license.[22] The brewery closed down briefly but reopened in April 1900; an advertisement claimed, "Proprietor Kidgell has

thoroughly renovated and filled it up and is now prepared to furnish the public with popular beverage."[23] Despite the renovation, the brewery closed its doors for a final time in late 1900 or early 1901,[24] and according to family histories, Kidgell went to work for the Amalgamated Sugar Company.[25] Of the brewery itself, nothing remains.

JACOB THEURER AND CACHE VALLEY BREWING COMPANY

There was a second brewery in Logan, the Cache Valley Brewing Company, whose notice of establishment appeared in April 1886 in the same paper that noted that Vogel succeeded Affleck and Beirdneau.[26] Beginning in May 1886, advertisements for the brewery appeared almost weekly in the *Utah Journal*; these ads listed Theurer and Bloom as the proprietors, and that "Orders left at J.R. Edwards', Main Logan, or at the Brewery, will receive prompt attention. Special attention paid to orders from a distance."[27]

Jacob Theurer was a Swiss immigrant who came to Utah in 1876. Anecdotal evidence suggests he took up brewing quite soon after moving to Logan.[28] According to Simmonds,

> In the mid-1870s George Bloom and Jacob Theurer established the Cache Valley Brewery in the grove of trees south of Logan and west of the Providence Lane. Aggressive businessmen, they later opened a stand at the mouth of Logan Canyon to serve the needs of drivers and loggers working on the construction of the Temple. Their successors as brewers to Cache Valley was a company which operated in the center of the

block behind J.R. Edwards Main Street Saloon during the late 1890s.[29]

The Logan Temple was begun in 1877 and completed in 1884, which suggests that the Logan Canyon beer stand was open at some point between these years.[30]

The *Utah Directory and Gazetteer* for 1889–1890 listed "Jacob Theurer, Cache Valley Brewing Co." as located one mile south of the Logan center.[31] Blogs and other modern web sources state the brewery was "known as Jake's" and "was built on the north side of the present state highway and south side of the Johnson grove,"[32] which is identified in other articles as about 900 South.[33] Bloom, who had begun as a proprietor alongside Theurer, quickly dropped out of all official notices and records related to the brewery.

One important point to note is that Theurer's wife, Barbara, was also deeply involved in the business. In the 1890s, the mother of nine children applied for a number of licenses for brewing and dispensing. As she was required to reapply quarterly, she appears in the records frequently. At one point she requested that the fee be reduced, but this was denied as it was asserted the fee was "the minimum fixed by law."[34] When county commissioners considered the question of whether to allow the town of Providence to incorporate in 1898, one of the reasons given for extending the town limits to just beyond the brewery was that the Providence people wanted to benefit from Theurer's license fees. The commissioners granted Providence's incorporation but restricted the town limits.[35]

The brewery was also the site of terrible violence. In 1891, the papers reported that Theurer's nine-year-old daughter had been viciously attacked and assaulted by a German man employed at the business.[36] The brewery was also the site of much drunken violence against men. In 1896, Peter Peterson, who had been held for ten days in jail for public drunkenness, was released. Peterson immediately went to a brewery on the "outskirts of town" (no doubt Cache Valley) where he proceeded to get drunk. Although he did not remember the attack which left him unconscious for over a day, he apparently had just left the brewery when he was beaten up, stripped, and almost killed.[37] The following year, Jacob Theurer was viciously attacked by a drunk at his brewery, and later that same year three men were arrested and fined for assault and battery committed during a drunken row at the brewery.[38] Then, in 1898, the sheriff arrested a man named Simon Jones for assault and battery committed at the brewery.[39]

I have found no further references to the Cache Valley Brewing Company after 1906. Alma and Hermann, Jacob's sons, may have continued their family's brewery, or they may have opened a saloon. The 1906 Logan paper did advertise an "old city brewery" for sale; although the brewery was unnamed, it could have been Jake's, or perhaps even the closed-down Logan City brewery.[40] Vance (as well as websites based on his work) asserts the Cache Valley Brewing Company did not shut its doors until 1912, but I am unable to corroborate this late date.[41] In 1911 most of Utah (with the exception of Salt Lake City, Ogden, and several other mining towns) banned the sale of alcohol.[42] By 1917 the entire state had joined the prohibition movement. This of course did not stop brewing but merely drove it underground. Prohibition was eventually repealed in 1930, but no breweries have operated in Logan (or Cache Valley) after that date, and the attitude toward alcohol continues to remain quite critical.[43] In the early 2000s, several people attempted to revive the Cache Valley Brewing Company, to no avail.[44]

Although I have uncovered a number of sources and references to Logan's early breweries, regrettably absent are accounts of local home brewers, including women, as well as more information about the breweries themselves, their beers, and their clientele. Hopefully those with unpublished family histories will be able to fill in some of the gaps of Utah's lesser-known history.

NOTES

1. The best source for the history of brewing in Utah is Del Vance's *Beer in the Beehive: A History of Brewing in Utah* (Salt Lake City: Ken Sander's Dream Garden Press, 2008). A. J. Simmonds, former Special Collections curator at Utah State University, also explored brewing in Logan in a series of newspaper articles for Logan's *Herald Journal* in the 1970s. This essay draws from both these authors' works while also correcting misinformation and expanding what is known about Logan's brewing history.
2. "Mormon Migration, Liverpool to New York, 25 Aug 1869–6 Sep 1869," http://mormonmigration.lib.byu.edu. Utah State University Special Collections has a photograph of Worley, USU_Aboard1, A-1584.
3. A. J. Simmonds, "Looking Back," *Herald Journal*, September 11, 18, and 25, 1986; see also Cache County Records, February 18, 1873, Merrill-Cazier Library, Special Collections, Utah State University, Logan; F. Ross Peterson, *A History of Cache County* (Salt Lake City: Utah State Historical Society, 1997), 95–99.
4. A. J. Simmonds, "The Lynching of Charles Benson in Logan on February 17, 1873," *Cache Valley Historical Society, Meeting of February 13, 1975*, Special Collections, Utah State University; A. J. Simmonds,

"A 'Wet' Valley's Distilleries, Breweries and Saloons," *Herald Journal*, April 1, 1977. Simmonds suggests that Worley may have been brewing as early as the 1860s in Logan, but since Worley only arrived in Logan in late 1869, it is safe to assume that his sales could not have begun in earnest until 1870.
5. "Suppressing the Liquor Traffic in Logan," *Logan Leader*, January 23, 1880.
6. According to Peterson (*History of Cache County*, 92), "alcohol was a major target of every city [in Cache Valley]. The city not only handled the licensing of the establishments but also threatened licensees who sold alcohol and allowed gambling, betting, or disorderly conduct.... The majority of convictions in the Logan and Hyrum justice of the peace records are for drunkenness, and the fine was usually five dollars. However, if the defendant pled innocent and was found guilty, the fine and the court costs appreciated dramatically" (92).
7. "Liquor Sellers Fined," *Logan Leader*, April 22, 1881.
8. "Items of Local Interest," *Utah Journal*, May 6, 1885. I have not found evidence to suggest that Beirdneau bought the business from Worley, although this is of course possible.
9. *Utah Gazetteer and Directory of Logan, Ogden, Provo and Salt Lake Cities*, compiled by Robert W. Sloan (Salt Lake City: Herald Printing and Publishing Co., 1884), 334. Online at http://archive.org/details/utah/1884.
10. Untitled, *Utah Journal*, May 9, 1885.
11. Ibid.; "A Hard Earned Spree," *Utah Journal*, July 4, 1885. For more advertisements, see, for example, Untitled, *Utah Journal*, August 5 and September 2 and 9, 1885, and "Where to Trade," *Utah Journal*, December 19, 1885.
12. Peterson describes the idea of the Mormon cooperative movement, including the telegraph office, which accepted "wheat, board, wood, potatoes, or milk," *History of Cache County*, 68.
13. William married Bel (Isabel) Affleck; Bel's father, Peter, worked as a founder in Logan.
14. "Local Points," *Utah Journal*, March 6, 1886; Untitled, *Utah Journal*, March 10, 1886; Untitled, *Utah Journal*, March 20, 1886; "Finance and Mining," *Salt Lake Herald*, April 11, 1886.

15. "Finance and Mining," *Salt Lake Herald*, April 18, 1886; "Affleck & Beirdneau, Brewers, Sold Out; Cache Valley Brewing Company, Just Commenced . . . Herman Vogel, Brewer, Succeeds Affleck & Beirdneau." Vogel's occupation in the 1880 and 1884 *Utah Directory and Gazetteer* was given as brewer in Salt Lake City, so he had solid experience in the business. In 1880, Vogel is listed as a brewer in Salt Lake City on "5 E between 5 and 6E." In 1884, H. Vogel was listed as a brewer in the city on 551 S. Sixth East (p. 598). See *Utah Directory and Gazetteer for 1879–80*, ed. Henry L. A. Culmer.

16. Untitled, *Utah Journal*, September 11, 1886; Untitled, *Utah Journal*, November 13, 1886. For more of Vogel's advertisements, see also "Read This," *Utah Journal*, May 26, 1888, and Untitled, *Logan Journal*, December 23, 1897.

17. "Local Points," *Utah Journal*, October 20, 1886.

18. Untitled, *Utah Journal*, June 13, 1888.

19. Sanborn Fire Insurance Maps, Logan, 1890: Sheet 08, Western Americana Division, Special Collections, J. Willard Marriott Library, University of Utah, Salt Lake City.

20. See, for example, "Attempted Suicide," *Logan Journal*, March 29, 1898; "A Frightful Tragedy," *Salt Lake Herald*, March 29, 1898; "Horrifying Case at Logan," *Salt Lake Tribune*, March 29, 1898; "Shooting at Logan," *Deseret Evening News*, March 28, 1898.

21. "Gone to Hospital," *Logan Journal*, March 31, 1898; "Died," *Salt Lake Herald*, April 4, 1898; "Logan Locals," *Salt Lake Herald*, April 6, 1898.

22. "Logan Locals," *Salt Lake Herald*, April 8, 1898; "A Dejected Stovepipe," *Salt Lake Herald*, January 6, 1899; "Logan Local Affairs," *Salt Lake Herald*, September 1, 1898.

23. See Renee Tomlinson Petersen, "Fred, Lily Jane, Stella and Fred Charles," *Whispers from the Past . . . Tales Told* (blog), October 15, 2011, http://honorancestors. blogspot.com/2011_10_15_archive.html, which includes a list of newspapers that list Kidgell as the proprietor. See also Renee Tomlinson Petersen, "Sure Enough—It Is Sarah Ann Cashmore Kidgell," *Whispers from the Past . . . Tales Told* (blog), April 27, 2011, http://honorancestors.blogspot.com/2011/04/sure-enough-it-is-sarah-ann-cashmore.html.

24. "Breweries Closed," *American Brewer's Preview* 14 (July 1900–June 1901): 402.

25. Renee Tomlinson Petersen, "What Next? Sell the Logan City Brewery?" *Whispers from the Past . . . Tales Told* (blog), May 15, 2011, http://honorancestors. blogspot.com/2011/05/what-next-sell-logan-city-brewery.html; Petersen, "Fred, Lily Jane, Stella and Fred Charles."

26. See also *One Hundred Years of Brewing: A Complete History of the Progress Made in the Art, Science and Industry of Brewing in the World, Particularly During the Last Century* (Chicago: H. S. Rich, 1901), which describes how Jacob Theurer started his brewery in 1886.

27. Untitled, *Utah Journal*, May 5, 1886. See, for example, Untitled, *Utah Journal*, May 12, 26, and 29, 1886; Untitled, *Utah Journal*, June 5 and 16, 1886; Untitled, *Utah Journal*, August 25, 1886.

28. "Death Notice," *Utah Journal*, May 24, 1905; "The Coming Company of Emigrants," *Deseret News* (Salt Lake City, UT), July 19, 1876. Jacob Theurer joined his brothers Frederick and John in Utah.

29. Simmonds, "A 'Wet' Valley's Distilleries," *Herald Journal*.

30. As the director of Utah State University's special collections, Simmonds was widely read in primary sources and also had the opportunity to speak to Cache Valley residents who were alive in the late 1880s. Unfortunately, he did not include sources in his newspaper articles.

31. *Utah Directory and Gazetteer for 1889–90*, ed. Henry L. A. Culmer (Salt Lake City: Herald Printing and Publishing Co., 1890).

32. "Early Logan City Government," Mendon Utah Net, http://www.mendonutah.net/history/cache_county/18.htm.

33. Johnson's Grove was "a popular area for recreation in the early part of the 20th century. It was a gathering place in a grove of trees located roughly between Walmart and the current Wells Fargo Bank at 889 S. Main. It was a place where people gathered to watch baseball games, get a hamburger or a hot dog, dance on the open-air dance floor or play on the rope swings suspended from the trees." Amy Macavinta,

"Local Businesswoman Celebrates 100 Years of Life," *Herald Journal*, April 21, 2015, hjnews.com.

34. For references to Barbara Theurer, see "County Court," *Logan Journal*, March 11 and July 9, 1893, and June 9 and September 8, 1894; "County Court Proceedings," *Logan Journal*, August 9, 1893; "Local News," *Logan Journal*, September 29, 1896; "County Commissioners," *Logan Journal*, December 12, 1896; and "County Court Minutes," *Logan Journal*, June 10 and September 7, 1897, and August 8, 1898.

35. "Will Be Incorporated," *Salt Lake Herald*, March 21, 1898.

36. "A Case of Rape," *Provo Daily Enquirer*, September 16, 1891; "An Important Arrest," *Salt Lake Tribune*, September 16, 1891.

37. "Almost a Fatality," *Logan Journal*, December 31, 1896.

38. "At Logan," *Salt Lake Herald*, April 13, 1897; Untitled, *Salt Lake Herald*, November 5, 1897; "Logan Locals," *Salt Lake Herald*, November 7, 1897.

39. "A Brute and a Child," *Salt Lake Herald*, September 3, 1898.

40. "City and County," *Logan Republican*, June 23, 1906.

41. *Utah State Gazetteer and Business Directory*, 1903–1904, vol. 2 (Salt Lake City: Polk, 1904), 175.

42. Those without prohibition included Farmington, Sandy, Midvale, and Price. Randy Harward, "Utah Brewing Timeline," *Salt Lake City Weekly*, August 24, 2011.

43. Ibid.

44. The Cache Valley Brewing Company's Facebook page has not been updated since 2009, and their blog's last post was in 2010 (http://cachevalleybrewing.blogspot.com).

27

THE FIRST KFC FRANCHISE

KYLIE SCHROEDER

Harman's State Street Restaurant in the late 1950s just prior to becoming the first franchise for Kentucky Fried Chicken. Courtesy Jay Alexander.

In 1941, Leon W. "Pete" Harman purchased a small restaurant on 3900 South and State Street in Salt Lake City. It was called the Do Drop In and contained only six tables and a counter. A decade later, in 1952, Harman received a call from Harland Sanders, a gentleman from Corbin, Kentucky, whom he had met a year earlier in Chicago at a national restaurant convention. Sanders wanted to stop in Salt Lake, on his way to Australia, specifically to meet with Harman.

The Harmans had plans to take Sanders to a nice restaurant, but Sanders had other plans. He was interested in selling his fried chicken recipe to existing restaurant owners so they could add it to their menus. Using the restaurant's pressure cooker and supply of spices, Sanders cooked a meal for the Harmans—one that would soon become America's most famous fried chicken.

Harman agreed to use the recipe and asked his friend Don Anderson to paint an advertisement on the window of the building. Without a proper name for the food, Anderson labeled it Kentucky Fried Chicken (now known simply as KFC), since Sanders was from Kentucky, and a worldwide label was born.[1]

When Sanders stopped on his return from Australia, he saw cars lined up all the way down the street waiting to order fried chicken. Based on this initial success, he began selling franchises throughout the United States and later around the world, creating the largest fast-food chicken chain[2] and one of America's most well-known and successful businesses.

Harlan Sanders became the "Colonel" when the governor of Kentucky gave him that designation in honor of his success.[3] But local lore holds that his other signature, his white suit, was the result of his association with Pete Harman and Utah. Sanders had arrived in town in a black jacket and pants, on a scorching summer day, to ride on a float in Salt Lake City's Pioneer Day parade. Fearing that he would be too warm to participate, Sanders was provided with a last-minute white suit, the press adored the look, and the rest, as they say, is history.

Though Harman's original location at 3900 South and State Street has been knocked down and rebuilt multiple times since 1941, today's visitors can still stop there to enjoy KFC as well as a display of photos and memorabilia honoring the friendship between Pete Harman and Colonel Sanders.

Statue of Colonel Harland Sanders and Pete Harman at the current KFC building at the site of the original restaurant. Photo by Carol A. Edison, 2018.

NOTES

1. "About Utah: Story of First KFC shows anything can happen by Lee Benson," *Deseret News*, January 19, 2012.
2. Colonel Harland Sanders: Chef (1890–1980), https://www.biography.com/people/colonel-harland-sanders-12353545.
3. Ibid.

28

FISH TRAPS, NETS, AND FOOD ON THE TABLE

Utah's Fish for Food Story

LISA DUSKIN-GOEDE

As early as 1847 and into the 1870s, Mormon pioneer settlers, under the direction of Brigham Young, overharvested the forests and overgrazed the land, destroying the natural habitat of other living things. Fish, a natural resource integral to the diets of nomadic Indian tribes, were also deeply impacted by this influx of settlers. Danish pioneer Peter Madsen reportedly grew flaxseed at Utah Lake, which, when harvested, was used to weave fishing line so people could fish for their food.[1] Mormon leaders during the late 1860s encouraged the consumption of fish over other forms of protein, such as beef or pork, saying in one general conference in 1868 that fish possess "brain making material to a greater extent than any other animal food."[2] Their quest to harvest as much fish as they could to survive the earliest years took a toll that required decades to reverse.

"Methods used to harvest fish included the use of 'giant powder,' dams, nets and traps. At the same time, changes in water use patterns (for irrigation and industry) began to adversely affect the fish populations. Streams were blocked, and large numbers of mature fish were taken prior to spawning. Young-of-the-year fish were lost to irrigation canals. As a result, populations of native fish in some areas were drastically reduced."[3] The unregulated introduction of nonnative species of fish into the waters of the Great Basin also impacted the health of the resource.

In 1853 the Utah Legislative Assembly passed "An Act to prevent the needless destruction of Fish."[4] In 1856 Utah's Deseret Agricultural and Manufacturing Society began fish planting programs, creating the first private fish hatchery. Then, in the 1920s, Utah began a program of propagation and stocking in order to provide enough fish for consumption for an increasing population interested in outdoor sports.[5]

Fishing as a livelihood was part of the story. Jean Calder, born in 1909, recalled how her parents made a living at Bear Lake. According to a 2014 newspaper story, "Her mother would can berries and sell them in Evanston and Kemmerer, Wyoming. Her father, meanwhile, caught fish and stored them in an ice house along the lake shore, layering the fish in ice with sawdust so he could sell them year round."[6] Bear Lake residents became proficient at using large nets to capture huge quantities of fish endemic to the lake, such as the Bear Lake whitefish and the Bonneville cisco. Up until regulations came into effect, there were no limits on the amount of fish an angler was allowed to take.

Meanwhile, using fish as food remained popular throughout Utah for many years, giving rise to family traditions of camping, fishing, harvesting, and preparing fish for family meals. What Boy Scout program has been without the ritual of camping, fishing, and learning how to cook the fish over a fire?

Bottling or home-canning of fish for long-term storage is also a Utah tradition, albeit not as popular an activity as it was a century ago. In a 1997 paper found in Utah State University's Fife Folklore Collection, Michele M. Nielson wrote, "Preserving food saves a lot of time and money, in the long run, and nobody has to go hungry or worry about getting enough food. I think that younger generations should learn and be a part of preserving techniques. We never know what the future will bring, but it's nice to know that we would be able to survive, because we know how." Instructions for bottling fish are given: "Take skins off fish and put the whole fish in the jar, if it is small. When the jar is filled with fish, add 1 tsp. salt and 1 tsp. lemon juice

Two men fishing for trout. Courtesy Special Collections & Archives, Merrill-Cazier Library, Utah State University.

(if desired). Cap with lids and rings and cook in a pressure cooker for 75 minutes at 10–12 pounds of pressure."[7]

Today, due largely to environmental concerns, catch-and-release is on the rise, but there are still a significant number of fishers who harvest their catch

In 2017 the King Nature Park in North Logan offered a fun place for the Oman family to fish. Photo by Lisa Duskin-Goede.

as food. Trout is the most popular harvest fish, and these are caught in the cooler waters of the northern and northeastern parts of the state. According to the Utah Angler Survey for 2011–2012, trout species include cutthroat, brown, rainbow, brook, tiger, splake, lake, kokanee, whitefish, and grayling. The survey reports that for trout caught in the northern and northeastern regions, 30 percent and 32 percent, respectively, of the fish caught were kept as harvest.[8]

Another popular activity is wintertime fishing, including ice fishing, in Utah's northern lakes and reservoirs. Bear Lake is the only home to the Bonneville cisco, a long, slender, pearly silver fish that rarely grows beyond seven inches.[9] Anglers often fry it on the spot or take it home to smoke. Other northern and central Utah reservoirs offer a range of perch, crappie, bluegill, bass, whitefish, and trout, providing both family fun and good food.

Today's trout farms—both public and private—provide another way for Utahns to catch and enjoy eating fish. Leland Barker (owner of Mountain Valley Trout Farm, a fee-to-fish facility west of Smithfield, Utah, which has been in business for over forty years) believes that eating fish and staying physically active is a healthy lifestyle—along with eating lots of fresh fruits and vegetables. His tan and lean figure attests to this. While he's not tending to his fish hatchery, filleting the fish caught by his customers, or selling at the Cache Valley Gardener's Market, he's out playing tennis someplace around the nation.[10]

Fishing for food was a vital activity in nineteenth-century Utah. Though the emphasis has shifted since then from fishing for sustenance to fishing for fun, fishing can still provide not only tasty fresh food but also a link to our heritage. We've learned through trial and error that we need to protect and manage this natural resource so that those who follow will have an opportunity to experience the thrill of catching fish from Utah's streams, rivers, and lakes and, if appropriate, take home some of nature's bounty to prepare and enjoy.

NOTES

1. *Peter Madsen, 1824–1911*, ed. Joyce M. Harrison and Leland G. Harrison (N.p., 1996).
2. Bradley Paul Hansen, "An Environmental History of the Bear River Range, 1860–1910," (Master's thesis, Utah State University, 2013), 33.
3. J. W. Sigler and W. F. Sigler, "History of Fish Hatchery Development in the Great Basin States of Utah and Nevada," *Great Basin Naturalist* 46, no. 4 (October 31, 1986): 583–84.
4. Edwin V. Rawley and LeeAnn Rawley, *Utah Fish and Game: A Brief History* (N.p., August 1, 1967).
5. Sigler and Sigler, "History of Fish Hatchery Development," 584.
6. Kristen Moulton, "105-Year-Old Utah Woman, Raised at Bear Lake, Feted with Raspberry Shake," *Salt Lake Tribune*, September 17, 2014.
7. Michele M. Nielson, "Food Preservation" (May 29, 1997), Utah State University Special Collections and Archives, Merrill-Cazier Library, FOLK COLL No. 8, Box 60, Folder 97-09.
8. R. S. Krannich, R. J. Liliholm, and J. Unger, *2011–2012 Utah Angler Survey Project Summary Report* (November 2012), Utah Division of Wildlife Resources, Salt Lake City. See Angler Catch and Harvest Data by Species and Region, 54, and Table 4-5, 55.
9. "Bonneville Cisco," Utah Fishing Info, http://www.utahfishinginfo.com/utahfish/bonnevillecisco.php.
10. Leland Barker (aquaculturist and owner, Mountain Valley Trout, Smithfield, Utah) in discussion with the author, August 1, 2014.

FOOD AND ME

My Story of Polynesian Food in Utah

ERUERA "ED" NAPIA

Haere mai ki te kai! (Come and eat!)

For most societies, food is at the top of the list of important things. Securing, distributing, cooking, and serving food are windows into understanding the practices and values of a group and how it will survive. Today, many of us don't really think about what food says about us, but for me, its tastes and its smells can take me to other places and other times.

Take *hangi* for example. At a recent birthday of mine, hangi was served. Hangi is *the* style of cooking for the Maori (New Zealand indigenous people), where large amounts of food which might include chicken, pork, lamb, and beef with potatoes, sweet potatoes, cabbage, and watercress are cooked in an earthen oven. Rocks are heated in a fire for hours and then put in the bottom of a pit. All the food is salted, wrapped in cloths, and put in wire baskets. Meat goes on the bottom, starches on top of that, and cabbage and watercress on top. Sometimes other vegetables might find their way in the hangi—as also might steamed pudding. Everything is covered with cloth and then burlap sacks soaked with water and then covered with dirt. The hangi is watched for about five hours to make sure no steam escapes. To me there is no sweeter food than hangi where foods are cooked in their natural juices and steam. The hangi prepared for my birthday in Bountiful, Utah, however, was different. The differences: The food was wrapped in tinfoil, the rocks were supplemented with rebar, and a few pieces of cherry wood were added for flavor. I was in a state of bliss as I bit into pieces of delicious cooked beef, potatoes, and yams. I only had a little pork because it was the more expensive, low-fat cut of pork—not the pork butt cut that I, and most of my Maori friends, like.

Utah-style Maori *hangi* consisting of pork, chicken, potatoes, sweet potatoes, yams, and cabbage. Food prepared and photographed by Eruera "Ed" Napia, 2018.

Pigs were brought to the various Pacific islands from Southeast Asia by early explorers who settled the distant regions of the Pacific Ocean long before Europeans arrived. For Hawaiians, pork continues to be a cuisine mainstay whether that be kalua pork (cooked in earth oven), pork *laulau* (steamed with taro leaves and wrapped in ti leaves), or teriyaki pork. However, for Tongans, pork is also a vehicle for showing respect and honor, and roast pigs, especially suckling pigs, continue to be an important part of Tongan gatherings in Utah. Although families may roast pigs on a spit in their backyard, some have refined the process by using mechanized rotating spits on the backs of trailers that can be rolled up to an event so pigs can be cooked on the spot. I have seen similar step-ups at city fairs for cooking *hulihuli* chicken (Hawaiian barbecue), dozens at a time.

In the islands or in Utah, there's a magic that happens when Polynesian women get together to cook, whether in a traditional cooking area or in a modern kitchen. It's like they had an assignment sheet of who is going to do what and when, as they become a finely tuned machine where each person seems to know exactly what to do. Younger family members are apprenticed as they watch and observe, and Mum or Aunty shows them what to do and how. But it is important to know that, as in many other societies, cooking is not totally a woman's domain. Men definitely have their roles in the food process.

In the islands, men, women, and children were involved in the meat-producing, fishing, and gathering parts of the process. I remember times at home when we would go to the beach to collect clams, mussels, and oysters. Some would go fishing or diving for crayfish. Some would pick watercress or cabbages, and others would dig potatoes and sweet potatoes. At Christmastime the women of my family would be peeling potatoes, preparing salads, and making desserts and preparing the elements for hangi. The kids would be washing the plates and polishing the silverware. The men would be outside heating the hangi stones in a fire and digging the hangi hole. When the stones were ready and the food to be cooked was packed in baskets, the men would place the food in the hangi and cover it, and a teen would be responsible for watching the hangi to make sure that no steam escaped. Food preparation and consumption can be about strengthening social and family ties whether it be preparing a hangi in a pit, roasting a pig in the backyard, or preparing for a large community gathering in a reception hall or church recreation hall; women, men, relatives, children, and friends all come together as a community. We celebrate living together in the high desert valleys of Utah.

Kava, an island beverage made from pounded stems and roots of a pepper plant, is another food product used to strengthen community ties. The ceremonial use of kava continues in Utah, especially at gatherings honoring people or welcoming important visitors. Traditions identify who should sit in the kava circle and in what position, who prepares the kava root, who mixes and pours the kava, who serves the kava, and the order in which people are served; for many Pacific Islanders, it is very important to adhere as strictly as possible to those practices. But kava has a recreational side, a side that thrives here in the form of kava parties. Although some Pacific Islanders may frown upon them, kava parties are based in cultural practices. In earlier times, men would return from the gardens or from fishing tired and in need of relaxation; the consuming of kava helped to accomplish that. Kava relieves anxiety and stress and relaxes the body without reducing mental clarity. Pacific Island men and their friends may gather as often as a couple of times a week to mix and drink kava. Following prescribed traditions at these parties is becoming less important than the pleasurable effects and resulting camaraderie.

In an indulgent moment of my own pleasant thoughts, I can call up images of being with my Aunty Toa, spending time with my best teen friends Lesa and Ferron Fruean, staying with the Halls when my parents were out of town and going with them to visit their Samoan relatives, and many other Samoans whom I miss. I remember Aunty Toa so well because she was the only Samoan woman in our little Polynesian community. I remember her not because of the food she cooked, but because she never ate until after Uncle Andy had eaten. I learned later in life that this was one of her ways of holding onto and respecting her Samoan upbringing. Then there was

Mrs. Fruean. Her table was filled with things that I took for granted and later learned the names of when I moved to Hawaii—*palusami*, a dish with canned corn beef, coconut milk, and greens; or my favorite, Samoan chop suey. I have eaten many types of chop suey: chop suey made with pork pieces, mince (hamburger), or beef pieces, seasoned with garlic, onions, celery, and carrots, and flavored with shoyu sauce, all mixed into bean thread noodles. For me, eating Samoan chop suey not only delights my palate, but also warms my heart.

Mind you, another of my favorites, fish and chips, would do the same thing but I have yet to find good fish and chips in Utah. A Navajo-Hawaiian-Gilbertese high school student once told me her favorite food was *panipopo* and I had a flashback of eating panipopo in Hawaii. Panipopo is a dish of rolls floating in a sort of coconut custard. One of my students at the University of Utah gave me what may be the Utah, or at least mainland, recipe. He bought frozen rolls from the store, baked them, and then poured a mixture of coconut milk, half and half, and sugar over and under them, put them back in the oven for just a bit, and presented them dripping with delicious coconut flavor. Coconut milk is as tasty with rolls as it is with boiled bananas and onions, another of my favorites.

If the coconut is the mother of the Pacific because she feeds us, clothes us, and houses us, then surely taro is her sister. The root of the taro is used throughout most of the Pacific. Whether it is boiled and sautéed in coconut milk and onions, or pounded into a paste that complements many Hawaiian dishes (many flavored with sea salt), taro continues to grace the tables of many island people in Utah.

I often wonder what it was like for the first Pacific Islanders who moved to Utah, most of whom were Hawaiian converts to the LDS Church. By the time they arrived, much of Utah had been settled by Mormon converts from both Europe and states east of the Rockies. Proselyting began in the Hawaiian Islands in the 1850s, but converts from Hawaii did not move to Utah until after 1875. Hawaiians were unlike any other Mormon pioneer groups because they were visible minorities that would not easily blend into the rest of the population. By the 1890s hundreds of Hawaiians had moved to Utah, most of them settling in the Beck Springs area in northwest Salt Lake City. LDS Church leader Joseph F. Smith was instrumental in purchasing land for them in Skull Valley, where Iosepa, a Polynesian colony, was established. Most Utahns don't know about Iosepa but I learned that in 1911 and 1912 Iosepa won recognition as an outstanding community. We would have to assume that at that time, the people of Iosepa must have had to adapt to foods that were locally available because it would have been close to impossible to raise foods in the part of the state that was least like their island homes, the west desert.

When the LDS Church announced the building of a temple in Laie, Hawaii, Iosepa was closed and Hawaiian Mormons and other Polynesian Mormons in Utah were urged to move back to the islands. There was a lull in Polynesian immigration until the 1970s, and most of those who moved here in the 1970s, 1980s, and even into the 1990s were predominantly Hawaiian, Tongan, or Samoan, many of whom came through Hawaii with a taste for Hawaiian food. As Polynesian restaurants began to open up, most of them featured Hawaiian-style food like

Tongan *otai* made with pineapple, coconut milk, watermelon, mango, and avocados. Prepared and photographed by Eruera "Ed" Napia, 2018.

I always look forward to *otai*. Otai is a Tongan fruit drink that may include apples, mangos, watermelon, (almost always) pineapple juice, pineapple, coconut water, milk, and sugar. I consider myself lucky if I find a vendor that sells *lupulu*, a dish made with corned beef, coconut milk or mayonnaise, taro leaves, and maybe onions. My friend Fahina tells me that originally lupulu did not include mayonnaise but that became popular because coconut milk used to be hard to get. I wonder about that, though, because when I lived in Hawaii, I learned to eat mayonnaise with almost every savory dish. It had to be Best Foods mayonnaise because that was the mayonnaise of choice in Hawaii. Coconut milk is now easier to get in Utah and more affordable. Words like *otai* and *lupulu* will always invoke memories of the Manns, the Hansens, and other Tongan families from my childhood, and especially memories of Queen Salote who reigned over Tonga at that time. When I was growing up, we rarely ate at restaurants. If we did eat out, it was at the local fish-and-chips shop. I believe that even though many Polynesians living in Utah may indulge in Utah's fast food array, when it comes to "homestyle" food, we do prefer to eat at home or at community gatherings when the best of island food comes out.

Island people relied on the natural flavors of the meat, fish, vegetables, and coconut. Salt, pepper, and curry were the only seasonings my mother used—I didn't even know what garlic was until I came to the United States. And yet the food was tasty, whether it was roasted or boiled.

Speaking of curry, my mother used to make a simple dish of sausages in curry quite regularly, but my romance with curry started when I met

shoyu chicken, pork dishes (more often than not Kalua pig with or without cabbage), pork ribs, and sweet-and-sour pork, served with rice and macaroni salad. People tend to prefer the dishes they were raised on, so one has to wonder if the restaurants feature Hawaiian dishes because the ingredients are easier to get or because Hawaiian food was more marketable. Regardless of the reason, Polynesians tend to cook their traditional foods at home and occasionally flock to the Hawaiian-style restaurants.

There are a couple of restaurants that feature foods from different Polynesian cultures, but one can experience a good assortment of Hawaiian and Polynesian dishes at "Living Traditions," an event sponsored by the Salt Lake City Arts Council that brings to one place the dances, music, crafts, and foods of the many groups that have settled in Utah.

my adopted Aunty Bev and Nana, her mother, in Los Angeles and I tasted their curry crab. In the months that had the letter "r" in the name, Nana and Aunty Bev would buy fresh crab, sauté it in a light coconut and curry sauce, and serve it over rice; that sits right at the top of the list of my favorite foods. Aunty Bev and Uncle John would take me out to sushi and Japanese restaurants in Redondo Beach and Santa Monica, and I developed a taste for Japanese foods, especially sushi. I think sushi is a natural match for Polynesians because we like some fish uncooked and the cooked fish that we do have can't be overcooked. Fresh, raw fish is not as readily available in Utah, but some fish merchants and seafood restaurants have fish flown in fresh daily from the west coast, and some Polynesians will have fish flown to Utah from Hawaii for special events. Today you can get almost any ingredient you need to make your favorite Polynesian dish such as taro, taro leaves, coconut milk, and *ufi* (kind of a white yam with a consistency similar to taro). Sometimes we can find poke (Hawaiian raw fish) and now and again you might find someone selling Hawaiian poi, a starch staple made from taro that is pounded and then cooked. You can seek out the Polynesian restaurants in the area or you can be explorative like my brother, who found a Mexican restaurant that serves good salmon cervice, pico de gallo, and chile sauce, which he mixes together into something that is close to spicy Hawaiian *lomilomi* salmon. Either way, I am always on the lookout for good sushi.

I love to eat. Physically, I am not a big person, but I enjoy eating good food, food that stimulates both my palate and my memories. We Pacific Islanders living in Utah are changing with the passing time, whether in terms of numbers or in practices. Utah cities continue to have among the highest mainland USA per capita percentages of Pacific Islanders. Many who live here are from Polynesia: Tonga, Samoa, Aotearoa–New Zealand, Tahiti, and Fiji. In recent years we have seen an influx of people from Micronesia, such as Kiribati and the Marshall Islands; in time their influence on Utah may become apparent. Regardless of where we came from or how long we have been in Utah, our lives are not without challenges. We adapt to a different climate, to societal values that may not be exactly the same as our own, to different foods, to a place where time moves at a different pace, and to lifestyles with different levels of physical activities. Culture is about what we do to enhance our survival and our cultures must change to ensure our survival. We, and our children, must revise our cultural practices. We need to establish new balances in our lives, balances that will allow us to maintain our culture but also our physical, mental, and social health.

We hope that our Pacific identities will continue to flourish here in Utah through our songs, dances, stories, memories, and food—those we brought with us and those that are shaped and reshaped. For me, as I think of food I cannot help but remember the people of my childhood with fond pleasure, and to happily celebrate my friends and family here.

30

ETHNIC RESTAURANTS IN SALT LAKE CITY

LINDA THATCHER

Since initial settlement in the mid-nineteenth century, Utah has had a significant foreign-born population. The Church of Jesus Christ of Latter-day Saints' emphasis on international missionary work, the need for laborers for railroads and mines (and now for tech workers), and the commercial opportunities offered by an ever-growing population are contributing factors. Initially, "immigrants poured into Utah from Great Britain, Canada and Australia"; "social and religious upheavals in Sweden, Denmark, and Norway attracted Scandinavians to Mormon missionaries, bringing the second-largest group of converts to Zion"; and Jewish merchants established businesses in Utah. They were followed by "immigrants from the Mediterranean, the Balkans, and a lesser number from Asia Minor and the Middle East to assume the unskilled laborer positions on the railroads and mines." "Italians, Finns, South Slavs, Greeks, and Mexicans came in large numbers to Utah," while the Chinese and Japanese remained after their jobs building rail lines were eliminated. "For mutual help and for the comfort of familiarity, each national group formed their own communities," and they also formed businesses to serve those communities—especially coffeehouses and eating establishments.[1]

The Salt Lake City Polk Directory shows that during the first two decades of the nineteenth century, the number of ethnic restaurants in downtown Salt Lake City steadily grew. Among the earliest eating establishments was the Vienna Café (1900), located at 141 South Main and owned by George W. Morgan. Morgan was prominent in Utah mining circles and was a former director of the New Quincy mine.[2] The café was "always open" and was "the headquarters for railway officials, mining, professional and commercial men."[3]

Branning's Chili & Tamales (1901) had both a retail and wholesale business and may have been the area's first Mexican restaurant. In 1904, one Chinese restaurant—Wing Duck and Tim—and one Japanese restaurant—Fujii and Miyazaki—both appeared. The same year there

ETHNIC RESTAURANTS IN SALT LAKE CITY, UTAH, 1890–1970

Year	Total # of Restaurants	Ethnic Restaurants	Chinese	Japanese	Italian	Mexican	Greek	Other (German, French and later Middle Eastern)
1890	44	0						
1900	46	1						1
1910	164	29	6	9	2		6	3
1920	149	24	7	5		1	7	4
1931	228	28	11	2	5	5	3	2
1940	187	12	8		1	1	2	
1951	312	30	14	2	4	7	3	
1960	280	30	13		3	5	4	5
1970-71	311	48	12	1	13	15	1	5

Source: The information for this chart was taken from the Salt Lake City Polk Directories for the specific years. There may have been other restaurants located in the city.

was one Greek establishment listed—Damascus Demosthenes. By 1907 there were seven businesses with Greek names listed under restaurants; by 1908, there were eight; and by 1909, there were thirteen. It's likely these were mostly coffee houses, characterized by historian Helen Papanikolas as "the [Greek] men's true home."[4]

In 1906 two German restaurants were operating—the Heidelberg and the Bismarck. The Bismarck was owned by Sig Simon and, according to their ad, was "famous [for] German Lunches and Delicacies, also the celebrated Imported Bavarian and Pilsener Beers, on draught and in bottles."[5] The other restaurant was Rathskeller & Co., conveniently located in the basement of Walker Bros. Bank (1910).

In 1909 a Scandinavian-American restaurant was listed and in 1910 a Yiddish dining parlor. The parlor was owned by Mrs. R. Lisser and advertised "Yiddish home cooking."[6] A newspaper ad seeking a waitress required that prospective employees speak German.[7] Another popular restaurant, the Louvre, featured "Daily table d'hotel luncheons [set course menu] for business men and ladies who may be shopping, at a nominal price, and with rapid service."[8] On August 25, 1911, the Louvre also featured Madam Detzel, a high operatic soprano, as their entertainment.[9]

In 1913 two Italian restaurants were listed—Ballino and Maloti, and the Roma Café; in 1917 the Albanian Coffee House was added, and in 1920 the American French Lunch Room. Aside from the war years, there were always between twenty-five and thirty ethnic restaurants listed in the directory for downtown Salt Lake City well through the 1960s.

In 1910 a popular eating place in Salt Lake City was the Heidelberg Bar and Café on 300 South. Used by permission, Utah State Historical Society. All rights reserved.

Besides coffeehouses and restaurants, in downtown Salt Lake City there have always been delicatessens serving immigrants looking for food from their home countries. Offering both prepared food and specialty grocery items, they attract not only foreign-born clients but also thousands of missionaries of the Church of Jesus Christ of Latter-day Saints who served in foreign missions as well as Utahns who have traveled abroad and developed a taste for their offerings.[10] One of the first delicatessens was opened in 1909 by Mrs. M. Obuchon[11] and through the next few decades a number of specifically Italian and

Jewish delis also opened. In the 1950s and 1960s German and Dutch delis became prevalent, including one owned by Lu Dornbush who emigrated from Holland and opened a deli in 1955 at 163 East Third South. A newspaper article in 1976 reported that

he does a large business with caviar and imported coffees and cheeses. Imports from Indonesia, Mexico, Russia, South America and Japan can be found among the Hebrew, French, Dutch, Greek and Scandinavian items lining his shelves. He prepares his own cheesecake and many of his meats. Although he once had restaurant facilities, he now only makes take-out orders for lunch. He said he has as many young customers as old, and that he is now serving third and fourth generations of his original clientele.[12]

After 1970, following national trends, the landscape of Utah restaurants experienced a dramatic change as more chains and fast-food eateries began operating in Salt Lake City. The face of immigration also changed. With the arrival of refugees from war-torn countries and with economic immigrants seeking education and a new life, the restaurants opening along the Wasatch Front began offering an even more varied cuisine from around the world. Utah is now home to an ever-growing and wide-ranging number of people from places like Thailand, India, Latin America, and the Middle East, as well as refugees from Vietnam, Tibet, the Balkans, Afghanistan, and Africa. All of these groups have established eateries that offer familiar food to their native communities and exotic alternatives for their new

162

neighbors. The wide-ranging ethnic restaurants along the Wasatch Front have become an integral part of the state's contemporary culture, expanding upon a more-than-century-old Utah tradition of sharing culture and heritage by inviting Utah's nonethnic majority to the table. In response, Utahns have proven themselves to be adventurous consumers as the popularity of ethnic restaurants continues to grow.

NOTES

1. Helen Z. Papanikolas, *The Peoples of Utah* (Salt Lake City: Utah State Historical Society, 1976), 2–7.
2. "Vienna Café Man Dies in Salt Lake," *Ogden Standard-Examiner*, March 3, 1929.
3. Advertisement, *Goodwin's Weekly*, May 30, 1908.
4. Papanikolas, *Peoples of Utah*, 417.
5. "The Bismarck," *Salt Lake Tribune*, August 13, 1906.
6. Advertisement, *Salt Lake Tribune*, February 27, 1910.
7. Advertisement, *Salt Lake Tribune*, February 26, 1910.
8. "The Louvre," *Goodwin's Weekly*, June 10, 1911.
9. Advertisement, *Salt Lake Tribune*, August 25, 1911.
10. Diane Baker, "New Clientele: S. L. Delis Business Gains," *Salt Lake Tribune*, March 21, 1976.
11. Advertisement, *Deseret Evening News* (Salt Lake City, UT), February 9, 1909.
12. Baker, "New Clientele."

31

NAVAJO MUTTON STEW

KIMBERLY J. MARSHALL, BEVERLY JOE, AND ELAINE JOE

Every year, young Navajo women from Utah, Arizona, and New Mexico gather to demonstrate their skills in the Miss Navajo Nation pageant. Organizers emphasize that this pageant honors beauty "within" in culturally appropriate ways for this matrilineal society, honoring the "grace, pride, and the teachings of mothers and grandmothers." The competition has contemporary, traditional, and linguistic components; contestants demonstrate talent, public-speaking skills, and fluency in the Navajo language. But one of the events that sets this pageant apart from others is when the young ladies, decked out in their traditional finery, butcher a sheep and cook it for the audience. In a contest that seeks to highlight the best of Navajo womanhood, the inclusion of this event suggests the continued importance of the connection between the Navajo people (*Diné*) and their sheep (*dibé*).[1]

In this article, we explore the foodways of the Native people of Utah through discussing the cultural significance and preparation of Navajo mutton stew.[2] Navajos are one of the largest Native American tribes in the United States; there are over 300,000 enrolled members. Their homeland spans over 27,000 square miles across the Four Corners area in Arizona, New Mexico, southwest Colorado, and southern Utah. The Navajo language is still widely spoken, and Navajo people maintain distinctive cultural traditions and foodways while simultaneously incorporating new technologies and ideas. We authors come to this discussion of mutton stew as one outsider and two insiders. Kimberly Marshall is a professor of anthropology at the University of Oklahoma. She encountered the preparation of mutton stew during fieldwork on the *Diné Oodlání* (Navajo neo-Pentecostal) religious movement, where the preparation of this dish was regularly undertaken by church women serving their community. Beverly Joe (a Navajo elder) was raised by her older sisters and learned to cook this and other mutton-based dishes from them. Elaine Joe (her daughter) has cooked with her mother her whole life.

Mutton stew begins with sheep, so we will start there. Sheepherding has been part of the traditional lifeway of Navajos for centuries, and the association of Diné and dibé constitutes deep and complex associations for Navajo identity. Sheep came to Navajo country through the Spanish-speaking colonists of New Mexico in the seventeenth century.[3] Sheepherding became crucial to the weaving activity through which nineteenth-century Navajos produced traditional clothing (*biil*), saddle blankets, and door coverings. The five-year internment of Navajos at Fort Sumner, New Mexico (*Hweeldi*), decimated Navajo herds in the late nineteenth century.[4] But through careful stewardship, Navajos increased the flocks abundantly during the first decades of the twentieth century, providing not only food staples but also financial resources through the market for Navajo textiles.

By the 1930s, Navajo herds had grown so large that the Bureau of Indian Affairs became concerned that overgrazing was having a serious ecological impact on the fragile high-desert landscape. Through a heavy-handed federal program of livestock reduction, sheep were taken from Navajo families, killed, and, because of a negative market price, left to rot.[5] This program was traumatic for Navajos who lived through it, as the reduction program failed to consider the cultural importance of sheep for Navajo people. As Marsha Weisiger has pointed out, large and healthy herds are important status symbols: They signify the owner's hard work, careful management, and ritual knowledge. Sheep herds are central to the maintenance of social networks, as they allow for the means to feed large gatherings of people and thus satisfy reciprocal kinship obligations. Therefore, the culling of sheep in the 1930s damaged the central Navajo economic reciprocity "that linked spiritual life with family and kin."[6]

Contemporarily, these deep-seated connections between sheep and people continue to orient Navajo lives. As Kathy M'Closkey notes, the traditional Navajo family unit is organized around the sheep herd, the family's land-use area, the head mother, and sometimes planted fields, and all these things

Indian Days fry bread contest, 1980, at Montezuma Creek. Photo by Carol Edison. Courtesy Utah Folklife Archives.

collectively can be identified as *shimá*—the Navajo word for mother.[7] The Joes live in a small rural community in the northern part of the Navajo Nation. They have a small sheep herd they care for that lives in a corral outside their front door. Because adult family members are often away working wage jobs in nearby Shiprock or Farmington, New Mexico, all the members of the extended Joe family take turns caring for the sheep. Ms. Joe's grandchildren will take the sheep out in the mornings to graze freely in the hills around their home. Her sons will stop by to bring the sheep in or give them water during the day. Ms. Joe or her daughters feed them alfalfa in their corral every evening, where they stay overnight protected by the proximity of the houses and the family's dogs. The health and increase of the herd, therefore, reflects the stability and closeness of the family.

The Joes are lucky in that they can keep their sheep herd close. Other Navajo families who have moved to housing projects in larger reservation towns (such as Shiprock) often maintain a family herd in the mountains, usually tended by elderly relatives. When this pattern is followed, sheepherding can be an important way of passing on cultural teachings, since even Navajo youth who are growing up off the reservation frequently spend their summer break at "shepherding school," helping their grandparents at the remote sheep camps across the Navajo Nation. The threatened existence of the endangered Navajo-churro stock of sheep has brought contemporary Navajo breeders of this hearty and ancient stock into contact with the Slow Food USA movement,[8] and numbers are recovering. Finally, mutton continues to be a staple of Navajo foodways, anchoring social and kin relationships through reciprocal food provision at communal gatherings. This holds true whether Navajo families are gathering for traditional ceremonials, special family events, or Christian tent meetings.

For Ms. Joe, the best part about keeping sheep is taking care of them: feeding them and taking them to graze. She also appreciates how many different ways they can be useful to Navajo people. The wool, for instance, is used to make the beautiful and intricate rugs for which Navajos are so well known. Ms. Joe didn't have sheep as a child, so she never learned to process the wool to ready it for weaving. She can weave, but only using store-bought wool.[9] Her granddaughter Meekal, however, is recovering this knowledge. Through a college course at San Juan College in Farmington taught by Navajo weaver and linguist Lorraine Begay Manave, Meekal learned to clean, card, spin, and dye the wool, and now she can weave rugs like her grandmother using wool from the sheep raised on their land.

MUTTON STEW
Courtesy Beverly Joe

Raw mutton meat: taken from hind leg and arm, cut into 1/2-inch pieces
2 bags celery, diced
2 bags carrots, diced
2–3 onions, diced
4 cans of corn
4 cans of diced tomatoes
2 bags of potatoes, peeled and diced

1. Bring water to boil in a very large pot (around 20 quarts).
2. Add mutton and boil 1/2 hour.
3. Add celery, carrots, onions, corn, and tomatoes; boil 1/2 hour.
4. Add potatoes, cook 15 minutes.
5. Serve with fresh fry bread, watermelon, coffee, and iced tea.

The meat from sheep (mutton) is an important ingredient in many traditional Navajo foodways. Mutton can be prepared in several ways, and Ms. Joe proudly points out that Navajos use every part of the sheep in their cooking. The head is roasted for a dish called *atsii'*. The intestines are used as well in a dish (somewhat of a delicacy) called *ach'íí*, which is made by roasting sheep intestines that have been coiled around sheep fat. A favorite local offering is the roast mutton sandwich, where roasted pieces of mutton are placed on a piece of fresh, hot fry bread and served with a roasted green chili.

We focus here on mutton stew because it is a more frequently served communal dish than either the roast mutton sandwich (which would be more expensive per person) or the ach'íí (which is more labor-intensive to prepare). Mutton stew remains a communal dish, intended to serve family and friends at any event where large groups of people gather. These include secular gatherings, such as birthday parties, graduation parties, or holiday barbecues; however, mutton stew is also served to those who have gathered for sacred and traditional observances as well, including coming-of-age ceremonials (like the *Kinaaldá*), seasonal ceremonials (like the *Ye'ii Bi Chei*), or healing and blessing ceremonials (like the *Hozhonji* or *Ana'í Ndáá'*).[10] Even Navajo Christians are sure to sacrifice a few lambs for stew when hosting a tent revival or camp meeting. Thus (despite its relative simplicity) mutton stew is a foodway that continues to hold social importance for the perpetuation of Navajo culture.

Ms. Joe uses her mutton stew recipe in the church kitchen to cook for a large group of people, and it would have to be scaled back significantly for home use.[11]

NOTES

1. For more on Navajos and sheep, see Elisa Regen, *The Contributions of Churro Sheep to Sustainable Livelihoods among Navajo Women* (Logan: Utah State University Press, 2005); Marsha Weisiger and William Cronon, *Dreaming of Sheep in Navajo Country* (Seattle: University of Washington Press, 2009); and Gary Witherspoon, "Sheep in Navajo Culture and Social Organization," *American Anthropologist* 75, no. 5 (1973): 1441–47.

2. For more on Navajo foodways, see Flora L. Bailey, "Navaho Foods and Cooking Methods," *American Anthropologist* 42, no. 2 (1940): 270–90; Frank Morgan, *Navajo Terminology for Foods and Nutrients: Kindness, Caring, and Blessings Through Our Food: A Guide to Standardized Navajo Translations for Nutrition Terminology in Navajo Language* (Window Rock, AZ: Navajo Nation, 2011); Suzanne Pelican and Karen Bachman-Carter, *Navajo Food Practices, Customs, and Holidays* (Chicago, IL: American Dietetic Association, 1991); Scott Christian Russell, "From Trading Post to Supermarket: Changing Food Marketing Systems on the Navajo Indian Reservation" (unpublished thesis, Arizona State University); and the magazine *Leading the Way: Wisdom of the Navajo People*, published in Gamerco, NM, by Kathleen Manolescu, https://www.facebook.com/Leading-the-Way-Magazine-130538826977944/.

3. Joy Vargo et al., "The Return of the Navajo-Churro Sheep," in *Conservation You Can Taste: Best Practices in Heritage Food Recovery and Success in Restoring Agricultural Biodiversity over the Last Quarter Century*, ed. Gary Paul Nabhan (Tucson: Southwest Center of the University of Arizona, 2013).

4. For more on the trauma of this removal to Hweeldi, see Jennifer Nez Denetdale, *Reclaiming Diné History: The Legacies of Navajo Chief Manuelito and Juanita* (Tucson: University of Arizona Press, 2007), 72–77.

5. Peter Iverson, *Diné: A History of the Navajos* (Albuquerque: University of New Mexico Press, 2002), 153.

6. Marsha Weisiger, "Sheep Dreams: Environment, Cultural Identity, and Gender in Navajo Country" (PhD diss., University of Wisconsin–Madison, 1998), 127–29.

7. Kathy M'Closkey, *Swept Under the Rug: A Hidden History of Navajo Weaving* (Albuquerque: University of New Mexico Press, 2002), 59.

8. Vargo et al., "Return of the Navajo-Churro Sheep."

9. For a critical history of the relationship between Navajo women, wool, rugs, and trading posts, see M'Closkey, *Swept Under the Rug*.

10. Thanks to Justin Lund for observations incorporated here.

11. Mutton stew is the basic recipe but is related to a host of other similar stews that can be created by altering the recipe slightly. For instance, adding dough makes dumpling stew, substituting steamed corn or Indian corn makes steamed or Indian corn stew (respectively), the addition of hominy can create hominy stew, and a favorite in the fall is corn and squash stew.

In addition to freezing, drying meat into jerky has always been a tasty way to preserve the bounty of the hunting season. Dan Winder's jerky on display at the 1979 Southern Utah Folklife Festival. Photo by Hal Cannon. Courtesy Utah Folklife Archives.

32

HUNTING FOR FOOD

HEATHER MAY

Aim for the head. Or, for the greenhorns, just behind the front shoulder. Kill in late August or early September. Be lucky.

Such are the rules for the (mostly) men who hunt deer and elk to make tenderloin steaks, roasts, and jerky. These men are a rare breed: Today it seems that many hunters aim for the bucks with the biggest rack. But Utah's past is filled with men in search of food for the table. Some of them still exist today, like Robert Wilcox, a deputy sheriff around forty-something years old from Blanding who shot his first deer with a bow when he was sixteen. He hunts for both deer and elk in Utah's Blue Mountains. "You can't eat the horns, so why shoot a big trophy? I'm sure it looks good on the wall [but] I'm more of a meat hunter than a trophy hunter," he says.[1]

Utahns can hunt deer, elk, black bear, moose, bison, bighorn sheep, cougars, mountain goats, turkeys, rabbits, quail—even skunks and raccoons. Although elk are one of the most sought-after big-game animals in the state, it is the mule deer that are the "most important game animal in Utah," according to the Utah Division of Wildlife Resources.

They show up in ancient rock art—in one study, up to 31 percent of inventoried drawings feature mule deer.[2] A petroglyph in Cache Valley's Blacksmith Fork drainage shows a human figure kneeling and pointing out a mule deer with branching antlers to a smaller figure.

Opinions on how widespread these deer were during the time of the Mormon settlement vary from common to rarely sighted. But for pioneers struggling to survive, deer were "relished and hunted whenever possible." By the early 1900s, they were so scarce that the state had to ban big-game hunting—though they were likely poached by the hungry—until 1913. A hundred years later they were the most prevalent big game in the state, with 332,900 estimated after the 2013 hunt.

Up until the last fifty or sixty years, hunters sought deer to put food on their table instead of seeking trophy antlers. Extra permits for antlerless deer were common in the 1950s and early 1960s—World War II veterans in particular wanted to hunt—and deer harvest peaked in 1961 with 132,000 deer killed.

"Today, I would say the largest share of the hunters are not hunting for food to sustain their families," says Bill Fenimore Sr., a hunter and former vice-chairman of the state's Wildlife Board.[3] "They're hunting for the sport and enjoyment of it, going out there and trying to outwit the wildlife.

"The size of the antlers has become more dominant," he continues, pointing to how a hunter bid on the right to kill a mule deer buck on Antelope Island by paying $265,000 for a hunting tag. "That's a guy who doesn't want a two-point" deer with a small antler rack. In 2015 a record $390,000 was spent on an Antelope Island trophy deer tag.

Fenimore recalls a hunter appealing to the board for another bear tag because the animal he had shot had a research collar "so it wasn't a beautiful coat for a rug." Fenimore's response was, "Give me a break. That's not what hunting is all about."

Fenimore was born in the 1940s in Pennsylvania when hunting and gathering were necessary to supplement the table. As a boy he'd trap muskrats and hunt rabbits and squirrels. He recalls dandelion-leaf salads and adults drinking wine made from the yellow flowers: "We would pick elderberries and wild cherries and acorns and all sorts of nuts. Those all made it on to the table. My parents, having just finished living through a Depression, they were very thrifty. They were always looking to save money where they could."

A waterfowl hunter, Fenimore owns a three-thousand-acre marsh in Corinne and eats everything he kills. In years past when he hasn't wanted to eat venison, he's donated it to a homeless shelter. But he still enjoys duck.

He either plucks his birds or dips them in wax to remove the feathers, then cooks them "pretty much like you would a chicken." He'll stuff a mallard like one does a Thanksgiving turkey. According to Fenimore, "There's nothing better than a duck with the right orange sauce. It's a base you put on the duck as you cook it with brown sugar, orange juice. It just creates a wonderful flavor.

"There's nothing more exciting to me than to be sitting in a marsh in the predawn light watching the sun come up over the mountain and the ducks flying into your decoys and sending your dog out to retrieve what you've managed to hit and spending [the] day with my son, my best hunting buddy," Fenimore adds.

The deer hunt has long been a part of many Utah family traditions, and largely a male one. Dennis Austin, a retired research scientist who worked as a wildlife biologist for the Utah Division of Wildlife Resources, estimates that more than 90 percent of Utah deer hunters are men or boys, with more than half between the ages of twenty-five and forty-four. They tend to stop after age forty-five. Utah hunters are more than twice as likely as the state's general population to come from rural Utah. And while Utah sportsmen have similar incomes to the rest of the state, a small segment appear to be richer, with 16 percent reporting annual incomes between $75,000 and $99,999 (compared to 11 percent of the general population), reinforcing the idea that hunting is more for sport than sustenance.[4]

Wilcox started hunting because he loved shooting and spending time alone with his father. Now he gets to hike with his teenage son, who recently shot his first deer with a bow.

"It was more exciting for me seeing him shoot a deer than any time I've ever shot one by myself," he says.

Wilcox's family eats deer meat, usually tenderloin steaks, from the previous season the night before the hunt as a "good luck charm."[5]

Superstitions are a good idea. Only about four out of ten mule-deer hunters, or 37 percent, in Utah will hit their prey, according to the Utah Division of Wildlife Resources. And while you'd think a hunter with more experience would be more successful, that's not necessarily true, according to Austin. "Much of the success in harvesting a buck," he writes, "depends upon plain 'hunter luck.'"[6]

Wilcox says hunting is also a cost-effective way to put protein on the table because he butchers the deer and elk himself, something he learned through trial and error. He figures he spends up to seventy dollars for a hunting tag and gas and ends up with 150 pounds of meat from one elk. He started hunting elk a decade ago, pointing out that it's healthier than beef—it's lower in fat and higher in protein than beef, chicken, and pork.[7] Companies that raise elk for meat also point out they are never given steroids, growth hormones, or antibiotics, unlike factory-raised meat. Utah State University once compared deer to beef in a blind taste test. Venison bested beef for tenderness, texture, and taste appeal. Beef won out for juiciness.

Wilcox, like other hunters who hunt for meat, wants premium cuts—roasts and steaks—from his elk because they taste better than deer. He recently started smoking his elk roast made from backstraps (the meat along the spinal column). "That's the best way I've ever cooked an elk roast. That's going to be my tradition going forward."[8]

Josh Lopez, who helps run Thompson's Smokehouse in Erda, butchers about 650 deer and elk during his busy season: He'll spend up to ninety hours a week processing wild game from the end of December to the middle of January.

"These individuals love wild game meat. They love the taste of it. There's the guys out there that do it for sport. Then there's the guys that come to me," Lopez says.[9]

Hunters prefer that Lopez make steaks, roasts, and burgers with elk meat. ("I don't eat none of it because I cut it every day," Lopez says.) Deer is usually saved for jerky.

"Hindquarters and backstraps [make] really good jerky," Lopez says. "They have the best chunks of meat right there. I trim it up real nice so there's no fat. Slice it with a slicer. Smoke it. . . . I change it up here and there. Right now I'm using apple wood."[10]

Wilcox also cuts his venison "almost paper thin" and dries it after flavoring it simply with salt and pepper. "It's really crispy and kind of melts in your mouth. [The jerky] usually lasts about a week around our place."[11]

No matter the preparation, there are some better ways to both hunt and care for the deer to make it the most palatable. Austin's book emphasizes the importance of a good shot. One bullet can damage up to eight pounds of meat. Still, he says only expert shooters should aim for the head and neck, since the target is so small—four inches in diameter—and is "usually moving." "The best place to aim is in the middle of the body cavity just behind the front shoulder. Any shot in that area is fatal and provides a quick death," Austin writes.[12]

His book cites a Utah State University study comparing the tastiness of deer based on the time it was killed. Late August to early September was determined to be the most palatable, and venison killed during the late summer and fall period was more nutritious.

The deer must be gutted in the field—and that should take under fifteen minutes, according to Austin—or else the meat will be ruined. "You have to get the guts out right away," says Lopez. "It can ruin the meat." Austin also says the deer should be skinned as soon as it's hung, and the hide shouldn't be left on overnight, or else the meat will taste too gamey.

Both Wilcox and Lopez say to hang the carcass for about a week. "The meat starts to break down and actually gets more tender, kind of like aging a steak or a cow," Wilcox says.

"You cut it too soon and it's rubbery," agrees Lopez. "When they bring it to me it's real pink. By the time I cut it, it's a good red color."[13]

For most of the years between the 1960s to the mid-1990s, more than 200,000 people participated in the state's mule deer hunt, with a high of nearly 250,000 deer hunters in 1988. But since then, the hunting landscape has changed. In 1994, the state required hunters to choose specific regions in which to hunt instead of allowing them to seek prey statewide. This new legislation broke up long-standing family hunting groups. According to Austin's book, relatives living in various parts of the state had to apply for permits for particular regions, forcing them to choose between hunting close to home for the entire season or hunting with family far away for only the opening weekend.[14]

At the same time, the state had to cap the deer hunt for the first time in the mid-1990s after a period of drought and a hard winter. The state has continued to reduce deer permits today, even as the number of hunters seeking them has increased. "As demand . . . continues to increase faster than supply, many hunters are giving up on the sport," according to the state deer management plan.[15]

Still, the number of hunting licenses issued for any animal—whether it's a hunting-only license or a combination hunting-fishing license—has been on the rise in the past several years, according to the Utah Division of Wildlife Resources. Nearly 228,000 licenses were issued in 2018.

But youth interest appears to be dropping, something the state tried to fix by creating a new license in 2014 that made it more economical for them to hunt and fish.

Declining interest is a trend that worries Fenimore. He watches children on the weekends playing soccer, remembering that when he was a boy he'd pretend he was hunting. His own grandson isn't interested in hunting. He recalls taking the then-five-year-old out with a pop gun. "He went out there twice and lost complete interest. He wants to sit home and play with his video games. . . . I believe there's a real importance in being close to nature and understanding what's holding this web of critters and so forth together."[16]

NOTES

1. Robert Wilcox discussion with the author, fall 2014 or winter 2015.
2. Dennis Austin, *Mule Deer: A Handbook for Utah Hunters and Landowners* (Logan: Utah State University Press, 2010).
3. Bill Fenimore Sr., discussion with the author, fall 2014.
4. Utah Division of Wildlife Resources and Department of Natural Resources, "Utah Mule Deer Statewide Management Plan," http://wildlife.utah.gov/hunting/biggame/pdf/mule_deer_plan.pdf.
5. Wilcox, interview.
6. Austin, *Mule Deer*, 137.
7. Wilcox, interview.
8. Ibid.

9. Josh Lopez, discussion with the author, winter 2015.
10. Ibid.
11. Wilcox, interview.
12. Austin, *Mule Deer*, 146.
13. Wilcox, interview; Lopez, interview.
14. Austin, *Mule Deer*, 19.
15. "Utah Mule Deer Statewide Management Plan."
16. Fenimore, interview.

Indian rice grass, a native perennial bunchgrass, is one of Utah's state symbols. In earlier times the seed was gathered, ground into meal or flour, and made into bread. Rice grass was a food staple especially when the corn crop failed. Courtesy Cassondra Skinner, hosted by the USDA–NRCS PLANTS Database.

33

FORAGING UTAH-STYLE

DEAN G. MORRIS

Utah has a great number of foragers. Gardeners sample their fruits, orchard growers test for ripeness, ranchers and farmers check seed heads, and trekkers, campers, hikers, and hunters eat on the trail. All are gathering food. Chewing on a stem of fresh-picked dandelion or a blade of grass qualifies as foraging.

While most Utahns recognize a sego lily[1] and would avoid disturbing the wildflower that provided life-saving sustenance to their pioneer forebears, an absentminded forager, wandering through a meadow or along a waterway in Utah, might nibble on the same rice grass that was a predominant source of food for Utah's earlier foragers, ancient hunter-gatherers. Found in all counties, rice grass,[2] joined the sego lily in status and was made the official state grass[3] of Utah in 1990. If you thought it was just something to nibble while moving along the trail, know that the bittersweet taste in your mouth is a living link to both ancient and more recent cultural foodways of Utah.

"Ten ounces of chewy subsistence raked in from out-of-doors and served with roughage" is not the most appealing description one could find on a restaurant menu.[4] Nor would many line up for an "all-you-can-forage buffet with handpicked freshness" or would crave State Fair fare offering "deep-fried roots, leaves, and berries—on its own stick!" But food is necessary for life and scarcity increases what we'll accept as food as well as the work we'll do to get it. Prior to the advent of systematic agriculture, forage (both gathered and hunted) was the only source of food.[5] Foraging skills make hunters better since knowing the favored forage of their prey, readily identifying it in the field, recognizing topography where stands may be found, knowing its phenology (the time of season when it will be ready to forage), and then having patience, brings the prey to the hunter. Native American hunters certainly understood the connection between rice grass and jackrabbits.[6] Forage is nature-supplied food and the primary reason to forage has always been survival.

HISTORY OF UTAH FORAGING

The history of foraging everywhere correlates directly with the availability of food. Plentiful food at hand means hands are free to pick up something else. But when food becomes scarce, the value of things in hand declines until they are abandoned to go forage.

Evidence of early native foraging has been studied in the Four Corners area. According to archaeologists from the Navajo Nation Archaeology Department, an archaic population lived in Dust Devil Cave on the northern part of the Rainbow Plateau near Navajo Mountain in southeastern Utah "some 9,000 years ago, up until…about AD 1,300."[7] "Fecal specimens reveal heavy reliance on foraged small seeds such as dropseed, goosefoot, and sunflower, along with prickly pear pads, pinyon pine nuts, hackberry, chokecherry, and rose."[8] In contrast, the earliest agricultural development found in the same area "is [from] no earlier than about 400 BC."[9] "Some argue that farming was adopted to maintain a foraging lifestyle—it was a means to continue a traditional way of life under altered circumstances."[10] Others say that

> most of the wild plants common in the Anasazi diet came from disturbed areas such as fields.…One of the key benefits of farming on the Colorado Plateau was not just domesticates but the weeds that proliferated in the fields [which] improved the nutritional basis of the population.…Archaic populations may have practiced weed encouragement well before the introduction of agriculture."[11]

Foraging was also vital for the Mormon pioneers who arrived in the Salt Lake Valley in the nineteenth century. As one observer described it,

There were a few bushes along the streams of City Creek, and other creeks south. The land was barren; it was covered with large black crickets, which seemed to be devouring everything that had outlived the drouth [sic] and desolation.… For the next three years we were reduced to considerable straits for food…thistle roots, segos, and everything that could be thought of that would preserve life, were resorted to.[12]

Much of what the pioneers learned about survival in this unfamiliar place was taught to them by the Indians.

While Emily [Stewart Barnes] and her relatives were hard put to avoid starvation, it is interesting to note what plants the Indians about her utilized for food, for…they did dry and store mashed seeds of the service berry.…They ate the wild onion,…the bulbs of the sego lily,…[and] cancer root.…[They] made bread from the seeds of the sunflower,…ate the seeds of the more common milkweed…[and] balsam root.…[They enjoyed] several species of *Opuntia*, prickly pears or cacti…and the Indians were smart enough to burn off the spines and eat the partially cooked body, sometimes roots as well. They treated the thistle in the same manner.…Spring beauty, the Indians ate its roots.…Wild rye…[and] bears grains, the Indians gathered and made into flour.…Indian parsnip, a member of the carrot or parsley family, the thick roots of which the Indians ate…as well as the dogtooth violets.…They ate the seeds of a goosefoot…made tea from mint...got their sugar from the common reed, the stalks and roots of which they gathered and ground into a flour....Watercress was gathered...for salad....The upshot of the matter is, that one need not starve if he knows his flora and is as wise as the chipmunk, which at least puts edible bits aside to dry for future use.[13]

FORAGING TODAY

As agriculture-based societies developed, foraging became more an optional means to diversify and extend food, to season and improve food, and to maintain cultural ties to food. With modern processing, preservation, and convenience preparation, foraging became a novelty used by outdoor enthusiasts, backpackers, and hunters.

One cannot, in my opinion, get food that is more directly attuned to the climate or more complementary to the current version of "eating local" than from forage. It is truly only your footprint you leave. Wild plants that haven't been hybridized to sterility, modified genetically, and coddled in chemically enhanced soil are more likely to have a greater diversity and higher concentration of the phytonutrients that may convey more protection to the consumer against the stressors that all organisms—we included—must face within our shared environment.

Utahns maintain websites[14] where people of similar interests register to organize foraging (often called wild food gathering), to attain survival skills, or to seek a hunter-gatherer or caveman diet (often called a Paleolithic or Paleo diet). Some natural and health food stores post a calendar of amateur and professional plant identification forays—often called herb walks. Boy Scout troops, Pioneer Girls, wilderness groups, botany and nature school clubs, and emergency preparedness and community emergency response teams ask those who are knowledgeable to help them identify edible plants and distinguish toxic plants.

With modern affluence, foraging is often perceived as unnecessary and even dangerous. Sadly, there are an estimated ten to sixty deaths per year in the United States caused by unintentional poisonous plant and mushroom ingestion.[15] (Need I say: figure it out before you forage. Train before you touch. Educate before eating.) But some of us still choose to take hold of it. Survivalists, minimalist outdoor enthusiasts, and even foodies are looking to savor the unique and original flavors of forage while gaining a greater appreciation for and desire to protect our dwindling natural resources.

As a child, weeding was awful work. Now as a forager I no longer pull any weeds. Knowing a use for whatever grows changes "weeds" into useful plants.

The work feels like foraging even when thinning or pruning. When harvesting garden vegetables and fruits, I work in a little forage too. I pick the purslane, lambsquarter, dandelion, salsify, and burdock that grow voluntarily and include them in the meal. One evening after being away from home all day and hungry, my family faced an empty kitchen. My wife and youngest daughter found driving to get burgers more appealing but I went to the backyard and harvested beets, greens, kale, okra, basil, a bowl full of tomatoes, and lambsquarter. By the time my wife returned I had a hearty, satisfying pot of stew and she wished she had not eaten those fries. We finished off the stew, put the refuse on the compost heap, and washed the pot while the fast food remnants—wrappers, bags, pouches of condiments, plastic ware, and polystyrene clamshells—filled the kitchen garbage. Learn your Utah flora and enjoy the forage.

SEASONAL FAVORITE

I do have a favorite combination during the morel mushroom season. Steam or parboil a fistful of nettle leaf, watercress leaf, or other mustard greens then add all the washed and chopped morel mushrooms you've found. If you want a thicker broth, you can throw in the crushed, well-washed rhizome (root) of bracken fern or bitterroot. Season to taste and enjoy.

NOTES

1. The sego lily has been the Utah state flower since 1911.
2. Stanley L. Welsh et al., *A Utah Flora*, 2nd ed. (Provo: Print Services Brigham Young University, 1993), 877.
3. Utah Code T63G C1 S601.
4. In 1999, a restaurant called Forage opened in Salt Lake City, with Bowman Brown as chief forager. *Food & Wine* magazine called it "ingenious modernist food." (Heather May, "Forage Lives up to Its Name with Nature-Based Menu," *Salt Lake Tribune*, May 29, 2013.) Sadly, it closed in 2016.
5. Even when miraculously supplied, "bread from heaven" forage had to be gathered (Exodus 16:21).
6. John P. Dunn, Joseph A. Chapman, and Rex E. Marsh, "Jackrabbits: *Lepus californicus* and Allies," in *Wild Mammals of North America: Biology, Management and Economics*, ed. J. A. Chapman and G. A. Feldhamer (Baltimore, MD: John Hopkins University Press, 1982), 124–45.
7. Phil R. Geib, *Foragers and Farmers of the Northern Kayenta Region: eEcavations along the Navajo Mountain Road; with Contribution by Jim Collette* (Salt Lake City: University of Utah Press, 2011), 1.
8. Ibid., 28–29, 172.
9. Ibid., 211.
10. Ibid., 229.
11. Ibid., 229–30.
12. President George A. Smith, Historical Address Delivered in the New Tabernacle, Salt Lake City, October 8th and 9th, 1868, in Brigham Young, *Journal of Discourses*, vol. 13 (Liverpool, London: Horace S. Eldredge, 1871), 120.
13. Claude T. Barnes, *The Grim Years; or, The Life of Emily Stewart Barnes* (Salt Lake City: Ralton, 1949), 38–41.
14. One example is www.meetup.com, with a Paleo group subsite: www.meetup.com/Paleo-People-of-Salt-Lake-City/.
15. In the same analysis it was reported that one is more than four hundred times more likely to die by being poisoned by the proper use of pharmaceutical agents. See Joe@EatThePlanet, "How Many People Die Foraging Plants and Mushrooms in the US Each Year?" Eat the Planet, accessed August 29, 2014, http://eattheplanet.org/archives/2427.

34

MEXICAN FOOD

A Recipe for Love

ELIZABETH ARCHULETA

Utah's Spanish-speaking population is the largest minority group in the state, comprising people with roots from Mexico southward to Argentina. Each group maintains their own unique food traditions. The earliest of these immigrants, descendants of the region's original Spanish colonists in neighboring New Mexico, were recruited during World War II to work in Utah's mines and railroads. Some of my family was part of that immigration, and our traditional cuisine, known simply as Mexican food, has been embraced by Utahns for nearly a century.

My identity partially stems from the foods I grew up eating and the customs involved with those foods. My family serves specific foods around certain holidays or other events, and we talk about food in the stories we share. However, there are many foods we no longer eat, revealing changes in my family's traditions over time. At the same time, the foods we used to eat weren't always as popular as they are now, so while they're disappearing from my family's homes, they are becoming more ubiquitous elsewhere. Most people are familiar with smothered burritos, carne asada, and tamales, or have maybe even had a glass of horchata. Tortillas can be found in any store, and there is a Mexican food section in most mainstream grocery stores. My mother was teased when she took tortillas to school in her lunchbox; indeed, generational and cultural changes are revealed through food.

Two changes that come to mind are modifications to recipes that have moved from the home to the mass market. One change comes with the abandonment of an ingredient that changes the flavor of certain foods I knew and loved. The other change comes in the name of a dessert that hides a main ingredient in order to make it more palatable to individuals who would never eat that ingredient voluntarily. But before I discuss these changes, I want to share a story about my

Tamales are another mainstay within Utah's Spanish-speaking community, but because making them is laborious they are usually saved for special occasions or holidays such as Christmas and Easter. Dried corn husks, pork loin, onion, garlic, dried Hatch, New Mexico chile (not chili powder), and masa harina made with Snowcap Lard are the author's favored ingredients. Courtesy Snixy Kitchen.

family by going back to my grandma's childhood and also discuss some of the ways food was used in our culture.

FROM NEW MEXICO TO UTAH

I like sharing stories I heard as a child about how grandma came to Utah. My immediate family originally came from northern New Mexico. Most of them lived in the mountain valleys of Peñasco, Chamisal, and Rodarte, located at the foot of the Sangre de Cristo Mountains. It was, and still is, a place of great poverty and economic hardship. My grandma Ida always wanted to escape the region's poverty, but in order to do this she had to leave her family and home. She and three other friends had long planned their escape together. They agreed to each get married and leave New Mexico as soon as they turned sixteen, which was the legal age to marry at that time, or so I was told. When that time came, everyone backed out except for my grandma. She left by herself for Tooele, Utah, to live with and work for her godmother, who ran a boarding house for enlisted men stationed at the Tooele Army Depot.

The story goes on to say that her father traveled to Tooele and brought her back home three separate times because it was not proper for a young, single woman to be around so many young, single men. Eventually she married one of those men, stayed in Utah, and started a family.

The story claims that my grandma helped most of her brothers and sisters relocate to Salt Lake City. As each one finished high school, she brought them here and helped them get established. Thus, my family roots shifted from northern New Mexico to Utah, my home state. Included in this story of family and place are the recipes that my grandma brought with her. My favorites to this day include enchiladas, tamales, biscochitos, chicos, and homemade tortillas.

My grandma brought and kept our family together during the holidays and for events that always involved too much food. That is, until her death. With her passing I have seen many of the foods and food traditions transform and disappear, at least in my family. Gone are the frequent family gatherings where everyone prepared food, shared company, and exchanged gossip.

FOOD AND CELEBRATIONS

When I think of the foods New Mexico families serve at funerals and weddings, I'm reminded of the recipes my grandma Ida brought with her when she moved to Utah. Funerals bring the living together to share stories and food with those who come to pay their last respects. Weddings also bring the living together to eat, welcome the blending of families, and celebrate the creation of new families.

Traditionally, families and friends supplied the food served at both events, but these days, younger people planning weddings rely more on caterers. While this might be convenient, it's leading to the loss of foods traditionally served at weddings and the customs linked with the events. This means that younger generations are slowly losing the food traditions that inform our identities and that tie us to New Mexico—a place that many of our older relatives call home. The foods that are disappearing at weddings and funerals are some of the same foods that my family served during the holidays.

Holidays brought out foods considered to be treats because that was typically the only time we ate them. These included tamales, chicos, and homemade tortillas, all of which have labor-intensive methods and were therefore served less often. The work connected with tamales involved washing and drying corn husks, making *masa* (dough), putting masa on the husks,

topping with meat, and then tying up each individual husk and cooking. This was typically a multiperson task that required a lot of preparation, so it was done as a family. I loved my family's tamales because they weren't small and thin like some I've eaten while searching for family comfort food at restaurants. Our tamales were hearty things; one was a meal in itself!

The making of chicos is also labor-intensive, making them less readily available and more expensive. Unlike dried corn kernels used to make posole, the dried corn that becomes a chico is prepared differently and presents an entirely different flavor when cooked. Whole ears of corn are steamed in the husk and then dried. However, the best chicos are those cooked the old-fashioned way—in *hornos* (outdoor adobe ovens), leading to a more smoky flavor that isn't found in chicos available for purchase in grocery stores. More often than not, chicos were added to pinto beans and cooked all day on the stove or much more quickly in a pressure cooker. My family never made chicos, but we knew the best ones came from New Mexico in Ziploc baggies tucked away in an auntie's pantry. For some reason, they are even harder to find now, making them much more of a luxury food item.

AN ABANDONED INGREDIENT

What else is disappearing? Homemade tortillas. Homemade tortillas are now considered a treat, and nothing replaces a hot tortilla right off the griddle, smothered in butter, and rolled up and eaten while still warm!

Norbert Martinez made tortillas available to a wider group of people when he opened up Mama

Maria's Tortilla Factory in Midvale, Utah, in 1981. With Mama Maria's popularity, the competition for manufactured tortillas heated up and homemade tortillas have practically disappeared. It wasn't until manufactured tortillas were so readily available that I began to miss the taste of a food that is now accessible only in memories. I recall my grandma Ida and great-grandma Sophia making masa for tortillas, pinching out small balls, and then taking those masa balls, rolling them out, flipping them over, rolling again, and repeating the process until each tortilla was perfectly round and flat. Only then would it be thrown on the griddle and carefully turned by hand over and over until it was cooked to perfection. In my opinion, the more brown spots, the better!

My grandma Kate always had a houseful of her own kids, grandkids, and extended families' kids, so I could never figure out how she was able to make enough tortillas for the next meal or to last for later meals. There wasn't bread in her house; there were only tortillas, so she had to make enough to satisfy all of us who eagerly grabbed the tortillas as fast as they came off the griddle. We always ate our fill, and those that remained uneaten were stored in a cupboard behind the strung-up cotton dishtowel that served as a cupboard door. My memories of my Grandma Kate are of her in the kitchen with a box of Rex Lard sitting on the stove.

One of the modifications that came with manufactured tortillas was the abandonment of lard, the key ingredient that made my grandmas' tortillas taste so good. Both of my grandmas always had Rex Lard or Morrell Snow Cap Lard close by. There was no vegetable oil; there was only animal fat.

Today, with consumers' increased attention to

PRUNE PIE
(MAKES 1 COOKIE SHEET)

8 c. flour
3 c. sugar, divided
1/2 tsp. salt (more if desired)
4 tsp. baking powder
2 c. lard (shortening works too, but please read article before attempting to substitute)
3 lbs. prunes, pitted
Cinnamon, to taste
Cloves, to taste

Heat oven to 350 degrees F.
　Mix together flour, baking powder, salt, and 1 c. of sugar.
　Cut in the lard until the mixture is crumbly. Add enough cold water to make a soft dough. Knead slightly and cut in half.
　Roll out each half of dough to 1/4-inch thick and line a cookie sheet with one. Save the other.
　Cook prunes in water until soft. Drain. Mash well, adding 2 c. sugar (to taste, you may not need it all). Season with cinnamon and cloves.
　Spread filling evenly over bottom crust. Cover with top crust; pinch seams and cut steam vents.
　Bake until crust is slightly brown.

ingredients, most people would not dream of buying tortillas made with lard. But people who have never tasted homemade tortillas made with lard have no point of reference, so they do not know what they are missing. I know, and I long for the days when I could go to my grandmas' houses, lift the dishtowel in which the tortillas were wrapped, and eat a homemade tortilla! Nowadays, tortillas are found in the fridge, wrapped in plastic that contains a company logo, a nutrition label, and an expiration date. Manufactured tortillas don't taste like home or love!

TORTILLAS

4 c. flour
3 tsp. salt
3 tsp. baking powder
2–3 c. warm water
4 Tbsp. lard

Mix all ingredients together and slowly add warm
water to form a firm, soft dough.

They taste like convenience that comes off of a conveyor belt.

Lard is also key to making the best refried beans. The much healthier olive oil is not even a choice for my family! Even biscochitos should be made with lard. These holiday cookies are flavored with anise, sprinkled with cinnamon and sugar, and served at weddings and for Christmas.

A HIDDEN INGREDIENT

Another family favorite for the holidays was my great-grandma Sophia's prune pie. Yes, you heard me right! I said prune pie. Wild red plums are abundant in northern New Mexico's mountains, and prune pie originated among the northern Pueblos, including Taos Pueblo. Prunes aren't the only filling used. There are also pumpkin mixtures, but regardless of filling, this dessert is still a favorite.

These pies do not look like traditional pies. Instead, my great-grandma's prune pies consisted of a flat piece of dough placed on a pizza pan, spread with a prune mixture, then another flat piece of dough placed on top, and sprinkled with sugar and cinnamon before baking. The mixture contains prunes,

raisins, sugar, cinnamon, and cloves. The pies can also be made to look like big, unfrosted, New Mexican pop tarts. We always gobbled up as many as we dared, knowing full well that we could not overindulge!

Like those who might turn their noses up at ingesting lard, others have turned their backs on this delicious dessert called "prune pie." After some family members married non–New Mexicans, they changed the name to "plum pie" in order to fool the unsuspecting eater of this delicacy. I prefer its original name if for no other reason than it means more for me to eat when others politely refuse to try it!

Two other staples that have never gone out of style are Hatch green chilis and red chili powder. In fact, if you eat at most any restaurant in New Mexico, you will be asked "red or green?" because chili is served with just about everything—including ice cream! And just like chicos, the best red and green chilies cannot be found in bags or cans in the Mexican food aisle.

FOOD AND VISITORS

The food practices my grandma Ida brought with her to Utah have also changed considerably. One of the food practices that reminds me of her involves guest-host relations. She planned her day around the potential arrival of unannounced guests. There always seemed to be a big pot of beans and rice on the stove whenever we visited her. She told me she always wanted to have food for company even if she was not expecting anyone because it would be rude not to feed company.

Guests were always fed, and this meant that we always had homemade food to eat when we visited her. The first question she asked us when we walked through the door was "Are you hungry?" She asked this even as we were already peeking in her cupboards, looking in the fridge, and opening up her dishwasher, which was where she stored cookies and other goodies.

Our health and wellness were always tied to food in my grandma's eyes, so even if we were not hungry, we ate. Being a little plump meant being happy and healthy. Moreover, it was rude to say no when she had gone through the trouble of preparing something for us to eat. Feeding us was a signal that she loved us: Aren't you feeling well, *mijita*? You don't look like you've been eating enough. Here, let me make you something to eat. This act of preparing food for guests and feeding loved ones is a custom that the modern world is neglecting with the easy availability of fast and processed foods. It is becoming a remnant of a bygone era where people are now too busy working and engaging in social media to interact with real people around a kitchen table.

CONCLUSION

Traditions and rituals around how and why we share meals always come to mind when I think about my family's foodways. Food keeps us connected to our roots, helps us maintain ties to one another, and, in doing so, helps nourish who we are. My grandmas were the matriarchs of large extended families. They made sure we always got together for holidays, birthdays, weddings, funerals, and just because we were family. Now those traditions are gone or quickly disappearing. I know that food kept us together, and I wonder what is happening to us as we slowly drift apart, eating in our separate homes. Since all of my grandmas have passed away, my families see each other less often, and we all indulge less and less in the food traditions, practices, and recipes they brought with them from New Mexico.

35

ASIAN FOODWAYS IN UTAH

EDITH MITKO

Utah is home to over thirteen Asian communities. The Japanese and Chinese, the state's largest Asian communities, were the earliest Asian immigrants. Both entered Utah in the 1860s, many coming as laborers with the transcontinental railroad. In the 1920s and 1930s, migrant laborers from the Philippines and Korea came; later in the century immigrants from Thailand began coming—many were members of military families stationed at the Hill Air Force Base. In the mid-1970s Utah became home to refugees from Vietnam, Cambodia, and Laos, resettling here after the Vietnam conflict. This group also included ethnic Chinese and the Hmong. In the early 1990s, a small group of Tibetan refugees were also resettled here. Over the years, immigrants from India and Pakistan have also chosen Utah, mostly for educational opportunities.

Today each of these Asian communities has contributed to the diversity of Utah with their religions, cultures, and cuisines. They have successfully introduced their favorite dishes and family recipes at religious and cultural festivals and at their ethnic restaurants. In the twenty-first century, Utah has become home to an even more diverse Asian population as refugees from Nepal, Bhutan, and Myanmar (Burma) have arrived. It's exciting to see the contributions they have begun to make to Utah cuisine.

CHINESE COMMUNITY

By the late 1800s, many of the Chinese who chose to stay in Utah after the completion of the railroad decided to go into business. They created a Chinatown on Plum Alley in downtown Salt Lake City filled with restaurants, laundromats, specialty shops, and living quarters. It was razed in the 1950s, a victim of mid-century progress, but the Chinese entrepreneur skills that built Chinatown are still evident today.

Daily fare for the early Utah Chinese family usually consisted of one dish served with white steamed rice, such as steamed pork with "fuyee" bean cake or steamed white rice covered with a rich stew and thick brown gravy. Today Chinese families often enjoy one-dish traditional foods

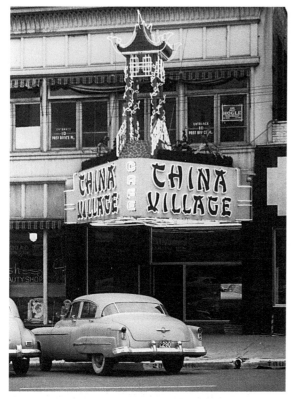

Chinese restaurants were among the first ethnic restaurants in Utah. In 1910 there were six, and by 1951 there were fourteen in downtown Salt Lake City including the popular China Village Café. Shipler Commercial Photographers Collection. Used by permission, Utah State Historical Society. All rights reserved.

at dinnertime—steamed white rice with fish, beef, chicken, or pork. Proteins can be stir-fried, slow cooked, sautéed, barbecued, or roasted; vegetables are steamed and then flavored with black bean, oyster, or one of many other favored sauces. Another favorite is soup—winter melon, lotus root, or vegetable—made with Chinese herbs.

In the 1950s and 1960s most of the Chinese restaurants were created through partnerships. Later they were family owned. For many years one could find a family-owned Chinese restaurant in even the smallest Utah towns. All served Cantonese-style dishes. During this period Johnny Quong, famous for his Hawaiian and Tiki Hut restaurants, opened Utah's first Chinese buffet, which closed after only two years—but in the 1980s Chinese Gourmet brought back the buffet. Today not just restaurants but Chinese buffets can be found throughout the larger cities and towns in Utah.

Today Chinese restaurants in Utah, like those throughout the country, typically offer the popular General Tso chicken, twice-cooked egg noodles, sweet-and-sour pork, walnut shrimp, orange and lemon chicken, as well as a number of spicy dishes. The first restaurant to offer the now popular "dim sum" was the old Golden Dragon, located on Main Street in Salt Lake City. Dim sum are individual servings of different specialties including pastries, spareribs in black-bean sauce, chicken feet, and shumai (ground meat steamed or fried in a pastry shell), among others. There can be more than thirty different dishes on a dim sum menu.

One iconic Chinese restaurant was the Jade Cafe. It was opened in 1954 in Salt Lake City by Bin Yee and his uncle Dick Yee and lasted for sixty years. The Yees owned the restaurant property, enabling them to keep prices very low while providing large quantities of both American and Chinese dishes. This remarkable business practice earned the Jade many loyal customers. In his book about growing up in Salt Lake City, Utah juvenile court judge Andrew Valdez remembers the wonderful sixty-five-cent egg foo yong sandwich.[1]

Utah's Chinese community has always been

generous in sharing its many holidays and festivals along with the sumptuous dishes made for each event. One example is Chinese New Year, celebrated with great public banquets as well as more private family dinners. For this holiday the menu always includes something round (a cake or perhaps an orange) symbolizing togetherness and abundance or achieving a higher goal, such as getting a promotion; a whole chicken representing prosperity or good fortune; a whole fish symbolizing lots of money with plenty to spare; noodles symbolizing a long life and good health; lettuce representing lots of money; an oyster to bring luck; a roast pork to bring fertility; and apples representing peace and health.

JAPANESE COMMUNITY

Since farming was held in high esteem by the Japanese, many Japanese immigrants became farmers. Their success in growing and introducing new products sometimes even aided in their acceptance. One example of the public admiration immigrants could win through their hard work and financial success was when the Sanpete County newspaper, the *Ephraim Enterprise*, paid tribute to the introduction of cauliflower and cabbage by the Japanese as profitable new crops. They wrote, "The Japanese are experts.... [L]et us welcome them." Incredibly, for a time, this "Sanpete Valley" produce was eagerly sought by buyers along the Atlantic Coast from Jacksonville, Florida, to Boston, Massachusetts.

Most Japanese farmers settled in Box Elder, Weber, and Salt Lake Counties. Besides cauliflower and cabbage, they were known for celery—the nationally acclaimed Sweetheart and Jumbo celeries—and for strawberries. The patent on the everbearing Twentieth Century strawberry was held by Utahn Taijiro Kasuga and made him a millionaire.

The tiny settlement of Keetley, midway between Heber City and Park City in the Wasatch Mountains, became a wartime home to the largest single group of Japanese Americans to resettle in a community that was not an internment camp anywhere outside of the West Coast. Keetley's Japanese farmers produced lettuce, potatoes, and onions. They became self-sufficient before the war's end, but the cost of transporting their produce prevented greater economic success.

In Salt Lake Valley, Japanese truck farmers peddled their produce door-to-door in suburban neighborhoods while also providing produce to local restaurants and grocery stores. At the same time, they grew Japanese daikon (long white radish), burdock root, and soybeans for their own families and the community.

The Japanese community had established their *Nihon Machi*, "Japan Town," on 100 South between 300 West and West Temple in Salt Lake City by the early 1900s. In those early days the California Market and Sage Farm Market sold hundred-pound bags of rice, gallon containers of shoyu (soy sauce), and essential ingredients for Japanese "must have" traditional dishes—*gobo* (burdock root), mochiko (sweet rice flour), daikon (radish), *nori* (sheets of seaweed for sushi rolls), and much more. Sunrise Fish Market provided the source for fish and the other proteins included in most Japanese *okazus* (stews)—the mainstay of nightly meals. The okazus in most homes consisted of many vegetables and a little very thinly sliced meat (beef, pork, or chicken)

At the height of World War II, California produce dealer Fred Wada and a cadre of "voluntarily relocated" Japanese farmers were living in Keetley, Utah, near Heber City, where they had leased thousands of acres for victory gardens. This 1943 photo with Mr. Wada in the center features land that was soon to become a strawberry patch. Peoples of Utah Collection. Used by permission, Utah State Historical Society. All rights reserved.

added only to flavor the veggies. Three thinly sliced pork chops and a large amount of vegetables served with bowls of *gohan* (white steamed rice) would easily feed a family of twelve.

While most early Japanese families in Utah indulged in American desserts such as pies, cakes, and cookies, for very special occasions they would make a trip to the Mihoya for *manju*, Japanese dough buns often filled with sweet red-bean paste. Today manju is available at Asian festivals, church and civic fundraisers, and of course at the many Asian food markets.

For dining out, the Japanese immigrants frequented the Pagoda Restaurant, Dawn Noodle, State Noodle House, Aloha Café, City Café, and Manhattan Café. Their Caucasian neighbors also enjoyed these establishments and they became even more popular after World War II and the Korean War as returning soldiers searched for the foods they had enjoyed in faraway places. Japan Town in Salt Lake City was destroyed in the early 1960s to make way for the Salt Palace Convention Center, and although businesses were encouraged to relocate, only Sage Farm Market survived, which in recent years was renamed Japan Market.

Probably the most popular contribution by the Japanese to the American food scene is sushi. Many people make the mistake of thinking that sushi (cooked vinegar rice combined with seafood, vegetables, or fruit) means raw fish or *sashimi*. Sashimi can be included in sushi, but not all sushi includes sashimi. Teriyaki is another popular Japanese sauce used in cooking chicken, pork, fish, and beef. Tempura seafood and vegetables, prepared with a light batter and then deep fried, are found on all Japanese restaurant menus.

KOREAN AND FILIPINO COMMUNITIES

The Koreans and Filipinos were the next Asian immigrants to settle in Utah. Both have established their share of markets and restaurants. The Utah public became more knowledgeable about Korean food during the 1980s and 1990s because of the annual Korean Food Bazaar, a fundraiser sponsored by Salt Lake's Korean Presbyterian Church of Utah. The church's women's group prepared an array of traditional dishes including *bulgogi* (BBQ beef), *chapchae*

LOBSTERS WITH MISO SAUCE
(SERVES 6)

6 to 8 lobster tails
1/2 c. butter

Cut lobster into 1-inch pieces. Sauté in butter for about 5 minutes.

Miso Sauce
4 Tbsp. miso (white)
2 eggs
1 Tbsp. sugar
1 tsp. salt
1/2 c. water

Pour miso sauce over sautéed lobster, cover and cook another 20 minutes over low flame. Vegetables, such as Chinese peas, may be added at last minute for color.[2]

Modifying tried and true recipes to meet individual taste is one way home cooks make a recipe their own. By adding slivered almonds and sliced green onions to a favorite recipe for lobsters with miso sauce, the Mitko family created a birthday meal of extraordinary flavor and beauty. Photo by Edith Mitko, 2019.

(clear noodles with vegetables), fried wontons, rice cakes, sushi, and Korea's signature dish *kim chi* (fermented cabbage), helping to develop a larger local following for Korean food. Today Korean barbecue, with its many individually served relish dishes, is a favorite along the Wasatch Front.

There are many signature and traditional Filipino dishes such as roasted pig, *lumpias* (egg rolls), chicken adobo, *pancit*, *caldereta* (beef stew), *kare-kare* (stew with peanuts), pork barbecue, chicken barbecue, and stir-fried vegetables. Many of these dishes are routinely enjoyed by Filipino Utahns—especially on special occasions.

For centuries the Philippines hosted foreign traders and colonizers and today much of their traditional food is inspired by foreign cuisine. In fact, adobo, the well-known Filipino dish featuring meat marinated in sauce, is actually a Spanish word for sauce. Adobo is basically a meat stew (a.k.a. CPA or chicken pork adobo) simmered in vinegar, garlic, black peppercorn, and bay leaf. "Adobo" also refers to the cooking technique of braising any meat or vegetable with the aforementioned ingredients, then adding spices that reflect personal preferences or regional variations. Spices can range from Chinese soy sauce

PHO BO

(MAKES EIGHT LARGE BOWLS)
Courtesy Jean Tokuda Irwin

Prepare the broth and cooked meat:
2 medium yellow onions (about 1 lb. total)
1 4-inch piece fresh ginger (about 4 oz.)
5–6 lbs. beef soup bones (marrow, oxtails, and knuckle bones)
5 star anise (40 star points total)
6 whole cloves
1 3-inch cinnamon stick
1 lb. beef chuck, rump, brisket, or cross-rib roast, cut into 2-by-4-inch pieces (weight after trimming)
1 1/2 Tbsp. salt
4 Tbsp. Vietnamese fish sauce
1 oz. (1-inch chunk) *duong phen* (yellow rock sugar is sold in one-pound boxes at Chinese and Southeast Asian markets; break up large chunks with hammer)

1. Use an open flame on grill or gas stove. Place onions and ginger on cooking grate and char the skin. (If using stove, turn on exhaust fan and open a window.) After about 15 minutes, they will soften and become sweetly fragrant. Use tongs to occasionally rotate. Discard any flyaway onion skin. It is not necessary to blacken entire surface.
2. Cool. Under warm water, remove charred onion skin; trim and discard root or stem ends. Smash ginger with flat side of knife to loosen flesh from skin. Use sharp paring knife to remove skin, and run ginger under warm water to wash off blackened bits. Set aside.
3. Parboil bones. Place bones in stockpot (minimum 12-quart capacity) and cover with cold water. Bring to boil. Boil vigorously 2–3 minutes. Dump bones and water into sink and rinse bones with warm water. Quickly scrub stockpot to remove any residue. Return bones to pot.
4. Simmer broth. Add 6 quarts water to pot, bring to boil, lower flame, and gently simmer. Skim scum that rises to surface. Add remaining broth ingredients and simmer, uncovered, for 1 1/2 hours. Boneless meat should be slightly chewy but not tough. Remove meat and place in bowl of cold water for 10 minutes to prevent from drying and turning dark. Drain meat; cool and refrigerate. Allow broth to continue simmering for 3 hours.
5. Strain the broth through fine strainer. Remove any bits of gelatinous tendon from bones to add to your pho bowl. Store tendon with cooked beef. Discard solids.
6. Use ladle to skim as much fat as possible from top of broth. Cool and refrigerate overnight. Reheat to continue. Taste and adjust flavor with additional salt, fish sauce, and yellow rock sugar. The pho broth should taste slightly too strong because the noodles and other ingredients are not salted. Add water to dilute and adjust taste. Makes approximately 4 quarts.

Prepare the noodles and bowls:
1 1/2 to 2 lbs. small (1/8-inch-wide) dried or fresh rice stick pho noodles (banh pho or Thai Chantaboon brands)
1/2 lb. raw eye of round, sirloin, London broil, or tri-tip steak, thinly sliced across the grain (1/16-inch thick; freeze for 15 minutes to make it easier to slice)
1/2 lb. bean sprouts
1 medium yellow onion, sliced paper-thin, left to soak for 30 minutes in a bowl of cold water
3 or 4 scallions, green part only, cut into thin rings
1/3 c. chopped ngo gai (cilantro)
ground black pepper

1. Thinly slice cooked meat.
2. Heat the pho broth and ready the noodles. To ensure good timing, reheat broth over medium flame while assembling bowls. If using dried noodles, cover with hot tap water and soak 15–20 minutes, until softened and no longer transparent. Drain in colander. For fresh rice noodles, just untangle and rinse in a colander with cold water.
3. Blanch noodles. Fill 3- or 4-quart saucepan with water and bring to boil. For each bowl, use long-handled strainer to blanch a portion of noodles. As soon as noodles have collapsed and lost their stiffness (10–20 seconds), pull strainer from water, letting water drain back into saucepan. DO NOT overcook. Place noodles into eight bowls. Noodles should occupy 1/4 to 1/3 of bowl.
4. Blanch bean sprouts for 30 seconds in same saucepan. They should slightly wilt but retain some crunch. Drain and add to the garnish plate.
5. Place slices of cooked meat or raw meat atop noodles. (If cooked meat is not at room temperature, blanch slices for few seconds in hot water.) Garnish with onion, scallion, and chopped cilantro. Finish with black pepper.
6. Bring broth to rolling boil. Check seasoning. Ladle broth into each bowl, distributing hot liquid evenly to cook raw beef and warm other ingredients.
7. Serve your pho with the garnish plate of fresh mung beans, Thai basil, cilantro, lime wedge, and sliced jalapenos.

Additional garnishes:
Sprigs of spearmint (*hung lui*); sprigs of Asian/Thai basil (*hung que*); leaves of thorny cilantro (*ngo gai*); red hot chilies (Thai bird or dragon), thinly sliced; lime wedges; thin slices of jalapeno

PHO BO VARIATIONS:

If you want to replicate options available at pho shops, head to the butcher counter at a Vietnamese or Chinese market. There you'll find white cords of *gan* (beef tendon) and thin pieces of *nam* (outside flank, not flank steak). While tendon requires no preparation prior to cooking, nam should be rolled and tied with string for easy handling. Simmer it and the beef tendon in the cooking broth for two hours, or until chewy-tender. Airy *sach* (book tripe) is cooked when purchased. Before using, wash and gently squeeze it dry. Slice thinly to make fringe-like pieces to be added to the bowl during assembly. *Bo vien* (beef meatballs) can be purchased in Asian markets in the refrigerator case; they are precooked. Slice each one in half and drop into broth to heat through.

Some pho restaurants also serve pho with a jar of hoisin sauce and sriracha hot sauce.

or *achuete* (basically Mexican achiote or annatto) to spices found in Southeast Asian cuisine such as onion, coconut cream, lemongrass, or turmeric.

Another well-known Filipino dish is pansit or pancit, an alternative to rice, and is presumably a Chinese contribution to the Filipino cuisine. Pancit is made from fresh or dry wheat noodles, rice noodles, vermicelli noodles, glass noodles, or soybeans. It can be stir-fried or served in a rich broth and is eaten as a snack, light meal, or side dish. Another Chinese-inspired food is *hopia*, a sweet pastry with mung bean filling made for special occasions using Filipino ingredients.

Eunice Jones, a leader in Salt Lake's Filipino community, explained that "we eat a lot of fresh vegetables, tropical fruits, seafood, fish, poultry, beef, pork, root crops and rice as a staple. . . . We buy most

of what we eat at all Asian Stores. They carry most of the Philippine products. They may have one or two aisles of our favorite food."

THAI COMMUNITY

Though the Thai community is quite small, they have made a significant contribution to Utah foodways. With a complex combination of flavors and aromas, Thai food has become a particular favorite as evidenced by the large and growing number of Thai restaurants in the state. Signature dishes like Pad Thai (noodle and vegetable salad), tom yam goong (spicy, sour soup), and massaman curry (sauce served with rice made from coconut milk and various spices) are well known and widely appreciated.

SOUTHEAST ASIAN GROUPS

Starting in the mid-1970s, many new Asian immigrant groups from Southeast Asia began arriving in Utah. The Vietnamese, Laotian, Cambodian, and Hmong brought food traditions from the jungles of Asia to Utah's desert.

When the first Vietnamese arrived in Utah, they couldn't find staples like lemongrass in the local stores but were delighted to discover that Utah is great for growing apple pears, persimmons, and jujube red dates. Most started growing gardens, not only as a food source but as a connection to their old life and to provide time for meditation. Families that grew the seeds for specific fruits and vegetables would share with the rest of the community. At home, a typical traditional Vietnamese dinner might include *cahchua* (sour soup), *ca' kho* (stewed fish), and a vegetable dish like *rau muons* (bok choy).

While some of their traditional foods were available in the Chinese markets, the Vietnamese quickly opened their own specialty markets and restaurants. Today the Vietnamese sandwich, *banh mi*, and their noodle dishes, *pho*, are local favorites in the state's many Vietnamese restaurants.

TIBETAN COMMUNITY

The Tibetan community in Utah has grown since 1983 when the first refugee families arrived. Today there are two Tibetan restaurants, as well as Tibetan food booths at both the annual Asian and the Living Traditions festivals. Traditional foods such as *momos*, steamed dough dumplings filled with beef or vegetables, are favorites at both events.

One of the most significant accomplishments for this very small community is the recent dedication of its Tibetan Community and Cultural Center in Salt Lake City. Through the dedication and leadership of Pema Chagzoetsang, the Tibetans now have a beautiful permanent home where they can share their celebrations with the larger community. These events often include Tibetan favorites such as hot spicy potatoes, momos, vegetables flavored with special herbs, pork or chicken dishes, and delicious sweet or butter tea.

ASIAN INDIAN AND PAKISTANI COMMUNITIES

The Asian Indian and Pakistani communities also have a distinct presence in Utah with many markets

and several restaurants. An influx of East Indians began in the early 1970s that included undergraduate and postdoctoral students as well as professionals with college degrees. Utah's Asian Indian community includes a large number of physicians, surgeons, business owners, attorneys, and educators. Along with a zeal for economic success, they brought along their traditional dishes, and some have opened restaurants featuring food from their regional homelands.

Indian families generally eat their dinner together daily. A lot of Indian men like to help with the cooking while children usually help with setting the table and getting the ingredients out. For most Indian and Pakistani families, a normal dinner includes bread, rice, salad, a vegetable, and *daal*. Daal is a diet staple made of boiled lentils garnished with fried onions, green chiles, and mild spice. Yogurt, with or without buttermilk, is a typical dessert.

Indian food is quite popular in Utah. The 1990s saw a rise in interest in nutritional Indian dishes as vegetarian and vegan diets flourished. Indian vegetables, main-course dishes, and premade frozen desserts are available from one of several Indian stores in Salt Lake City, and many Indian restaurants not only serve a wide variety of customers but also cater traditional food for family events.

FOOD BRINGS US TOGETHER

Asian food traditions offer an interesting and tasty addition to Utah's food landscape, and the groups who have come to Utah have found a receptive audience for their cuisine. For many Asian Utahns food has become a marker of culture and heritage within both families and the larger community. According to Vietnamese refugee Victoria Dong, "Family and food are connected. When you want to get the family together, you make a big pot of pho." Making traditional meals is always a sacrifice and is often quite expensive, but it is always worth the effort. Having a messy house needn't be used as an excuse for not having a family gathering. Food brings everyone closer together. Each person has their own way of cooking traditional meals, so each tastes slightly different. Good cooks don't have precise measurement—they measure by taste. And maybe that's why there still aren't many Asian franchise restaurants.

ACKNOWLEDGMENTS

The author wishes to thank the following community members for their help in telling the story of Asian food in Utah: Jo-Ann Wong and Margaret Yee (Chinese community); Eunice Jones (Filipino community); Victoria Dong (Southeast Asian community); Pema Chagzoetsang (Tibetan community); and Sudhir Nadkarm and Malavika Deo (Asian Indian and Pakistani communities).

NOTES

1. Andrew A. Valdez, *No One Makes It Alone* (Marina del Rey, CA: Juniper Press & Oxide Books, 2006).
2. Martha Kawada, *Nisei Favorites* (Kansas City: North American Press of Kansas City, 1967), 160–61.

36

GARDENING AS PLACEMAKING IN UTAH COMMUNITIES

DANILLE ELISE CHRISTENSEN

On May 17, 1851, not quite four years after the first Mormon scouts entered the Salt Lake Valley, a single page of the fledgling *Deseret News* referred to the challenges of settling country so different from the climate and infrastructure of the eastern United States. While the March and April mail had still "not been heard from" and heavy rain had leaked "thro' the houses not shingled, and some that are," not all was bleak: A new pottery kiln was set to burn its first lot of crockery, five wagons had arrived from Fort Laramie "laden with bacon, &c," and the "first University dance of Deseret" (commended for an absence of both alcoholic spirits and "profane, wanton, or uncivil language") had gone off splendidly. In the midst of this general news, an icon of a pointing hand called readers' attention to that fact that

> Jeremiah Woodbury of the 7th ward has a cherry tree in his garden, which sprang from the stone last season, and the tree is now in full bloom, May 5. Mr. Woodbury also sowed half a pint of wheat, and after the mice and fowls had destroyed a considerable portion, he threshed 135 pounds of wheat from the produce of the half pint.[1]

This oddly specific notice underscores the practical and ideological importance of small-scale domestic food production in Utah. While wheat was a hard-won treasure that could be traded for other resources, the flowering cherry in Woodbury's yard promised color and flavor in an otherwise unfamiliar and often dusty landscape; furthermore, it represented a long-term investment and signaled hope for residential stability.

Vital to sustaining life in a region more given to sagebrush than to snap peas, cultivated vegetables, trees, berries, and flowers have also been central to sustaining cultural and moral identities among the state's inhabitants. From the Mormon shaping of village landscapes, to Native affirmations of traditional ecological knowledge, to spaces created by "relocated" Japanese Americans and political refugees, Utah's gardens have both caused and responded to human displacement.

DOMESTIC GARDENS IN MORMON SETTLEMENTS

Commodity crops like Woodbury's wheat were central to the economy in early territorial days as Mormon settler colonists staked out claims to Utah lands; further, many field crops that did not need to be traded could be eaten. But "kitchen" or "subsistence" gardens were also important provisioning tools, especially since the Latter-day Saints' experiences with mobbing in the East had compelled them to choose both geographic and economic isolation. Good garden seed promised one step toward self-sufficiency in valleys surrounded by famously arid lands and limited commercial distribution systems.[2] By early 1853, in addition to sugar beet seed, Edward Sayers of Salt Lake City's Twelfth Ward advertised the availability of "rutabaga or Swedish turnip, carrot, parsnip, onion, radish, lettuce, early June pea, cucumber, melon, cabbage" and other garden seeds that had been grown the previous season and were "warranted of good quality."[3] These vegetables supplemented basic starches, such as sweet corn and potatoes, grown in small quantities on home lots.

Three-quarters of a century later, in 1926, Porter-Walton Co.—a nursery and mail-order business in Salt Lake City—offered many of the same vegetables enjoyed by Sayers's early clients. In addition, the company advertised perennial "asparagus and rhubarb roots" and seeds for starting spinach, cauliflower, tomatoes, and peppers.[4] Though much produce was eaten fresh during the growing season, these garden vegetables also made possible the relishes and sauces that brightened winter meals and improved diets. Old Utah cookbooks and tin recipe boxes are filled with instructions for pickles, chow-chow, piccalilli, piquant sauces called "catsups," and other modes of combining and preserving produce. For instance, Mary Verona Cox Smyth (b. 1880, Manti, Utah) bottled "Sandwich Spread" made from ground (and then salted) cucumbers, green tomatoes, onions, and peppers grown in her Fountain Green garden; she flavored the drained mixture with vinegar, celery seed, mustard, sugar, and turmeric and bound it with mayonnaise and flour.[5]

Fruit trees also secured an early place in Utah's nineteenth-century domestic landscapes. Peach pits and apple seeds were planted almost as soon as Latter-day Saint companies unhitched their wagons, and Utah fruit has generated glowing reviews, fond remembrances, and economic profit for decades since. In 1857, however, territorial governor and LDS prophet Brigham Young (b. 1801, Whitingham, Vermont) chastised Great Salt Lake City's residents for not investing more fully in food production that could offer both self-sufficiency and pleasure:

> Go round this city now, and probably you will not see one garden out of twenty, even where men have lived here four or five years, that has a single fruit tree growing in it. Have they set out anything? Yes, some cottonwoods; but they would not set out a peach tree, if you would give it to them. In many lots there is not a fruit tree, or currant bush, or anything to produce the little necessaries to make a family comfortable.

To those hesitant to put down roots because they feared being forced again from their homes, Young promised that if they "live[d] their religion, walk[ed] humbly before their God, and deal[t] justly with each other," they would "never be driven from the mountains."[6] His exhortations carried weight: By August 1863, one visitor from Idaho, exulting over a peach "seven and a half inches in circumference," described the capital city as "one vast peach orchard" interrupted only by the business district.[7] In the red-rock south, Mary Ann Stucki Hafen (b. 1854, Bern, Switzerland) recollected that in the 1860s fellow citizens of Santa Clara "drove all the way to California to buy young fruit trees and grapevine cuttings. In our mild warm climate of southern Utah we soon had peaches, apples, and luscious grapes to vary the diet."[8]

Though some of this fruit was cultivated in large orchards and vineyards, many home lots had several fruit trees close to the house—a pattern that persists in Utah today. Towns platted by Latter-day Saints throughout the territory favored "nucleated settlements" that clustered homes at the intersections of large blocks and permitted each family space for outbuildings, garden, pasture, and orchard; 80 percent of these towns laid out city house lots that were at least one acre in size.[9] Edna Eliza Porter Little (b. 1908, Porterville, Utah), who worked for her cousin in the Porter-Walton mail-order department from 1925 to 1938, grew up in the city of Centerville on a "lot with a small rock home and orchard that was situated at the foot of the Wasatch Mountains." Even though the Porters' yard had its own apricot, peach, cherry, and plum trees—fruit that young "Ted" helped dry and bottle for winter use—her stories of childhood in the first quarter of the century include several about the consequences of borrowing fresh apples and peaches from neighboring yards.[10]

Anne Jensine Marie Rasmussen Christensen (b. 1883, Ervik, Norway), great-grandmother of the author, takes a midday irrigation turn in Ephraim, Utah, c. mid-1920s. Her Danish husband, Christen P. Christensen, died in 1916 after an altercation with a neighbor about water rights. Courtesy Danille Elise Christensen.

Local gardens featured sweet things, too. In typical "Mormon village" fashion, Edna's parents, William Ira and Zina Porter, also kept chickens, pigs, and a cow on the property and irrigated "a nice garden with some strawberry plants."[11] Melons, pumpkins, and squash vines—which had long been successfully cultivated via irrigation in the Southwest[12]—grew quickly and became important parts of white settlers' kitchen gardens. Salt Lake Stake Relief Society president and civic leader Mary Isabella Hales Horne (b. 1818, Rainham, England), who arrived in Utah with one of the first pioneer companies, remembered that melon preserves and squash butter compensated in early years for scarce sugar and for vegetables that had to be let go to seed. Offering a refreshing burst of color, sweetness, and moisture, melons were given as gifts to newcomers and dignitaries in the early years of Anglo settlement, and slices were dried for later use.[13] These sweet fruits were also popular with marauding youngsters. In a letter from Cedar City dated February 13, 1851, and later published in the *Deseret News*, LDS apostle George A. Smith (b. 1817, Potsdam, New York) counseled his nine-year-old son (back home in northern Utah) to help his younger siblings, avoid swearing, check in with his mother frequently, and use a dictionary; as a final bit of advice he cautioned, "Never rob a melon patch or fruit garden, a meaner act cannot be done than to steal melons."[14]

The nineteenth-century garden that Isabella Horne grew behind a wattle (woven sapling) fence included flowers in addition to the melons and squash she so appreciated—and it seems that in Utah, *garden* has commonly been used in this broadly inclusive sense. In 1889, reflecting on LDS Church leaders' platting of Salt Lake City, one writer (probably editor Emmeline B. Wells, b. 1828, Petersham, Massachusetts) recalled that "each lot had

sufficient room for a little garden, where trees, and flowers, and shrubbery might be cultivated as well as vegetables for table use."[15] As part of her regular *Woman's Exponent* column, in 1874 a writer called Flora had led readers through a Dixie garden of fragrant honeysuckles and peonies, tasty strawberry plants and edible nasturtium, vining scarlet cypress, and dozens of other blooms that would require just twenty minutes of maintenance each day, perhaps during a visit from the neighborhood gossip. The work of spading new ground, Flora suggested, could be done by husbands or sons, especially if the idea were raised just after presenting them with a new pair of pants or a custard pie.[16]

Otherwise, these "little [nineteenth-century] gardens" were often female spaces—Brigham Young, for instance, invited Utah women to "go into the garden and raise the salad and numerous other articles within your judgment and strength."[17] Fields beyond the town centers, on the other hand, produced the cash crops—including peas, cabbage, tomatoes, beans, corn, celery, and onions—that sustained truck farming and supplied the local commercial canneries that dotted the state before the 1930s, when industry consolidation and refrigerated train cars and trucks began to bring cheaper "products from outside."[18]

Despite these changes in commercial food production and distribution, small-scale gardening in Utah remains an important cultural symbol. Central to a sense of Mormon identity, for instance, especially along the Wasatch Front, is the notion that an ethical, harmonious society is marked by a vegetatively productive landscape that shows evidence of human shaping. LDS apostle Orson Pratt (b.

The home and garden of a Northern Ute family in Whiterocks, Utah, on the Uintah and Ouray Reservation, c. 1964. Notice the woman working near a cookstove in her outdoor kitchen. Used by permission of Fort Lewis College, Center of Southwest Studies.

1811, Hartford, New York) verbalized such an ideal in 1879: "You will see a thickly populated country, inhabited by a peaceful people, having their orchards, their fruit trees, their fields of grain, their beautiful houses and shade trees, their cities and towns and villages. And you may ask—Who are all these people? And the answer will be—Latter-day Saints."[19] And when Mormon leader Spencer Kimball preached gardening from the pulpit in the late 1970s, he stressed not only economy and beauty, but also morality: Gardens could teach children to work, and to work together.[20]

GARDENING AS RESPONSE TO DISPLACEMENT

Though Utah's gardens have been promoted in terms of health, self-sufficiency, and social cooperation,[21] they have also been vehicles of cultural memory and continuity for the state's foreign-born residents. In the nineteenth century, articles in the LDS periodical *The Woman's Exponent* encouraged Utah readers to grow native plants like yucca, cacti, *Agave utahensis,* desert catalpa (*Chilopsis linearis)*, penstemons, and desert lilies (which together would produce graceful spaces "vieing with the best gardens of the East"),[22] but most of the Mormon gardeners new to the Great Basin sought to re-create the green, colorful, fragrant places they'd left—generally farms or villages in New England or the Midwest, the United Kingdom, or northwestern Europe.[23] In an 1888 letter to the *Exponent* titled "The Old Home," one woman lamented the sale of her family's Utah homestead— with its vegetables, fruit trees, and transplanted wild golden currant bushes—in part because there, in the shade, her mother had woven flower wreaths and told "lovely stories of the old New England home, with its woods, and brooks, and bushes, long rows of lilacs and roses, and the dear old grandfather drawing the maple from the trees," tales that the writer and her siblings listened to with "wonder" and "delight."[24] In 1960, artist and author Alice Morrey Bailey (b. 1903, Joseph, Utah) wrote that items in her great-grandmother's frontier garden—an "unplanned" mix of sweet William and rhubarb, squash and hollyhock, beans and columbine, lilac and corn—acted as "mementoes of a distant land," with the food plants offering nutrients, while the flowers disguised the roughness of her ancestor's adobe home: "With flower and leaf her moral proof / She claimed this spot her own."[25]

In subsequent decades, other new arrivals also used gardens to meet nutritional, cultural, and personal needs. Immigrants from Italy, many of whom came to labor in Utah mines and on Utah railroads between 1880 and 1920, settled in both the northern and southern parts of the state. Though conditions in early mining camps were harsh (one camp in Carbon County was known as Rag Town) and prejudice toward southern Europeans prevalent, Italian residents maintained cultural touchstones like local

musical groups and gardens that supported familiar foodways. These gardens included herbs important to the distinctive flavor profiles of Italian cuisines— basil, oregano, fennel, parsley, and garlic—as well as foundational foods like peppers, fava beans, zucchini, squash, and grapes. Intensive planting reflected agricultural norms of southern Italy (where the landscape was not dissimilar to that of Carbon and Tooele Counties); happily, this style also suited the exigencies of irrigation. Distinctive garden structures and *barrache* (outbuildings) for growing and processing food—including tomatoes grown on wooden lattices and sheds for canning produce and making wine— have also marked Italian-American homeplaces in Utah. During the Great Depression, writes Philip Notarianni, "an emphasis on family gardens and the importance of family-produced and stored food carried [Italian immigrants] through these lean years." Mary Anselmi-Ravarino (b. 1924, Wyoming), whose parents were Tyroleans from the Alps in northern Italy, remembers that they "transformed" the "desolate, treeless, sandy hills" of Reliance, Wyoming, with "vegetable gardens, flowers, and trees so they could have food for the body as well as for the soul," then repeated the process after the family moved to a farm in Ogden in the early 1930s. In the late 1980s, the Helper, Utah, homeplace of John Bruno (b. 1910, Italy) and Yolanda Spodafora Bruno (b. 1915, Green River, Utah), featured many of the aforementioned Italian staple foods, as well as apple, apricot, peach, pear, cherry, nectarine, plum, and walnut trees, raspberry bushes, horsebeans, peas, string beans, and a variety of flowers.[26]

This kind of placemaking occurred among many other groups as well. In just one example, the more than eleven thousand people of Japanese descent who endured the Topaz Internment Camp near Delta, Utah, used gardening as a way to bear the dislocation and indignity of their imprisonment between 1942 and 1945. Though people living near War Relocation Authority camps throughout the United States sometimes accused the WRA of pampering camp residents and contributing to local food shortages, food in the camps was in fact often meager, unhealthy, or culturally out of sync: Rations were dominated by sauerkraut, processed meats and canned hash, commercially canned fruit, and starches like boiled potatoes and bread. Residents in several U.S. detention camps protested, and self-governing committees soon focused on improving the food situation by encouraging the production of daikon, leafy greens, beets, strawberries, corn, watermelon, and napa cabbage. Many of Topaz's eventual residents had spent the summer of 1942 in whitewashed horse stalls at the Tanforan racetrack "assembly center" near San Francisco, where some grew tiny gardens outside their units in order to fill out government rations and perhaps stave off boredom and worry.[27]

At Topaz, the camp's weekly newspaper started a "Food Fancies" column that featured creative recipes that could be made using the limited resources and technology available in the hastily tarpapered barracks (which had coal potbelly stoves and hotplates, but no refrigeration or running water); in addition, camp manufacturing projects eventually generated $7,000 of bean sprouts and $25,000 of tofu. Most Topaz internees had lived near San Francisco, and only about 250 had been farmers; furthermore, alkaline soil, fluctuating temperatures, high winds, dust storms, unpredictable frosts, and irrigation difficulties made growing fresh food on the edge of the Sevier Desert difficult. However, camp residents longed for landscapes that felt like home. Author Yoshiko Uchida (b. 1921, Alameda, California), who lived in Topaz for eight months before receiving a scholarship to Smith College, felt "cautiously optimistic" when she saw the "pleasant little farms, green fields, and clusters of trees" surrounding the nearby town of Delta, but was stunned to see the surroundings turn "bleak as a bleached bone" just a few miles outside the city limits. One seventh grader wondered in a 1943 essay whether her family's abandoned Bay Area garden had "withered and died" from lack of care, or whether roses and violets still bloomed among the weeds; she hoped that if her house had not been torn down, its new residents had chosen to plant a victory garden.[28]

Nearly all the ornamentals and trees trucked into Topaz died, and it was difficult to maintain small garden beds near the living quarters, even with bucket brigades organized to bring water from central washhouses. Nevertheless, photographs show tall asters and other foliage outside Topaz residences. And in larger plots, internees produced more than 1.4 million pounds of vegetables—including tomatoes, peppers, eggplants, cucumbers, cantaloupes, and squash—in the three years they were confined to Topaz, supplying most of the center's fresh vegetables. Despite the challenges of an unfamiliar lifestyle and distressing conditions, the displaced residents also created beauty: Produce from Topaz's gardens won accolades at the Millard County Fair.[29]

Tragically, by rooting themselves along the Wasatch Front, newcomers dispossessed the peoples who already lived in and managed these lands, with disastrous results. Even the wide-ranging and regionally dominant Utes were starving by 1856, less than a decade after Mormon gardens and fields began to cordon off harvesting grounds long maintained by means of indigenous ecological knowledge.[30] Thus, in 1851, the Utah territorial government began a program of Indian pacification, containment, and assimilation, paying white settlers to grow food for Native groups; organizers hoped that in time the farms would become fully staffed by male Indians, who would be trained in what Brigham Young called "a more certain way of obtaining a living," one that would "advance themselves in the habits, means, and appliances of civilized life."[31] In 1855, federal Indian agent Garland Hurt (b. 1819, Russell County, Virginia), a Kentucky physician committed to an agrarian ethic of self-sufficiency, established Indian Farms in earnest. Hurt designated farm-reservations on fertile ground at Spanish Fork River (near Utah Lake), Twelve-Mile Creek (in the Sanpete Valley), Corn Creek (near Fillmore), and later Deep Creek (near what is now the Nevada-Utah border). However, by 1865 these farms had been abandoned due to a number of factors, including inadequate federal funding and unratified treaties, conflict between government superintendents and local agents, and broader disruptions such as the Civil War and ongoing tension between Mormons and the federal government. Pressure from white settlers who desired the prime but sometimes underused farmland also played a role, and Indian "trainees" themselves often viewed as risky the relatively undiversified livelihood represented by sedentary agriculture. In addition, some resisted attempts to alter gender roles and power

structures (in many Native communities, women, rather than men, had traditionally worked the soil). By 1861 Abraham Lincoln had approved the removal of some Ute groups to a reservation in the Uintah River Valley, and in 1865 nearly 170,000 acres of Indian farmlands in Utah Territory were opened to white settlement.[32]

Native populations struggled to develop new food resources in their own spaces of dislocation. For example, after the 1863 Bear River massacre in present-day Idaho—in which hundreds of Northwestern Shoshone were killed by a U.S. cavalry unit—survivors established (but were soon displaced from) a series of cooperative farms in northern Utah. One historian has marked 1928 as "the height of Ute [mostly subsistence-based] farming" on the Uintah-Ouray Reservation and notes that by 1920 "nearly every family maintained a home vegetable garden." But a collapse in seed prices and the rise of corporate agriculture elsewhere in the nation contributed to a vast reduction in farming on the reservation by the 1960s; according to oral interviews, only a few families continued to grow alfalfa, and most had stopped gardening.[33]

GARDENS IN DECLINE

The very vigor and frequency with which home gardens have been promoted by government and social leaders in Utah suggests that many of the state's residents have opted not to embrace the difficulties of producing food on a small scale. The mismatch between local environments and recreated homeplaces of origin became glaring when irrigation was abandoned. In 1954, Matia McClelland Burk (b. 1899,

Tombstone, Arizona) offered the following lament in the *Relief Society Magazine*:

I cannot bear to visit any more
The desert homestead where I was a child,
And see that dry and thorny weed-grown ruin,
My Mother's lovely garden, now grown wild.

Without dedicated attention, a "tangled bed of orange poppies" was all that marked the former habitation.[34]

Several ethnographers noted in the late 1970s that rapid urbanization of the Wasatch Front and the expansion of pressurized culinary (drinking) water systems had reduced lot sizes in the larger cities and disrupted irrigation schemes throughout Utah; in rural areas, better roads, new grocery stores, and shifts away from marginal farming lifestyles meant that "the subsistence agriculture for which the [large house] lots were used" had been largely abandoned, especially by rising generations. By 1978, due to population loss and little demand for land in poorer and less fertile areas, the in-town microfarms that characterized nineteenth-century settlements often included neglected orchards and "weed-infested lots in an uneasy conjunction with a garden, lawn, and home." Researcher Richard Francaviglia observed that among older people, flowers—especially roses and gladiolas—were "the real pride and joy," noting that the "bright patches of color in an otherwise drab unpainted landscape are impressive."[35]

But uneven investment in home gardens was not just a twentieth-century phenomenon. In May 1889, even as *The Woman's Exponent* editorialized on the importance of efficient and shared work and

beauty in Latter-day Saint homes, the piece's writer noted that Salt Lake City had already moved away from engagement with the soil: "I remember how much more homelike the city looked while the gardens remained. But though all may not have gardens, the home may be made attractive in other ways."[36] Nearly a century later, subsistence gardening continued to wax and wane in the Mormon West. In August 1967, while Barbara Thompson Dowdle's husband Jack was in Vietnam, she set out to reclaim the quarter-acre of her lot that had returned to weeds. But Dowdle knew little about gardening and nothing about irrigating. Turning to her father for expertise, she and her five young children managed to last the season, learning that melons grew well and that fresh and ripe tasted better than store-bought. Her account in the *Relief Society Magazine* also emphasized the moral benefits of home gardening: By monitoring and harvesting their own food, she wrote, "I feel the children learned a little more about responsibility and work."[37]

TWENTY-FIRST-CENTURY GARDENS

Utah gardens continue to help maintain cultural identities and display cultural values in the twenty-first century. Despite steady urbanization, rising land prices, and changes in irrigation options along the Wasatch Front, small-scale agriculture within city limits persists. In the oldest sections of towns like Providence, Manila, or Ephraim, open-ditch irrigation turns still keep extensive household gardens watered, and fruit trees, unpainted outbuildings, and the occasional horse jostle with RVs and backyard trampolines. City and county governments also partner with nonprofit organizations like Wasatch Community Gardens, which in 2014 facilitated thirty neighborhood and school gardens in Salt Lake County and coordinated a "Sharing Backyards" online exchange. In the latter program, households with underused garden plots negotiate trades of space, labor, water, expertise, and produce with interested but unlanded gardeners.[38] Even in the gated communities that have mushroomed on old orchards and hayfields throughout parts of the state, it's not uncommon to see stalks of corn showing over the back fences of million-dollar homes.

Part of this enthusiasm may be due to the continued encouragement of home food production and preservation among members of the Church of Jesus Christ of Latter-day Saints,[39] but it's also congruent with a national uptick in homegrown fruit, vegetables, berries, and herbs. According to a 2014 survey conducted by the National Gardening Association, between 2008 and 2013 household participation in food gardening across the United States grew 17 percent, with substantially increased participation among young adults, city-dwellers, families with children, and those on the high ($75,000+) and low (<$35,000) ends of the socioeconomic spectrum.[40] In western Utah (Logan, Salt Lake City, Kaysville, and Park City), surveys of farmers markets in 2011 found that 63 percent of shoppers—mostly college-educated, upper-income, middle-aged married women with three-person households—had their own gardens.[41] That same year, journalist Caleb Warnock published *The Forgotten Skills of Self-Sufficiency Used by the Mormon Pioneers*, and within three months the book had gone into a third printing and become a regional no. 1 and national no. 5 bestseller. *Forgotten*

Skills emphasizes the environmental, social, and character-building benefits of subsistence gardening, offering a defense of the "self-provident home garden" as well as practical strategies for everything from growing heritage varieties and seed-saving to designing raised beds and extending the harvest.[42]

Today's Utah gardens represent some of the oldest and newest examples of small-scale food production in the state. Between 2002 and 2012, the Ute Ethnobotany Project—a collaboration of Northern Utes, anthropologists at the University of Northern Colorado, and several federal agencies—documented plant-based knowledge among elders of the Uintah-Ouray Reservation. In addition to other results, the project encouraged the creation of a 2.5-acre Ute Learning Garden near the Mesa County Fairgrounds in Grand Junction, Colorado, and another in Fort Duchesne, Utah. The gardens recreate diverse growing conditions and have been used to produce food as well as educate locals and visitors about indigenous cultural practices, histories, and mores.[43] Additionally, in recent years the International Rescue Committee and the Utah Refugee Coalition have partnered with Salt Lake County to develop New Roots, a nonprofit organization that offers refugees access to community gardens and small farm plots. Like the gardens of earlier immigrants, these offer comforting taste experiences and encourage social interaction, utilize existing skills and build new ones, and generate savings as well as income. Chinese and African eggplants, Egyptian spinach, okra, the Armenian or snake cucumber (a kind of muskmelon), and roselle (hibiscus) grow well in Utah and are prized by new residents who have been displaced from Bhutan, Myanmar, Burundi, Chad, the Democratic Republic

The following recipes offer historical examples of how Utahns have preserved garden produce; the written instructions for heat processing and long-term storage are incomplete and outdated, so do not attempt to bottle these recipes at home. Wording and spelling from the original documents have been retained. For the most current guidance on home canning, see the National Center for Home Food Preservation.

SANDWICH SPREAD

Courtesy Mary Verona Cox Smyth[44]

Grind 1 gal. cucumbers, 1 gal green tomatoes, 6 large onions, and 4 green peppers. Let stand over nite in 1 cup of salt. Drain. Add 4 red peppers, 1 tablespoon celery seed. Cook until tender in 1 qt. vinegar, 1 pt. water, 3 cups sugar, and 3 oz. mustard. Make a paste of 1 1/2 cups of flour, 3 tablespoons turmeric, and 1 qt mayonase. Add to above mixture just before vegetables are done. Cook until the flour is well done. Stir constantly to prevent sticking. Put in bottles and seal.

STEWED TOMATOES AND ZUCCHINI (SOUP BASE)

Courtesy Carolee Noss[45]

1 bucket tomatoes
2/3 stalk celery
4 large onions
4–5 large green peppers
5 small peeled zucchini
1 head cauliflower (optional)
Salt
Pepper
Onion salt

Blanch and peel tomatoes. Chop celery and onions. Cut peppers, zucchini, and cauliflower into small pieces. Put all ingredients in large kettle. Season to taste. Cook covered for 1 to 1 1/2 hours. Bottle and pressure for 35 minutes. Or, cook 2 hours in open kettle and cold pack for 55 minutes.

of Congo, and Sudan. Plants grown along sidewalks and berms as part of the program revive city beautification strategies advocated a century earlier.[46]

In 1978, Francaviglia observed that even as some gardens in his survey of small-town Utah had fallen on hard times, gardens and gardening were still an important focus of conversation and cultural instruction; the mere fact that garden plots were located so close to homes indicated some measure of their social importance.[47] Of course, gardening can produce fresh, healthy, life-sustaining food. But in addition to this critical role, gardens act as "moral proofs": they illustrate intangible ideas about cause and effect, effort and hope, harmony and respect, and production and consumption, and thus they feature prominently in culture-specific articulations of these concepts. Gardens also stimulate the senses, acting as sites of memory, beauty, belonging, and celebration. At the same time, clashing definitions about what "counts" as plant cultivation and struggles to control the resources that make gardening's physical and social benefits possible have resulted in displacement and destruction alongside bounty and growth.

NOTES

1. "Jeremiah Woodbury," *Deseret News* (Salt Lake City), May 17, 1851.
2. Leonard J. Arrington and Dean May, "'A Different Mode of Life': Irrigation and Society in Nineteenth-Century Utah," *Agricultural History* 49, no. 1 (1975): 3–20.
3. "Garden Seeds for Sale," *Deseret News* (Salt Lake City, UT), February 5, 1853.
4. Porter-Walton Co. advertised regularly in *Relief Society Magazine*.
5. Mable Smyth Christensen, "Sandwich Spread," *Smyth Family Recipes* (Richfield, UT, 1983), 6. Typescript

in possession of author. One cookbook compiled by an LDS congregation in the late 1970s suggests that cucumbers and summer squash yielded prodigious harvests: The spiral-bound book includes recipes for pickle relish, mustard pickles, kosher dill pickles, three recipes for bread-and-butter pickles, sweet pickles, sweet zucchini pickles, dill zucchini, sweet and sour zucchini, zucchini relish, stuffed zucchini, Zucchini-Cheese Delight, six versions of zucchini casserole, and three recipes for zucchini bread, as well as zucchini cake and zucchini cookies; *Happiness Is Homemade: Jordan North Ninth Ward Relief Society Cookbook*, ed. Salt Lake Granger South Stake, Granger, UT (Kansas City, KS: Cookbook Publishers, 1977). Copy in possession of author.

6. Brigham Young, "The Power and Importance of Economy—Domestic Extravagance and Mismanagement, with Their Bad Results" (April 6, 1857), in *Journal of Discourses* 4 (Liverpool: S. W. Richards, 1857), 312–20, quotes on 315, 319.

7. Jill Mulvay Derr, "'I Have Eaten Nearly Everything Imaginable': Pioneer Diet," in *Nearly Everything Imaginable: The Everyday Life of Utah's Mormon Pioneers*, ed. Ronald W. Walker and Doris R. Dant (Provo, UT: Brigham Young University Press, 1999), 222–48, quote on 235–36; see also Brock Cheney, *Plain but Wholesome: Foodways of the Mormon Pioneers* (Salt Lake City: University of Utah Press, 2012).

8. Mary Ann Stucki Hafen, *Recollections of a Handcart Pioneer of 1860: A Woman's Life on the Mormon Frontier* (Denver, 1938; reprint, Lincoln: University of Nebraska Press, 1983), 44–45, 50. The trees supplemented garden produce grown from seeds her mother had brought from Switzerland. Like many others in southern Utah, the Stuckis and Hafens sold dried peaches to breweries and mining camps up north.

9. Richard H. Jackson, "Religion and Landscape in the Mormon Cultural Region," in *Dimensions of Human Geography: Essays on Some Familiar and Neglected Themes*, ed. Karl W. Butzer (Chicago: University of Chicago Department of Geography, 1978), 100–27, quote on 107; see also Richard V. Francaviglia, *The Mormon Landscape: Existence, Creation, and Perception of a Unique Image in the American West* (New York:

AMS Press, 1978), and Lowry Nelson, *The Mormon Village: A Pattern and Technique of Land Settlement* (Salt Lake City: University of Utah Press, 1952). The layout of Iosepa, the Polynesian colony established in Skull Valley between 1889 and 1917, also followed this pattern; see Sarah Miley, "Remembering Iosepa," *Honolulu Magazine*, October 21, 2008; and Tracey E. Panek, "Life at Iosepa, Utah's Polynesian Colony," *Utah Historical Quarterly* 60 (1992).

10. Edna Eliza Porter Little, *My Life Story: Edna Eliza Porter Little, May 29, 1908–May 31, 2000*, typescript, ed. Douglas R. Little (Ivins, UT, c. 2008); copy in possession of author. Little remembered two types of apricots: "one for bottling and a Chinese brand, which were quite small and a dark orange and made very good jam. The stones in the Chinese were sweet. We would spread them out to dry, then crack them to go in the jam, and also use them in place of store-bought nuts," 14.

11. Little, *My Life Story*, 11.

12. Douglas R. Hurt, *Indian Agriculture in America: Prehistory to the Present* (Lawrence: University Press of Kansas, 1987).

13. Derr, "Pioneer Diet," 224, 235–36. See also excerpts from Emily Stewart (b. 1846, Bedfordshire, England) Barnes's biography, in Kate B. Carter, *Pioneer Recipes: Lesson for May, 1950* ([Salt Lake City, Utah]: Daughters of Utah Pioneers, Central Company, 1950), 330–35. A jar of "Melon Prepared" was collected in 1873 from Paiute cooks by John Wesley Powell and is archived at the National Museum of Natural History (Ethnology Division, no. E14787-0).

14. *Deseret News* (Salt Lake City, UT), May 31, 1851.

15. [Emmeline B. Wells?], "The Home of Childhood," *Woman's Exponent*, May 1, 1889; Wells's poem "The Dear Old Garden" extols the social and personal significance of spaces beautified by apple trees, hollyhocks, and honeysuckle (*Woman's Exponent*, June 1, 1889).

16. Flora, "Floral Hints," *The Woman's Exponent*, June 1, 1874.

17. Young, "The Power and Importance of Economy," 1857, 317.

18. *Utah: A Guide to the State* (Washington, DC: Federal Writers' Project, Work Projects Administration,

1941), 99; Don Strack, "Utah's Canning Industry," *Utah History Encyclopedia* (Salt Lake City: University of Utah Press, 1994), online at http://utahrails.net/industries/canning.php.

19. Orson Pratt, *Journal of Discourses* 21 (September 7, 1879), 135. Such a stance aligns with the broader Jeffersonian ideal sometimes called "American agrarianism": the belief that small-time, self-sufficient, and socially integrated farmers form the bedrock of a morally sound democracy; Michael Hardt, "Jefferson and Democracy," *American Quarterly* 59, no. 1 (2007), 41–78; Jackson, *Religion and Landscape*.

20. Spencer W. Kimball, "Family Preparedness," *Ensign* (May 1976), 124, and "Welfare Services: The Gospel in Action," *Ensign* (November 1977), 78.

21. For example, Perceny D. Greaves, "What Is to Be Gained from the Home Garden," *Relief Society Magazine* (April 1915), 175–78; Ezra Taft Benson Agriculture and Food Institute, *Home Production and Storage: A Study of Church Doctrine and Policy* (Salt Lake City, UT: Church of Jesus Christ of Latter-day Saints, 1976), 68–69, available in L. Tom Perry Special Collections, Lee Library, Brigham Young University, Provo, UT.

22. "Wildflowers and Native Plants," *Woman's Exponent*, February 1, 1875, reprinted from *Utah Pomologist*. Some of these native plants were also edible.

23. Cf. Jackson, *Religion and Landscape*, 126.

24. A. W. C., "The Old Home," *Woman's Exponent*, April 15, 1888.

25. Alice Morrey Bailey, "Frontier Garden," *Relief Society Magazine* (July 1960), 444.

26. Philip F. Notarianni Jr., preface to "Book 5: Italian Community," in *Missing Stories: An Oral History of Ethnic and Minority Groups in Utah*, ed. Leslie G. Kelen and Eileen Hallet Stone (Salt Lake City: University of Utah Press, 1996), 248–54, quote on 250, and "Italianita in Utah: The Immigrant Experience," in *The Peoples of Utah*, ed. Helen Z. Papanikolas (Salt Lake City: Utah State Historical Society, 1976), 303–31; "Mary Ravarino," in Kelen and Stone, 295–301. The book *Old Ties, New Attachments: Italian-American Folklife in the West* (ed. David Alan Taylor and John Alexander Williams, 1992) summarizes much of the ethnographic

data collected between 1989 and 1991 during the American Folklife Center's Italian Americans in the West project (AFC 1989/022). In it, three essays address Italian American gardens in Utah: Notarianni, "Places of Origin: Calabresi in Carbon Co., Utah" (68–79); Steve Siporin, "Folklife and Survival: The Italian Americans of Carbon County, Utah" (80–93); and Thomas Carter, "The Architecture of Immigration: Documenting Italian-American Vernacular Buildings in Utah and Nevada" (94–111).

27. Jane Dusselier, "Does Food Make Place? Food Protests in Japanese American Concentration Camps," *Food and Foodways* 10, no. 3 (2002), 137–65; Topaz Museum Foundation, http://www.topazmuseum.org/; Leonard J. Arrington, *The Price of Prejudice: The Japanese-American Relocation Center in Utah during World War II* (Delta, UT: Topaz Museum, [1962] 1997), http://digital.lib.usu.edu/cdm/compoundobject/collection/Topaz/id/8175/rec/3; Sandra C. Taylor, *Jewel of the Desert: Japanese American Internment at Topaz* (Berkeley: University of California Press, 1993), plate 4.

28. Arrington, *The Price of Prejudice*; Dusselier, *Does Food Make Place?*; Taylor, *Jewel of the Desert*; Yoshiko Uchida, "Topaz: City of Dust," *Utah Historical Quarterly* 38 (Summer 1980), 234–43, quote on 235–36; "Little Citizens Speak: 7th Graders of '43," *All Aboard* (Spring 1944), 31, Topaz Japanese-American Relocation Center Digital Collection, Utah State University Library.

29. Arrington, *The Price of Prejudice*, 38.

30. Floyd A. O'Neil, "The Utes, Southern Paiutes, and Gosiutes," in Papanikolas, *The Peoples of Utah*, 27–59. In the early 1870s, government researchers reported that Indians in the area acknowledged that they could "no longer live by hunting, fishing, and gathering the native products of the soil," given that "their hunting grounds are spoiled, [and] their favorite valleys are occupied by white men." The agents recommended removal to reservations as the best solution. G. W. Ingalls and John Wesley Powell, *Report of Special Commissioners J. W. Powell and G. W. Ingalls on the Condition of the Ute Indians of Utah; the Pai-Utes of Utah, Northern Arizona, Southern Nevada, and Southeastern California; the Go-Si Utes of Utah and*

Nevada; the Northwestern Shoshones of Idaho and Utah; and the Western Shoshones of Nevada (Washington, DC: Government Printing Office, 1873), 2–3.

31. Beverly Beeton, "Teach Them to Till the Soil: An Experiment with Indian Farms 1850–1862," *American Indian Quarterly* 3, no. 4 (1977): 299–320, quotes on 301, 305. Young echoed longstanding American sentiments and policies. For example, treaties with the Creek and Cherokee in 1790 and 1791 incorporated clauses for agricultural aid and instruction, and in 1796 Quaker missionaries began trying to convince Six Nations men to take up the plow; Thomas Jefferson was also an ardent supporter of Indian Farms (Hurt, *Indian Agriculture in America*, 96–100). On agrarian idealism and U.S. Indian policy, see also David Rich Lewis, *Neither Wolf nor Dog: American Indians, Environment, and Agrarian Change* (New York: Oxford University Press, 1994).

32. Beeton, "Teach Them to Till"; Lewis, *Neither Wolf nor Dog*. In his June 1873 report to the Commissioner of Indian Affairs in Washington, John Wesley Powell commended Kanosh, chief of the Pahvant Utes and an "Indian of great ability and wisdom," for "doing all he can to induce his people to cultivate the soil" near Corn Creek (Ingalls and Powell, *Report of Special Commissioners*, 1).

33. Mae Parry, "The Northwestern Shoshone," *Utah History to Go* (Salt Lake City: State of Utah, [c. 1999] 2014), http://historytogo.utah.gov/people/ethnic_cultures/the_history_of_utahs_american_indians/chapter2.html; Lewis, *Neither Wolf nor Dog*, 1994, 65.

34. Matia McClelland Burk, "Deserted Garden," *Relief Society Magazine* (May 1954), 297; the rock gardens of Topaz are similar relics on the Utah landscape.

35. Jackson, *Religion and Landscape*, 108; Francaviglia, *The Mormon Landscape*, 28. Despite public pronouncements of Utah's beauty, the state suffered from rubbish and bare dirt earlier in the century as well; in 1915, Hazel Love Dunford decried lack of lawns at church buildings, animals that wandered the streets, and broken vehicles in barnyards; see "Civic Beauty," *Relief Society Magazine* (April 1915): 169–71.

36. [Wells?], "The Home of Childhood."

37. Barbara Dowdle, "Our Garden," *Relief Society Magazine* (August 1967), 580–82, quote on 582.

38. *Wasatch Community Gardens*, accessed May 29, 2014, http://wasatchgardens.org/.

39. For example, Allie Schulte, "Seeds of Self-Reliance," *Ensign* (March 2011).

40. National Gardening Association, *Garden to Table: A 5-Year Look at Food Gardening in America* (South Burlington, VT: National Gardening Association, 2014), available at www.garden.org. This increased interest in home-grown food continued in subsequent years, with six million new American gardeners in 2016 (more than 80 percent of them millennials); George Weigel, "More Herbs, More Indoors: Millennials Shape Gardening Trends for 2017," *PennLive.Com*, December 30, 2016.

41. See, for example, reports made available through the Utah State University Cooperative Extension: Kynda R. Curtis and Jean Dominique Gumirakiza, "Consumer Motivations for Attending Utah Farmers' Markets" (PDF, Finance and Economics: Utah State University, March 2013), and Jean Dominique Gumirakiza and Kynda R. Curtis, "Exploring Consumer Spending at Farmers' Markets: Who Spends More?" (PDF, Finance and Economics: Utah State University, April 2013).

42. Caleb Warnock, *The Forgotten Skills of Self-Sufficiency Used by the Mormon Pioneers* (Springville, UT: Bonneville Books, 2011); and "Good News! My Book Goes into Third Printing," Backyard Renaissance with Caleb Warnock, October 2011, http://calebwarnock.blogspot.com/2011/10/good-news-my-book-goes-into-third.html.

43. Betsy Chapoose et al., "Planting a Seed: Ute Ethnobotany, A Collaborative Approach in Applied Anthropology," *Applied Anthropologist* 32, no. 1 (2012): 2–11, online at http://www.hpsfaa.org/page-1488664; Raleigh Burleigh, "BLM Recognizes Ute Learning Garden for Education and Outreach," KOTO-FM Community Radio, June 19, 2018, https://www.koto.org/koto-news/2018/6/19/blm-recognizes-ute-learning-garden-for-education-and-outreach; Ute Tribe Education Department and Ute Tribe Cultural Rights Protection Department, "Ute Learning Garden Project," Ute Tribe Education

Department, accessed April 28, 2014, http://www. uteed.net/ulg.htm.

44. Christensen, *Smyth Family Recipes*, 20–21.

45. *Happiness Is Homemade: Jordan North Ninth Ward Relief Society Cookbook*, ed. Salt Lake Granger South Stake, Granger, UT (Kansas City, KS: Cookbook Publishers, 1977), 21.

46. Peter Rosen, "West Valley Farm Giving Refugees a Way to Put down New Roots," KSL.com, July 24,

2012. International Rescue Committee, "New Roots: The Food Is Local, the Story Is Global," International Rescue Committee, accessed May 29, 2014, http://www.rescue.org/us-program/us-salt-lake-city-ut/newroots- food-local-story-global-0; cf. Janette A. Hyde, "Conservation and City War Gardens," *Relief Society Magazine* (October 1917), 572–75.

47. Francaviglia, *The Mormon Landscape*.

37

ETHNIC FESTIVALS

Food and Ethnic Identity in Utah

CAROL A. EDISON

Utah's ethnic populations may be small in comparison to many states, but their impact and contributions to the cultural climate—and especially to food heritage—are great.

Gatherings within ethnic communities have taken place in Utah since there were enough people of the same national origin to get together. Some events began as a way to commemorate a national holiday or re-create a traditional celebration from the old country. Some were tied to the religious calendar. Others were designed as family picnics or adult dinner-dances. All of these gatherings provided an opportunity for friends and family with old-world ties to leave their individual lives of hard work and come together as a group. Whatever the motivation to gather, there was always food—recipes from the old country, ingredients not always found in the local grocery store, and dishes prepared in special ways that reminded everyone of their family and heritage.

INSIDER EVENTS

Many ethnic celebrations in Utah have been going on for years but are not widely known within the general population. They are generally sponsored by churches or national or ethnic clubs and associations. While they often welcome visitors, most are not widely advertised because their primary purpose is to bring people together to celebrate a shared heritage.

The Basque Club of Utah, reestablished in the early 1970s by families whose progenitors came here decades earlier to herd sheep, always serves Basque specialties like leek soup and chicken spiced with peppers and chorizo each winter at their annual dinner-dance. At the same time of year, the Utah Scottish Association holds three Robert Burns suppers in Provo, Ogden, and Salt Lake City, featuring a traditional menu that even includes haggis![1] Hand-crafted klobase,

Fleeing oppression after the communist takeover of Vietnam, a community of Hmong refugees established themselves in Utah. In 1984 they held a festival in Ogden where they celebrated their new home by sharing traditional music, dance, and food. Photo by Carol Edison. Courtesy Utah Folklife Archives.

cabbage rolls, and strudels are still a mainstay of the Slovenian Picnic in Price, which began in 1981 and draws a crowd from three local chapters of the Slovene National Benefit Society. And for over eight decades, since 1934, the Italian American Civic League has hosted a picnic at the All-Italian Day at Lagoon that features not only a bocce ball competition but also a pasta-eating contest.

It might also surprise many Utahns to know that Utah Swedes get together in local parks to celebrate traditional Swedish holidays that mark the summer season—the Midsummer Solstice and a traditional crawfish party at the end of the summer. Bonfires, group singing, dancing around maypoles, and tables laden with traditional Swedish food are all part of the fun.

CELEBRATIONS OF HISTORICAL AND CONTEMPORARY ETHNICITY

On the other end of the spectrum are several well-known and publicly advertised ethnic festivals that actually have more to do with local history than the makeup of contemporary communities. Swiss Days in Midway, Swiss Days in Santa Clara, and Scandinavian Days in Ephraim honor the ethnicity of their respective towns' original settlers in spite of the fact that those ethnic traditions are more historical than contemporary. They put on what is, in reality, a town homecoming celebration with costuming, performance, displays, and food, re-creating the ethnic heritage of which they are so proud.

There are also Utahns for whom ethnic heritage plays a vital role in everyday life. Over time, some of their get-togethers have grown beyond their own community into larger, annual events designed with the express purpose of sharing ethnic culture, traditions, and cuisine with the general public. Like rural festivals that celebrate traditional crops and livelihood, they have become grander, sometimes multiple-day celebrations that draw thousands of visitors. And, more often than not, traditional food is one of the major attractions.

In the 1920s and 1930s, respectively, the Japanese Buddhist churches in Ogden and Salt Lake City invited the larger community to join them in celebrating Obon, a traditional religious holiday that

Many ethnic festivals began as small in-community gatherings or picnics like this Japanese Church of Christ picnic at Lagoon Amusement Park in 1921. Peoples of Utah Collection. Used by permission, Utah State Historical Society. All rights reserved.

honors those who have passed away. Today those celebrations feature beautiful dancing by Japanese community members and their guests, performances of taiko drumming, and an array of foods that are traditional to the holiday. And just like the Scottish Festivals held each year in Lehi and Payson, a number of Native American powwows throughout the state, a cluster of St. Patrick's Day events, the annual Asian Pacific Festival, and the relatively new Brazilian Festival, the events typically draw large crowds. Their success is due, in part, to the fact that they offer tastes of ethnic fare perpetuated within ethnic families and communities—tastes that are not always available to the wider public.

BUILDING BRIDGES WITH FOOD

Utah's premier ethnic festival, especially when one thinks about food, is the Greek Festival held each September in downtown Salt Lake City. Ogden hosts an older Greek Festival, started in 1964; a smaller event, dating from 1987, also continues in Price. But the Salt Lake festival, known at one time as the "largest Greek Festival west of the Mississippi,"[2] is undoubtedly Utah's largest and most popular annual ethnic event.

The festival's origins are tied to a 1935, one-day "mother's" bazaar that gradually drew more and more interest from outside the Greek community until, in

211

For many years master cook Ellen Furgis was an integral part of the Greek community's year-round preparation of food for the annual Greek Festival. She also wrote a Greek–American cookbook and in 1990 was awarded the Governor's Service to Folk Arts Award. Photo by David Stanley. Courtesy Utah Folklife Archives.

In 1986 the Salt Lake City Arts Council and the Folk Arts Program of the Utah Arts Council joined together to produce Living Traditions: A Celebration of Salt Lake's Folk & Ethnic Arts. Every year since, this festival has provided an opportunity for a variety of ethnic communities to share their traditional cuisine with the public while raising money for their ongoing arts programs. Seen here is the 2016 Basque Club of Utah booth. Photo by David Vogel. Courtesy Salt Lake City Arts Council.

1976, the women's organization joined with the parish council to produce a three-day event.[3] The festival is held the first weekend of September on the campus of the Holy Trinity Cathedral in the middle of Salt Lake's legendary Greek Town, the section of downtown Salt Lake that, during the first few decades of the twentieth century, looked like a Greek village with outdoor bake ovens, large vegetable gardens, coffeehouses, ice cream parlors, and hotels. Today the festival draws tens of thousands of visitors who enjoy performances of choreographed folk dance by community members of all ages, several church choirs, tours of the cathedral

ETHNIC FESTIVALS IN 2018

All events are still taking place and the public is invited.

Date	Name	Location	Began	Organization	Contact information
January–February	Robert Burns Suppers (first in SLC, then Provo, then Ogden)	SLC	1974	Utah Scottish Association	http://www.utahscots.org/
February	Basque Dinner-Dance	SLC	1974	Utah Basque Club	http://www.utah-basque.com/
April	Nihoni Matsuri Japan Festival	SLC	2007	Coalition of Japanese churches and community groups	http://www.nihonmatsuri.com/
May	Living Traditions Festival	SLC	1986	Salt Lake City Arts Council	http://livingtraditionsfestival.com/
May	Scandinavian Heritage Festival (originally Scandinavian Jubilee)	Ephraim	1976	City of Ephraim and Snow College	http://www.scandinavianfestival.org/
June	Swedish Midsummer Celebration	SLC	1963	Swedish Heritage Society of Utah	http://www.swedishheritagesociety.com/
June	Utah Asian Festival	SLC	1977	Coalition of Asian community groups	http://www.utahasianfestival.com/index.html
June	Utah Scottish Association Festival and Highland Games	Lehi	1974	Utah Scottish Association	http://www.utahscots.org/games/
July	Greek Festival	Price	1977	Greek Orthodox Church	http://www.castlecountry.com/Greek_Festival_Days
July	Payson Scottish Festival	Payson	1984	City of Payson	http://www.paysonscottishfestival.org/
July	Japanese Obon Festival	SLC	c. 1930	Salt Lake Buddhist Temple	http://www.slbuddhist.org/calendar.html
July	Japanese Obon Festival	Ogden	c. 1930	Ogden Buddhist Church	http://ogdenbuddhistchurch.org/obon.html
August	Slovenian Day Picnic Lodges	Price	1982	Lodges 113, 689, and 757 of the Slovene National Benefit Society	http://www.snpj.org/
August	Midway Swiss Days	Midway	1947	Midway Boosters	https://midwayswissdays.com/
September	Greek Festival	SLC	1975	Greek Orthodox Church of Greater Salt Lake	http://www.saltlakegreekfestival.com/
September	Festa Italiana (originally Ferragosto Italian Cultural Street Fair)	SLC	2003	Italian–American Civic League	https://www.festaitalianaslc.com/
September	Swiss Days	Santa Clara	1990	City of Santa Clara	https://sccity.org/swiss-days/
September	Greek Festival	Ogden	1964	Transfiguration Greek Orthodox Church	http://www.tgoc.ut.goarch.org/festival.html

DOLMATHES

STUFFED GRAPE LEAVES
Courtesy of the Salt Lake Greek Festival Website

2 large onions, chopped
1 c. green onions, thinly sliced
3/4 c. fresh parsley, minced
3/4 c. fresh dill, chopped
2 c. rice (short-grain rice is recommended, but long-grain may be used)
1/2 c. lemon juice
3/4 c. extra virgin olive oil
Salt and pepper to taste (salt may be omitted or reduced because the grape leaves are salty)

Broth
1 can vegetable broth, 15 oz.
1 can water
1/4 to 1/2 c. lemon juice

Sauté onions until tender, about 5 minutes. Add rice and sauté for approximately 2 minutes, stirring continuously. Remove from stove and add remaining ingredients.

Rinse, drain, and separate grape leaves. Prepare the dolmathes by placing a spoonful of the mixture in the center of each grape leaf. Fold over, fold in sides, and roll up. Cover the bottom of a large saucepan with leaves. Pack the dolmathes closely together to prevent unraveling during cooking.

Combine vegetable broth, lemon, and water. Pour this mixture over the rolled leaves. Add additional water to just cover the dolmathes. Place an inverted plate directly over the top to weigh down the packed rolls. Bring to a boil, reduce heat and simmer 1 hour or until done. Let cool. Garnish with lemon and lemon juice.

These are delicious as *mezedes* (appetizers).

and museum, a midway with rides for kids, cooking demonstrations, and plenty of food!

Preparations for the festival begin at least four months in advance as parishioners work shifts at the cathedral's industrial-style kitchen making and freezing foods like spanakopita and baklava. When visitors arrive, they wind their way through the enormous church activity hall past lambs cooking on spits to a cafeteria-style setup and face the challenge of choosing from among the meatballs, lemon soup, salad with feta cheese, lemon rice, souvlakia, green beans, cheese triangles, lamb, calamari, gyros, stuffed grape leaves, and every other Greek treat to be imagined. Then, after eating more than one can comfortably hold, there's always a visit to the bakery where a festival-goer can choose from a dozen different kinds of pastries to take home. The volume of delicious food prepared and consumed is hard to imagine. To provide a sense of it, here are the numbers from 2014, the thirty-ninth annual event: The community made "25,000 dolmathes (stuffed grape leaves), 10,000 pieces of baklava, 14,500 pieces of spanakopita (spinach pie), 11,540 meatballs, and 2,700 almond cookies."[4]

Each year, after nearly a hundred committee chairpeople and five hundred volunteers donate well over ten thousand hours of preparation before the event even begins, they share the financial proceeds of their hard work with the larger community. Besides funding scholarships and educational programs for the Greek community, festival proceeds are also donated to a long list of nonprofit organizations that serve the medical and educational needs of local elderly, troubled youth, and homeless populations. In return, the Greek community has the pleasure of sharing their revered ethnic heritage and their amazing food traditions with a general public that "has become aware of our religion, culture and heritage."[5]

ETHNIC FOOD IS IN!

In Utah today, there are opportunities to enjoy someone else's traditional cuisine on nearly every urban street corner. The growth in the diversity, number, and popularity of ethnic restaurants is mindboggling and for many it has become as commonplace to enjoy Japanese sushi, Indian naan, or Thai curry as it is to eat a hamburger. Many eager diners had some of their first experiences with ethnic foods at these festivals. Utah's ethnic communities have certainly learned that sitting down and eating a meal together opens an important door to interacting with others on common ground. They know that sharing their "exotic" food is a wonderful way to build bridges between people of differing backgrounds—bridges that often begin with simple appreciation but end with

increased respect. One can only guess that as time goes by Utahns will have more and more opportunities to become friends with a wider group of people and that ethnic festivals and their food offerings will help make this happen.

NOTES

1. Though sheep products needed for haggis are banned in the United States, the Utah Scottish Association modifies the traditional recipe using venison products. Leslie Dorius, in discussion with the author, August 9, 2019.
2. 2000 Festival Brochure in the author's possession.
3. "History," Salt Lake City Greek Festival, accessed 10/19/2016, http://www.saltlakegreekfestival.com/history.php.
4. Paul Rolly, "A Big Fat Greek Festival," *Salt Lake Tribune*, September 5, 2014.
5. "The community has received great exposure—the general public has become aware of our religion, culture, and heritage." https://saltlakegreekfestival.com/?page_id=61.

PART III LATTER-DAY SAINT INFLUENCE

38

LATTER-DAY SAINT INFLUENCE

ERIC A. ELIASON

This book's "Icons" section introduction noted how some foods are emerging as state identity touchstones that transcend religious boundaries and unite Utahns of all stripes. This section, on the other hand, fully embraces the considerable influence the LDS religion has had on the way people eat in Utah. This affects not only active Mormons, but "gentiles" and "jack-Mormons" as well. Food traditions often persist with those for whom the torch of faith has gone out or has transformed, or whose ancestors did not pass it on.

Those outside Utah's predominant religion are sometimes irked by "the Mormon Church's" role in inconveniencing their alcohol consumption, but are delighted by the plate of cookies or the casserole they are personally gifted when grieving thanks to the Mormon culture of giving food as compassionate service. Of course, many neighborhoods, regardless of any religious influence, have a culture of bringing food as a service to their neighbors. And many cultures, like the Mormon culture, sometimes think that their special customary ways are unique when they are really not so much. Even so, in Utah, perhaps more often than not, it is the Mormon cultural context through which many such food experiences come. Ronda Weaver gives us a glimpse into the LDS ideology of service, complete with scripture references and quotes

A number of small publications featuring Mormon pioneer and/or contemporary Mormon cuisine have been produced for tourists. Most contain a few recipes for Lumpy Dick, flapjacks, or other foods imagined to provide sustenance along the pioneer trail with a smattering of contemporary recipes for homestyle comfort foods. None has yet captured the range of both everyday American foods and more distinctive regional foods that are actually enjoyed by members of the Church of Jesus Christ of Latter-day Saints in Utah. Photo by Katherine Neish.

Locally produced hot chocolate, in a variety of gourmet flavors, satisfies Utah's sweet tooth. Photo by Carol A. Edison, 2018.

from LDS General Authorities. She does so in a personal manner from the point of view of a seasoned insider participant.

Carol Edison provides a thick description of the traditional Utah Mormon Sunday dinner—often a family affair, in a very family-oriented faith. Often, in Mormon discourse, family means nuclear family; for Sunday dinner it can mean extended family. In the United States, people move to a new place away from relatives more often than they do in Europe. The American West displays this tendency even more dramatically—except for Utah, where people have traditionally been more likely to live close to relatives and the place of their birth. (One ancestral migration was enough, thank you.) In preparing a meal for a large family, each member might have specific likes and dislikes. Busy days make long hours of complex preparation with ingredients that are hard to procure

and store a nonstarter. To the rescue comes a meal option from Mormonism's early missionary efforts in the South Pacific. These endeavors not only paid off in converts and pineapple plantations, but in a convenient yet oddly named Western Mormon food icon, the Hawaiian Haystack. Perhaps this name is not so strange when one considers that Utah's state bird is the California gull and the state tree was long the Colorado blue spruce until recently replaced with the quaking aspen.

Canning apricots and other fruits and vegetables has traditionally been a central feature of Mormon "preparedness" and "provident living" culture. Growing, storing, and knowing how to prepare food in case of events ranging from a personal financial setback to a worldwide apocalypse has long been part of Mormon religiosity. As concern about such possibilities has become a nationwide phenomenon in the growing "prepper" subculture, Mormons' many decades of experience have positioned them well to provide expertise and products. Randy Williams looks at the famous Mormon food-storage phenomenon. In another section of the book, Danille Christensen examines preparedness from a home-gardening perspective.

Often religions are defined by what they don't consume rather than what they do. Hindus? No meat. Jews and Muslims?

No pork. Mormons? No alcohol, coffee, or tea. Such obstructions do not necessarily lead to less emphasis on food. In fact, they might lead to compensating creativity. Many conversions to Hare Krishna began with attendance at one of the lavish and deliciously spiced free meals society members regularly provide. Normally voluminous pork-eating Southern Evangelical pilgrims often return from Jerusalem with tales of mouthwatering lamb dishes provided by competing Jewish and Arab street vendors. No coffee? How about Postum? A Utah-made, grain-based coffee substitute with even more bracing bitterness but none of the caffeine of coffee. No beer? How about Apple Beer? A frothy nonalcoholic brew concocted by a returned LDS missionary who served in Germany. Substitutions are not always so direct and obvious. Is it surprising that Utah towns seem to have a smoothie shop on the very corners other cities might have a Starbucks? Or that ice cream consumption, variety, and ritualization are

Hot chocolate with marshmallows souvenir pin, 2002 Salt Lake Winter Olympics. Used by permission, Utah State Historical Society. All rights reserved.

well developed in Utah? Or that many nationally recognized candy manufacturers are based here? Much of this might have happened anyway, but certainly some of it can be traced to the Mormon influence in Utah.

Beyond just Postum and Apple Beer, other national products seem to be based in Utah not just by chance but because of LDS influence. Consider Lehi Roller Mills, which makes prepackaged mixes of home-baked food for busy households, as well as Stephen's Gourmet Hot Chocolate, which makes a sweet substitute for other hot beverages. Food storage companies are especially plentiful: Family Storehouse in American Fork; Deseret Food Store in Kaysville; Honeyville in Brigham City; LindonFarms in Lindon; MyFoodStorage in Spanish Fork; LegacyFood in Layton; and Wise Company, Legacy Premium Emergency Food Storage, and Live Prepared in Salt Lake City.[1]

NOTE

1. Grant Olson, "Food Storage Taste Test: 9 Companies, Reviewed," KSL-TV, March 10, 2015, http://www.ksl.com/?nid=1010&sid=33767179.

39

MORMON FOOD STORAGE

A Performance of Worldview

RANDY WILLIAMS

As a child, the chore of retrieving bottled food—fruit, jam, pickles, chili sauce, beets, grape juice—from my grandparents' spider-filled cellar often fell to me.[1] This food represented my family's hard work and deep-seated beliefs in provident living. Early on, I was taught the skills that helped produce the carefully stored food: planting and weeding the garden, harvesting the produce, sterilizing canning jars, chopping ingredients, stirring boiling pots, and filling and topping off jars with new lids and old rings. For my Latter-day Saint family and others like ours, home food production, preservation, and use are not only a temporal way of life, but also a manifestation of religious beliefs.

Foodways are a conduit of culture used to teach and perpetuate group identity and values.[2] Ripe with semiotic meaning and functions, foodways are often used to express a group's collectively held beliefs (think eggs used for Christian Easter celebrations, roasted lamb shank bone during the Jewish Passover Seder, or dates to break fasting during the Muslim commemoration of Ramadan). Because folk ideas reflect a group's "traditional notions" about their place in the world, folk ideas contain their "underlying assumptions" and serve as the "building blocks" used to construct the group's worldview.[3]

For many members of the Church of Jesus Christ of Latter-day Saints, the belief in and practice of food storage conceptualizes their millennial worldview. In preparation for Christ's second coming at the onset of the millennium, church members are taught that they are "to prepare a people for the second coming of the Son of Man...[to] lay the foundations of Zion" as a means of preparing the world for this experience.[4] Prior to these events, Latter-day Saints believe the world will experience signs heralding Christ's second coming, including "wars and rumors of wars," earthquakes, famine and pestilence, and sickness, with the "whole earth in commotion."[5]

Display of canned foods including chicken breasts, green beans, pickles, and a variety of fruit jam at the Southern Utah Folklife Festival, 1989. Photo by David Stanley. Courtesy Utah Folklife Archives.

The preparation of Zion for this auspicious event is both spiritual and temporal, and the earthly directive to store food in preparation for this and other times of need has long been a part of Latter-day Saint teachings.

Under the direction of President Heber J. Grant, the church's First Presidency inaugurated the church security plan in 1936, the forerunner of the modern-day Church Welfare Program.[6] At the April 1937 General Conference, members were counseled that "every head of every household [should have] . . . on hand enough food and clothing, and, where possible, fuel also, for at least a year ahead."[7] The Great Depression influenced this push for preparedness. This counsel was a continuation of early church teachings.[8] Church founder Joseph Smith Jr. believed

the Church of Jesus Christ of Latter-day Saints to be the vehicle that would prepare the world for Christ's second coming, an act of divine intervention that could not occur until the saints established "moral, social and political conditions congenial with the presence of a divine ruler on earth."[9] These conditions include that members become independent and self-reliant.[10]

Isolationism also factors into church members' long history with preparedness. After Smith's murder in Illinois at the hands of local militia members, President Brigham Young directed the saints west to what would become the Utah Territory, where they could live in relative isolation to practice their religion and politics. There they "established a virtual Mormon kingdom . . . [a] unique, cohesive, economically self-sufficient, and thriving society."[11] Brigham Young preached self-reliance, urging the faithful to be self-sustaining, noting, "This is what the Lord requires of this people."[12] Following Young's admonition, Latter-day Saints worked feverishly to build Zion in the Intermountain West.[13]

Like other Euro-American settlers, Latter-day Saint pioneers believed they were destined to succeed. Embracing the Christian ethos of dominion, most worked doggedly to make the West, their Deseret, blossom like the proverbial rose.[14] Evidence of their zeal is demonstrated in the unique Latter-day Saint settlement patterns and in their attempts to live a United Order, a Christian communal and collectivist economic system. Today, indicators of this worldview are seen in church members' irrigation systems scattered throughout Utah and the West, church welfare farms, church-owned canneries, Welfare Square in Salt Lake City, Deseret Industries (employment training center and thrift store), and the worldwide humanitarian program of the church, all of which affirm and reinforce Latter-day Saint ingenuity, self-reliance, and charity. The beehive, the Utah state symbol and motif used in church buildings, publications, and in a youth organization and jewelry, is a reminder of this ingenuity.

Endeavors such as these, refashioned from time to time, have been consistent and ongoing. Food storage, explained Steven Peterson, managing director of the Church Welfare Services, "is a skill passed down from . . . pioneer ancestors. . . . From the moment the pioneers started their westward trek," he recently told a group of food journalists, "growing and storing food was critical."[15] As in Heber J. Grant's day, the mid-1910s to mid-1940s, contemporary church members are admonished to store food where permissible by law.[16] Today the church recommends storing a three-month supply (and some do), but many of the reasons to store food are the same as in past times.[17] "Self-reliance is a product of our work and undergirds all other welfare practices," imparts the late church president Thomas S. Monson. "It is an essential element in our spiritual as well as our temporal well-being."[18] Concepts of provident living, such as food storage; being good stewards of resources (land, animals, skills); being prepared in the cases of temporal emergencies like loss of job, economic downturns, and crop failures; and today, perhaps even cyberattacks, are all related to the faith's millennial beliefs, which, as a folk idea, permeate all areas of Latter-day Saint life. Others too are aware of church member preparedness; veteran newscaster Ted Koppel discusses the church's preparedness program in his book *Lights*

In this 1940 Farm Security Administration photo from Box Elder County, Mrs. Marinus Hansen proudly surveys some of the five hundred quarts of home-grown and home-preserved fruits and vegetables she cans, or puts up, every year. Courtesy Library of Congress, Prints & Photographs Division, FSA/OWI Collection, LC-USF34-014110-D.

Out: A Cyberattack, A Nation Unprepared, Surviving the Aftermath.[19]

When asked the question of how church members should respond to possible calamities, Bishop Gordon K. Bischoff of Citrus Heights, California, stated, "Church leaders have never laid down an exact formula for what to store," noting that "no single formula is adequate because what to store, how much to store, and how to store depend on a number of factors, including customs, climate, preferences, and resources."[20] Church doctrines, such as the need for food storage, often evolve and are worked out within families, wards, and in countless Latter-day Saint neighborhoods through lay leadership and members.[21] Suggestions for basic storage include grains, legumes, fats, oils, powdered milk, salt, sugar, honey, water, vitamins, garden seeds, medical supplies, fuels, and scriptures.[22] Wherever feasible, church members are also encouraged to produce as much as possible through gardening and animal husbandry, for both immediate use and storage.

Today, as in past times, many church members store food, learning techniques such as home canning, freezing, and drying foods from preservation publications, classes, family, neighbors, friends, and fellow church members. Doctrinal and folk teachings concerning food storage are prevalent on the official church website: churchofjesuschrist.org.[23] In addition, social networking sites such as Pinterest (cyber bulletin boards) have proven particularly popular among Latter-day Saint women, and even some men. The site hosts *many* boards devoted to food storage and self-reliance.[24] There are online message boards that answer questions like, "Why do church members store up food and water?"[25] and blogs dedicated to Latter-day Saint food storage and philosophy that share know-how and tips such as "How to Shop at Food Storage Case Lot Sales" from the Food Storage Organizer[26] and "Ten Baby Steps" from Food Storage Made Easy.[27]

Church members are part of the larger societies in which they live; thus, some Latter-day Saint food storage activities are informed by the seasonal eating, modern farm-to-table, locavore, and sustainable food systems movements.[28] As well, church members the world over, where it is legal, are encouraged to store food; no doubt these endeavors are flavored by the cultures in which the members are situated.

Although food storage directives come from the top down, Latter-day Saints believe they (individually and collectively) help to *lay* the foundation for the millennium through the *act* of being prepared. Participation in food storage activities puts the trowel of this work in members' hands. Without exception all of the Latter-day Saint individuals I interviewed, read about, or personally interacted with who stored food did so as a reaction to the "command" to store food. However, for most it was also a response of family or community tradition.

So, how do Latter-day Saints in Utah comply with their church's admonition to store food? Letters (directives that teach, clarify, or announce) are routinely sent from the Church First Presidency, the presiding authority of the church, to area authorities, with the intent that they be read over the pulpit to all church congregations. When I asked J. Wilson, president of a North Logan Church of Jesus Christ stake, what activities his stake had implemented, he noted that "welfare is one of our major quests."[29] Allowing that his views are not necessarily representative of the church, he explained how meetings in his stake were held every three months to examine welfare issues in the stake.[30] Church members are taught that welfare activities are not only for self and family, but for others as well, for building Zion.[31] Even though Wilson's family did not plant a garden the year I interviewed him, he noted that "we have neighbors who are constantly supplying us with corn, beans, and zucchini. We all share somehow and the neighborhood becomes an open market to help each other." In fact, a joke told during summer months amongst church members humorously illustrates this point. A visitor to Utah was chastised for trying to lock car doors at homes, stores, and businesses, but was cautioned to "lock them at church." When the confused visitor questioned this, he was informed that "if we don't lock the doors, our car will be filled with zucchinis."[32]

The object of food storage figures prominently into these welfare activities. On a more personal level, Wilson recalled:

> My dad raised a family on a bare minimum salary. However, my mother made sure that we did not go without food. We had fruit trees, a garden, and we canned. We were all involved in the process. Mother did the greatest amount of work, but we all did things like peel apricots, prepare the bottles—we all had assignments. . . . It is one of the feelings I carried from my home life—a need to can, a need to be prepared to feed your family for the winter, and beyond.[33]

Personal narratives are part of the Latter-day Saint experience. Church members teach official doctrines like food storage through oral tradition, including personal stories, legends, and testimonies. Members are encouraged to use "personal experiences" to influence those they teach at home and in church.[34] At a Latter-day Saint Relief Society (women's organization) evening activity in North Logan, Utah, women were invited to "A Garden Tour: Walk, Talk and Taste." Here, women participated in a tour of several members' gardens to learn gardening techniques and food storage ideas. Afterward, presentations were given on childrearing, self-sufficiency, home food production, and storage. These

presentations were peppered with personal experience narratives and testimonials of the creative things ward members did to fulfill the command to store food.

Personal narratives are also found in the church's monthly periodical, the *Ensign*. In a 2012 issue, Elder Randall Bennett, a member of the Seventy (General Authority of the church), shares an example of the "promptings" he and his fiancée had during their 1976 engagement to sell Shelly's engagement ring in order to buy food storage.[35] These narratives can be empowering. For instance, J. Osborne, a young woman in the process of building her first home, short on time and long on tasks, had this to say:

> [W]e have an under-the-porch area that is nice and cool and would be a great storage room. But, I was having fears of running out of money on our house, and I asked my husband how long it would take before we could put some nice shelves in there, and he said, "Oh, we'll just have to wait and see." Anyway, I could see it was going to be like everything else; where we would be waiting and waiting until we had saved enough money, and how many other things might come up first? And so I just told him one day, "Let's go down and buy all the stuff that we need [for our storage room] and add it to the bill, that little bit of money will never make a dent in the money that we have spent on our house."[36]

The fact that the Osbornes' food storage room was the first room completed in their home indicates the faith this young family put in obedience to food storage practices—a fact that is not lost on Latter-day Saints who hear this story. Church members who exchange food storage narratives do so as a way to manifest personal control of their theological beliefs. It is a way to personalize the official directives of church leaders. These "reported events" deal with food storage activities, anecdotes, and testimonials which members use to sustain and perpetuate their unique point of view.[37]

Food storage narratives give both the orator and the audience a feeling of believability.[38] Narratives I collected are often instructive and frequently cautionary. Like all folk groups, Latter-day Saints begin teaching group mores and beliefs to their children at an early age. One young mother stored items all over her two-bedroom trailer, including in her two-year-old daughter's bedroom. Every night when her daughter went to bed and every morning when she awoke, the first things she saw were five-gallon buckets of wheat, beans, and rice. Perhaps to an outsider this might not be considered a room with a view, but to a Latter-day Saint child, it is the molding of group identity. In this case, the apple didn't fall far from the tree, as this young mother was also taught the meaning of Latter-day Saint food storage by her mother. She and her sister both recalled home canning with their parents and siblings as one of their favorite childhood memories:

> We canned everything. I especially remember one summer when I was about eight; we were in the garage doing corn. My mom was about eight months pregnant and we five kids ranged in ages from twelve to three. We got an assembly line going, but after a while things started to drag out, so my older brother went inside the house and came out a while later with paper hats for everyone with our job title written on it. I got the "scrapper" hat. We all laughed, and although it didn't take the work away, things seemed to go better after that. Even to this day, I can't see corn without thinking of that day over twenty years ago. I think all that canning, working together, and having fun…has sparked the food storage bug in me.[39]

Along with narratives dealing with the temporal realities of storage, there are personal narratives that convey the millennialist underpinnings of the Latter-day Saint faith. J. Huppi, whose parents always had a one-year supply of food, noted that her food storage took on greater importance after the death of her infant son. "Now when I think about my storage, it isn't what will get us through in an emergency, what I can get by with, but what I will need during the millennium when I am reunited with Nicky. I wonder, 'Will I need formula and diapers?'"[40] Her very personal narrative connects Latter-day Saint listeners to their millennial beliefs. While interviewing S. Natividad regarding her "Food Storage Support Group," she shared her millennialistic views while showing me the spices in her food storage.[41]

> [Y]ou know that people are going to come here in the last days and this is going to be a place of refuge. And we don't know what kind of people are going to come and what they are going to want to eat and I would like them to feel welcomed when they come. To feel like, you know,

at least if all the people are strange and a different color from them that at least there is some food that they recognize and something that they know how to cook.[42]

Not all Latter-day Saint children grow up participating in food storage at this level. But, whatever the level of involvement, many of these children are nurtured in the foodways, practice, and belief of food storage.

A church bishop recalled his mother's glorious food storage, but also the "mess" they had to contend with when she died because she had not rotated her storage. Much, if not all of it, was spoiled, he related, and had to be "dumped."[43] Such cautionary stories are prevalent among members who store bottled and canned foods, and are encapsulated in the proverbial phrase "waste not, want not." The potential for waste has caused some to turn away from large-scale practice of food storage. "Years ago I helped clean out my…grandmother's food storage," commented a respondent on the internet site "Recovering from Mormonism." "She was 90 when she died. I just shook my head thinking of all the time that was wasted over the years. There must have been 60 years' worth of effort (canning, rotating food, etc.), that was my wakeup call about food storage; I never did buy the brainwash on that one."[44]

Most who participate in food storage attempt to use the foods they store; and most church members would also find the waste distasteful. In fact, most of the individuals I spoke with grow a family garden with the idea that they will add to their stores from its bounty, having used up most of the previous year's foodstuffs during the winter and spring months.

Many have carefully planned systems for storing and rotating this bounty. Many date their goods, whether home preserved or store bought, with a permanent marker, noting the month and year. This allows the consumption of older products first. Some rotate by always placing the newer items behind the older, somewhat like a grocer would do when stocking a supermarket. The first house my husband and I purchased in Logan, Utah, had a food storage room under the front steps built by the previous Latter-day Saint homeowner with angled shelves that allowed the canned goods to roll ever downward, enabling the oldest item to be removed and the next oldest taking its place. Today there is a market for can storage and rotation systems. But, commercial products notwithstanding, the free exchange of storage room ingenuity was evident among the individuals I interviewed; they were all conscious of using their stores and all had a recollection of who told them how to build their shelves or shared strategies for "using up" old fruit.

Keeping alive the skills to produce and store food is the companion command to food storage. Thus, the old women in both stories who continued to

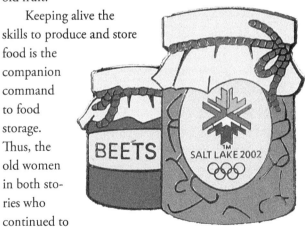

Souvenir pin honoring canning, 2002 Salt Lake Winter Olympics. Used by permission, Utah State Historical Society. All rights reserved.

BOTTLED FRUIT CAKE
*Recipe attributed to
L. Binns; provided by L. Thompson*

1 qt. bottled fruit
2 c. sugar
2 eggs
1/2 c. oil
4 c. flour
4 tsp. soda
2 tsp. cinnamon
1 c. raisins
1 c. shredded carrots
1 tsp. nutmeg
1/2 tsp. cloves
1 tsp. salt
1 c. chocolate chips (opt.)

In blender, put quart of fruit, including juice, sugar, oil, and eggs and blend. In large bowl put all other ingredients, add blended mixture, and mix. Bake in 2 greased Bundt pans at 350 degrees for 55 minutes. Drizzle icing over top and sides. Freezes well.

"beautiful Bundt cake" to her.[45] The giver noted: "I like to keep one of these [cakes] in my freezer at all times. When my fruit gets old, what I do is make these cakes and freeze them and then I can take them to people."[46] Another woman shared with me her collection of several Relief Society cookbooks that listed recipes for "Dump Cake" or "Any Bottle of Fruit Cake."

Food storage, asserts Rick Foster, manager of LDS North American Humanitarian Services, is "about helping all of us individually to get through these bumps that occur in our lives.... If members are prepared, they can help themselves and others in times of need."[47] An online forum writer noted: "It seemed that when I was growing [up] food storage was encouraged as a preparation for the Second Coming and the related natural disasters, but more recently I've noticed a change in emphasis towards it being more of insurance during difficult financial times."[48] For many, stewardship over their resources (including garden plots) is an important philosophical, doctrinal belief. Latter-day Saints who store food, I believe, do so not only because it is a commandment, but in great part because it addresses the temporal realities of their otherworldly beliefs.

Along with perpetuating and sustaining the skill sets of food storage among folk groups, verbal traditions are used by church members to emphasize food storage. One such legend circulated throughout northern Utah involving a male hitchhiker who was picked up by a Latter-day Saint motorist. When the hitchhiker asked the woman about her food storage, she told him that she didn't store food. After admonishing the woman on the virtues of preparedness in the last days, the hitchhiker vanished from the car.[49]

produce and keep food long after their families had left home, most likely did so as a means of showing obedience to the dual command of storing foodstuffs (in case their family may have need) and keeping the *skill set* of preservation alive. For many church members in Utah, food storage is an active and informed pursuit, whether they preserve their own foodstuffs or purchase canned goods at the grocery store or through food storage companies. Many church members work creatively to use up their older storage, making interesting recipes from wheat chili to dump cakes. One woman shared a story of how her visiting teacher (now called ministering sister), hearing of the stillborn birth of a grandchild, brought a

As a barometer of current church doctrinal teachings, folklorist William A. Wilson believes that the Three Nephites (characters from the Book of Mormon) legends "reflect the attitudes, values, and concerns of the people telling the stories."[50] Legends and personal experience narratives are often used in church lessons, talks, and testimonies to create solidarity and confirm group belief.

Food storage is a significant expression of Latter-day Saint identity. Not only does it meld the physical and mental acts of keeping a commandment, but it continues a folk tradition handed down over time and space by family and friends. One family never begins tilling the ground in preparation for planting until "most" of the snow is cleared off the Oquirrh Mountains, while another family begins nursing seeds inside the kitchen window during late winter. My elderly neighbor, W. Skidmore, showed me the *correct* way to "eye" a potato before planting. He also strung my pole beans properly so they would not sag or touch the ground and invite pests; he also advised me about the best way to weed. To all this there is a stewardship: first to self, including work, self-reliance, and provident living and preparedness; and second, to care for others through love, service, and consecration of one's surplus.[51] It also connects to a very deep-seated belief in preparation for a millennial, Godly time. "Latter-day Saints believe in being prepared and self-reliant....Most importantly, we believe in preparing spiritually for the Second Coming of Jesus Christ and for living with our Father in Heaven again. This approach to preparedness is called provident living."[52]

This process of provident living is reflected by walking barefoot in a garden to pick cucumbers, onions, and dill in preparation of canning pickles, while recalling similar steps as a child with a parent in order to add to the family's food stores. It includes the story that comes to a child on the correct way to husk corn or the warning testimonial to a new bride on the dangers of pressure cookers, all link action to event, novice to expert, custom to belief. "Never bury corn seeds deeper than a pinkie width or they won't take," taught my father-in-law. "Yes, that size cuke; anything larger and your dills will taste woody," instructed my Grandma Sarah. "Use Kerr jars and lids," she advised, "I've always had good luck with them; and never use mayonnaise jars—they'll surely break on you." "We are a people of faith *and* works," my mother declares. "If we are prepared, we shall not fear." Words of wisdom garnered over a lifetime of doing cannot be fully taught to a congregation in church, but only in a well-cultivated garden and a well-lived-in kitchen among intimate folk.

NOTES

1. In August 2018, The Church of Jesus Christ of Latter-day Saints issued a statement requesting the disuse of the name *Mormon* to identify the Church and its members, with an allowance given for the use of Mormon as an adjective in titles and historical expression, like the "Mormon Trail." I use "Mormon Food Storage" as a historical expression.

2. Many scholars utilize foodways as a means of interpreting culture. See, for example, Theodore Humphrey and Lin Humphrey, *We Gather Together: Food and Festival in American Life* (Logan: Utah State University Press, 1988); Ruth Gruber Fredman, *The Passover Seder: Afikoman in Exile* (Philadelphia: University of Pennsylvania Press, 1981); *Ethnic and Regional Foodways in the United States: The Performance of Group Identity*, ed. Keller Brown and Kay Mussell (Knoxville: University of Tennessee

Press, 1984); *Foodways & Eating Habits: Directions for Research*, ed. Michael Owen Jones, Bruce Giuliano, and Roberta Krell (Los Angeles: California Folklore Society, 1983).

3. Alan Dundes, "Folk Ideas as Units of Worldview," *Journal of American Folklore* 84, no. 331 (1971): 96.

4. Bruce R. McConkie, "Building Zion," *Liahona* 23, no. 8 (1977): 12–15. (English version https://www.lds.org/liahona/1977/09/building-zion?lang=eng.)

5. Dallin H. Oaks, "Preparation for the Second Coming," *Ensign* 34, no. 5 (May 2004).

6. The security plan was an effort to help church members with their temporal needs. David O. McKay, "Timeline: A Look Back at the Church Welfare Plan," *Church News* (Salt Lake City), March 22, 2011.

7. J. Rueben Clark, "Conference Address," *Conference Report* (Salt Lake City: Church of Jesus Christ of Latter-day Saints, April 1937), 26.

8. Leonard J. Arrington and Wayne K. Hinton, "Origin of the Welfare Plan of the Church of Jesus Christ of Latter-day Saints," *BYU Studies* 5, no. 2 (1964): 68.

9. Klaus J. Hansen, *Quest for Empire: The Political Kingdom of God and the Council of Fifty in Mormon History* (East Lansing: Michigan State University Press, 1967), 18.

10. "The Most Frequently Asked Questions about Home Production and Storage," *Ensign* 7, no. 8 (1977): 20–27.

11. Donald Scott, "Mormonism and the American Mainstream," National Humanities Center, revised August 2004, http://nationalhumanitiescenter.org/tserve/nineteen/nkeyinfo/nmormon).

12. Brigham Young, *Discourses of Brigham Young*, ed. John A. Widtsoe (Salt Lake City: Deseret Book, 1978), 293.

13. Utah, southeastern Idaho, southern and eastern Nevada, western Wyoming, as well as portions of California and Mexico.

14. Many church members both now and earlier see these activities, customs, and traditions as fulfillment of Isaiah's prophesy that "the wilderness and the solitary place shall be glad for them; and the desert shall rejoice, and blossom as the rose."

15. Kathy Stephenson, "Food Storage Today a Byproduct of Mormons' Pioneer Past," *Salt Lake Tribune* (Salt Lake City), November 8, 2013.

16. On January 20, 2002, the First Presidency of the Church of Jesus Christ of Latter-day Saints sent a letter to the worldwide church membership through priesthood leaders. The letter stated: "Priesthood and Relief Society leaders should teach the importance of home storage and securing a financial reserve," including food storage. Gordon B. Hinckley, Thomas S. Monson, and James E. Faust, "Letter from the First Presidency," *Liahona* 27, no. 4 (2003): 1.

17. In 1975, the church noted that only 30 percent had a two-month supply, with the remaining membership having little or no food storage. H. Burke Peterson, "The Welfare Production-Distribution Department," *Ensign* 5, no. 11 (1975): 116–17. Although I could not locate current statistics, concepts of self-reliance and Zion-building are continually taught and reinforced to LDS people ("Provident Living: Self-Reliance and Welfare Resources," The Church of Jesus Christ of Latter-day Saints, https://providentliving.lds.org/?lang=eng).

18. Thomas S. Monson, "Guiding Principles of Personal and Family Welfare," *Liahona* 33, no. 2 (1987): 2–8.

19. Edward J. Koppel, *Lights Out: A Cyberattack, A Nation Unprepared, Surviving the Aftermath* (New York: Crown Publishers, 2015): 179–98.

20. Gordon K. Bischoff, "I Have a Question," *Ensign* 27, no. 9 (1997): 67.

21. Doctrine of the Church of Jesus Christ of Latter-day Saints comes from a priesthood authority–based ecclesiastical government, with a prophet at the helm who receives divine revelation regarding the beliefs and practices of church members. The official church doctrines are taught and "worked out" in familial, ward/neighborhood, and regional groups. Peter Crawley, "Parley P. Pratt: Father of Mormon Pamphleteering," *Dialogue: A Journal of Mormon Thought* 15, no. 3 (1982): 20–21.

22. "Home Storage: Build on the Basics," *Ensign* 19, no. 6 (1989): 39–42.

23. The site references curriculum materials, videos, General Conference talks, Church magazines that include sections where members present their ideas, such as "Random Sampler," "Mormon Journal," and

"I Have a Question." Personal narratives are often used in articles and talks by LDS Church authorities and members. Thus, the official is interpreted by the laity and taught and perpetuated in local congregations on a folk level.

24. Mormon Women, "Food Storage/Self-Reliance" (board), Pinterest, accessed April 18, 2019, http://www.pinterest.com/mormonwomen/food-storage-self-reliance/.

25. "Why Do Mormons Store up Food and Water?" *Yahoo Answers!*, last modified 2007, accessed April 18, 2019, https://answers.yahoo.com/question/index?qid=20071205181941AAzurNq.

26. Valerie Albrechtsen, "How to Shop at Food Storage Case Lot Sales," *Food Storage Organizer*, accessed April 18, 2019, https://www.foodstorageorganizer.com/2012/07/how-to-shop-at-food-storage-case-lot.html.

27. Jodi and Julie, "Ten Baby Steps to Building a Food Storage," *Food Storage Made Easy* (blog), accessed April 18, 2019, http://foodstoragemadeeasy.net/babysteps/.

28. Rural people have long participated in food production and storage, but urbanites are increasingly participating in gardening, food preservation, and small-animal farming. While for some this may have been a necessary reaction to the economic downturn of 2008, others simply desire a more intimate connection to their food. For these, participation in food production and storage is a reflection of their personal and folk beliefs. Chef Justin Soelberg, a member of the church, considers Latter-day Saint food a "part of a larger Western tradition of hearty meals, seasonal eating and food preservation that is in keeping with modern farm-to-table ideas" (Julia Moskin, "Not Just for Sundays after Church: A New Generation Redefines Mormon Cuisine," *New York Times*, January 24, 2012.

As with "LDS traditions," relates historian Kate Holbrook, locavores emphasize "food from gardens and farmer's markets, as well as the slow-food movement, which encourages a trend away from fast food and the conveniences of preservatives." Wendy Leonard, "University of Utah Fellow to Study Origins of Mormon Food Subculture," *Deseret News* (Salt Lake City), May 17, 2010.

29. J. Wilson, interview by Randy Williams, September 2002, North Logan, Utah, Fife Folklore Archives, Folk Collection 59, Utah State University.

30. Ibid. A stake represents approximately 3,500 to 5,000 members, represented by seven to ten wards of 500 to 800 members each. A stake is presided over by a stake president with two counselors, all male; a ward is presided over by a bishop with two counselors, also all male.

31. Church members are advised to heed the words of Moses found in *The Pearl of Great Price*: "And the Lord called his people Zion, because they were of one heart and one mind, and dwelt in righteousness; and there was no poor among them" (Moses 7:18, *The Pearl of Great Price* [Salt Lake City: Church of Jesus Christ of Latter-day Saints], 22).

32. Vorpal Blade, "RE: #58907 Garden Rash," Theboardboard.org, July 1, 2008.

33. J. Wilson, interview.

34. Richard Nash, "Telling Personal Stories," *Ensign* 32, no. 9 (2002): 49.

35. Randall K. Bennett, "Follow the Prophet," *Ensign* 42, no. 3 (2012): 19.

36. J. Osborne, interview by Randy Williams, September 2002, Logan and Hyde Park, Utah, Fife Folklore Archives, Folk Collection 59, Utah State University.

37. Richard Bauman, *Story, Performance, and Event: Contextual Studies of Oral Narrative* (Cambridge: Cambridge University Press, 1986), 33.

38. Erving Goffman, *Frame Analysis: An Essay on the Organization of Experience* (New York: Harper & Row, 1974), 503–4.

39. J. Osborne, interview.

40. J. Huppi, interview by Randy Williams, December 1992, Logan Utah, Fife Folklore Archives, Folk Collection 59, Utah State University.

41. In the spring of 2002, S. Natividad and her friend started the Food Storage Support Group as a means of sharing recipes and tips on food storage with ward members, neighbors, and anyone who was interested through the use of a website. The group also bought storage items together in bulk.

42. S. Natividad, interview by Randy Williams,

September 2002, Logan, Utah, Fife Folklore Archives, Folk Collection 59, Utah State University.

43. B. Bastian, interview by Randy Williams, December 1992, Logan, Utah, Fife Folklore Archives, Folk Collection 59, Utah State University.

44. Marcionite, "Mormon Sister Rants about Food Storage and the Waste It Has Been," Recovery from Mormonism, February 2012, http://exmormon.org/d6/drupal/Mormon-Sister-Rants-about-food-storage-and-the-Waste-it-has-been.

45. L. Thompson, interview with Randy Williams, April 1995, Logan, Utah, Fife Folklore Archives, Folk Collection 59, Utah State University. Visiting teachers, now called ministering sisters, "visit and watch over and help another woman in their Latter-day Saint ward or branch."

46. Ibid.

47. The LDS Church maintains many "grocery store–like storehouses across the Americas to provide food to members in need" and allow other members to can dry goods in an effort to add to their own stores. Brady McCombs, "Mormon-Centric Utah Epicenter for Food Storage," Salt Lake Tribune, December 23, 2013. These storehouses are affected by the economy and economists take note, calling it the "Mormon Index." Economy writer Daniel Gross said that "the Mormon Index and similar boutique economic clues are often more reliable than big-gun barometers, such as housing starts and the unemployment rate" (Tim Townsend, "The Mormon Index is a rising

sign of troubled economy," St. Louis Post-Dispatch, January 22, 2009).

Along with the Bishop's storehouses, food storage companies that sell everything from freeze-dried goods to rotation shelving systems do swift business amongst church members and others. Utah-based Daily Bread, which specializes in packaging and selling dehydrated and freeze-dried foods, "had more than $300 million in sales" in 2012 (Kathy Stephenson, "Food Storage Today a Byproduct of Mormons' Pioneer Past," The Salt Lake Tribune, November 8, 2013).

48. Omni, "What Is the Purpose of Food Storage?," in Mormon Dialogue and Discussion Board, October 26, 2013, http://www.mormondialogue.org/topic/62070-what-is-the-purpose-of-food-storage/.

49. This narrative is typical of other Three Nephite legends permeating Latter-day Saint culture. Based on three characters from the Book of Mormon, the legend invariably involves a "kindly male stranger" who gives advice or help to someone in distress and then mysteriously leaves the scene without giving his name or being thanked.

50. William A. Wilson, "The Paradox of Mormon Folklore," BYU Studies 17, no. 1 (1979): 43.

51. Harold B. Lee, "Providing in the Lord's Way," in Teachings of Presidents of the Church: Harold B. Lee (Salt Lake: Church of Jesus Christ of Latter-day Saints, 2000), 165–74.

52. "Provident Living Prepares Us for the Future," in What We Believe, Ensign 42, no. 10 (2012): 12–13.

LEAH WIDTSOE AND DOMESTIC SCIENCE IN UTAH

KATHRYN L. MACKAY

Many of the food traditions collected in this text are expressions of family experiential traditions that define ethnicity and region.[1] Some have been recorded in the popular genre of community cookbooks which thereby reflect the cultural and social history of their time and place.[2] However, there have also been significant contributions to food traditions by domestic science or home economics—an educational movement that promised modernization and science in the kitchen.[3] An influential promoter of home economics was Leah Widtsoe, whose work as writer, educator, political activist, and speaker guided the food choices of hundreds of Utahns in the first half of the twentieth century. Her 1943 book, *How to Be Well*, became the trusted handbook she intended in many a Mormon household.[4]

Leah Dunford Widtsoe (1874–1965), born in Salt Lake City, was raised by her father, Alma B. Dunford, after her mother, Susa Young Gates, divorced Alma. Leah called her home life a "nightmare."[5] However, in her mid-teens, she rejoined her mother's family and went on to become well educated—studying at the University of Utah, Brigham Young University, the Pratt Institute in Boston, and a summer session at Harvard. While at the University of Utah (then the University of Deseret), she studied with scientist James E. Talmage, whose book on domestic science had been adopted for use in all territorial schools.[6] While earning her B.S. degree from BYU, she was put in charge of the Department of Domestic Science.

Dunford married John A. Widtsoe in 1898 and had her first child the following year in Germany, where Widtsoe was studying chemistry. Upon their return to the United States in 1900, John became, in succession, director of the Experimental Station in Logan, the founder and chair of the Department of Agriculture at Brigham Young University, president of the Utah State Agricultural College, and president of the University of Utah.[7] Accompanying her husband in his many career changes, she gave birth to eight children (only three reached maturity) and became a pamphleteer and lecturer on homemaking and health. Her first major publication was "Labor Saving Devices for the Farm Home," published in 1912 as a circular for the Utah Agricultural College Experiment Station. Prepared for the first International Congress of Farm Women held in Colorado Springs, Colorado, in 1911, which she helped organize, its purpose was "to stimulate thought on the part of the home-workers—the women; and to induce a spirit of interested cooperation on the part of the home providers—the men."[8] It included advice and illustrations about equipment, utensils, and costs.

Widtsoe concluded the circular with a plea for support of national legislation being sponsored by Utah senator Reed Smoot to appropriate funds to

Leah Dunford Widtsoe's 1943 cookbook *How to Be Well* was the culmination of her extensive research into nutrition and health. She shunned white bread, cola drinks, and sugar, and promoted the consumption of a variety of vegetables. Her book was well received by Utah Mormons. Photo by Carol A. Edison, 2016.

agricultural experiment stations for research in home economics. Although the bill did not pass, she doggedly kept up a correspondence with Smoot and other supporters until the Purnell Research Act was passed in 1925 providing federal money to facilitate the scientific investigation of vitamins and rural home-management studies. By then, however, she was no longer involved in studying farm family conditions.[9]

She was, however, continuing to promote a scientific approach to domestic work. Her papers are filled with notes and drafts about "Healthful Cooking," "Foods to Avoid," "Fabricated Food," "Natural Vitamins Necessary," and "Importance of Minerals in Food."[10] And she connected her scientific work to her religious beliefs, arguing that Brigham Young was a pioneer in health education.[11]

How to Be Well is the culmination of her research. Characterized as an outgrowth of the 1937 book she and her husband wrote on LDS health,[12] John Widtsoe extolled in the preface of the 1943 book that

the author has dared to break away, in the interest of human welfare, from the traditional contents of cook-books. Instead, she has related all material used to sound nutritional knowledge.... [There] are numerous recipes for the use of the housewife, but all comport with the modern knowledge of bodily requirement....It is a handbook for the kitchen of every intelligent, health-loving woman.[13]

And so the book includes sections on "The Role of Vitamins in Nutrition," "Family Diet Changes

BREAD PUDDING

(A GREAT WAY TO USE LEFTOVER BREAD)
Courtesy of Leah D. Widtsoe

Cook 1/2 cup brown sugar with 3 tablespoons butter; add 1 quart scalded milk. In it soak 2 cups stale bread or cake pieces or crumbs; cool. Beat 2 or 3 eggs lightly; add 1/2 teaspoon salt, 1 teaspoon vanilla and mix with the crumbs and milk; add more milk and sugar if needed. Grated nutmeg or cinnamon may be added also. Bake 1 hour in a moderate oven (325 degrees). Serve hot with vanilla sauce (see recipe) or cold with cream, plain or whipped, or any preferred sauce, or applesauce or any fruit.

Vanilla Sauce
(This is a basic pudding sauce. It may be varied with different flavorings.)
Mix 1 cup of sifted brown sugar with 1/8 teaspoon salt and 2 teaspoons corn starch. If brown sugar is in lumps, mash before sifting. Slowly pour over this 2 cups boiling water. Boil 5 minutes. Add 4 tablespoons butter and 1 teaspoon vanilla extract. Serve hot with any desired pudding.[14]

for Better Health," and "Food for Mothers and Food Habits of Children." However, most of the text is some one hundred recipes for each food group such as: "Bread and Cereals," "Salads and Salad Dressing," "Healthful Drinks," and "Vegetable Cookery."

Leah Widtsoe also gives much advice, such as: "There is no excuse for using white bread"; "All the different kinds of vegetables should be used as good and all members of the family should learn to enjoy them"; "The use of cola drinks on such outings [church affairs and picnic] cannot be too strongly condemned. It is a pernicious thing for them to take any drug laden food or drink, no matter how weak

the drug content may be"; and "Avoid the over-use of sugar." She also includes advice on table settings, invalid cookery, and party menus.

Only the scientific sourcebooks are cited in the book. No attributions are given for the hundreds of recipes, although there are rare labels such as "Maria's Norwegian Dumplings" and "Beverly's Nectar." Several recipes do seem to be the consequence of Leah's marrying a Norwegian immigrant. But in her practical, easy style, Leah Dunford Widtsoe made a solid contribution to food traditions in Utah.

NOTES

1. Danna R. Gabaccia, *We Are What We Eat: Ethnic Food and the Making of Americans* (Cambridge: Harvard University Press, 1998).
2. Alison P. Kelly, "Choice Receipts from American Housekeepers: A Collection of Digitized Community Cookbooks from the Library of Congress," *Public Historian* 34, no. 2 (Spring 2012): 30–52.
3. Megan J. Elias, *Stir It Up: Home Economics in American Culture* (Philadelphia: University of Pennsylvania Press, 2008); Dolores Hayden, *The Grand Domestic Revolution* (Cambridge, MA: MIT Press, 1981).
4. Leah D. Widtsoe and John A. Widtsoe, *How to Be Well: A Health Handbook and Cookbook Based on the New Knowledge of Nutrition by a Member of the Mormon Church* (Salt Lake City: Deseret Book Co., 1943).
5. Mary Jane Woodger, "Leah Widtsoe: Pioneer in Health Lifestyle Family Education," *Journal of Family and Consumer Science* 92, no. 1 (2000): 50–54; Virginia F. Cutler, *A Twenty-One Gun Salute for Leah Dunford Widtsoe* (Logan: Utah State University College of Family Life, 196?).
6. James E. Talmage, *Domestic Science: A Book for Use in Schools and for General Reading* (Salt Lake City: George Q. Cannon & Sons, 1892). The book did not contain any recipes but rather information about the science of air, water, food, and cleansing agents.

7. John Andreas Widtsoe Papers, Special Collections, J. Willard Marriott Library, University of Utah.

8. Leah D. Widtsoe, "Circular No. 7: Labor Saving Devices for the Farm Home," *UASE* (Lehi, UT: Lehi Publishing Co., June 1912).

9. Alison Cornish Thorne, "Visible and Invisible Women in Land-Grant Colleges, 1890–1940," USU Faculty Lectures, Paper 2, 1985.

10. Leah D. Widtsoe Papers, 1939–1963, LDS Church History Library.

11. She published a biography of the church leader: *Brigham Young: The Man of the Hour* (Salt Lake City: Bookcraft, 1947).

12. John Andreas Widtsoe and Leah D. Widtsoe, *The Word of Wisdom: A Modern Interpretation* (Salt Lake City: Deseret Book, 1937). The Word of Wisdom, a code of health dealing primarily with human nutrition, was supposedly received as divine revelation in 1833 by Joseph Smith Jr., founder of the LDS Church. The writers explained the purpose of the book: "First, to make clear the meaning of the Word of Wisdom in terms of modern knowledge. Second, to show that the learning of the last century confirms the teachings of the Word of Wisdom. Third, to furnish some information for the guidance, through proper nutrition, of those who seek to retain, improve or recover their health."

13. Widtsoe and Widtsoe, *How to Be Well*, 4.

14. Ibid., 132.

41

SUNDAY DINNER

CAROL A. EDISON

A typical Sunday dinner at the Edison home features roast beef, potatoes and gravy, vegetables, salad, rolls, and pickled condiments. Courtesy Carol Edison, 2015.

Nearly every Sunday, since before I can remember, my mother cooked roast beef for dinner.[1] She grew up eating hot Sunday meals, but when she married my father, she quickly learned that in his family Sunday dinner meant roast beef, served with potatoes and gravy, carrots, and a green salad. That's what he liked and wanted, so that became our family tradition.

I know Grandma cooked her potatoes and beef roasts in the oven—an easy and efficient way to cook food for a group, especially when one wanted to return from church to a nearly completed meal. But my mother, fresh from the 1950s home economics classes at the university, quickly discovered the joys of the pressure cooker. This enabled her to first brown the roast to perfection and then cook it until it was incredibly tender. But the real test of her cooking ability was how she transformed the drippings into tasty gravy—a skill no one in the family has quite matched.

Koosharem is one of the few Utah communities that still holds an annual Old Folks Day—a day of celebration initiated in 1875 by Mormon leaders to honor the older members of the community. The day-long event features a midday meal, a variety show, an evening meal, and an old-fashioned pioneer dance. Sunday dinner—roast beef with all the trimmings—is always on the menu. Photo by Carol A. Edison, 1984. Courtesy Utah Folklife Archives.

Over the years, the menu only occasionally varied. For Easter, we'd have ham and scalloped potatoes and, once in a while, a pork roast, both cooked in the oven while we attended church. While I don't remember either rolls or special desserts being part of the meal when I was young, they've now become staples as the family has grown from two girls to an extended family with grandchildren and spouses, who still meet at my parents' home every Sunday.

Aside from the tradition of getting together

every week and almost always eating roast beef, we also love the homemade condiments Mom always served with the meal. We've always had pickled beets, never from a tin can but always home-canned in a recipe of vinegar and spices, providing a savory accompaniment to the meat and potatoes. Only recently, as my mother approached her ninetieth decade, did she give up the annual (and often disappointing) quest for the perfect one-and-a-half-inch-diameter beets. She found a laborsaving strategy:

238

MOM'S ROAST BEEF AND GRAVY
Courtesy of Alice Nelson Edison

Start with a 2– to 3–pound rump roast; trim off any excess fat.

Put the roast in the pressure cooker and, using a little Crisco, brown it well on all sides.

Add half a cup of water for every 1 pound of roast. Generously season with Lawry's Seasoned Salt.

Tighten the lid and bring the cooker up to full pressure. Cook for 20 minutes per pound.

Cool down, remove lid, and remove the meat.

To make the gravy, heat the drippings while stirring in a mixture of flour and water to thicken. Add water from the cooked vegetables to increase the volume, season with salt and pepper, and boil long enough to cook the flour.

Serve the meat with condiments (pickled beets, bread & butter pickles) alongside potatoes and gravy, a vegetable (carrots in our family), and a green salad.

Besides deep red, pickled beets, we've always enjoyed eating the well-cooked but tender roast beef with another home-canned, vinegar-based condiment we call piccalilli. For many years, every fall, on one special day, the house would be filled with the enticing and pungent smell of simmering piccalilli—a combination of thinly sliced green tomatoes, onions, vinegar, and spices—made from a recipe that Dad's mom had used for years. Then, somewhere along the way, Mom rediscovered another recipe from her side of the family. It was made from cucumbers and onions and she initially called it bread-and-butter pickles. This variation soon became our new favorite, and before long we were calling it piccalilli and introducing it to all the new husbands and grandsons as one of the cornerstones of our roast beef Sunday dinner.

buying commercially canned beets, cooking up the pickling juice using her family recipe, and then hot-packing them into her store of glass-bottom pint jars in the basement. The result is the same without the need to grow or hunt for the right-sized beets, or boil and peel them!

NOTES

1. A version of this essay was previously published as a sidebar, "Sunday Dinner," in "Every Summer of My Life" by Elaine Thatcher, *Sojourns* (Peaks, Plateaus & Canyons Association) 3, no. 1 (Winter/Spring 2008): 34.

42

COMPASSIONATE SERVICE CASSEROLE

Identity Performance in the Lives of Mormon Women

RONDA WALKER WEAVER

I vividly remember walking the five blocks home from Rigby High School and being so hungry and tired I could not wait to get home and have a snack and take a nap. I would enter the house through the back door and, more often than not, be greeted by the smell of bread, cookies, cinnamon rolls, or soup. This was a regular occurrence, one which consistently meant two things—Mom was baking, and someone in our LDS ward needed help.

More than twenty-five years later, nothing much has changed except two more generations have also picked up the tradition. I make cookies, banana bread, or fresh salsa and deliver these to my neighbors, who are mostly ward (congregation) members of the Church of Jesus Christ of Latter-day Saints; my daughter is making brownies or sharing fruit from her orchard; and my mother is still baking goodies, particularly cinnamon rolls, for anyone in need. This tradition extends far beyond my own family: My friend Ann laughingly refers to LDS hymn no. 219, "Because I Have Been Given Much"—a song about choosing to give to those in need—as the "Zucchini Song," highlighting how intimately connected the concepts of service and food are.

Within my family and my Mormon culture, I have begun to ask "why?" about many of the roles foods have in our culture. Mormon women take their cooking and baking seriously, and we take serving others quite seriously too. My hunt for answers to this query has led me to explore the messages LDS leaders have given regarding service and the way LDS women have interpreted and personalized these messages. I have looked at issues of the LDS Church's *Relief Society Magazine* from 1950 to 1970, the LDS Church's *Ensign* from 1970 to 2013, and LDS songs and scriptures, and I have had conversations with more than a hundred LDS women of various ages, in an attempt to answer my question, "Are food and service intricately connected?"

COMPASSIONATE SERVICE

The LDS Church has a term, uniquely Mormon, which best describes the kind of giving LDS women are expected to provide: compassionate service. Scriptures, talks, and lessons about this type of service abound in the church. A definition of compassionate service comes from Matthew 25:35: "For I was an hungered, and ye gave me meat; I was thirsty, and ye gave me drink; I was a stranger, and ye took me in."

Compassionate service is charity, most often born from the perception of being Christ's representative here on earth and spreading the pure love of Christ. This type of service comes from a woman's heart. An LDS woman sees herself as giving that love and answering prayers or pleas, proving both that the Lord does watch out for one's needs, and that one is blessed in serving.

LDS RELIEF SOCIETY

The LDS Church's *Relief Society Magazine*, dedicated to LDS women, was not published after December 1970; the *Ensign*, a magazine for adults in the church, took its place. LDS Church leaders' instructions on how to serve can be found in both magazines. In the January 1970 issue of the *Relief Society Magazine*, church president Joseph Fielding Smith describes the responsibilities of Relief Society women: "This is a charitable Society, and according to your natures; it is natural for females to have feelings of charity and benevolence. You are now placed in a situation in which you can act according to those sympathies which God has planted in your bosoms." President Spencer W. Kimball, in the November

1978 *Ensign*, similarly said, "We encourage the sisters of the Church—young and older—to be 'anxiously engaged' in quiet acts of service for friends and neighbors.... Acts of service help not only the beneficiaries of the service, but they enlarge the giver."

Relief Society general president Elaine L. Jack, in her 1996 *Ensign* message, said serving God is not new to LDS women. She observes, "Your efforts to assist and help others have become so much a part of your personal style that, for the most part, they are spontaneous, instinctive, and immediate." Jack states that giving of oneself is truly giving charity. In agreement, Gail, forty-seven, shares, "Growing up ... I wasn't LDS. After joining the Methodist Church I learned about service, but it wasn't until I joined the LDS Church at age eighteen that I learned service was a way of life, for the LDS people, and thus, me."

HOW TO SERVE

A January 1957 *Relief Society Magazine* article speaking of pioneer women read, "We all have something to give; we must reach a little deeper into the bin.... If there was no flour in the bin and no other food to share, they gave of themselves in compassionate service.... They learned that encouragement, compassion, and faith may be given to others, as they become a part of a shining light undimmed and unlimited." If followed to a logical conclusion, does this then mean women are to first give food and then give of themselves, or are they so intricately tied together that there is no distinction between food, self, and service? Kay, seventy-eight years old, wrote that she believed the food she makes for her family and friends is a source of comfort for them: "They know I make it with love."

Food is more than physical sustenance. Roland Barthes said food is "a system of communication, a body of images, a protocol of usages, situations, and behavior."[1] Food becomes this prop in identity performance. Laurie, twenty-one, writes that she feels guilty when she visits someone without taking a treat. LDS women communicate through food, giving them a chance to share a portion of themselves, to use a God-given talent—an outward expression that can be seen as a humble offering. Food communicates for an LDS woman—as providing both physical and spiritual nutrition.

The recipe for "Compassionate Service Casserole" is an example of Barthes's body of images. I received this as a portion of a Visiting Teaching message in the late 1970s:

If an LDS woman is to first focus on her family and caring for them, then this compassionate service is an extension of a woman and her home. In extending this, wouldn't sharing of one's homemaking skills, the making of food in particular, be a part of this logical sequence? Virginia Newman, in a 1962 *Relief Society Magazine* article, wrote,

"No Half Loaf, This"
Friendly were the words you said,
Tendering the loaf of bread,
Oven warm and savory;
How much that gesture meant to me,
Almost a stranger, lonely too,
And gladdened by the sight of you.
I would repay you if I could.
Oh yes, the bread was extra good.

(I'd like the recipe some day.)
But let me ask you if I may,
How you acquired the finer art
Of nourishing the hungry heart?
I never had the knack, somehow.
(I'd like *that* recipe right now.)

DO THE WOMEN OF THE LDS CHURCH SEE SERVICE AND FOOD GOING HAND-IN-HAND?

Definitely yes.

LDS women are taught that compassionate service is charity, and charity is the pure love of Christ. But can LDS women give intangibles without giving tangibles? As Elaine Jack states, "sharing intangibles, not easily left on the doorstep but easily deposited in the heart"? My research has shown that women need something in their hands when making a doorstep visit, regardless of the purpose. One way women give of themselves is in the sharing of traditional food items. These then take on new meanings as they go from one hand to another, as the motivation of the giver and the response of the receiver are of one heart. Cooking becomes a vehicle for artistic expression, a source of sensory pleasure, and an opportunity for power.[2] Kristin, thirty-eight, writes that sharing food with one in need can be one way of saying, "Let me worry about the mundane; you worry about the important stuff." Foodways bind people together; food defines a group's identity and serves as a means of communication.[3] Peggy, forty-six, writes: "I loved it when my mom took food into another home, because she always made enough for our family too! I think that's important to do. As a child I

COMPASSIONATE SERVICE CASSEROLE

2 ears for listening
2 eyes that see what needs to be done
1 mouth, open to speak the words of the Spirit
1 neck, easy to move and not stiff
1 shoulder, ready for crying on (may use 2 shoulders
   if desired)
2 elbows (don't drain the grease)
2 hands, willing to serve
1 heart, ready to open
2 knees, prepared for kneeling
2 feet, ready to go where needed

Put all ingredients in whatever modest container is desired: jeans and a sweatshirt, skirt and sweater, or dress. Proportions of the finished product don't matter, as long as all the parts, especially the heart, are in the right place. Sprinkle liberally with the scriptures. Bake under various degrees of prayer until there's a burning in the bosom. Remove from heat and serve those who cannot help themselves. Feeds the multitudes much like the Savior's loaves and fishes—the more served, the more there seems to be available.

felt my mother was serving her own family also. And it made me feel special along with the family she was serving."

HAS COMPASSIONATE SERVICE TRANSCENDED TIME?

There is an apparent change in the style and focus of writing from the *Relief Society Magazine* to the *Ensign*. Fictional stories and personalized recipes no longer play a prominent role in the newer church magazine. Few personal experiences, namely those with an inspirational message, are apparent. Past Relief Society general president Barbara B. Smith, in the May 1978 *Ensign*, wrote, "My Aunt Martha is soon to be ninety-five years of age. I'd challenge almost anyone to keep up with her.... In a time of need she is the first one to render compassionate service. I've heard many people say that the bowl of hot soup she brought was just what they needed."

There is nearly a ten-year gap before another article regarding women, service, and food appears. The January 1985 *Ensign* has a personal narrative written by Lori Boyer, a woman who, upon hearing about the death of a sister in the ward, looks back on her own lack of compassionate service. She didn't want to visit her empty-handed, but every time she purchased fruit to take over to this woman something inconsequential came up that kept her from visiting. Boyer writes, "I try to remember this hard-won lesson whenever I see a moving van pull into the neighborhood. I know that if I wait until I have a plate of cookies to meet the new neighbors, they may never find me *or* my cookies at their front door." She added, "A sister in our ward who is crippled and lives alone told me once that she loves to see a visitor come to her door with two trays of food. 'It means she is going to stay and eat with me, rather than just drop the food off and leave me to eat alone.' That is coming with both your heart *and* your hands full."

Appearing in June 1985, an *Ensign* article titled "Fresh Crab and French Bread," by Garnee Faulkner, discusses a woman who, while visiting San Francisco, was prompted to purchase fresh crab and San Francisco French bread to take home to a recently widowed woman. Faulkner felt letdown when the

MOM'S BANANA BREAD
Courtesy Alice Jensen Walker

1/2 c. butter, softened
1 c. sugar
2 eggs
1 c. mashed bananas
3 Tbsp. milk
1 tsp. baking soda
2 c. flour
1/2 tsp. salt
1 tsp. vanilla
(Nuts if desired)

Mix all ingredients together, pour into a large, greased loaf pan (or pour into 2 small loaf pans, and share one loaf with a neighbor). Bake at 350 degrees for 30–40 minutes.

Photo by Ronda Walker Weaver, 2018.

Photo by Ronda Walker Weaver, 2018.

woman did not wholeheartedly receive this gift. However, Faulkner received a note from this woman thanking her for helping make her wedding anniversary easier by bringing a gift only her husband would have brought her.

This article was the last one I could find regarding this topic until the December 2003 *Ensign* article, "I Can Make Rolls." Glenda Anderson, author of the article, mentions that a new family moved into her neighborhood, and she looked for some way to serve, to reach out, to this family. She wrote, "I can make rolls. . . . They have to eat something, and rolls are easy to make." Anderson says giving the rolls was a way of showing her love and concern for them. "When I went to their home with my humble offering, I realized that my visit offered a small bit of consolation—the rolls were not necessary, but they had given me a reason to visit."

Gifts of food have changed over time. We may not be receiving casseroles and Jell-Os, but instead crab and French bread, or perhaps frozen lasagna and packaged salad—even now the evolution also

FRESH TOMATO SALSA
Courtesy Irma Lopez

6 large ripe red tomatoes
1 large green pepper
1 large white onion
2 peppers (Anaheim or Jalapeno)

1. Dice all ingredients (can blend, but I prefer it chunky).
2. Add 1 bunch cilantro, 1 teaspoon fresh lemon juice, and salt and pepper to taste.
3. Blend all together, refrigerate.
4. Share with your neighbor by placing salsa in a throw-away plastic container and adding 1 bag tortilla chips to the gift.

includes candles, lotions, and seasonal crafts. Yet giving or receiving, whether it is homemade bread or a package of store-bought cookies, is still appreciated, and this has not gone out of style. Carol, fifty-five, explains, when writing that she believes compassionate service among LDS women is genetic, "Maybe even DNA!" Laurie, in her twenties, writes that one evening her visiting teachers offered to bring her family dinner. "They brought sandwiches from Subway. It wasn't hard, but it showed they cared, and it helped ease our burden after a long day."

Today the *Ensign* publishes few articles teaching LDS women homemaking or compassionate-service skills, but the pattern of serving others with food, set in the years of the *Relief Society Magazine*, now plays forth because of repetition, imitation, and adaption. Traditions do change. This adaption keeps the tradition of giving of oneself through "compassionate service" alive. Maria, thirty-nine, writes, "I think when

you do cook for someone else it gives you a sense of sharing yourself with them that isn't too encroaching, but maybe will open the doors if there is more of a need there than what meets the eye."

By no means do LDS women have a market on this type of service. Women, service, and food are an everyday aspect of most women's lives. My friend Angie, who is not LDS, moved to Utah from Washington State. Upon arriving in Utah, she was having a hard time meeting people in her neighborhood. One day she decided to make and deliver coffee cake to her neighbors and introduce herself. She shared and served, and within days she was receiving knocks on her door by women with their accompanying identifying factor: food.

On a recent February visit, women from my ward came visiting. These two ladies did not come empty-handed. But, rather than a loaf of banana bread or a plate of cookies, they brought a wood craft: three cut-out hearts painted in bright colors. Their gift was meant to be a constant reminder that I can have faith in my Father in Heaven if I listen with an open heart. Although I would have loved a plate of cookies, it is not about the food, but about the love that delivers it. Kamelle, in her twenties, agreed when she wrote, "It doesn't matter what you give, but how and why you give. I think it is when we eternalize these principles that we truly serve." The gift I received is still in keeping with the call to action—to show that love by word and deed.

One little side-note: I recently attended the funeral service of a dear friend who died at the age of ninety-two. LDS women usually furnish a meal for the deceased's family after the service. Usually all of the meal is donated, as is the service of these women. Typically, at the bottom of the typed funeral program, there is a note mentioning that the meal is provided by (for instance), Brigham City 13th Ward Relief Society Sisters. In the case of this program, the wording was different. It stated, "Compassionate Service: Brigham City 13th Ward Relief Society Sisters." Even here, food and compassionate service go hand-in-hand.

NOTES

1. Theodore C. Humphrey and Lin T. Humphrey, *We Gather Together: Food and Festival in American Life* (Logan: Utah State University Press, 1991), 2.
2. Warren Belasco and Philip Scranton, eds., *Food Nations: Selling Taste in Consumer Societies* (New York: Routledge, 2001), 8.
3. Linda Keller Brown and Kay Mussell, *Ethnic Regional Foodways in the United States: Performance of Group Identity* (Knoxville: University of Tennessee Press, 1984).

CANDY

KATHRYN L. MACKAY

"More sugar is consumed in Utah than in any other state," is a statement often made but not possible to document. Accompanying that statement is the follow-up explanation that Utahns eat lots of candy. As one confectioner explained, "Salt Lake City is a candy capital because people give a three-pound box of chocolates here rather than a bottle of wine."[1]

Major ingredients in candy were imported into the area that became Utah long before the 1847 arrival of the Mormons. Chocolate was brought in via Native American trade routes from central Mexico where the Mayans and then the Aztecs had developed the cacao beans into a ceremonial drink.[2] New research suggests ancestral Puebloan people living in a village near Blanding, Utah, were consuming chocolate as early as AD 750.[3]

Refined sugar—"Havana brown" and "Havana white"—were popular trade items at the fur-trapping rendezvous of the 1820s and 1830s.[4] These products were made by slave labor in the Caribbean and denote the international dynamics of this ingredient. Many of the fur trappers themselves, coming into the Utah area from Canada, Santa Fe, and St. Louis, carried with them hard or boiled candies flavored with lemon or peppermint oil.

However, not until Mormon immigrants settled in Utah was candy produced—both at home and commercially—in any great quantity. Building the Kingdom of God included satisfying the "sweet tooths" of its inhabitants. By 1851, there were in several settlements not only lumber and grist mills, but molasses mills turning out sweet syrups from sorghum.[5] By the end of the nineteenth century, Utah candy companies dominated the Intermountain West and vied with major national companies for overseas markets. Today, forty-five candy companies are listed with Utah's Own, a state program established to "create a consumer culture of choosing Utah products."[6]

The development of the candy industry in Utah parallels national and worldwide developments—from mom-and-pop by-hand operations to mechanized industrial operations to contemporary artisan operations. And the use of candy in Utah also parallels national and worldwide uses—whether medicinal, commercial, or cultural. Utahns have succumbed to the same notions as other Americans about the supposed necessity of candy in a child's world, the notions about

Processing sugar beets into sugar was a dream of Utah's earliest leaders, and by the end of the 1800s Utah Sugar was doing just that. The company later expanded to become Utah–Idaho Sugar, which remained a strong presence in the region until the 1980s. Photo by Bill Shipler. Used by permission, Utah State Historical Society. All rights reserved.

chocolates as status symbols, and the notions about candy making and giving as behaviors of sociability. But there are also uses of candy that are idiosyncratic to the Mormon Corridor. Candy making has been part of sustaining LDS leaders' quest for self-sufficiency. Candy manufacturing has been encouraged with the expansion of LDS church-owned businesses. And candy making has been enshrined as fostering family and community connections and reinforcing reverence for the pioneer past.

In the early years of the Mormon settlement of Utah, most candy was made at home, usually

CANDY CONSUMPTION IN THE UNITED STATES: A COMPARISON

	1880	1920
pounds of candy	110 million	1.4 billion
retail value of candy	$44.7 million	$1.2 billion
per capita consumption(in pounds)	2.2	13.2

Women in the Candy Industry in Chicago and St. Louis: a Study of Hours, Wages and Working Conditions in 1920–1921," *Bulletin of the Women's Bureau*, no. 25, Washington, D.C.: GOP, 1923.

for special occasions such as holiday celebrations. But candy making also strengthened community ties. Joseph Cooper, upon returning to Utah with a "down-and-back" wagon train which brought emigrants and supplies from St. Louis, noted: "Here some of our boys friends met us and we had some sorgum [*sic*], we had a Candy Pull and had a real good time."[7]

Mary Ann Hafen emigrated from Switzerland to Utah with her Mormon family in 1860 at age six. In her memoir, she described her life in Nevada, where she had moved in 1891 as part of a polygamous family. "Sugar, or sorghum, cane we took to the town sorghum mill and got our year's supply of molasses. Sugar and honey were almost unknown in those times, so sorghum served as sweetening. Candy pulls around the shining molasses mill were favorite evening pastimes for the young people."[8] On the other hand, Clarissa Jane Wilcox, born in 1863 in Mount Pleasant, as an old woman confessed: "I couldn't stand to eat another bit [of molasses candy] to this day."[9]

TAFFY

1 c. honey
1 c. half and half
1 c. sugar

Combine all ingredients in a heavy saucepan. Cook over medium heat until it comes to a medium hard-ball stage. Pour equal amounts into two well-greased cookie sheets. Allow to cool only until it can be easily handled. Pull until light and glossy. Twist into a rope and cut into bite-size pieces. Wrap individually in wax paper.[10]

A version of pulled candy often reproduced in Utah pioneer cookbooks is made with honey rather than molasses. Norma Matheson contributed this recipe to the *Salt Lake Tribune*'s *What's Cooking in Utah Kitchens* in 1978 with a note: "This recipe is of Parowan origin and is a Matheson favorite."

In territorial Utah, most of the candy not made at home was made by small, family-operated businesses, often in connection with a grocery. Henry Wallace, who migrated from England to Utah in 1862, is credited with establishing the first candy store in Salt Lake City. In 1863, John Taffe McDonald, whose son founded the J. G. McDonald Company, began selling out of his saddlebags the taffy he and his family made at home. William Startup is credited with bringing into Utah in 1869 the first machinery: scales, iron edging bars, hand-cranked drop machines, shears, and hooks.[11]

Henry A. Tuckett, whose English parents had converted to Mormonism in the 1850s, built his Wasatch Candy Company in the 1880s using the first steam plant in Utah. He also took advantage of increased availability of sugar, produced from sugar beets, the first sugar beet factory having been built in Lehi in 1891. Tuckett's company became the largest one in Utah, doing an annual business in 1892 of $150,000, with forty-two operators.[12] By the time Tuckett died in 1918, however, five companies dominated the Utah candy industry: the Startup Candy Company of Provo, the Shupe-Williams Candy Company of Ogden, the Murdock Candy Company of Logan, and the Sweet Candy Company and the J. G. McDonald Company, both in Salt Lake City.

These companies also came to dominate candy making in the Intermountain West. With access to rail transportation, a tradition of low wages, and the expansion of the Utah–Idaho Sugar Company, owned and controlled by the LDS Church, Utah became a "candy capital."[13] As reported in 1905: "Leaving out smelting, ore refining, and kindred industries of mining, the manufacture of Utah sugar stands at the head of the list of Utah's industrial enterprises." This report on the resources of the state continued exultantly: "The present annual consumption of Utah is 9,464.8 tons of sugar. Her production surpassed her consumption some time ago, and now the State is shipping over 20,000 tons of sugar to Missouri River points and other markets."[14]

Not only in Utah, but nationwide, sugar consumption was increasing exponentially and the confectionery trade flourished. By 1890 the industry was valued at $179,276 and just five years later at $712,552. And what was not exported was consumed domestically. By 1910, the national output per year equaled nine pounds of candy at fifteen cents a pound for every man, woman, and child in the country—a total worth of $135 million.[15]

The candy industry was booming not just because of increasing supplies of sugar and increasing efficiencies of machinery but also because of the expanding international trade. In 1920, Don W. Conover rhapsodized about the ingredients used in the thousand varieties of candy and chewing gum he claimed were produced by the Startup Candy Company of Provo: "Perfumes from the Balkans and Persia, egg albumens from Russia and China, agaragar [a gelatin from algae] from the Japanese seas, coconut from Ceylon, colors from Central Europe, chicle from South America."[16]

The same Industrial Commission of Utah that reported in 1918 the above statistics also offered the oft-repeated mantra:

[T]he per capita consumption of sugar in Utah is larger than anywhere else in the world. Several reasons are assigned: One is that a large proportion of the people abstain, as a matter of principle, from the use of narcotics and stimulants. It is quite frequently noted that the man who does not smoke or drink is a larger user of candy than the man who does. A physiological cause is assigned, but the fact remains that the consumption of candy in Utah is by no means confined to the young woman with the "sweet tooth." Then too, Utah is a sugar-producing state; and with a supply of sugar always available, it is only to be expected that its consumption would also be heavy.[17]

That same year, Leon Sweet of Sweet's Candy Company declared, "No commodity manufactured in Utah has a wider distribution that her confectionary. Fully one hundred salesmen cover the territory from the Missouri River to the Pacific Coast exploiting Utah's chocolates and confectionary."[18] A grandson described such a salesman, not for Sweet's, but for Shupe-Williams:

> Grandpa covered a territory in Nevada for the Shupe-Williams candy company. The area he covered was broiling hot in the summer, mighty cold in the winter, and desolate all year round. I can vividly remember how Grandpa would load his sample cases into the trunk and take off in his Nash Rambler (no air conditioning, of course) to make his rounds for a week or more, stopping at small grocers, drugstores, gas stations, motels—anybody who might carry candy near the checkout counter or on the shelves.... Grandpa liked the people who were his customers, and apparently they liked him. They bought a lot of candy from him.[19]

Logan's Bluebird Candy Company has been in business since 1914, offering beautiful and tasty hand-dipped chocolates. Photo by Andrea Graham, 2001. Courtesy BRHA Survey, Special Collections & Archives, Merrill-Cazier Library, Utah State University.

Most of the candy manufactures in Utah were, not surprisingly, from LDS families who had emigrated from Northern Europe. The Startup family, for example, had been in the candy business in London since 1823 before some members moved to Utah in the 1860s. There were, however, immigrants from other traditions. Sebastiani and Ruffati are confectioners listed in the 1909 Business Directory of Salt Lake City. And several members of the Greek community in Ogden were candy makers. James G. Karas established the Orpheum Candy Company in 1916. By 1920 the business was described as "manufacturing all of its own candies, confections and ice cream, and something of the volume of their trade is

CONFECTIONERY MANUFACTURING IN UTAH

Year	Number of Firms	Salaried Officers	Wage Earners	Wages paid
1899	9	45	153	$51,000
1904	12	54	335	$103,000
1909	17	150	586	$204,000
1919	31	184	1013	$540,000
1927	21	162	617	$474,000

Source: "Confectionary and Bakery Products," *Report of the Industrial Commission of Utah, 1917–1918*, Utah Public Documents, vol. 2, no. 19, 153.

indicated in the fact that they now employ eight people."[20] Some of those employees in turn started other companies. George and brother John purchased Orpheum and established Dokos Candy, which operated until the 1970s. John Bockeas and George Poulis organized the Little Sweet Shop in 1922, which was open through the 1940s.[21]

These were modest local businesses. The major companies had become industrial factories, employing hundreds of workers, a majority of them women. Women worked as chocolate dippers, as piece sorters, and as packers. Most of the women were under the age of twenty-five, and daughters of immigrant working-class families. Their earnings, about $5.50 per week in 1914, contributed to the family income.[22]

W. F. Jensen, manager of his own candy company in Logan, supposed that

the wholesome and pleasant nature of the work is an incentive to women to enter the industry. Where could one find a line of work with fewer objectionable features than is presented in the

positions in these factories or behind the counters in these stores which making and selling dainty, delicious confections?[23]

Such a cheery description is countered by the indictment of candy factories reported by the investigators from the Consumers' League of New York in 1928. It is likely that conditions were not dissimilar to those in Utah factories:

The facts disclosed in the present study, supplemented by the figures furnished by the State Department of Labor would indicate that the two major tragedies of the industrial worker's life—low wages and unemployment—are particularly keen in the case of the candy worker. Perhaps no other group of women workers in our midst is so unorganized, so young, and so inarticulate—therefore so helpless.[24]

Candy is a commodity made mostly by women in businesses run mostly by men, and is culturally constructed as feminine. Most people enjoy candy;

yet advertising and language expressions assume women have a particular fondness for it.[25] Certainly women are encouraged to make candy at home as an expression of maternal care. In fact, the publication of candy-making manuals and candy cookbooks increased dramatically between 1880 and 1930, the same period that witnessed the explosive growth of machine-made candy.[26]

In Utah, LDS church magazines often printed recipes for candy and other treats, especially around the holidays: "Nine Tips for Perfect Candy," *Ensign*, December 1975; "Incredible Edible Valentines," *New Era*, January 1985; "Christmas Workshop," *Friend*, December 1990. Assumptions about candy making and maternal responsibilities were not particular to Mormon culture, even though they may have been more intense in terms of defining the good housewife.

Intense interest in homemade candy recipes also accompanies the LDS passion for all things pioneer. For example:

How about celebrating Pioneer Day the way the pioneers would have, with an old-fashioned candy pull?

David Bench, executive chef at the Lion House, teaches occasional classes called "Old-Fashioned Pulled Candy" with his mother, Karla Bench, of Moroni. Children can also hone their candy-pulling skills during birthday parties at the Lion House, where they dress in pioneer bonnets and play games that were popular during the 1800s.[27]

And candy has a role in the increasingly popular activity of going on treks, which involve dressing up in pioneer fashion, packing handcarts and other wooden vehicles, and hiking for some days in various places in the Mormon West. The time-honored use of candy as bribery does not seem to be forbidden, as evident in this report from the *Eastern Arizona Courier* about members of the Duncan and Pima LDS Stakes:

The Pioneer Trek also included many fun activities like a stick-pull and tug-of-war competition, a three-legged race and a taffy pull. They had fiddlers and square dancing and singing. The youths experienced Dutch oven cooking, black powder rifle shooting, tomahawk throwing, and making apple fritters.

Some of the famous true pioneer stories involved crossing icy streams along the way. To simulate that experience, the leaders brought out a tub of ice water and told the youths that anyone who stood barefoot in the icy water would receive four Tootsie Rolls for every three minutes they endured.[28]

Candy is a cultural artifact. As historian Samira Kawash notes: "Candy provokes strong feelings in many people, feelings that seem much larger and more complex than the simple substance itself."[29] In America it carries meanings about consumption, commercialization, nostalgia, gentility, and gender. In Utah it also carries meanings about sophistication, internationalism, and heritage.

NOTES

1. Marie Cavanaugh of Mrs. Cavanaugh's Candies, as quoted in *The Intermountain Food Retailer* 58, no. 6 (June 1982): 57.

2. Sophie D. Coe and Michael Coe, *The True History of Chocolate* (New York: Thames & Hudson, 1996), 37–39.

3. Brent Gover, "Was Chocolate on the Menu in the Ancient Southwest?" *Rand McNally Classroom, The Weekly Buzz*, February 8, 2014, http://education. randmcnally.com/classroom.

4. "Invoice of merchandise shipped on board S.B. Diana C.M. Halstead Master bound for the upper Missouri River and consigned for account and risk of upper Missouri outfit 1835 under mark in the margin," *Papers of the St. Louis Fur Trade*, Reel 7, vols. 86 and 98, http://user.xmission.com/~drudy/mtman/html/diana.html.

5. Hubert Howe Bancroft, *History of Utah, 1840–1886* (San Francisco: The History Company, 1889), 328.

6. "Food & Beverage," Utah's Own, http://utahsown.utah.gov/list. php?id=58&name=Candy&user_type=Member.

7. "Joseph Cooper," in *Utah Pioneer Biographies* (Salt Lake City, 1935–1964), 7:134–35; https://history.lds. org/overlandtravel/pioneers/14555/joseph-cooper?; George W. Givens, *The Language of the Mormon Pioneers* (Springville, UT: Bonneville Books, 2003).

8. Mary Ann Hafen, "A Mormon Woman's Life in Southern Utah," in *Memories of a Handcart Pioneer, with Some Account of Frontier Life in Utah and Nevada* (Denver: Privately printed for her descendants, 1938); http://historymatters.gmu.edu/d/4931/.

9. Becky Bartholomew, "The Lives of Six Pioneer Girls," Utah History to Go, September 1996, http:// historytogo.utah.gov/utah_chapters/pioneers_and_cowboys/thelivesofsixpioneergirls.html.

10. Donna Lou Morgan, ed., *The Salt Lake Tribune's What's Cooking in Utah Kitchens* (Salt Lake City: J. W. Gallivan, 1978), 173.

11. Leon Sweet, "A Few Facts and Some Figures Relative to the Candy Industry of Utah," *Utah Payroll Builder* 9, no. 8 (May 1921): 67; "Unique Treats and Flavorful Past Help Startup Candy Stay Sweet," *Deseret News*, April 8, 1992; "Startup Candy Factory," National Park Service, National Register of Historic Places, 1983.

12. Robert Mitchell, "Candy Industry Makes Big Gains," *Deseret News* (Salt Lake City, UT), December 27, 1956.

13. For information about the Utah-Idaho Sugar Co., see Matthew C. Godfrey, *Religion, Politics, and Sugar: The Mormon Church, the Federal Government, and the Utah-Idaho Sugar Company, 1907–1921* (Logan: Utah State University Press, 2007).

14. *Resources of the State of Utah*, 12th ed. (Omaha: Union Pacific Railroad, 1905), 68–69.

15. Wendy A. Woloson, *Refined Tastes, Sugar, Confectionary, and Consumers in Nineteenth-Century America* (Baltimore: Johns Hopkins University Press, 2002), 6; the 1914 Census of Manufactures as quoted in U.S. Department of Labor, *Wages of Candy Makers in Philadelphia*, Bulletin of the Woman in Industry Service, no. 4 (June 28, 1919): 11–12. CMOS: By 1936, even as the nation was in the midst of the Great Depression, per capita consumption of candy was 16.0 pounds: H. Dewy Anderson and Percy Davidson, *Occupational Trends in the United States* (New York: Stanford University Press, 1940), 326.

16. Don W. Conover, "Startup Candy Company of Provo," *Utah Payroll Builder* 8, no. 1 (June 1920): 26.

17. Ibid.

18. "Confectionary and Bakery Products," *Utah Payroll Builder* 6, no. 5 (October 1918): 19.

19. Tom Sant, *The Giants of Sales: What Dale Carnegie, John Patterson, Elmer Wheeler, and Joe Girard Can Teach You About Real Sales Success* (New York: AMACOM Books, 2006), iv.

20. Noble Warrum, Charles E. Morse, and W. Brown Ewing, *Utah Since Statehood, Historical and Biographical*, vol. 4 (Chicago: S. J. Clark, 1920), 576.

21. John Sillito and Sarah Langsdon, *Images of America: Ogden* (Charleston, SC: Arcadia Publishing, 2008), 80.

22. Madeline Stauffer Lambert, "Women at Work in Salt Lake City" (Master's thesis, University of Utah, 1914), 40–43.

23. W. F. Jensen, "The Candy Industry and What It Means to Cache Valley," *Utah Payroll Builder* 7, no. 6 (April 1920): 24.

24. *Behind the Scenes in Candy Factories* (New York: Consumers' League of New York, 1928), 58.

25. "Bonbons, Lemon Drops, and Oh Henry! Bars: Candy, Consumer Culture and the Construction of Gender, 1895–1920," in *Kitchen Culture in America: Popular Representations of Food, Gender, and Race,* ed. Sherrie A. Inness (Philadelphia: University of Pennsylvania Press, 2001).

26. Samira Kawash, *Candy: A Century of Panic and Pleasure* (New York: Faber and Faber, 2013), 124–25.

27. Valerie Philips, "Pulling Together: Celebrate Pioneer Day with an Old-Fashioned Candy Pull," *Deseret News* (Salt Lake City, UT), July 22, 2008.

28. "Pioneer Trek Teaches Life Lessons," *Eastern Arizona Courier,* April 10, 2013.

29. Kawash, *Candy,* 18.

By 1915, Sweet Candy Company was sending their Utah-made goods to international markets. Photo by Bill Shipler. Used by permission, Utah State Historical Society.

44

ICONIC UTAH CHOCOLATIERS

CAROL A. EDISON

Since the early twentieth century, commercial candy making has been big business in Utah. That's when well-known Sweet's Candy, originally of Portland, Oregon, moved their operation to Salt Lake City—presumably to take advantage of Utah's sugar beet industry.[1] About the same time J. G. McDonald's, which had begun peddling taffy in the 1860s, expanded their candy production with the construction of a widely acclaimed four-story factory in downtown Salt Lake City.[2] Both companies soon marketed their products worldwide while also serving an appreciative local audience.

A number of smaller, family-owned businesses were also established in the first half of the century. They often began with a talented home candy maker and expanded from there. Many specialized in hand-dipped chocolates. Today most of these companies, including Sweet's, still produce and sell candy. Utahns' well-known love of candy was recognized and memorialized on pins created for the 2002 Olympics in Salt Lake City including one for salt water taffy and another for Fernwood's popular thin mint.

Here is a list of some of Utah's most well-known and longstanding chocolatiers.

1900 – Sweet's Candy Company, Salt Lake City[3]

1914 – Bluebird Candy Company, Logan (originally affiliated with the Bluebird Restaurant)[4]

1916 – Glade Candy Company, Salt Lake City (now known as Taffy Town and specializing in saltwater taffy)[5]

1938 – Cummings Studio Chocolates/C. K. Cummings, Salt Lake City[6]

1942 – Garden Gate Handmade Chocolates and Toffee, Salt Lake City (originally an ice cream parlor with hand-dipped chocolates; now open only at Christmas)[7]

1947 – Fernwood Candy Company, Salt Lake City[8]

1947 – Maxfield Candy Company, Salt Lake City[9]

1964 – Mrs. Cavanaugh's, Bountiful[10]

Fernwood Candy Company's still-popular mint sandwiches date back to 1947. Chocolate mint sandwich souvenir pin, 2002 Salt Lake Winter Olympics. Used by permission, Utah State Historical Society. All rights reserved.

NOTES

1. "History," Sweet Candy, http://www.sweetcandy.com/history.
2. "The World Wants Our Candies and Chocolates," *Goodwin's Weekly* (Salt Lake City), July 14, 1917, 16.
3. Sweet's Candy Company, https://www.sweetcandy.com/.
4. Blue Bird Candy, http://www.bluebirdcandy.com/.
5. "About Taffy Town," Taffy Town, https://www.taffytown.com/about-3/.
6. "Tradition," Fine Candies, https://www.finecandies.com/tradition.php.
7. Jacob Stringer, "Garden Gate," December 18, 2012, http://www.cityweekly.net/utah/garden-gate/Content?oid=2286041.
8. "Fernwood Story," Fernwood Candy, https://www.fernwoodcandy.com/fernwood-story/.
9. "Our Story," Maxfield Candy, http://www.maxfieldcandy.com/our-story.html.
10. "Meet Mrs. Cavanaugh," Mrs. Cavanaugh's, http://mrscavanaughs.com/meet-mrs-cavanaugh/.

45

ICE CREAM

JEAN LITTLE

In Utah, ice cream has been part of the local economy and culture for over a century. Companies such as Farr Better Ice Cream and FatBoy Ice Cream, which are known throughout the United States, got their start right here. As the nation's eighth largest ice cream consumer per capita,[1] Utah also has a number of local shops and manufacturers that have helped make this delectable dessert such a vital part of the Utah identity. Fendall's and Snelgrove were two of the first ice cream manufacturers in the Salt Lake Valley. Leatherby's Family Creamery opened in 1984 and quickly became known for its gargantuan ice cream sundaes. In 2004, a BYU alumnus opened Sub Zero Ice Cream and Yogurt, a revolutionary business where each ice cream creation is combined and frozen to order using liquid nitrogen. Over the years, Utah has clearly become a center of innovation for this sweet treat. In addition to playing a significant role in the local economy, college students, children, and families have all formed their own ice cream traditions.

ICE CREAM INNOVATION

In 1910, just six years after the ice cream cone debuted at the St. Louis World's Fair, Fendall's opened in Salt Lake City.[2] The sit-down section of the parlor closed in 1997, but until 2013 customers could still custom-order uncommon flavors such as ginger or black licorice, or they could take a trip down memory lane with burnt almond fudge. Another ice cream innovator, Casper Merrill, started making ice cream bars on a stick, covered them in chocolate and nuts, and sold them at the 1925 Independence Day celebration in Richmond, Utah. Soon after, he made the ice cream sandwiches that would later be known as FatBoys.

Double-scoop chocolate and strawberry cone souvenir pin, 2002 Salt Lake Winter Olympics. Used by permission, Utah State Historical Society. All rights reserved.

From 1929 until it closed in the 1990s, the family-owned ice cream company Snelgrove's was such a Salt Lake City institution that when Dreyer's bought the company, they retained the iconic double-dip ice cream sculpture at the flagship Sugarhouse store and factory. Courtesy Clint Gardner.

Another one of the oldest ice cream manufacturing plants in Utah actually started as an ice maker. Steve Farr's Farr Better Ice Cream began in March 1929.[3] As an increasing number of families bought in-home refrigerators, people no longer needed to buy ice from the store. To stay in business, the Farr Better Ice plant really had to scramble. They were able to continue using a lot of their existing equipment by shifting production to something a little sweeter.

In the early days, Farr's Ice Cream shop and Snelgrove competed heavily for business. While Snelgrove Ice Cream Parlor focused primarily on local customers, Farr's bought out Russel's Old-Fashioned Ice Cream of Salt Lake City and established a line of ice cream that would eventually sell in grocery stores throughout the region. In 1989, Dreyer's bought out Snelgrove and discontinued it in 2008. Farr's Ice Cream has continued to flourish, and even expanded by establishing Farr's Fresh in 2010 to compete with increasingly popular frozen yogurt shops.

Although most of the old-time parlors have gone out of business, they still have a place in Salt Lake culture. Even today the store sign for Fendall's can be seen at its original Salt Lake location at 450 South 700 East. And Snelgrove's iconic double-decker ice cream cone still adorns the original building at 850 East 2100 South.[4] Snelgrove's logo also appeared on one of the 2002 Olympic pins. Postcards, signs, and other memorabilia continue to circulate among vintage collectors and ice cream enthusiasts.

COLLEGE ICE CREAM RIVALRIES

With such a rich ice cream history, it is no surprise that the tradition found its way into institutions of higher learning. Both Brigham Young University and Utah State University operate creameries that feature signature ice cream flavors designed to celebrate elements of their own unique cultures.

Founded as Utah's agricultural college in 1888, Utah State has always had a creamery. By 1922, it had become a place where students could learn how to make milk, cheese, ice cream, and a number of other things. The founders of Casper's, Snelgrove, and Farr's all learned their technique as students there. According to the Utah State University website, Aggie Ice Cream was also the first ice cream to make it to outer space. It's no secret that Utah State is proud of the work they do at their creamery.

Crystal Ice Cream Parlor, Mount Pleasant, Utah, circa 1910. Used by permission, Utah State Historical Society. All rights reserved.

Walking through campus, you are likely to hear students bragging that USU ice cream is much better than BYU's. Some even accuse BYU of copying Utah State's recipe, though this rumor has never been substantiated.

Today, Utah State's four signature flavors are Aggie Birthday Cake, Aggie Bull Tracks, True Aggie Night, and Aggie Blue Mint. One of the most popular flavors, Aggie Blue Mint is actually blue—a commemoration of their school color and their true-blue loyalty to the institution. In addition to its creamy texture, what makes this ice cream really stand out is that it has chunks of Oreo and white chocolate mixed in. Another favorite, True Aggie Night, has a vanilla base with raspberry swirls and raspberry-filled dark chocolate hearts. This ice cream makes special reference to a school tradition that says a student can only become a "True Aggie" by kissing someone who has already received the designation at the block "A," a sculpture at the top of the Old Main Hill on campus, under a full moon at midnight. If neither member of a given couple is already a "True Aggie," they can only obtain the status by kissing each other on Homecoming day or on A-Day.

Aggie ice cream. Courtesy USU College of Agriculture.

A few hours south of USU, in Provo, BYU has its own kissing traditions that feature ice cream. According to a tradition that has been passed down from one generation of students to another, students are required to buy ice cream for their roommates every time they kiss someone for the first time. This is just one part of a tradition that also calls for M&M's for holding hands and a steak dinner for getting engaged; like all good traditions, there is considerable variation. Having fun with this tradition, one group of girls would tease a roommate by tapping an empty ice cream carton to the outside of the

door to the apartment on nights she had a date. For some students, even the flavor of ice cream has symbolic value. In an entry from the William A. Wilson archives, Anna Tueller describes Rocky Road as the ice cream a girl buys "when the ice cream has been anticipated for a long time."[5] Tueller is careful to note, however, that there aren't set rules for the type of ice cream that the girl buys, but that the choice is dependent on how she would characterize her feelings about the relationship.

When it comes to buying interesting ice cream flavors for roommates, students have a considerable number of options to choose from. The BYU Creamery currently has forty-three different flavors, a number that has dropped significantly since the on-site creamery closed and production began at Welfare Square in Salt Lake City. A few of BYU's signature concoctions are Bronco's Cocoa Bean and LaVell's Vanilla. Named for former football coach Bronco Mendenhall, Bronco's Cocoa Bean ice cream is the successor to LaVell's Vanilla,[6] which memorializes the name of LaVell Edwards, BYU's head football coach from 1972 to 2000. This ice cream is still sold at the creamery. In a school that has such a strong athletic tradition, it is fitting that sports teams would have their own ice cream customs. Since 2006, BYU's football team has taken BYU Creamery ice cream to every bowl game for its players to enjoy.

So far, there have also been two flavors named after BYU presidents. Whoosh Cecil is a chocolate ice cream with caramel swirls and pecans, and makes reference to a BYU tradition in which the student section calls out "Whoosh Cecil" every time a BYU player makes a foul shot.[7] In response, President Samuelson would give a thumbs-up.[8] One

GRAHAM CANYON ICE CREAM

1 pint heavy whipping cream
1 can sweetened condensed milk
1 tsp. vanilla
8 crushed honey graham crackers
1/2 c. crushed chocolate honeycomb candy

In a large bowl, use a hand mixer to beat whipping cream for about ten minutes or until peaks form.

Add sweetened condensed milk and vanilla and continue to whip the mixture until it is smooth. With a rubber spatula, stir in the graham cracker crumbs.

Finally, mix in the crushed honeycomb candy.

Transfer mixture to an airtight container and place in the freezer for 6 to 8 hours before serving.

For people who are nostalgic for the type of old-fashioned ice cream sold by Snelgrove and Fendall's, there are also several copycat recipes floating around, most notably Burnt Almond Fudge, which both companies sold at the height of their popularity.[9]

BYU Creamery ice cream. Photo by Sara Hill. Courtesy *Daily Universe*.

of the most popular flavors, Ernestly Chocolate, was named after Ernest L. Wilkinson, BYU's president from 1951 to 1971.

Even though USU and BYU ice creams seem to be rivals, there is one thing that they definitely have in common: they both use their ice cream to commemorate important people and traditions in their own schools.

CULTURAL INFLUENCES

Undoubtedly, ice cream makes an important contribution to Utah culture—especially in college towns. While there are many potential reasons for this, including the characteristically hot, dry weather in the summer, one reason may have to do with the LDS faith, which prohibits traditional party beverages. For many people in Utah, the phrase "going out for a pint" is more likely to refer to a pint of Ben & Jerry's than a pint of beer; and when they are looking for a pick-me-up, a sugar buzz is their version of an alcohol buzz.

For many Utah residents, ice cream is linked to religious traditions. Following the Priesthood session of General Conference, which is a semiannual church meeting specifically for men above the age of twelve, it is common for fathers and sons, groups of friends, or even entire elders quorums to go out for ice cream or root beer floats.[10] Also beginning at age twelve, young church members of both genders are invited to participate in trips to the temples. Across the street from the Ogden temple is a Farr Better

BURNT ALMOND FUDGE ICE CREAM

1/2 c. cocoa powder (we have a really rich cocoa powder
  so I measure slightly below the rim)
3 c. half-and-half (or 1 1/2 c. milk and 1 1/2 c. cream, same thing)
1 c. heavy cream
8 egg yolks, large
9 oz. sugar
2 tsp. vanilla
1/2 c. almonds
1 Tbsp. butter

Mix the cocoa with 1 cup of the half-and-half in a medium saucepan over medium heat, whisking to combine. Add the remaining half-and-half and the heavy cream. Bring the mixture just to a simmer, stirring occasionally, and remove from the heat.

In a medium bowl, whisk the egg yolks until they lighten in color. While whisking, slowly add the sugar until it has all been added and combined. Temper the cream mixture into the eggs and sugar by gradually adding small amounts (I use the half-cup used to measure the cocoa) and whisking constantly, until about 1/3 of the cream mixture has been added. Pour in the remainder and return the entire mixture to the saucepan and place over low heat. Continue to cook, stirring frequently, until the mixture thickens slightly and coats the back of a spoon or reaches 170 to 175 degrees F. Pour the mixture into a container and allow to sit at room temperature for 30 minutes. Stir in the vanilla extract. Place the mixture in the refrigerator; once it is cool enough not to form condensation on the lid, cover and store for 4 to 8 hours or until the temperature reaches 40 degrees F or below. (I've never waited that long...)

While the mixture is cooling, toast your almonds. Preheat oven to 325 degrees F. Spread the almonds out on a rimmed baking sheet. Cut the tablespoon of butter into a few pieces and scatter over the almonds. Put the almonds in the oven. Check and stir them every couple of minutes. The almonds can burn quickly so don't neglect them! Once you've reached a satisfied level of toastiness, remove from oven and allow to cool. Once cool, chop and set aside.

Pour the mixture into an ice cream maker and process according to the manufacturer's directions. When the ice cream is almost done, add the almonds to the ice cream maker. Serve as is for soft serve or freeze another 3 to 4 hours to allow the ice cream to harden.[11]

Ice Cream shop,[12] which plays an important part in the temple trip tradition for many Ogden residents. Not only do youth groups go out for ice cream afterward, but many people continue the tradition into adulthood.

Throughout Utah, many people carry on their own family ice cream traditions by trying their hand at making the frozen dessert in their own kitchen.

In the last few years one of the most popular recipes circulating among Utah food bloggers is a copycat of BYU's Graham Canyon. While there are several different versions, one of the most popular recipes can be made without an ice cream maker.

Both of these recipes are perfect for people who want to re-create days when some of their favorite ice cream flavors were a little bit more accessible, or share a favorite dessert with friends or relatives. Although it is hard to trace exactly when or why ice cream became such an integral part of Utah culture, one thing is certain: This delicious treat continues to be part of many traditions that are passed down from one generation to another.

NOTES

1. Julie Zeveloff, "These Cities Love Ice Cream the Most," *Business Insider*, July 20, 2012.
2. Valerie Phillips, "Frozen in Time: Fendall's Celebrates 100 Years of Making Ice Cream," *Deseret News* (Salt Lake City), March 17, 2010.
3. "Our History," Farr Better Premium Ice Cream, http://www.farrsicecream.com/#/History/.
4. In the early 1990s Dreyer's Ice Cream purchased Snelgrove's and in 2008 stopped making ice cream under that name. But they kept the beloved store sign on display for another generation, until 2019, when they removed the name Snelgrove but retained the iconic double-decker ice cream cone.
5. Anna Tueller, "Ice Cream," FA 14 Series 1 Subseries 1 1.1.3.7.2., L. Tom Perry Special Collections, Harold B. Lee Library, Brigham Young University, Provo, Utah.
6. Kathy Stephenson, "Top 10: Utah's Signature Foods," *Salt Lake Tribune*, May 17, 2011.
7. Kathy Stephenson, "Creamery Rivalry: USU vs. BYU," *Salt Lake Tribune*, October 1, 2008.
8. Sugene Lee, "BYU Basketball Cheer Becomes Tradition," *Daily Universe* (Brigham Young University, Provo, UT), April 2, 2013.
9. Katie, "No Churn Graham Canyon Ice Cream Recipe," Clarks Condensed, https://www.clarkscondensed.com/food/graham-canyon-ice-cream-recipe/.
10. Joseph Walker, "Priesthood Session Traditions 'Must Be Served,'" *Deseret News*, March 26, 2012.
11. Audrey, "Burnt Almond Fudge Ice Cream," The Dirty Dish Club, http://dirtydishclub.com/burnt-almond-fudge-ice-cream/.
12. "Farr Russell Ice Cream," Farr's Ice Cream, http:// www.farrsicecream.com/#/History/.

If your Coffee-Pot has boiled too often

If too many cups of coffee have set your stomach and nerves on edge, put the pot on to boil again—

But this time use

POSTUM CEREAL

in place of coffee

Boil it a full fifteen minutes after boiling starts and you will bring out its rich, satisfying flavor.

The benefit to health will soon be apparent.

"There's a Reason"

Made by
Postum Cereal Company, Inc.
Battle Creek, Michigan.

POSTUM

Naturally Caffeine Free

ELAINE CLARK

Postum wasn't born in Utah. Why would it have been? The dietary restrictions on alcohol, tobacco, and "hot drinks" that are found in the LDS Church's Word of Wisdom weren't commandments when church founder Joseph Smith Jr. wrote them through divine revelation into the Doctrine & Covenants—one of the foundational bodies of scripture of the Mormon Church.[1] They were a principle, a good idea, and in 1895 when C. W. Post started making the coffee substitute in Michigan,[2] drinking tea and coffee had little to do with being a Mormon in good standing.

Postum has become part of the Mormon story, but the journey to that association was as much about being accepted in the national community as it would later be about setting faithful LDS adherents apart.

THERE'S A REASON

When you flip through the magazines at your local check-out stand, it would be hard to deny that Americans are given to diet crazes and health fads—and that's nothing new. Scholar Ruth Clifford Engs documented three major American health movements—she refers to them as "Clean Living Movements." Postum was a child of the second of these, which coincided with the Progressive Era of 1890 to 1920.[3] But while the temperance movement gets all the attention when looking at this era, there were many other theories about what a person should or should not be consuming.

There was a lot of anxiety in industrialized nineteenth-century America, and it exhibited itself in symptoms that may seem familiar to people today: sleeplessness, fatigue, bad digestion. And like today, many people were looking for a cure. Charles William Post was one of them.[4]

"Sanitariums" around the country offered respite to invalids like Post. In 1891, his search for a cure led him to Michigan, home to Dr. John Harvey Kellogg's Battle Creek Hydropathic Sanitarium. Kellogg was a Seventh Day Adventist and a physician. His cure came in the form of exercise, sunshine, rest, and a vegetarian diet that restricted, among other things, alcohol, tea, and coffee.[5]

Post found a renewed vitality in his time at "the San," and Battle Creek offered a bustling community serving people on a similar health journey. Post stayed in Michigan and set his sights on creating a commercial line of products like those he had encountered under Kellogg's care. The Postum Cereal Company was founded in 1895 and began offering its eponymous beverage, "a sure relief from the many ails of coffee,"[6] followed two years later by Grape-Nuts "to meet a well-defined need of humanity."[7]

THEY SUPPOSED THEY HAD REASONS

The Word of Wisdom—a health code that LDS members are instructed to follow—was recorded in the Doctrine & Covenants on February 27, 1833.[8] It would be more than sixty-two years before Postum hit the scene, and some twenty-five years after that before adherence to dietary restrictions—including coffee and tea—would be required to gain access to the temple, where the most sacred rites of the religion are conducted.[9] It's fair to say that the Mormon relationship with coffee was complicated.

In March of 1855, Elder George A. Smith gave a talk in the Salt Lake Tabernacle. Smith told stories of people who had fallen away in the earliest days of the Mormon Church and recalled one family who

traveled a great distance to join the church body in Kirtland, Ohio, in 1833.

The Prophet asked them to stop with him until they could find a place. Sister Emma, in the meantime, asked the old lady if she would have a cup of tea to refresh her after the fatigues of the journey, or a cup of coffee. This whole family apostatized because they were invited to take a cup of tea or coffee, after the Word of Wisdom was given.

Smith scorned their lack of faith.[10]

Coffee made the journey westward with the believers, but there were voices decrying its use. In January of 1851, the *Deseret Evening News* printed a letter written by a person using the pseudonym "Homer." In it, he introduced himself as one of the "best customers to the store keepers for tea, coffee, &c," but after reading an earlier article about the Word of Wisdom, he had a vivid dream. In it, the land was ravaged with cholera, but the homes of the saints "were like paradise." He was led to a table where he saw stricken people who had drunk coffee and tea. The saints, though, drank "cold water . . . and the destroying angel shall pass by them as the children of Israel."[11]

The Word of Wisdom was a focus of the October 1851 General Conference of the LDS Church, and in an 1855 sermon, Brigham Young encouraged "young, smart gentlemen" to leave "tobacco, whiskey, or a little tea and coffee" to "the old fogies."[12]

Still, in 1893 the *Deseret Evening News* reported that church members in Utah consumed 325,000 pounds of coffee annually at a cost of $45,000.[13] The health benefits of abstinence were touted, as were the economic benefits of using that money to pay off debts and benefit the church body as a whole.

There was a response a few days later that challenged those numbers, suggesting they represented a little less than one pound per capita. The real concern, the unattributed piece went on to say, was sending money outside of Utah to buy coffee, tobacco, and even dry salt bacon.[14]

GRAIN IS GOOD FOR THE FOOD OF MAN

Postum was advertised in Utah in late 1896 in the *Salt Lake Herald*, a paper published by two elders in the LDS Church. The ad didn't make a moral appeal to readers though; it made a scientific argument for replacing coffee with the "health-giving properties" of Postum.[15]

The timing couldn't have been better. It was only earlier that year that Utah had been admitted to the Union, and the efforts to secure statehood had meant a significant change in church practice to align with the moral goals of the Progressive Era. Statehood had meant abandoning plural marriage.[16]

The outcry against polygamy was part and parcel of the larger moral campaign throughout America. That same fervor drove the temperance movement, and religious groups, like the Women's Christian Temperance Union, aimed to stamp out both alcohol consumption and plural marriage.[17]

In Utah, LDS Church leadership was still divided over whether to enforce the Word of Wisdom and what parts of it should be emphasized. Church president Lorenzo Snow focused particularly

on not eating too much meat, while others made a point of suggesting that beer shouldn't be among the beverages that were forbidden.[18] Historian Thomas Alexander points to the succession of the church presidency following the death of Snow as the turning point. Joseph F. Smith, who became president in 1901, began emphasizing restraint from coffee, alcohol, and tobacco, and his 1918 successor, Heber J. Grant, was deeply involved in the state's prohibition movement.

Aligning Utah with national sentiment was politically advantageous[19] and much easier in the case of prohibition than it had been for polygamy. It didn't take a new revelation to command the faithful to be "temperate in all things." It simply meant underscoring church teachings that were already in place. In turning to the Word of Wisdom, coffee felt the sting of the same hatchet that came down on alcohol.

And there was Postum, boasting the very ingredient that the Word of Wisdom encouraged by stating that "all grain is good for the food of man" and suggesting that wheat was chief amongst those.

DO YOU KEEP THE WORD OF WISDOM?

The Eighteenth Amendment to the U.S. Constitution was ratified in January of 1919, and the following year it went into effect, banning "manufacture, sale or transportation of intoxicating liquors."[20] Though there is some argument as to the exact date, adherence to the Word of Wisdom became a requirement to enter the temple in the early presidency of Heber J. Grant, likely sometime between 1919 and 1921.[21] This meant that to demonstrate a person's worthiness to perform the sacred rites and rituals of

> ## BAKED POSTUM CUSTARD
>
> 3 c. milk
> 1/4 c. sugar
> 2 Tbsp. instant Postum
> 3 eggs, slightly beaten
> 1/4 tsp. salt
> 1/2 tsp. vanilla
>
> Scald milk with Postum. Combine eggs, sugar, salt, and vanilla; add hot liquid gradually. Pour into greased baking dish or custard cups. Place in pan of hot water and bake at 325 degrees F for 45 minutes or until knife inserted comes out clean. Chill; serve plain or with cream. Shredded coconut may be sprinkled over the top. If custard is to be carried in lunch box, bake in unwaxed paper cups.[22]

their faith,[23] coffee was off the table.

The first state ratified the Twenty-First Amendment in early April of 1933.[24] In Utah, the debate over prohibition was on many people's minds, so much so that church auxiliary groups were instructed to teach their members on the Word of Wisdom. Newspapers around the state ran articles touting the wisdom. The *Deseret News* emphasized the one-hundred-year history of the document and underscored its provenance: "Not by commandment or constraint, but by revelation . . . for the order and will of God."[25]

It was the Utah legislature that rang the death knell for prohibition when it ratified the Twenty-First Amendment in December of 1933,[26] but it was against the wishes of church leadership. The prohibition for the Mormon faithful against strong drink, tobacco, and "hot drinks"—interpreted by early and current church leaders as tea and coffee[27]—stayed in place. It's one thing to repeal a constitutional amendment; it's another thing entirely to go back on a religious dictate.

POSTUM TODAY

In an online, nonscientific survey conducted for this chapter, it was clear that abstinence from coffee was and continues to be a marker to define a person as a good Mormon. One young man in his early twenties, who was raised LDS in Provo, explained his family's attitude toward coffee:

> [Coffee] was openly talked about as dangerous. Whenever it was mentioned, the family was referring to an uncle or cousin that left the church "out of bitterness." Coffee drinkers were all as bitter as their coffee.[28]

For some faithful believers, the idea of drinking coffee is as bad as abandoning other particularly Mormon practices, such as wearing prescribed Mormon temple garments:

> Almost all kids in my family left the church. . . . Five of us were/are coffee drinkers. My parents are not coffee drinkers. They are "good" Mormons. Two of my brothers go to church, but claim to be agnostic and don't wear their garments. One of them has the only coffee maker in the neighborhood (just east of BYU). When he was first allowed to have it in the house, it was a big hit in the neighborhood. Many kids came over to see it. Some thought it was bad.[29]

Don't confuse drinking Postum with a longing for something faithful Mormons feel is missing. Mormon arts and culture blogger William Morris put it this way:

> Funnily enough, I never thought of it as a coffee substitute—not until I started buying it as an adult and saw that it was marketed that way. As a kid I saw it as something Mormon.[30]

The association between Mormons and their Postum wasn't confined to the beverage. It served as a substitute in vocabulary when referring jokingly to a "Postum table" instead of a coffee table[31]; prominent Mormon Cleone Skousen appeared in ads for Postum while he was Salt Lake City police chief in 1959;[32] and it was used in a variety of recipes in place of coffee.

It's clear in both the Postum survey and in discussions on Mormon blogs that Postum holds a place of nostalgia. An LDS woman from Texas associates Postum with her grandmother, who "mixed Postum with warm milk and brown sugar. I have fond memories of a steaming glass of Postum."[33] Another woman thinks of time she spent with her mother, who "has always been a great Anglophile and appreciates the beauty of a good hot drink. . . . We would brew up a cup of Postum and watch her favorite British show, *Coronation Street*."[34]

One LDS man in his late sixties, who was raised in California, talked about his family's Saturday breakfast ritual:

> We drank Postum as kids every Saturday with my father's famous buttermilk pancakes. The

POSTUM CAKE

6 eggs (separate yolks and whites)
4 Tbsp. cold water
2 tsp. baking powder
1 1/2 c. sugar
1 1/2 c. flour
4 Tbsp. Postum

Beat egg *yolks*. Add half of the sugar, beat again, then add water, then beat. Now beat egg *whites* until part stiff, then add the rest of the sugar and beat stiff. Take 2 tablespoons of the white mixture and fold into yellow mixture. Sift dry ingredients into mixture, fold the rest of the whites into the yellow mixture, and beat for a few minutes. Pour into 3 layer pans, preferably circular. Bake at 350 degrees F for 15–20 minutes.[35]

pancake recipe has passed from generation to generation but not the Postum.[36]

And therein lies a problem. Postum use—and subsequently sales—began to decline. Despite an ad campaign in the mid-1990s[37] which brought sales up to $12 million a year,[38] it wasn't enough for Kraft Foods to continue production. In late 2007, Postum was taken off the market.

There was an outcry from the Postum-drinking public. They took to the internet to mourn the loss of their favored beverage, they lobbied Kraft Foods, and they started an online petition to try to revive Postum. They also began scrambling to find remaining stock in grocery stores. Some customers learned that Kraft Canada had a larger stock and ordered it online until that was depleted. One person reported a listing on eBay in October 2011 that priced a jar of Postum at $150.[39] In the summer of 2014, there

POSTUM ICING

2 Tbsp. butter
2 squares bakers' chocolate
2 c. powdered sugar
2 Tbsp. milk or Postum
1 tsp. vanilla

Melt chocolate and butter together in double boiler;
sift sugar and add a little at a time, beating smooth
after each addition. Add flavoring and milk or Postum
until of a consistency to spread.[40]

were eBay listings for a "new" jar going for $24.05, and even a half-used jar for $7.50.[41] In 2016, it was still possible to buy an unopened red-label jar for $29.95, along with store signs, matted advertisements, and vintage Postum tins.[42]

People were saddened at Postum's demise, though admittedly not everyone noticed right away. In February of 2012, one woman posted on an online Postum discussion:

Use it rarely, so the bottle in my pantry is still half full and at least 25 years old. (It still smells and tastes great!) I obviously haven't helped the cause. With consumers like me, they can't keep making it.[43]

Postum drinkers began looking for an alternative, as others had already tried to dethrone the reigning champ of coffee substitutes. In 1908, a company called College Pure Food, based in Logan, Utah, offered "Koffee-et," a product they claimed superior to the other options, each of which "has

found it necessary to add a little caffein [*sic*], tannin, or some other deleterious substance to secure the coffee flavor."[44]

In 2007, the merits of Postum versus its rivals, like the European-produced Pero, herbal teas, or the ubiquitous hot chocolate, were being adjudicated in the Mormon blogosphere. Unsurprisingly, the reviews were mixed, with some finding acceptable alternatives and others finding that the substitutes simply "just don't do it."[45]

Dayle and June Rust fell into the second camp. The Rusts live in North Carolina and are both members of the LDS Church. Dayle was raised Mormon, and Postum is part of his family memories, like wanting to be like his older brothers who drank it and added copious amounts of sugar to his cup. For him, nothing could take Postum's place. It was made from wheat, while Pero and other alternatives like Roma or Cafix are barley-based and, in Dayle's words, "weak and unsatisfying." And with a now-mature palate and the sweet tooth left behind, hot chocolate wouldn't fit the bill either.

So the Rusts set out not just to remake Postum, but to secure the trademark for it. They had already developed a recipe they felt matched the taste of the original, but being able to use the label would give the mom-and-pop shop the cultural edge over rivals. After securing the rights, the Rusts, under the name Eliza's Quest Foods, rolled out their "new" Postum to market in 2011.

Not all Postum drinkers were convinced. In 2013, Ardis Parshall of the blog "Keepapitchinin" dedicated a post to comparing some of the last of her original Postum store to the Rusts' product. Her verdict was that it wasn't the same. She declared it sweeter and weaker than the original, but drinkable. She suggested that Eliza's Quest Foods was "marketing nostalgia…but not Postum."[46]

The Rusts weren't discouraged though. Since their first roll-out, Dayle says they have improved the product manufacturing so that it more closely matches the flavor of the original. Their goal has been to "get back to Postum as people remember it."[47]

"New" Postum is now available in more than four hundred stores, primarily in the Intermountain West. The Rusts are targeting LDS and Seventh Day Adventist customers, but like C. W. Post nearly 120 years ago, they are also trying to meet the desires of health-conscious Americans. They have secured "non-GMO" certification as well as vegan and kosher status to market their product to consumers with various food concerns.

HOW ABOUT A DIET COKE?

It would be unfair to call Postum a fad. It held its place on Mormon tables for some eighty years and continues to be a touchstone in Mormon culture, though perhaps the memory is fading. But the association of Latter-day Saints with Postum didn't begin with Postum itself. It was based on adherence to a religious dictate to avoid beverages with ill effects.

Consider this corollary. There's a longstanding association between the LDS faithful and modest dress. What form that modest dress takes, though, is subject to trends and fashion in the community. Being modest in the 1980s or 1990s didn't look the same as being modest today does. Nor will it look the same as modesty in just a few years.

Americans in general significantly altered their beverage habits in the second half of the twentieth century. In 1945, we drank four times more milk than soft drinks. By 1997, we were drinking two-and-a-half times the soft drinks over milk.[48] There's been an explosion of beverage choices on the scene: soda varieties (including many noncaffeinated choices), flavored waters, fruit blends, etc. In 2012, the Church of Jesus Christ of Latter-day Saints clarified that the Word of Wisdom does not ban drinking caffeine, which came as welcome news to cola drinkers.[49] There is debate about whether that violates the spirit of the Word of Wisdom, or whether cola is just bad for you, but maybe there is at least a cultural replacement for Postum. As ex-Mormon blogger Emily Henderson explains, "It's a thing—Mormons love some Diet Coke."[50]

NOTES

1. Thomas Alexander, "The Word of Wisdom: From Principle to Requirement," *Dialogue: A Journal of Mormon Thought* 14, no. 3 (Autumn 1981): 78–88.
2. *This Journey Through the Pure Food Factories That Make Postum and Grape-Nuts* (Battle Creek, MI: Postum Company, Inc., 1906), 3.
3. Ruth C. Engs, *Clean Living Movements: American Cycles of Health Reform* (Westport, CT: Praeger, 2001), 3.
4. Nancy Rubin, *American Empress: The Life and Times of Marjorie Merriweather Post* (New York: Villard Books, 1995), 10.
5. Engs, *Clean Living Movements*, 114–15.
6. *This Journey*, 6.
7. Ibid., 7.
8. Doctrine & Covenants, The Church of Jesus Christ of Latter-day Saints, https://www.lds.org/scriptures/dc-testament/dc/89?lang=eng.
9. Alexander, "The Word of Wisdom," 82.

10. George A. Smith, in *Journal of Discourses* (London: Latter-day Saints' Book Depot, 1854–1886), 2:211.

11. Homer, Letter, "For the News," *Deseret News*, January 25, 1851.

12. Brigham Young, Sermon of April 8, 1855, in *Journal of Discourses*, 2:271.

13. "Words of Wisdom," *Deseret Evening News*, August 19, 1893.

14. "Shall We Answer Yes, or No?" *Deseret Evening News*, September 2, 1893.

15. "Drink at Meals," *Salt Lake Herald*, October 24, 1896.

16. Edward Leo Lyman, "Utah Statehood," in *Encyclopedia of Mormonism*, ed. Daniel H. Ludlow (New York: Macmillan, 1992), 1502–3.

17. Joan Smyth Iverson, *The Antipolygamy Controversy in U.S. Women's Movements, 1880–1925* (New York: Routledge, 1997), 8.

18. Alexander, "The Word of Wisdom," 78.

19. Ibid.

20. Daniel Okrent, *Last Call: The Rise and Fall of Prohibition* (New York: Simon and Schuster, 2010), ix.

21. Peterson, *Word of Wisdom*, 90.

22. Josephine B Nichols, Cooks Corner, *Improvement Era* 50, no. 9 (September 1947): 599.

23. "Being Worthy to Enter the Temple," *Ensign* 40, no. 8 (August 2010): 8.

24. Okrent, *Last Call*, 354.

25. "The Word of Wisdom," *Piute County News*, March 3, 1933.

26. Okrent, *Last Call*, 353.

27. "Word of Wisdom," *Handbook 2: Administering the Church* (Salt Lake City: Church of Jesus Christ of Latter-day Saints, 2010), 21.3.11.

28. Elaine Clark, *Postum Survey*, 2014, Male, 18–24, Provo.

29. Ibid., Male, 35–44, Provo.

30. William Morris, "Mormons Mourning Postum: A Consumer Culture Post," *A Motley Vision: Mormon Literature and Culture* (blog), December 17, 2007, http://www.motleyvision.org/2007/mormons-mourn-postum/.

31. Thom Duncan, comment on Morris, "Mormons Mourning Postum," December 18, 2007.

32. Ardis Parshall, "For All You Cleone Skousen Fans," *Keepapitchinin* (blog), January 5, 2009, http://www.keepapitchinin.org/2009/01/05/for-all-you-cleon-skousen-fans/.

33. Clark, *Postum Survey*, 2014, Female, 45–54, Texas.

34. Ibid., Female, 25–34, Utah and Illinois.

35. From Postum.com.

36. Ibid., Male, 64–74, California.

37. Stuart Elliott, "Move Over, Norma Desmond: Postum, The Coffee Substitute, Is Looking for a Comeback, Too," *New York Times*, April 19, 1995.

38. Dayle Rust, phone interview with author, May 26, 2014.

39. Melanie, online comment on Morris, "Mormons Mourning Postum," October 15, 2011.

40. Adah R. Naylor, Foods for Health, *Improvement Era* 34, no. 2 (December 1930): 128.

41. Ebay listings, June 8, 2014.

42. Ibid., February 9, 2016.

43. Donna, online comment on Morris, "Mormons Mourning Postum," February 3, 2012.

44. "A New Drink," *Inter-Mountain Republican* (Salt Lake City), October 20, 1908, http://udn.lib.utah.edu/cdm/compoundobject/collection/imr2/id/66676/rec/283.

45. Bob, online comment on Morris, "Mormons Mourning Postum," February 27, 2010.

46. Ardis Parshall, "Little White Lab Rat: The Postum Showdown," *Keepapitchinin* (blog), January 18, 2013.

47. Dayle Rust, phone interview with author, May 26, 2014.

48. Rick Diamond and Mithra Moezzi, "Changing Trends: A Brief History of the US Consumption of Energy, Water, Beverage and Tobacco," in *Proceedings of the 2004 Summer Study on Energy Efficiency in Buildings, American Council for an Energy Efficient Economy* (Washington, DC, August 2004).

49. Peggy Fletcher Stack, "OK, Mormons, Drink Up—Coke and Pepsi Are OK," *Salt Lake Tribune*, September 5, 2012.

50. Emily Henderson, "How to Be Culturally Mormon," *Style by Emily Henderson* (blog), July 7, 2012, http://stylebyemilyhenderson.com/blog/.

APPLE BEER

FRANK CHRISTIANSON

Faussbrause, a regional beverage unique to Berlin, Germany, was popular with LDS missionaries serving there in the early 1960s. Larry Stillman, of Salt Lake City, Utah, obtained the marketing rights after completing his missionary service and founded Apple Beer Corporation in 1964. First served on the soda fountain at local Wasatch Front establishments such as Snelgrove's, an ice cream parlor, and Heap's Brick Oven, Apple Beer soon appeared in a twelve-ounce can and became a fixture in independent grocery stores across the state. Over the next three decades Apple Beer enjoyed a local following as "Utah's Original Gourmet Soda," as well as cult status through specialty distribution in other parts of the country and abroad.

In the mid-1990s Apple Beer adopted an amber glass bottle package and began expanding its distribution; it has grown in sales and distribution consistently since, and now enjoys a strong presence in fountain, can, and bottled products throughout the Intermountain West. Apple Beer's unique relationship with Utah certainly began as a missionary import. Over time it has come to be identified with the local culture as a traditional soft drink—think root beer or ginger beer—or a nonalcoholic beer (something Mormons can safely enjoy). Certainly, part of its staying power is its unique profile as an apple soda with a dry, crisp finish.

Courtesy Apple Beer Corporation.

HAWAIIAN HAYSTACKS

SPENCER GREEN

Hawaiian Haystacks are a quick, easy convenience food made from various ingredients heaped like a haystack over rice. Enjoyed in homes throughout Utah, and made largely from canned foods, including items that are typically part of Mormon food storage, Hawaiian Haystacks likely originated during the Depression. Since then the recipe's simplicity and ability to feed many people have kept it popular with large families in Utah ever since.

Few, if any, Hawaiians have eaten or even heard of Hawaiian Haystacks because the dish has no gustatory roots in Hawaii. Hawaiians may even consider the name funny or possibly offensive, a symbol of how little mainlanders understand them and their culture.[1] One food blogger did report encountering it at a Utah Polynesian wedding—but made with pork rather than chicken.[2] So perhaps it is the canned pineapple and rice that lend the dish its name.

Hawaiian Haystacks show up on family dinner tables, at group get-togethers, and at church events. Served buffet style with each ingredient in its own dish, it allows each person to create their own haystack, including as much of their favorite ingredients as they like while excluding any ingredients they don't like. Hawaiian Haystacks are offered by some caterers,[3] but the dish has not yet found its way into restaurants where, except at a buffet, it would be unduly complex due to its wide range of ingredients.

Though Hawaiian Haystacks use a wide variety of possible ingredients, it seems that rice, chicken, gravy, cheese, and chow mein noodles are the most essential. Diced tomatoes, pineapple, green onions, and green peppers are also commonly used. Some recipes call for coconut, mandarin oranges, toasted or sliced almonds, celery, cashews, and raisins or craisins—ingredients often found in Asian salads. Perhaps that explains why some call this dish "Chinese sundaes" or "Oriental sundaes." A few recipes also include avocados, peanuts, peas, carrots, broccoli, and even maraschino cherries. In many of the recipes, nuts seem somewhat interchangeable, although interestingly none specify macadamia nuts, the nut most closely associated with Hawaii.[4] One Utah cookbook includes Hawaiian Haystacks among many family staples like casseroles and slow-cooker meals. It recommends using chicken gravy, a can of cream of chicken soup, and "canned or cooked chicken or turkey,"[5]—all items typically included in the food storage found in Mormon households.

In addition to names already mentioned, recipes for Hawaiian Haystacks also call this dish "chicken sundaes" or "Mormon haystacks." The name Hawaiian Haystacks is itself something of an oxymoron—the Hawaiian alluding to the Pacific, the haystack to Utah's pioneer and agrarian past. But Utah is perhaps a state comfortable with or at least used to oxymorons as their state bird is the California seagull and, until 2014, the state tree was the Colorado blue spruce.[6]

Yet there seems to be a good reason why "*Hawaiian* Haystacks" is the name that stuck. There are many Mormon connections with Hawaii and Hawaiians. In the nineteenth century the LDS Church was very successful in making converts throughout Polynesia, and the first temple built away from church headquarters was dedicated in Hawaii in 1919 by Heber J. Grant.[7] Before church leaders began encouraging converts to stay in their countries of origin instead of coming to Utah, there was even a Polynesian colony, named Iosepa, near Tooele, Utah.[8] Many Mormons believe Polynesians, including native Hawaiians, are descendants of a figure briefly mentioned in the Book of Mormon named Hagoth.[9] Today there are still large numbers of LDS Polynesians throughout Utah and California; BYU Football's website even remarks on the "Polynesian pipeline" to explain their many Polynesian players.[10] And finally, throughout the 1970s and into the early 1990s, a joint venture between the LDS Church and the Boy Scouts of America sent many teenage boys from the Intermountain West with returned missionaries to pick pineapples in Hawaii. The program,

Photo by Kylie Moe, 2018.

whose stated objective was to build character in the boys, eventually partnered with Dole and was profitable for some years.[11]

277

Beyond these historical connections, Hawaiian Haystacks are also a practical solution for overworked mothers who need quick and easy meals to feed their large families. Providing the ingredients and letting each person create their own dish can save preparation time and be especially useful in large families that may have a wide variety of food aversions or allergies.

As noted earlier, since most of the ingredients are available in cans, Hawaiian Haystacks also align with Mormon traditions of emergency preparedness and food storage.[12] Latter-day Saint prophets and leaders have emphasized food storage and emergency preparedness since at least the 1970s and it continues to be a prevalent topic on the church's website, in church instruction, and in women's Relief Society activities. And, until emergencies arise, the eclectic nature of the ingredients allows Mormon families to make good use of their food storage by using older items and replacing them with newer ones.[13]

Interestingly, there are other culinary "haystacks" connected with other small religious groups. The term "haystacks" turns out to be a blanket term for layered, potluck-style foods, and variations are found among both the Seventh-day Adventists and the Mennonites. The Seventh-day Adventist version has been around since the 1950s and is called simply "Haystacks" or "Hartlein Special"—after the Adventist who started making it. The Mennonite version is called "Amish Haystacks" and includes taco-seasoned meat and spaghetti sauce. Both Seventh-day Adventists and Mennonites versions have more of a Mexican influence and resemble taco salads, with corn chips or Fritos coming first, then beans or meat, lettuce, and other condiments to top them off.[14]

SPENCER'S HAWAIIAN HAYSTACKS

3 c. cooked rice
1 lb. cooked chicken, shredded
1 can cream of chicken soup to 1 c. sour cream

Toppings
Cheese
Diced tomatoes
Pineapple
Green onions
Green peppers
Celery
Cashews, peanuts, or almond slivers
Shredded coconut
Chow mein noodles

Cook rice and chicken. Heat cream of chicken soup and mix in sour cream. Top it with your favorite toppings.

NOTES

1. See Lehua Parker, "Paul Theroux's Hawaiian Haystacks," *Lehua Parker Talking Story* (blog), accessed January 21, 2016, http://www.lehuaparker. com/2012/05/20/paul-therouxs-hawaiian-haystacks/.
2. Tiffany, "Slow Cooker Hawaiian Haystacks," *Crème de la Crumb* (blog), accessed January 21, 2016, http://lecremedelacrumb.com/2014/10/slow-cooker-hawaiian-haystacks.html.
3. For example, see "Hawaiian Haystacks," You're the Boss Catering, accessed January 21, 2016, http://www.yourethebosslunchandcatering.com/hawaiian-haystacks/.
4. John F. Mariani, "Hawaiian Haystacks," *The Encyclopedia of American Food and Drink* (New York: Bloomsbury Publishing, 2013), 249.
5. Jane P. Merrill and Karen M. Sunderland, *Feasting on Food Storage: Delicious and Healthy Recipes for Everyday Cooking* (Springville, UT: Front Table Books, 2013), 10.
6. "Utah State Tree—Quaking Aspen" and "Utah State

Bird—Sea Gull," Utah Online Library, accessed January 22, 2016, http://pioneer.utah.gov/research/utah_symbols.

7. "Laie Hawaii Temple," LDS Church Temples, accessed January 14, 2016, http://www.ldschurchtemples.com/laie/.

8. See Tracey E. Panek, "Life at Iosepa, Utah's Polynesian Colony," in *Proclamation to the People: Nineteenth Century Mormonism and the Pacific Basin Frontier*, ed. Laurie F. Maffly-Kipp and Reid L. Neilson (Salt Lake City: University of Utah Press, 2008), 170–81.

9. See Armand L. Mauss, *All Abraham's Children: Changing Mormon Conceptions of Race and Lineage* (Chicago: University of Illinois Press, 2003), 150, and Jerry K. Loveland "Hagoth and the Polynesian Tradition," *BYU Studies* 17, no. 1 (1976): 59–73.

10. See "Polynesian Tradition," BYU Cougars, accessed January 15, 2016, http://byucougars.com/m-football/polynesian-tradition.

11. Tom Harvey, "Teenage Boys Get a Taste of Hawaii Pineapple-field Labor," *Deseret News* (Salt Lake City), January 30, 1985.

12. See "Emergency Preparedness" The Church of Jesus Christ of Latter-day Saints, accessed January 28, 2016, https://www.lds.org/topics/emergency-preparedness?lang=eng; "Food Storage," The Church of Jesus Christ of Latter-day Saints, accessed January 28, 2016, https://www.lds.org/topics/food-storage?lang=eng.

13. A manual created by members for members but not produced by the church can be seen here: Christopher M. Parrett, ed., "LDS Preparedness Manual," The Survival Mom, accessed January 28, 2016, http://thesurvivalmom.com/wp-content/uploads/2010/08/LDS-Preparedness-Manual.pdf.

14. Wilona Karimabadi, "Haystacks or Hartlein Special?" *Adventist Review*, accessed January 22, 2016, http://archives.adventistreview.org/article/2976/archives/issue-2009-1533/loaves-and-haystacks/haystacks-of-hartlein-special; see also Kevin Williams, "Amish Haystacks," accessed January 22, 2016, http://www.amish365.com/haystack-stuff-5-amish-haystack-recipes/.

49

GENERAL CONFERENCE FOODS

ERIC A. ELIASON

Twice a year, for two two-hour sessions on the first Saturday and Sunday of April and October, Mormons tune in at home on the television to the General Conference broadcast from church headquarters in Salt Lake City. LDS leaders encourage and instruct the members in a subdued style of prepared talks. To keep restless children engaged, parents may make a "general conference mix" with fun food items to munch on while watching. Sometimes families play "general conference bingo" where these food items are eaten or placed on a bingo card every time a church leader mentions a familiar phrase or topic. Often, extended families gather during these times. Prepared meals may tend toward iconic Utah comfort foods. Making scones is a particularly popular activity between the morning and afternoon sessions.

General Conference Mix

 = love, charity, or service

 = pray or prayer

 = missionary or mission

 = repent, repentance, or atonement

 = gratitude, grateful, thanks, or thankful

www.pinningwithpurpose.blogspot.com

Kristen Dastrup, *Pinning with Purpose* (blog), 2014.

PART IV LOCAL SPECIALTIES

50

LOCAL FOOD TRADITIONS

CAROL A. EDISON

From one end of the state to the other, Utah communities are famous for local crops and distinctive local food traditions. Ice cream and cheese from Utah's dairy cows, fruit and berries from orchards and fields, and summertime tomatoes and corn from farms and backyards are just some of the products that Utahns have always enjoyed.

Variations in altitude, soil, and climate have resulted in a wide range of animal and crop production, and the essays in this section illuminate many of those differences. Elaine Thatcher chronicles the full range of products home to northern Utah's Cache Valley while explaining their cultural impact and role in daily life. Other contributors explore some of the region's specific producers long known for their quality berries, ice cream, and cheese. Box Elder County's famed Fruit Way, a stretch of road that continues to host family-owned fruit stands, is featured, as is the chili sauce made to complement meat and egg dishes by generations of Grouse Creek cooks who live on the county's western border.

David Allred and Roger Baker cover the distinctive food culture of central Utah. They focus on the Sanpete County traditions of sheep and turkey production and, not surprisingly, the remnants of Danish cookery grounded in the area's much-cherished pioneer-era Scandinavian cuisine.

Several essays feature the food traditions of southern Utah's Dixie, a region with a distinctly different climate located in the southwest corner of the state. Actually part of the Mojave Desert, much of the terrain is two thousand feet lower than the rest of Utah. Pioneer leaders sent settlers there believing it would be a good place to grow cotton, which is likely why the region became known as "Dixie." Though cotton growing wasn't successful, the region produced an abundance of fruits and vegetables, including the grapes that pioneers made into wine and the pecans and pomegranates that are crucial to making Dixie Salad at Thanksgiving time. Sun-dried fruit and meat and unique foods like jelly made from the fruit of prickly pear cactus are also part of this food heritage. Lyman Hafen's reminiscences of growing up in St. George on the bounty of local fruits and vegetables, and some unusual local products like sorghum, create a beautiful portrait of food and family.

For over a hundred years Utahns have honored the fruits of their labors, often literally, at annual agricultural festivals that mark the end of the working season. Events taking place in every corner of the state provide folks with time to renew ties while celebrating the success of local crops or livestock production. These harvest or food festivals not only market crops to a wider audience but also reinforce membership in a community of shared interest and shared identity. Festivals continue sometimes long after the local crop is a thing of the past. And as illustrated by the "beetdiggers" of Jordan High, a school in the southern end of Salt Lake Valley where sugar beets were once grown, those crop-based identities persist.[1]

Some Utah foods have gained special status over time and we value them whether or not we've even tasted them! Everyone knows that Green River's melons—casabas, canaries, cantaloupes, honeydews, or, queen of them all, watermelons—are delicious.[2] We also know that in south-central Utah, in a little town named Bicknell, there's a lady who makes legendary pies from pinto beans and pickles that everyone is eager to try.[3] We hunger for those famous Bear Lake raspberry shakes, best at the peak of the summertime harvest. We celebrate these and many other foods because they are part of food traditions that have influenced our taste buds since childhood.

Around the turn of the twenty-first century, in concert with ideas being shared across the country, Utah's government, local businesses, and the general population began to acknowledge the cultural and economic advantages of supporting food production and of keeping money spent on food within the local economy. Well-advertised agricultural festivals continue to illustrate this strategy while, in recent

Southeastern Utah's hot summers offer the perfect climate for growing melons, and since 1906 the town of Green River has celebrated this crop at their annual Melon Days. Throughout the season visitors can buy juicy and sweet watermelons from the Vetere family which has operated out of the same stand for over fifty years. Photo by Carol A. Edison, 1989. Courtesy Utah Folklife Archives.

years, three initiatives have increased enthusiasm and awareness of locally produced foods.

In 1996, as part of the state's Centennial Celebration, the Utah Department of Agriculture and Food joined the national Century Farms and Ranches Program. Its purpose was twofold: to honor farm families and to increase public awareness of the role agriculture plays in the state. The program encouraged Utah farmers and ranchers whose property had been in production for over one hundred years to apply for the Century Farms designation. Nearly five hundred farms and ranches now display a Century Farm sign, offering a visible reminder of the many families in rural areas, and even in areas

Cula Ekker's famous Pickle Pie from the Sunglow Café in Bicknell. Photo by Lisa Duskin-Goede, 2014.

that are now quite urban, that continue to supply our tables with livestock, orchard goods, and fresh vegetables.[4]

In 2002, the Utah Department of Agriculture launched Utah's Own,[5] another program designed to increase public awareness of homegrown products by labeling goods and consolidating marketing efforts. Today they assist farms and businesses in Utah that grow, raise, or manufacture food and beverage products for human consumption as well as companies that use agricultural products to make value-added skin care products such as goat-milk soaps, beeswax lip balm, and herb-infused oils.[6]

Then in 2006, a group of business owners and community-minded residents organized Local First, one of the first business alliances in the country devoted to branding and jointly marketing all locally owned businesses.[7] Working in tandem with Utah's Own, they have raised general awareness of the availability and quality of local products, contributing to the success of many businesses and the ability of local producers, including local food producers, to continue participating in the lifestyle and culinary heritage they cherish.

Nationally, Utah ranks as the top producer of brine shrimp (yum fish food!) and second for tart

CULA EKKER'S SUNGLOW CAFÉ SWEET PICKLE PIE

Prepare pie dough using the following:
6 c. sifted flour
2 tsp. salt
2 1/2 c. lard
3/4 c. water
2 Tbsp. vinegar
2 eggs

For the pie filling, mix together the following:
5 eggs
2 c. sugar
1 tsp. cinnamon
1 tsp. nutmeg
1 tsp. lemon extract
2 Tbsp. corn starch
1 c. + 2 Tbsp. light cream
1/8 c. margarine
12 oz. sweet pickles, drained and ground

Fill unbaked pie shells with filling and bake at 350 degrees for 60 to 90 minutes until a knife comes out clean. Cool and serve with whipped cream, if desired. Makes two pies.

cherries (think dried cherries in granola snacks or luscious pie filling), with apricots, sweet cherries, and peaches not far behind. The production of beef, hogs, and sheep account for almost half of the total farm income.[8] Utahns, with their penchant for self-sufficiency, have always produced most of what they needed. And today, even though international marketing and modern transportation enables us to enjoy products from around the globe, we produce and consume more and more fresh, tasty food

raised by our neighbors and fellow Utahns. Bring on the grass-fed beef, the handcrafted cheese, the newly picked corn, tomatoes, and berries—and let's have a feast!

NOTES

1. "The mascot dates from the school's early days when students were dismissed from school each fall to help farmers harvest the sugar beets. Although the sugar beet industry is now gone, the school proudly continues the 'Beetdigger' spirit and traditions. Each year at the opening assembly student government officers top sugar beets and take a bite." From "The Story of Jordan High School," Jordan High School, accessed March 8, 2017, http://jhs.canyonsdistrict. org/the-harvest.html.

2. Valerie Phillips, "Melon Mania; Green River Produce Just Can't Be Beat," *Deseret News*, September 17, 2008.

3. Donna Lou Morgan, "Sun Glow Restaurant and Cula Ekker Pie Recipes," *Relaena's Travels* (blog), accessed March 3, 2017, https://relaena.wordpress.com/resources/ sun-glow-cafe-history-and-cula-ekkers-pie-recipes/.

4. "Century Farm Registration," Utah Department of Agriculture and Food, Utah.gov, accessed March 8, 2017, http://ag.utah.gov/licenses-registrations/41- licenses-regulations-and-registration/201-century- farm-registration.html.

5. "Thank You to Utah's Own for Joining the Local First Leaders Circle!" Local First, May 16, 2016, https://localfirst.org/think-local/blog/item/339- thank-you-to-utah-s-own-for-joining-the-local-first- leaders-circle.

6. Ibid.

7. "Who We Are," Local First, accessed March 8, 2017, https://localfirst.org/about-local-first-utah/ mission-and-history.

8. "A Look at Utah Agriculture," National Agriculture in the Classroom, updated August 2016, http://www. agclassroom.org/teacher/stats/utah.pdf.

PUTTING IT UP

Foodways of Northern Utah

ELAINE THATCHER

During every summer of my life I have sat in the kitchen with an apron, a paring knife, and bowls piled high with fruit to preserve for winter. Peaches, apples, cherries, apricots, pears, and plums—the summer's bounty—are all committed to mason jars in a steaming hot kitchen in the dog days of summer. When I was young we would open the windows wide to let in whatever cooling breeze might happen by, but an open window also posed a danger for the jars hot out of the canner—the cool air we craved could cause a jar to crack, and a whole quart of our labors would be lost. So, we covered the ranks of hot jars with a dishtowel to protect them and took the heat in stride.

Our efforts didn't stop at fruit. When I was young, we canned green beans in steel cans. Later, we switched to freezing the vegetables—corn, beans, and peas. My mother also made pints of jams and jellies, with our favorite being her special peach-pear marmalade with pineapple, maraschino cherries, and locally grown peaches and pears. I could almost finish a whole pint by myself when it was spread on Mom's homemade bread.

Before white settlers came to the area, the Northwestern Shoshone knew how to live in a land with little water. They fished the streams, hunted game, and gathered things like chokecherries and piñon nuts.

When European immigrants came, they learned foodways from the Indians and layered them with traditions from their places of origin. This was an ecosystem much different from the home places of most new immigrants. In northern Utah, the annual precipitation ranges from about 10 inches in parts of Box Elder and Rich Counties to 18 inches in Cache County. (The national average rainfall is about 37 inches per year.) The growing season is fairly short, averaging from 57 days in Woodruff (Rich County) to 163 days in Brigham City (Box Elder County).[1]

The Mormon settlers dug canals to carry fresh water from the mountain rivers into all parts of the valleys, making agriculture possible. They brought the idea of raising domestic animals for food, fiber, and other needs. They planted seeds of fruits and vegetables from other parts of the world, watering them with precious water from the canals. They learned over time how to make their crops grow in the semi-arid, cold West.

Subsistence farming became the norm. My grandfathers were both teachers—one in the LDS Church education system, the other a shop teacher at North Cache High School. But both maintained large plots of land with cows, chickens, and huge gardens because teaching didn't pay much, especially during the Great Depression. I remember walking down the steep hill behind Grandfather Wood's house in 1956 to the barn and pastures below to watch my grandfather milking his few cows (maybe four) with a new milking machine.

My own father, upon retiring from being a professor at Colorado State University in 1973, returned to his hometown of River Heights, Utah, bought a house with a large lot, and promptly planted a small orchard and laid out a big garden. He spent the rest of his life working that land.

That is not unusual. Although old-time Cache Valley residents are often reminded condescendingly by newcomers that they live in a desert, they continue to go about their traditional business of planting gardens, growing fruit, and "putting it up" for the winter. The community memory of the trials of settlement and a harrowing Great Depression remains, and self-sufficiency continues to be a closely held value.

Haystacks near Bear Lake. Photo by Lisa Duskin-Goede, 2006. Courtesy Bear River Heritage Area.

Agriculture has changed, of course. In the early twentieth century, Mormon scientist and apostle John A. Widtsoe studied, refined, and taught the techniques of dry farming,[2] allowing farmers to grow grain in arid lands. Where as recently as the 1950s, the majority of northern Utahns had a couple of cows, some chickens, and a garden, most livestock (except for the recent resurgence of backyard chickens) is now the exclusive domain of large farming and ranching operations, and most Utahns buy food from a store. Yet northern Utah is still a rural place with an agricultural identity. To confirm this, just drive down any county road and count the number of old plows, harrows, tractors, and wagon wheels that are used as yard decorations, and the number of backyard gardens. Or you can take a look at the list of community festivals honoring agricultural products in northern Utah: Trout and Berry Days (Paradise), Raspberry Days (Garden City), Black and White Days (as in Holstein dairy cattle; Richmond),

Commercial canning of Utah's abundant vegetable crop by both national and local canning companies has been a significant part of the state's economy for over a century. Used by permission, Utah State Historical Society. All rights reserved.

Apple Days (River Heights), Peach Days (Brigham City), etc. County fairs also thrive, and cities within those counties create wonderful temporary murals featuring produce at the fairs.

When Congress passed the Morrill Act in 1862, Utah quickly took advantage of it to establish a state land grant agricultural college. Cache County competed with Utah County for the honor of being the site of the new college. With the support of Weber County, which had its piece of the pie in the new Reform School and could afford to be generous, Cache County was the chosen site; the Agricultural College of Utah (UAC), later to become Utah State University (USU), was chartered in 1888.[3] Later, in 1914, the Utah Cooperative Extension Service was founded and based at "the AC."

MOM'S PEACH-PEAR MARMALADE
Courtesy Zella Wood Thatcher

3 lbs. peaches and pears, peeled and cut up (4 1/2
    c. after cut up)
2 oranges, peeled and chopped
1 no. 2 can crushed pineapple, drained
1 small bottle maraschino cherries, chopped
    (reserve juice)
1/2 tsp. salt
6 c. sugar

Combine chopped oranges, peaches, and pears with
salt, sugar, and cherry juice.
    Boil 30 minutes.
    Add cherries and pineapple and cook until thick.
    Bottle.

Elaine Thatcher (author) and her father, Ted, in their
backyard garden in River Heights, adjacent to Logan. Photo
by Andrea Graham, 2001. Courtesy BRHA Survey, Special
Collections & Archives, Merrill–Cazier Library, Utah State
University.

The specific charge of the land grant school was
to teach research-based agriculture and mechanical
arts. Thousands of students have graduated and pur-
sued agricultural careers, and the Extension Service
assists them and home gardeners all along the way,
providing information on best varieties for growing in specific areas, best horticultural and livestock
practices, and the safest ways to preserve and prepare
food. This continues to affect foodways throughout
the state.

Important food industries have varied over the
years. Food-canning plants were part of the northern Utah scene beginning in 1904 when the Utah
Condensed Milk Company built a milk-condens-
ing plant in Richmond. Later, in 1916, the Borden
Western Company built a condensery, as they were
called, on the south side of Logan.[4] When my father
was a youngster in the 1920s, he and his brothers
used to take a toy wagon holding two cans of fresh

milk down to the Borden plant, which was located
near the railroad tracks so canned milk could easily
be shipped out of the valley.

The Morgan Canning Company started in Morgan, southeast of Ogden, in 1908, canning peas. The
company expanded by building a cannery in Smithfield in 1920.[5] This plant still stands, and the name
"Morgan Canning Company," along with the slogan,
"Those Good Peas," can still be seen built into the
brickwork of the building. Another architectural remnant of the pea industry that remains on the Cache
County landscape is the pea vineries, where farmers
took their peas to be weighed and removed from the
vines before being sent to the cannery. Farmers were
then able to return to the vinery and take the pea
vines, without peas, for use as cattle feed.

CORN CHOWDER BISQUE

(SERVES 8)

Courtesy Phebe Ricks Wood and Zella Wood Thatcher (author's grandmother and mother)

2-3 slices bacon, diced
4 small onions, minced
6 medium potatoes, cubed
4 tomatoes, peeled and diced (or a can of
   tomatoes)
2 tsp. salt
¼ tsp. pepper
¼ tsp. baking soda
1 quart milk, heated
1 Tbsp flour
1 Tbsp margarine
1 pint boiling water
2 c. corn (may be fresh, frozen, or canned)

Fry bacon until crisp, remove from pan. Add onions, potatoes, tomatoes, salt and pepper to grease and sauté briefly. Cover with boiling water and simmer until vegetables are nearly tender. Add corn and cook 10 minutes. Put ¼ tsp. of baking soda into the tomato mixture and stir. It should foam slightly. In a separate bowl, make a roux of the flour and margarine and add it to the hot milk and stir or shake to mix. Add the milk mixture to the soup, stirring rapidly. Cook for a few more minutes to make sure the flour is cooked.

Later sugar beets and eggs became cash crops, along with processing plants for turning the beets into refined sugar. The sugar beet business died after cane sugar from Hawaii was sold for lower prices. Cache Valley still has a large egg farm just across the state line in Franklin, Idaho.

For many years, Cache County was the top agricultural producer in the state. It is still number one in barley production and number two in the production of wheat (both winter and spring), dry beans, corn for silage, and apples. It is third in production of alfalfa. In addition, Cache has the largest number of dairy cows of any county in Utah, plus a smaller but still significant number of beef cattle. In overall agricultural production, it is now in fifth place among the twenty-nine counties in the state.[6] Box Elder County raises similar crops, but adds dry onions, apricots, peaches, and cherries to the mix. Rich County is best known for beef production and hay.

Many northern Utah foodways are descended from these agricultural roots. Dairy has contributed to the cheese industry, ice cream shops and factories, and chocolate candy makers. Traditional foodways like Mormon funeral dinners consisting of ham, "funeral potatoes" (an easy and glutinous variation of potatoes au gratin), canned green beans, Jell-O salads, and bread are based in farming, home gardening, dairy, and canning. One reason funerals have a fairly traditional menu is that these foods will "hold" until the funeral is over, however long it is, without losing too much quality.

Today's northern Utahns still gather things that the Shoshone did. Chokecherries grow wild in the canyons and make a wonderful jelly—if you don't mind working with a fruit that's almost all seed. Trout fishing is a favorite pastime, and trout can be found on many local restaurants' menus. Many families make sure they "get their deer" each fall and stock their freezers with venison. We even have a few mushroom gatherers who head to the forest after a rain. You haven't tasted peaches until you've had some that were grown along Box Elder

County's Fruit Way, picked ripe, and home-canned in mason jars.

In spite of the fact that I enjoy cooking fresh foods, I find myself falling back on a lot of my Cache Valley–born mother's recipes that relied on foods from the pantry—canned, dried, and frozen—whether homegrown or purchased from a local farmer or a chain supermarket. Mormon recipes emphasize ways to use foods from long-term food storage and are passed around in women's Relief Society meetings at church, from friend to friend, and nowadays on Facebook, Pinterest, and blogs. I recently asked my friends on Facebook to share their favorite Jell-O recipes. Almost none of them required fresh ingredients but used canned or frozen fruit. Some cooks added toppings made from whipped or sour cream.

Northern Utah has long been one of the primary breadbaskets of the state, and the agricultural products grown there have profoundly influenced local foodways. European immigrants brought most of these foodways with them, and then adapted them to the climate and soil conditions found in Utah, bending the environment to their will so that such things

as peaches and corn could be grown. They topped that with a strong penchant for self-sufficiency and preserving foods for long-term storage, and there you have the primary influences on northern Utah foodways.

NOTES

1. E. Bruce Godfrey et al., County Agricultural Profiles (Rich County, Cache County, and Box Elder County), Utah State University Cooperative Extension, 2005; online at http://extension.usu.edu/files/publications/publication/AG_Econ_county-2005.
2. Widtsoe's famous book, *Dry-Farming: A System of Agriculture for Countries Under a Low Rainfall* (New York: Macmillan, 1920), is still available online (http://soilandhealth.org/wp-content/uploads/01aglibrary/010102/01010200frame.html), in reprints, and as a collectors' item.
3. Joel Edward Ricks, *The Utah State Agricultural College: A History of Fifty Years, 1888–1939* (Salt Lake City: Deseret News Press, 1938): 19–20.
4. Don Strack, "Utah's Canning Industry," Utah Education Network, http://www.uen.org/utah_history_encyclopedia/c/CANNING.html.
5. Ibid.
6. County Agricultural Profiles.

52

UTAH'S FAMOUS FRUIT WAY

VALERIE PHILLIPS

Getting freshly picked produce from the Box Elder County "Famous Fruitway" is a longtime tradition where roadside stands dot the ten-mile stretch of US 89 from Willard to Brigham City.

Peaches are the Fruitway's major claim to fame, although you'll also find cherries, berries, apricots, apples, plums, pears, and "row crops" such as corn, squash, tomatoes, peppers, cucumbers, and melons.

Box Elder County's peachy history goes back to the early pioneer settlers, who brought seeds and fruit-tree stock with them. To celebrate the peach harvest, Brigham City Peach Days was begun in 1904. Governors, senators, and once even a presidential candidate, Franklin Roosevelt, came to the annual celebration during its early years.

But according to Randy Lemon of Grammy's Produce, fruit-growing along the hillsides of Perry and Willard didn't really become viable until the 1930s, when a canal system was built from Ogden Canyon to Brigham City. Randy's parents, Helen Jane and Roy Lemon, were among the early Fruitway growers. Some of the others were Gay and Helen Pettingill, Don and DeeRae Christiansen, Jay and Joyce Matthews, Don and DeNece Barker, and Motaharu and Chiyo Sumida.

Another early grower was George Nielson Sr., a Box Elder High chemistry teacher who farmed to supplement his $600-per-year teaching salary. In 1941, Nielson bought property in Perry. In a 1999 interview, his son Ralph (now passed away) recalled selling raspberries door-to-door in Salt Lake City for five cents per cup. During World War II, the family set up a fruit stand in the parking lot of the Bushnell military hospital in Brigham City.

The Pettingill family began farming the Fruitway in 1947. Today, you can buy a fresh peach milkshake at their stand while you're shopping. Steve Pettingill recalls that during the 1960s and 1970s, customers often bought a bushel or more of fruit at a time for home canning. "That tradition went away for a while, but it's come back somewhat," he said.

Peaches make up about 50 percent of the sales at Grammy's Fruit and Produce, where twenty-three different varieties are grown in order to extend the season. The Flamin' Fury peach ripens as early as July 4, and other varieties ripen in succession through mid-October.

The late Paul Valcarce, owner of Paul's Patch, was one of over a dozen vendors who have been selling produce along old Highway 89 between North Ogden and Brigham City for decades. Photo by Lisa Duskin-Goede, 2015. Courtesy Bear River Heritage Area.

Beautiful displays, informational signs, and recipes suggesting how to best prepare the fruit and produce are the hallmarks of Grammy's, a stand run by matriarch and grandmother Helen Jane Lemon and her family. Photo by Lisa Duskin-Goede, 2015. Courtesy Bear River Heritage Area.

In 2015, the area had only about half the farmland than existed fifteen years before, said Randy Lemon. "I've seen five or six fruit stands close and their property has been developed. As the old farmers die, a lot of the children don't want to carry on the farming tradition."

It's a physically demanding lifestyle, with planting, pruning, thinning, and picking. And at any time, frost, heavy rain, or hail can negate several months' labors in just a few hours. That's why some growers consider the early summer crops of apricots and cherries as "sacrificial"—there's a good chance of losing them.

GRAMMY'S APPLE CRISP
Courtesy Grammy's Fruit and Produce

Filling
6 c. peeled and sliced apples
1 c. sugar
1 1/2 Tbsp. flour
1/4 tsp. salt
1 tsp. cinnamon
1/2 tsp. nutmeg

Topping
3/4 c. oatmeal
3/4 c. flour
3/4 c. brown sugar
1/4 tsp. baking powder
1/4 tsp. baking soda
1/2 c. melted butter

Mix filling ingredients together and place in a 9-by-13-inch pan.

Mix all topping ingredients together except butter. When mixed, mix in melted butter.

Crumble topping over the filling mixture.

Bake at 350 degrees F for 35 to 40 minutes until apples are bubbly.[1]

Randy Matthews is a fourth-generation farmer. His family began farming Perry in 1881. But, at sixty-five years old, and after losing much of his peach crop to a hailstorm in 2015, he hoped to sell off some of his land. "When you lose half your acreage to Mother Nature, you can only weather so much of it," he said. "It's harder each year."

And yet, it's also rewarding when generations of customers keep coming back and telling them it's the best-tasting fruit they've ever tasted.

NOTE
1. Grammy's Fruit and Produce, Willard, UT, Facebook page: https://www.facebook.com/Grammys-Fruit-Produce-145987868766486/timeline/

53

SMALL FRUIT AND BERRY PRODUCTION IN CACHE VALLEY AND BEAR LAKE

AMY MAXWELL-HOWARD

Similar to their neighbors in Brigham City and Perry who are famous for peaches and cherry production, farmers in Cache Valley, at one time, produced large quantities of peaches, pears, cherries, sweet apples, apricots, cantaloupe, grapes, and berries. The Providence Bench, the foothills above the town of Providence at the south end of the valley, was particularly known for its high-volume fruit production.

Cache Valley has a good climate for producing sweet and succulent strawberries, raspberries, dewberries, and, more recently, blackberries. Pioneer settlers of Cache Valley included berries in their family gardens, and in the early to mid-twentieth century farmers in Cache Valley grew them commercially. But over time rising land prices, blights, and competitive markets led many farmers to slowly abandon fruit production.

Today Cache Valley is known for its apples, produced most famously by Zollinger's Fruit and Tree Farm in River Heights, the oldest remaining fruit farm in the

Weeks Berries of Paradise grows and sells fresh blackberries, strawberries, and blueberries and also makes jam, juice, and syrup. Courtesy Scott Bauer for the United States Department of Agriculture; image is in the public domain.

area, and for the U-pick berries at newer farms such as Weeks Berries of Paradise. The current U-pick berry operations, a variation on past methods of fruit production and distribution in Cache Valley, continue the berry-growing tradition by combining aspects of commercial berry production, small-scale garden production, and even foraging traditions. Weeks Berries of Paradise along with the City of Paradise formally honor the heritage of Cache Valley berries once a year with their Trout and Berry Days celebration.[1]

To the north, the Bear Lake area has long been known for its raspberry production, originally initiated by German immigrant Theodore Hildt in 1910.[2] Since that time, production has increased as Bear Lake's climate is especially conducive for sweet, flavorful berries. Multiple generations of northern Utah and southeast Idaho residents have participated in the tradition of going to Bear Lake during the summer to pick raspberries for local farmers as the crops are quite large and the fragile berries must be hand-picked. Each year Raspberry Days is held in Garden City, Utah, to celebrate the tradition. Vacationers and raspberry fans travel to Bear Lake

BEAR RIVER RASPBERRY SHAKE

3 c. ice cream, divided
1/2 c. milk
3/4 c. fresh raspberries, divided

Place 2 cups vanilla ice cream in blender. Add milk and 1/2 cup raspberries. Blend well. Pour into a bowl. Add remaining 1 cup ice cream. Stir by hand. Gently stir in remaining raspberries. Pour into a tall ice cream glass.[3]

looking forward to fresh raspberry shakes and other commercial items.

NOTES

1. Elizabeth Betty Allen, "History of Paradise Utah," Paradise Utah, https://paradise.utah.gov/about.
2. Elizabeth Kolbert, "Great Shakes in a Small Town," *New York Times* online, last modified May 28, 1989, https://www.nytimes.com/1989/05/28/travel/great-shakes-in-a-small-town.html.
3. Mary Jane Griffith, "Bear Lake Raspberry Shake Recipe," Cookbook Project, https://www.familycookbookproject.com/recipe/912988/bear-lake-raspberry-shake.html.

54

GOSSNER CHEESE

A Family Legacy of Cache Valley Cheesemaking

ROSA THORNLEY

A Swiss chalet nestled in the industrial area west of Logan, Utah seems a bit out of place, but it is the heart of cheesemaking in Cache Valley. Gossner Cheese stands as the oldest locally owned and operated plant in the area. Painted shutters and flower boxes filled with brilliant red geraniums reflect the rural alpine setting of the family farmhouse in Edliswiel-Waldkirch, Switzerland that Ed Gossner left in 1930 to apprentice as a cheesemaker in America. Gossner's Swiss roots are also reflected in the alpenhorn player featured on the company logo and their signature product, Swiss cheese. There is even a Swiss proverb painted on the building near the front entrance that illustrates his family's commitment to agriculture:

> You good faithful farmers,
> How are you valued by our country?
> If God does not bless
> And the farmer does not work,
> I ask, who has something to eat?

Immigrating first to Wisconsin, Ed worked with his brother, honing his knowledge of and skill in the seven-thousand-year-old tradition of cheesemaking. His career progressed when he accepted an opportunity in California to convert a cheese plant from a Monterey Jack to a Swiss facility. Ed surprised skeptics when he developed a new concept utilizing milk produced by cows fed on silage, a fermented feed commonly used in U.S. dairy production.

During a vacation one summer, he discovered that the high peaks and lush green valleys in Cache Valley resembled his childhood home in Switzerland. He moved his young family and

Photo by Lynne S. McNeill, 2018.

leg. Supervisors are involved in decisions to purchase new equipment, paying particular attention to processes that will benefit the teams who work with them. The third leg is Gossner's customers. Cheese is routinely shipped to far-flung places like Australia or China and to American troops overseas. During many natural disasters, truckloads of dairy products are shipped to worldwide destinations. Local customers are served directly through the doors of Gossner's storefront—the Swiss chalet. Along with a full line of dairy products, locavores can sample a traditional favorite—fresh curds, or, as grandma called it "squeaky cheese."

Cheese connoisseurs reap the benefits of Ed Gossner's work by savoring the mild, nut-like flavor of the Traditional Swiss made from the highest quality, heat-treated (not pasteurized) milk. Others appreciate the Old Country Swiss made from imported cultures, which offers a full-bodied flavor typical of European cheese. Younger taste buds develop their palate on the milder Baby Swiss made from pasteurized milk, giving it a milder taste. Weight-conscious cheese lovers will also find a Reduced Fat Swiss.

Although the family's European roots are part of the Gossner legacy, the company's board of directors, which includes seven members of the Gossner family, has adopted the Japanese approach of *kaizen*, which translates to continuous improvement for the company. Cheese made from Ed's formula remains a mainstay of the business today as the company dedicates resources to assuring extraordinary milk products for its customers and developing markets for dairy farmers in the region.

went to work perfecting his Swiss cheese varieties. A steady supply of milk provided by hundreds of local dairymen in Utah and southern Idaho provided Ed with the resources needed to build his own cheese plant in 1966.

Edwin's daughter, Dolores Gossner Wheeler, who leads the cheesemaking tradition today, uses a metaphor of the three-legged milking stool to describe the multigenerational network of people who have worked to make the company stand strong for over forty years. Farmers and milk haulers are one of the supporting legs, harvesting and transporting quality milk free from chemicals and artificial hormones. Some suppliers are grandchildren of those who provided milk for the very first vat of cheese. The employees are another important

CASPER'S ICE CREAM

NELDA R. AULT-DYSLIN

Few other towns in northern Utah scream "Dairy!" louder than Richmond. From Black and White Days every spring (the longest-running Holstein cow show west of the Mississippi)[1] to the silhouette of a long-defunct milk-processing factory on the outskirts of town, Richmond's roots in the dairy industry run deep. One of the most iconic dairy products to come out of Richmond is the FatBoy, a thick ice cream sandwich manufactured by Casper's.

Casper Merrill, a Richmond native, took over his family's Thornwood Dairy Farm in 1925 after graduating from Utah Agricultural College, now Utah State University. Maintaining a dairy herd and bottling milk were not enough to keep the dairy financially afloat, so Merrill began experimenting with making ice cream. His first innovation consisted of a small block of vanilla ice cream dipped in chocolate and rolled in nuts, placed on a stick for easy handling. After the success of the "nut sundae on a stick," Merrill and his family members continued to develop new products. By the 1980s, the company's signature thick slab of ice cream between two chocolate wafers was called the FatBoy.[2]

FatBoys are sold commercially throughout the United States and in local ice cream shops. Many people are introduced to the sandwiches while attending large gatherings, such as family reunions and church activities. Large boxes of FatBoy "rejects"—sandwiches with faulty wrappers, missing one of the two wafers, or any other defect that makes the ice cream unmarketable—are sold at a discounted price at Casper's Malt Shoppe in Lewiston, Utah. Students from nearby Utah State University make frequent trips to pick them up while folks throughout the nation, and especially the Intermountain West, look forward to enjoying this summertime treat from the heart of Cache Valley.

Courtesy Casper's Ice Cream.

NOTES
1. Marlin W. Stum, *Richmond: A History in Black and White* (Richmond, UT: Richmond City, 2007).
2. "FatBoy Premium Ice Cream," Casper's, http://www.fatboyicecream.com.

GROUSE CREEK CHILI SAUCE

CAROL A. EDISON

Chili sauce is, by definition, a condiment—a sauce or a relish eaten with other foods to add flavor or spice. Growing up, I never paid much attention to chili sauce. It was just something my mom sometimes made in the fall from one of her mother's recipes that we always ate with meat loaf. Then I spent a week in Grouse Creek, where the world of Utah chili sauce opened up for me.

Grouse Creek is a small (very small) ranching community on the west side of the Great Salt Lake. The population peaked at just over three hundred in the 1920s, and today only about a hundred people call the place home. Both Nevada and Idaho are just a stone's throw away. It's one of the more isolated—hence one of the more traditional—places in the state. And it's a community where nearly everyone still makes chili sauce.

So, what exactly is chili sauce? It's basically a relish made from fresh tomatoes, onions, vinegar, and salt that is cooked down and home canned. Some people also include spices—allspice, cinnamon, cloves, ginger, or nutmeg—while others add green peppers, chili peppers, or even apples. But the cooks in Grouse Creek use another basic ingredient: sugar. The result—a unique combination of savory and sweet, rather than hot and spicy—may account for its continued popularity.

According to Ella Tanner (1905–1990), ranch wife, cook, and home-canner extraordinaire, her family ate chili sauce, or one of her other home-canned pickle specialties, at every meal. Each fall she canned bread-and-butter pickles, sweet dills, mustard pickles, sweet tomato relish, cabbage relish, and chili sauce to accompany their ranch-style meat-and-potatoes diet. Ella continued to make home-canned specialties well into her eighties, as does most everyone in Grouse Creek.

Though it's impossible to substantiate, it seems that the use of condiments to spice up a meal of meat and potatoes might well represent a remnant of British culture in Utah. Think about classic British cuisine—a hot meal of roasted meat with brown sauce, mint sauce, horseradish, or chutney, or the cold ploughman's lunch of bread, cheese, and eggs served with pickled vegetables. The addition of sweet or savory flavors is the hallmark. A large percentage of Utahns do have British ancestry, and another large percentage have roots in rural and ranching heritage. Grouse Creek was largely settled by second-generation British Mormons from Utah towns like Henefer or

Ella Tanner (1905–1990), ranch wife, cook, and home canner extraordinaire. Photo by Carol Edison, 1985. Courtesy Grouse Creek Cultural Survey, Special Collections & Archives, Merrill-Cazier Library, Utah State University.

GROUSE CREEK CHILI SAUCE

This recipe, similar to others in Grouse Creek, was passed from Melissa Tanner to her daughter-in-law, Kathleen Tanner.[1]

9 medium-sized tomatoes, peeled and pared
9 medium-sized yellow onions, peeled and put
   through grinder
2 c. sugar
2 c. cider vinegar
1/2 tsp. nutmeg
1/2 tsp. cinnamon
1/2 tsp. cloves
1/2 tsp. allspice
2 Tbsp. salt

Combine all of the ingredients. Boil "fast" until the mixture starts to thicken, then boil slowly and stir. Be careful not to scorch. Cook until desired consistency. Prepare canning jars and fill with mixture. If the lids don't seal, hot pack the bottle for 10 minutes.

Tooele who picked the undeveloped area west of the Great Salt Lake to raise cattle. They likely all grew up in families that enjoyed adding sweet or savory condiments to their meals.

A recent survey of the women throughout Utah in charge of the home-arts competitions at the county fairs reveals both strong memories of chili sauce and the reality that the number of people making chili

sauce has dropped dramatically. The earlier popularity of home-canned condiments is evident in the historical categories at the 2014 Sevier County Fair, which still include pickled vegetables, sweet pickles, dill pickles, relishes, sauces, and salsas. But a quick tally revealed that most submissions in the condiment category were salsas, and that chili sauce, as well as other old-time, home-canned condiments, are on the wane. Yet many of the fair directors reminisced about chili sauce in their own families, remembering the wonderful smell that filled the house when "mom made chili sauce," or the time when "dad was in the hospital and asked us to smuggle in chili sauce."

Today chili sauce is not that well known, and salsa, in its many variations, seems to have become the condiment of choice. But it also appears that most native Utahns, at least those with pioneer or rural heritage who were raised during the 1960s or earlier, know all about chili sauce and have fond memories of enjoying it with roast beef, venison, scrambled eggs, fried potatoes, or just a piece of toast with a tablespoon or two of grandma's homemade chili sauce. That's unless you're from Grouse Creek.

In that case you might have enjoyed chili sauce with your most recent meal!

NOTE

1. Thomas Carter and Carl Fleischhauer, *The Grouse Creek Cultural Survey: Integrating Folklife and Historic Preservation Fieldwork* (Washington, DC: Library of Congress, 1988), 53.

57

TURKEY, LAMB, AND AEBLESKIVERS IN SANPETE COUNTY

DAVID A. ALLRED AND ROGER G. BAKER

Benjamin Franklin made no mention of eating turkey when he compared it to the inferior bald eagle adopted as the official symbol of the United States. His main complaint was that the eagle was of low morality. So now that we are clear on the idea of a turkey as a bird of high moral character, we can consider more important issues, like proper cooking and the turkey traditions of Sanpete County. We can also quit with the turkey jokes—except for the one about there being more turkeys than people in Utah thanks, in large part, to Sanpete County.[1] In fact, at one point the county had 6 million of the birds.[2] With a population less than 30,000 people, there were over two hundred times more turkeys than people in the central Utah county that locals simply call Sanpete.

Previously inhabited by the Ute people, the area known as Sanpete was settled by Mormon pioneers fairly early in territorial history; Brigham Young sent the first groups to the valley in 1849, where they established towns such as Manti, Mount Pleasant, Ephraim, and Spring City. Throughout the nineteenth century, many Scandinavian converts to Mormonism immigrated to Utah and were sent to the county. That heritage carries on through today in celebrations like Ephraim's Scandinavian Days and in the food traditions of many families. Recipes for Danish beer (supposedly nonalcoholic) can still be found, and the family of Ephraim residents Kim and Jan Cragun still bake aebleskivers every Christmas Eve, carrying on the tradition Kim learned from his Danish grandmother.

The Scandinavian influence is also reflected in the local lore, which includes a story cycle of humorous tales narrated by Brother Peterson, who is described well by Sanpete scholar Ed Geary: "[He is] the generic Sanpete Dane, square-headed, pious, kindly, viewing the world with eternal wonder, and never quite at home with the English language."[3] For example, local historian Grace Johnson recorded a funeral sermon Brother Peterson attempted to give: "Oh grave, vare is

SANPETE MARINATED TURKEY

In Sanpete County, if you attend a family reunion, church party, or neighborhood barbecue (or attended the LDS Church's former Manti pageant), there is a good chance that the main dish will be marinated Sanpete turkey. One of the largest employers in the county is the turkey plant in Moroni, and residents can purchase turkey steaks there in bulk.

Marinade
1 c. soy sauce
1 c. vegetable oil
2 c. Sprite

Soak the turkey in the marinade overnight using zip-lock bags and then grill it.

If expecting a large group, some people find that old ice cream buckets or even five-gallon buckets are useful to soak the turkey. Of course, variations exist. One resident explained that she uses peanut oil instead of vegetable oil. Another noted that soy sauce gives the best results. Others will add a tablespoon of horseradish or a teaspoon of garlic powder. Finally, there are differences of opinion on how long to soak the turkey in the marinade: some say that it needs to be at least twenty-four hours.

A grill filled with Sanpete County's famous marinated and barbequed turkey. Nancy Rappleye, *Somethin' So Let's Eat* (blog) 2013.

Victoria? Oh death, vare is thy stinger?"[4] The Scandinavian influence is also shown by the fact that Danish-language Mormon services persisted into the mid-twentieth century and the continued preponderance of Sanpete surnames like Olsen, Larsen, Lund, Christiansen, and so forth, including their Swedish equivalents with *–son* endings. In fact, one local resident likes to highlight the difference between Swedish and Danish ancestry, while hinting at the tension among the British and American settlers in Sanpete.

The joke goes, "There are only three kinds of people in Sanpete: the *–sen*'s, the *–son*'s, and the SOBs."

The architectural jewel of the county graces the hill north of Manti: the Manti Temple. Completed in 1888, the structure symbolizes the deep Mormon presence in central Utah. However, the temple continues to have not only a religious function but also a cultural one. It is a favorite location for LDS students from nearby Snow College to walk the grounds, and many a youth has gone dizzy after rolling down the steep, grassy hill south of the temple on a dare.

In a blend of civic and religious cooperation, for over fifty years each June Manti hosted tens of thousands of visitors who came to view the LDS Church's outdoor pageant, the Mormon Miracle Pageant. While being an economic boon to the local communities (if nothing else, pageant time was *the* time to hold a yard sale), the influx of so many visitors to a small Sanpete town created public safety, sanitation, and hosting problems. Residents of Manti and nearby

Advertisement for the 2016 Pageant BBQ. Photo by David Allred.

communities banded together to prepare traditional Sanpete turkey dinners for hundreds of people each night of the pageant. Visitors to Sanpete County experienced a real turkey barbecue: chunks of white turkey meat marinated in a patented broth replaced beefsteaks on a smoking grill that was made from half of a fifty-gallon drum. The turkey juices were seared into the tender bites, and everyone was allowed preliminary snitches and seconds occasionally resulting in a drip mark or two on a clean blouse or shirt.

The trimmings were traditional, too: Dutch-oven potatoes properly buttered and seasoned; a small tossed salad (included to enable the claim that the meal was balanced); and sourdough biscuits fresh from a sheep-camp stove made the meal complete. Cups of root beer from a bubbling cauldron of homemade root beer acted as a chaser. (In earlier times the drink of choice was wine.) The meal also included desserts. For example, Pam Baker of Ephraim remembers using the community recipe for pageant brownies, which are sweet and rich. In

PAGEANT BROWNIES
Courtesy Norma Wanless Barton

These brownies were made by LDS wards each year to be sold at concession booths at the pageant. Sweet rolls were also sold. A different ward was assigned the task of baking the brownies each year.

Today, many of the women who used to make the brownies still make them for special occasions like family reunions and get-togethers. There are at least three different versions of the recipe floating around Ephraim.

At one point it became too difficult for Manti to serve a dinner and also make the brownies and sweet rolls, so the responsibility was given to the Ephraim Stake. They typically made seven to eight pans of brownies for each night of the pageant.

3 c. flour
3 c. granulated sugar
1 1/2 c. margarine
1/2 c. cocoa
dash salt
6 large egg yolks, beaten (save whites)
1 tsp. vanilla
1 c. chopped nuts

Blend together sugar, margarine, and cocoa until creamy. Add six beaten egg yolks. Add three cups flour, dash salt, one teaspoon vanilla, and chopped nuts. Fold in beaten egg whites. Pour into greased pan (a half-sheet cake pan or large cookie sheet) and bake for 35 minutes at 350 degrees. When cool, ice with frosting.

Frosting
1/4 c. cream or canned milk
1/4 c. cocoa
1/2 c. margarine
3/4 lb. powdered sugar
pinch salt

Beat frosting ingredients until fluffy.

Shearers at work on Crawford's sheep herd in Manti, mid-1880s. Photo by George Edward Anderson. Used by permission, Utah State Historical Society. All rights reserved.

recent years, the food services had become more regulated by food-safety standards and were organized by the city. Still, the month of June was so dominated by the pageant that Manti resident Melanie Jenkins recounts deadpan jokes from her neighbors: "Is there a pageant in town or something?"

Turkey farming is not the only agricultural industry to affect the culture of Sanpete County. Earlier settlers tried their green thumbs at peas, and there was a pea factory in Ephraim. For a while, Ephraim settlers were called carrot eaters, as this was an agricultural option they tried. ("Carrot Eater" was

not a term of endearment.) Sugar beets were planted in Sanpete as part of a statewide effort at beet production, and for a time the Utah and Idaho Sugar Company was a successful statewide project.

The sheep industry also has deep significance in the region. In the nineteenth and early twentieth centuries, herds of sheep covered the local mountainsides and brought relatively great wealth to the county. Many of the largest homes of the era in the county were purchased with sheep revenue. Before the Depression years, lamb was the staple food at the gatherings. This is not to be confused with eating mutton, the meat from sheep that have died of old age, which is like sitting up to eat a fresh bowl of Crisco. This is lamb—juicy chops from the Dutch oven or slices from a roast wrapped and cooked in the ground on hot coals and rocks. A couple slices of bacon on the top of the roast add a hint of flavor and seem to make the lamb tallow less likely to stick to the roof of the mouth.

The herds were so numerous, however, that the groundcover in the mountains was depleted, leading to devastating floods during summer thunderstorms. The federal government used the Sanpete mountains as a test area for reforestation and built a field station in Ephraim Canyon that still stands: the Great Basin Environmental Education Center. There are still many sheep ranchers in Sanpete, and the herders are increasingly multinational, with many coming from Latin American countries. Thus, the carvings on quaking aspens, a traditional form of expression for sheep herders high up on mountains, are increasingly written in Spanish. Another manifestation of the sheep industry occurs every October. Students from Snow College, especially those from the Wasatch Front or other urban centers, stand and gawk as the sheep herders lead hundreds and even thousands of the sheep from their mountain grazing past the college to the West Desert.

While aebleskivers, barbecued turkey, and mutton are not unique to the county, taken together, they certainly capture much of the history and culture of the region.

Of course, Sanpete County is changing. The historic Mormon tabernacle in Ephraim was razed years ago, and the LDS meetinghouse built in its place was torn down recently for a new bank. Throughout the county, hay and alfalfa fields are transforming into housing subdivisions, and national chain businesses are moving in. The issues of the *Saga of the Sanpitch*, which appeared annually for thirty years with essays recounting local history, are no longer published. However, traditional Sanpete foodways and culture persist as locals adapt to a new era in rural Utah.

NOTES

1. Matt Canham, "Utah Effect: Watch Out, People, You're Outnumbered by Turkeys," *Salt Lake Tribune*, November 24, 2015.
2. Personal interview with Jed Worthington, employee at the Moroni Turkey Plant, July 29, 2019. The current number of turkeys is lower than the 6 million number.
3. Edward A. Geary, *The Proper Edge of the Sky: The High Plateau Country of Utah* (Salt Lake City: University of Utah Press, 1992), 127.
4. See Grace Johnson, *Brodders and Sisters* (Manti, UT: Messenger-Enterprise, 1973), 56.

58

DIXIE SALAD

CAROL A. EDISON

If you already know what Dixie Salad is, there's a good chance you have some kind of connection to Utah's Washington County. If you haven't heard of it before, it's a sure bet you'll want to try it now!

The southwest corner of Utah, known for over 150 years as "Dixie," has a different ecosystem than the rest of the state. It is red-rock desert country, home to Zion National Park, and a good part of the county is less than three thousand feet above sea level and one thousand feet lower than any other part of the state. The area's unique climate allows the production of crops not found in the rest of Utah. In fact, Dixie was originally settled for the express purpose of growing southern crops like cotton and grapes. It was settled by Mormon converts, some of whom were actually from the American South. They were called to settle this southern outpost by Brigham Young in order to complement products made in northern Utah and to help reach the Mormon goal of self-sufficiency.

Pecans and pomegranates are two of the low-elevation crops still produced in the region today. Warm temperatures, a long growing season, and chalky, alkaline soil all contribute to their success. According to Tim Thompson, who operates the county's largest pecan farm, pecan trees were originally brought to Washington County by missionaries who had served in the Southern states.[1] The origin of the pomegranates is more of a mystery. Known as Utah Sweet Pomegranates, their willowy bushes are found in backyards throughout the county and they produce a terracotta-colored fruit that is more thin-skinned than those from other climes.[2] When local pecans and pomegranates are combined with apples, which also grow well in the county, and grapes or raisins, also historically local products, with just enough whipped cream to thoroughly moisten everything, the result is Dixie Salad.

For many Washington County residents, Dixie Salad is a Thanksgiving fixture (which coincides with harvest time for pomegranates) and a favorite at most every church social, school function, and community get-together. Although many folks say that the recipe was handed down from pioneer times, others attribute it to a salad-making demonstration at Dixie Academy in St.

DIXIE SALAD

(SERVES 6)[5]

1 medium can pineapple tidbits
Pulp of 3 pomegranates
3 bananas, sliced
2 apples, sliced
2 oranges, sliced
6 pitted dates, sliced
2 clusters Thompson seedless grapes
1/2 c. chopped pecans
1/2 pt. whipping cream
Sugar to taste
Vanilla to taste

Drain pineapple; reserve half the juice for future use. Combine pineapple, remaining juice, pomegranates, bananas, apples, oranges, dates, grapes, and pecans. Whip cream; add sugar and vanilla. Fold into fruit mixture. Vanilla ice cream may be substituted for whipped cream.

Dixie Salad—one of the best ways to celebrate Thanksgiving in southern Utah. Courtesy Ashley Amundsen, blogger at wanderzestblog.com.

George in 1911.[3] Some give the credit to home economics teacher Mrs. Emily T. Woodward;[4] still others credit a visiting cook. According to that version of the story, "There was to be a demonstration on salad making by an out-of-town guest. They expected to find salad making materials in the local grocery store. None was available at that time of year. From private cellars and storerooms came the ingredients for the first Dixie Salad."[6]

Today one can find recipes for Dixie Salad both in published cookbooks that feature recipes "tested in Mormon kitchens" and in recipe collections on the Internet. All recipes have the basics—apples, pecans, grapes, pomegranate seeds, and whipped cream—but many then add fresh, canned, or dried fruit as well as miniature marshmallows and maraschino cherries. And, without fail, all cooks who share these recipes have roots in this special quarter of Utah. They come from St. George, Hurricane, or

New Harmony, Utah, or from nearby Las Vegas or Henderson, Nevada. They may also live in northern Utah, southern Idaho, or in other places where the sons and daughters of southern Utah's original pioneers migrated, taking with them a bit of the uniqueness and wonder of Dixie.

NOTES

1. Valerie Phillips, "Thompson Family Pecan Fam in Southern Utah," Chew & Chat, last modified May 7, 2013, http://chewandchat.com/2013/05/thompson-family-pecan-farm-in-southern-utah.html.

2. "Pomegranate Trees," Bay Flora, last modified March 8, 2017, http://bayflora.com/pomegranates.html.

3. Pamela Perry Norris, "St. George, Utah's Dixie, Dixie Pioneer Recipes," pamphlet compiled for the Washington County Convention and Visitors Bureau.

4. Ibid.

5. Jeanette Christian, *Favorite Mormon Recipes* (Carson City, NV: Montgomery Second Branch of the Church of Jesus Christ of Latterday Saints, 1968), 81.

6. Carol Kemple, *Color Country Traditions II: A Holiday Supplement to* The Spectrum (St. George, UT: *The Spectrum*, 1995): 21–23..

59

WINE IN NINETEENTH-CENTURY UTAH

LYNNE S. MCNEILL

In the early 1860s the LDS Church made a push to further colonize southern Utah, sending more than three hundred families to found the city of St. George and, perhaps surprisingly, to make wine "for the Holy Sacrament," Brigham Young explained, as well as "for medicine, and for sale to outsiders."

Grape growing and wine production were also intended to support the cotton mission of southern Utah—the origin of the name "Dixie" for the region.[1]

A number of Swiss families from wine-producing regions of Switzerland were among the company that traveled south, as was horticulturist Walter Dodge, who planted his vines at Dodge Springs. Perhaps the best-known winemaker in southern Utah, John C. Naegle (whose wine was known locally as "Nail's Best"), arrived in 1866 and built a two-story home in Toquerville to house both his polygamous family and his wine cellar, press, and distillery. The building can still be visited today (though no one has since managed to turn it back into a winery).

By this time, about a third of the cultivated acreage in southern Utah was orchards and vineyards, and the product was a source of pride for many in the LDS Church. Young himself remarked, "I anticipate the day when we can have the privilege of using, at our sacraments, pure wine, produced within our borders."[2] The LDS Church itself joined the wine-making business, largely from member tithes paid in grapes.

Despite common expectations to the contrary, wine was consumed socially in southern Utah and wasn't considered a sin (there was a distinction between drinking and drunkenness—the latter was frowned upon). Suggestions that the "wine" consumed by church members was actually unfermented grape juice are contradicted by comments from natives to the region, who made observations such as "It isn't wine, unless it's fermented."

The tide began to turn on Utah wine production around 1890 for a variety of reasons. Mining operations were slowing down, so much of the customer base for commercial wine was dropping off. Temperance was also becoming an issue for the LDS Church, which was tightening its

Jacob Hamblin was an early Mormon leader, founder of Santa Clara and missionary to the Native Americans. His home, built in 1863, is now a museum and today grape vines are still cultivated in front. Photo by Kenneth R. Mays.

restrictions on wine consumption for purposes outside of the sacrament, and eventually even within, switching to the use of water during services.

The southern Utah wine traditions live on,[3] if not in drink, then in memory and song, such as the local favorite, "Sweet Dixie Wine," which extols the virtues (and headaches) of different local vintners' brews.[4] Utah musician Moses Gifford penned his song "The Good Old Keg of Wine" from personal experience:

> When the weather is warm, like bees they
>   will swarm
> With the good old keg of wine.
> And when it is cold, if a wife she will scold
> At the good old keg of wine.
> When the stomach grows sour, they'll heave
>   for an hour
> When called to a meal they'll decline,
> They try not to show it, think the women
>   don't know it,
> With the good old keg of wine![5]

NOTES

1. Dennis Lancaster, "The Dixie Wine Mission," *Sunstone*, online at https://www.sunstonemagazine.com/pdf/003-74-84.pdf.
2. Ibid.
3. Also see Olive Burt, "Wine Making in Utah's Dixie," in *Lore of Faith and Folly*, ed. Thomas E. Cheney (Salt Lake City: University of Utah Press, 1971), 147–48; and Loren Webb, "Southern Utah Memories," KCSG.com, July 15, 2012.
4. http://discover.lib.usu.edu/iii/encore/record/C__Rb2181881__Ssweet%20dixie%20wine.
5. https://www.sunstonemagazine.com/pdf/003-74-84.pdf.

60

THE BREAD (AND MILK) OF LIFE

Eating Close to Home in Utah's Dixie

LYMAN HAFEN

I recently sat down with my family at a table brimming with food freshly harvested from our neighborhood garden in Santa Clara, Utah: tomatoes, cucumbers, zucchini, summer squash, new potatoes, beets, onions, lettuce, and corn. It was the simplest meal I've had in a long time, yet perhaps the greatest feast in ages. There is something comfortably sustaining about eating from the ground you stand on. Something satisfying to more than just the stomach. Wouldn't it be great, I thought, if I ate like this every day?

One of the things I remember most about my grandparents' house on Tabernacle Street in St. George is the garden that grew just east of it. My grandfather Hafen was the grandson of original Swiss converts to the Church of Jesus Christ of Latter-day Saints who settled in Santa Clara, Utah, in the 1860s. Grandma was the granddaughter of original Mormon pioneers from upstate New York. The house, in the middle of downtown, is still there, but the once-fertile ground where the garden grew is now a parking lot capped with asphalt. I remember fence lines draped in grape vines and long rows of corn, green beans, peas, carrots, radishes, and a small pasture of alfalfa they called the Lucerne patch. Fig trees grew liberally throughout the neighborhood. Their fruit was dried or found its way into luscious cookies. I remember pomegranate bushes, apricot and pecan trees, and water running in ditches where asparagus grew like weeds.

My grandparents' garden, and all the food-producing plants surrounding my grandparents' house, had grown for decades under their careful care. It had existed not as a hobby or some quaint diversion, but as the key source of sustenance for a family of fourteen children who grew up during the roaring twenties, the depressed thirties, and the war-weary forties. When I appeared on the scene the ground was still producing, though more and more of everyone's sustenance was coming off the grocery store shelves. By then there were two or three grocery stores in St. George, including the new Safeway that seemed to me like the largest building in the city,

Drying fruit in the sun has been an important method of preservation since pioneer times. Used by permission, Utah State Historical Society. All rights reserved.

though today you couldn't fit a Harmon's produce section in the same floor space.

In the March 10, 1942, edition of *Look* Magazine there's a photo of my grandma and grandpa Hafen and eight of their children kneeling at their chairs turned backward to the dining room table—a table set for dinner and brimming with food. The photo is one of many illustrating an article by novelist Maurine Whipple, of recent *Giant Joshua* fame, on the peculiar lifestyle of Mormons in southern Utah. That week, early in World War II, my

grandma's table was exposed to millions of *Look* readers across America. On it I can identify a plate of meat (perhaps fried chicken), a large bowl of mashed potatoes, a bowl of gravy, individual plates with freshly cut tomatoes, a tall stack of thickly sliced home-baked bread, and individual bowls containing some sort of salad (could it be Jell-O?).

My father can't be more than ten years old; he is kneeling in the foreground, fingers clasped beneath his chin, with his closed eyes pointing toward the ceiling as if he is offering his own prayer for my grandfather to finish quickly so he can turn his chair around and dive into the meal. I recently asked my father about what and how they ate in that wonderful old house. He talked of white beans and ham-hock for lunch and dinner on Mondays, which was his mother's wash day. It was a handy meal to prepare ahead of time, as washing started before daylight and didn't end until after dusk. On Sundays it was always potatoes and gravy and usually roast beef, with green beans and beets fresh from the garden or from the bottle. Breakfast was often cracked-wheat mush with sugar, or cooked rice with sugar and milk or cream. On some mornings they had ham or bacon with eggs and hash browns. Grandma made chocolate and white cakes, and bottled in two-quart jars bushel after bushel of peaches, apricots, and cherries. She baked bread a couple of times a week and for much of her child-rearing years made her own butter from the rich milk of a Jersey cow. (They always had a Jersey cow—Dad was quick to remind me of that when he told me his milking stories. Jerseys gave the richest milk.) In summertime, melons abounded: crenshaw, casaba, muskmelon, watermelon, and cantaloupe. In winter, Dad said their family, like most in St. George and the surrounding towns, might not have survived without the venison hunted in the fall, the delectable meat of the mule deer that ran in the high country.

Much of the above has made it down another generation or two to my table and the tables of my children. Even green Jell-O, which has become cliché in Utah, is still a staple at our family gatherings; in our case it's my mom's long-honored recipe including cottage cheese and pineapple. But one item in particular continues to hold the generations of our family together: Dixie Salad. It comes in many iterations and can be traced back to the earliest days of St. George. For it to qualify as Dixie Salad it must contain apples, whipped cream, and pomegranates. Some will tell you nuts (almonds, pecans, or walnuts) are also mandatory to make it authentic, but that has not been the case in my experience. These days bananas and all manner of fruits are used. The key is thick, almost decadent, whipped cream, and juicy, purple-red, tart-sweet pomegranate seeds that explode in your mouth with the glorious burst of decades past.

One night in the late 1950s, we stopped in for an evening visit at my grandparents' house. For me, stepping into that house was like walking into a sacred shrine. It was a quiet place; the only sound was the tick-tock of the clock on the mantle and the soft and soothing voices of my grandparents. On the night I remember, there was a fire in the wood stove in the kitchen where my grandmother cooked and baked her bread; the house was full of the glorious smell of risen and freshly baked dough. My grandpa sat at the kitchen table eating what I would later learn was the late-night snack he had cherished all his life: bread and milk.

When I say bread and milk, I mean freshly baked homemade bread torn into small pieces and soaked in the richest whole milk a Jersey cow ever gave. My dad later told me Grandpa would sometimes change it up a little by plopping some freshly picked grapes into the mix, or a slice of onion, or a dollop of sorghum.

I only tried sorghum once (the homemade molasses pressed from cane stalks that grew in the fields south of town). I was given to think that a taste

Sorghum mill and evaporating pans in Utah's Dixie, circa 1900. Photo by F. S. Dellenbaugh. Used by permission, Utah State Historical Society. All rights reserved.

for sorghum was something I should have been born with. For decades our sports rivals in Cedar City had called us "Sorghum-lappers," a term that was supposed to be derogatory, but one my dad was always proud of because he'd been taught as a little boy it was the iron in sorghum that made Dixie boys athletically superior to the boys in Cedar City. I can still feel the guilt that gripped me when, to my father's displeasure, I gagged on the strong, harsh taste of the same substance that had been like candy to my forebears.

Never since have I been tempted by sorghum. But sometimes late in the evening a craving comes over me and I feel I might give anything for one mouthful of fresh baked bread soaked in rich Jersey milk.

AGRICULTURAL FESTIVALS

An Expression of Community Identity and Heritage

CAROL A. EDISON

The signature annual event in many rural Utah towns is a celebration that brings everyone together—residents, former residents, and visitors—to enjoy shared activities and celebrate life in their community. Often that celebration highlights a local food product—Apple Days, Raspberry Days, Dairy Days, and Orchard Days, to name just a few.

On the surface these agricultural and harvest festivals mark the end of a long season of work and the realization of shared goals. But they also function in other, more significant ways. Though most were started primarily as a means of advertising local products, they became much more than that. As folks embraced these events, they became symbols of local pride, occasions to honor local history, and ultimately an acknowledgment of their shared and highly treasured way of life. Perhaps that is why many of these events, including several that are over a century old, continue today, and why new festivals are still emerging in the twenty-first century.

THE BEGINNING OF UTAH'S AGRICULTURAL FESTIVALS

A number of Utah's harvest festivals were started during the early 1900s. This was a time of rapid change and the fruits of the Industrial Revolution were becoming evident. Indoor lighting, indoor plumbing, radios, telephones, and cars were coming onto the scene or were just around the corner for almost everyone in Utah. Everyday life was changing quickly and people's view of the world was expanding. Utahns interacted not only with family and immediate neighbors but also with people around Utah and beyond.

The state's economy was growing at a fast pace too. Programs like 4-H, Extension Services, and the Utah Farm Bureau were established to help farmers grow crops and raise livestock more

Small-town celebrations in Utah sometimes grew out of Mormon Relief Society bazaars that showcased and sold local crafts. Notice the display of beautiful quilts above this flower display at the 1933 Peach Days celebration. Courtesy Compton Collection, Special Collections & Archives, Merrill-Cazier Library, Utah State University.

effectively and efficiently, and to find wider markets for their products. Many areas had already experienced over fifty years of agriculture and people had discovered what grew well in their own fields and orchards. As they started to specialize in specific crops, they wanted to tell the world about their treasures. Creating a festival offered a great way to do just that. Before long, festivals were popping up from one end of the state to the other.

The reasoning behind creating Cherry Days, a celebration still held in north Ogden, probably reflects the motivations of community leaders in other rural Utah towns during the same period of time. "In 1932 a group of civic and church leaders . . . formed a committee to improve the cherry market throughout the Western states. They started an annual community celebration to call attention to the size, color and flavor of their cherries and to acquaint people with the beauty of the area and the high quality of community and family life."[1] In other words, decades before there was a state agency devoted to tourism, harvest festivals promoted not only local products but also the state's natural beauty and way of life.

A SAMPLING OF THE BEST

Utah's oldest agricultural celebration is likely Brigham City's Peach Days, started in 1904 as a day off from the harvest and a time to celebrate "an abundance of the best peaches in Utah."[2] Peach Days thrives today and is advertised as the oldest continually running harvest festival in the state. Early photos of the event document the breadth of activity: parades with marching bands, Peach Day royalty, and floats sponsored by local clubs and businesses; displays of peaches, flowers, and quilts; amusements such as a ring-toss booth, wrestling contest, horse races, and carousel and Ferris wheel rides. Today some features have been modernized, but similar activities are still part of nearly every community harvest festival throughout the state.

The Turkey and Sauerkraut Dinner, which began in the 1920s in the small Cache Valley town of Providence, is another early community food celebration.[3] It started as a church bazaar and dinner at which homemade sauerkraut, a product of the many Swiss and German immigrants in the area, was featured. Made from the local cabbage crop and served with turkey, Providence's sauerkraut was not only the centerpiece of the dinner but was also sold to visitors for later enjoyment. As the population grew, the celebration faltered for a few years. It was ultimately

The fame of Brigham City's peach crop is due in part to the century-old Peach Days celebration. Photo by Lisa Duskin-Goede, 2015. Courtesy Bear River Heritage Area.

adopted by the city and, even after the cabbage crop diminished and the health department prohibited the sale of homemade sauerkraut, a commercial sauerkraut supplier was contacted and the event continued.[4] Today it brings together the area's growing and more diverse populace, while still honoring a town that was first known as "Little Germany."

Peaches were also the focal point in southern Utah when the town of Hurricane started a fruit festival a few years after the town was established in 1896. By 1911 the event had grown into Elberta Days and by 1915 it, too, was called Peach Days. For

Black and white (aged class) 1936

A 1912 competition to pick the finest local cow expanded into Richmond's Black & White Days, a town celebration that has been going strong since 1915. This 1936 photo captured the judging of the Holstein cows that are the backbone of the local economy. Courtesy Special Collections & Archives, Merrill-Cazier Library, Utah State University.

many years Peach Days was part of the Washington County Fair, but today it is once again a standalone celebration honoring Hurricane's history of fruit production. According to the promotion on the city's website:

Peach Days wouldn't be complete without the rodeo, entertainment, parade, Pioneer Corner, 12K Fun Run, and the Peach Cook-Off. The Hurricane Canal Trek, quilt show, and a wide variety of booths displaying commercial and homemade goods will also be included. The traditional displays, always a staple of the event, will be featured in the Hurricane Elementary building. Plan now to prepare an entry.

Categories include home arts, fine arts, garden, and baked or bottled goods."[5]

Utahns are just as proud of their livestock as they are of their fruits and vegetables, and over the years they have established competitions and festivals to acknowledge and celebrate their quality. Perhaps the most well-known and certainly the longest-running livestock festival is Richmond's Black and White Days which began in 1915. The original idea was to parade the finest local Holstein-Friesian dairy cows through town and auction them off. But organizers quickly realized that rather than selling their animals, owners really just wanted to have a beauty contest by corralling the animals on the public square where judges—and everyone else—could admire them.[6] Today Black and White Days is a full-fledged town celebration with all the requisite competitions and entertainments found elsewhere. It might, however, be the state's only festival that features "Mooing, Hay Throwing, Milking, and 'Cowpie' Eating" contests.[7]

Another long-lived livestock-based event was Plain City Dairy Days, which started in 1926 and continued for over fifty years, growing into a well-respected livestock show. This Weber County event celebrated not only Holstein cows but also Jersey and Guernsey breeds. It was started to finance the town's baseball team. For many years it included a dance and a banquet that featured locally grown asparagus, a crop that today has almost disappeared from commercial production.[8]

Interestingly, a few festivals with origins in the first half of the twentieth century persist despite the decline, if not loss, of the heritage crop for which they were created. Pleasant Grove's Strawberry Days, established in 1920, and Payson's Golden Onion Days, established in 1929, continue to celebrate what are now historical crops.

Even when fields and orchards have been replaced with roads and subdivisions, the need to celebrate local heritage can remain strong. Residents cherish whatever makes their community unique, even if it represents a bygone era. In describing Strawberry Days, the Pleasant Grove City website explains:

> Although the berry fields of yesterday are all planted with houses and the threshing competitions have been replaced by a carnival, we gather every June to celebrate some good old Pleasant Grove history.... Everyone has favorite Strawberry Days memories that are told around the fire on dark winter nights. Sunburn and sticky cotton candy hands are commonplace. Almost every red-blooded PG or Lindon native remembers going down to the rodeo grounds with Dad or Grandpa to see the bulls when they come in and we all tend to get teary eyed as we smell those wonderful combined aromas of rodeo hamburgers and cow pucky. Throw in some berries and cream and its PG heaven on earth![9]

Similarly, the Payson Historical Society website proudly displays the original proclamation by which Mayor L. D. Stewart established the Onion Harvest and Home Coming celebration, urging the schools and businesses to close so that all could enjoy the parade and contribute to "making Payson and vicinity popular as an agricultural district and outstanding in the production of the onion."[10] Today Onion Days includes a parade, crafts fair, carnival, live entertainment, 5K and 10K runs, and a Dutch-oven cook-off. Sadly, the only onions are those that might happen to be used in the Dutch-oven recipes!

The 1920s saw the creation of at least three more Utah food festivals that have survived. Hooper Tomato Days, established in 1925,[11] Green River Melon Days, formally organized in 1925 after two decades of informal "melon busts,"[12] and Garland's Wheat and Beet Days, established in 1930,[13] each continue to offer a highly anticipated weekend of community reunion and camaraderie. While tomatoes are still grown in Hooper on a smaller scale, and melons are still a very important crop for Green River, Garland's sugar-beet industry is definitely a thing of the past.

ONE OF UTAH'S CLASSIC FESTIVALS

So, in addition to their advertising function, what did festivals really offer rural Utah communities, and why did they become so popular in the early twentieth century?

Food blogger Sarah Jampel writes,

The earliest history of food festivals is much like the history of autumn harvest holidays; they were closely tied to the celebration of the autumn bounty and the veneration of earth gods. It was in the midst of the Great Depression, however, that food festivals (at least those in the United States) really got their start. According to Harvey Levenstein in his book *Paradox of Plenty: A Social History of Eating in Modern America,* the 1930s coincided with a surge in concern for regional culinary practices. In this decade of instability, Americans sought to reinforce familial and community bonds by preserving rich traditions. And what better way to do that than to hold communal eating festivals?"[14]

That's exactly what the folks in Fountain Green, Utah, wanted to accomplish when, in 1932, they created Lamb Days—one of Utah's classic festivals because it so purposely commemorates not just a "crop" but also a way of life.

Fountain Green, with a population of about six hundred, is located at the northern end of Sanpete Valley. Until turkeys became the most important regional commodity, its claim to fame was its sheep industry started during pioneer times by Danish immigrant Andrew Aagard. In its heyday, Fountain Green's population was around two hundred people while the sheep population was thirty thousand. Almost everyone in town was either a sheep owner, herder, or shearer. During the 1920s Fountain Green was known as one of the wealthiest towns in the country, per capita, because of the sheep industry.[15]

The origins of Lamb Days are classic, following a storyline that can be attached to many of the food festivals Utahns enjoy today.

It began in 1932 as an attempt to counteract a slow market for wool that was being aggravated by long-term drought and the Depression. A local organization, the Jerico Wool Growers' Association, specifically designed and initiated the celebration to promote the consumption of

Pit-roasted lamb is the highlight of the annual Lamb Days celebration in Fountain Green. The lambs are slipped onto poles, wrapped with wire, and cooked overnight in specially built sandstone pits. The next day they are whisked away to the park where they quickly become delicious lamb sandwiches. Photo by Carol A. Edison, 1984. Courtesy Utah Folklife Archives.

lamb. Association members each donated lambs for a community barbeque, and Hyrum Jacobsen, a local man who had had some experience with pit barbequing, provided the expertise. Everyone was invited and all the lamb was given away without charge.... During these early days, the celebration succeeded in developing a taste for local lamb, ... raised public awareness of the sheep industry's potential for meat production

and helped promote its longevity as a vital local industry.[16]

As participation grew, activities were added. Among the earliest offerings were boxing and wrestling matches and dancing outdoors to the local Wool City Band. Although producers continued to donate lamb, a charge for the lamb sandwiches was gradually instituted to offset the cost of other

ONGOING RURAL FOOD FESTIVALS

Except where noted, all events are still taking place and the public is invited.

Date	Name of Festival	Location	Year began	Contact
May	Black and White (Holstein) Days	Richmond	1915	http://www.richmond-utah.com/bwdays.html
June	Strawberry Days*	Pleasant Grove	1920	http://www.strawberrydays.org/schedule/
June	Testicle Festival	Woodruff	2000	Last event held in 2013; hope to resume soon
June	Dairy Days	Gunnison	2012	http://gunnisonvalleydairydays.com/
July	Apple Days*	Torrey	1982	http://www.torreyappledays.com/
July	Cherry Days*	North Ogden	1932	http://www.northogdencherrydays.com/
July	Lamb Days	Fountain Green	1932	http://fountaingreencity.com/lamb-days.html
July	Wheat and Beet Days*	Garland	1930	http://www.garlandutah.org/wheat--beet.htm
July–August	Orchard Days	Santaquin	1980s	http://www.santaquin.org/orchard-days
August	Harvest Days*	Midvale	1938	http://www.midvaleharvestdays.com/
August	Raspberry Days	Garden City	1984	http://www.gardencityut.us/rasberry-days-2011.htm
August	Corn Fest	Enterprise	1990	http://enterprisecornfest.wix.com/enterprisecornfest
August	Trout and Berry Days	Paradise	1991	http://www.paradise.utah.gov/about
August	Apple Days*	River Heights	1998	http://www.riverheights.org/2015/03/24/apple-days-2015/
September	Tomato Days*	Hooper	1925	http://www.hoopertomatodays.com/
September	Onion Days*	Payson	1929	http://www.paysonutah.org/news_events.oniondays.html
September	Peach Days	Brigham City	1904	http://peachdays.org/
September	Peach Days	Ferron	1906	http://www.ferroncity.org/peach-days.htm
September	Peach Days	Hurricane	1911	http://www.cityofhurricane.com/categories/about/events/peach-days/
September	Melon Days	Green River	1925	http://melon-days.com/
September	Apple Festival	Glendale	1998	http://glendaletown.org/Glendale_Apple_Festival.html
October	Turkey and Sauerkraut Days*	Providence	1920s	http://www.providencecity.com/sauerkraut-festival.htm
October	Cedar Livestock Heritage Festival	Cedar City	2006	http://www.cedarlivestockfest.com/

*Food no longer produced in enough quantity to market.

activities. As the festival grew, its fundraising potential was obvious; when the local LDS congregation needed a way to generate matching funds for a new meetinghouse, the local church became the new organizers. After the church was built, the city took over sponsorship of the festival, using the profits to buy grills and other equipment needed for the event. After festival needs were met, profits were used to fund a variety of city improvements and local projects that included upgrading the park and the cemetery, purchasing a new ambulance, paying for EMT training for several residents, and supporting local ball teams, 4-H clubs, and other small organizations. In 1968, when the city decided they could no longer produce the event, a town meeting was called and local residents appointed a four-person committee to coordinate Lamb Days. Victor Rasmussen, the committee chair, explained, "The people wanted it to continue because they were proud of it and because they wanted to pay tribute to those who had started it."[17]

Today's Lamb Days includes a jam-packed weekend of activities designed to appeal to all ages. People look forward to talent shows, a parade with royalty, sports competitions, a carnival, children's games, and an open-air dance. But the central activity—the preparation and consumption of pit-barbecued lamb—is still the focus of the event. Local sheep producers still donate dozens of lambs to be barbecued in the town's permanent barbecue pits built for this celebration. Each pit is approximately four feet wide, four feet deep, and twenty feet long, lined with sandstone quarried from a nearby canyon. The floors of the pits are covered with metal sheets. After a bonfire of wood from the canyon has burned down, the metal sheets and remaining coals are carefully lifted out and twenty to twenty-five lambs, wrapped in chicken wire and slipped onto long poles, are lowered into the pit and quickly covered with successive layers of tin, cardboard, canvas, and then dirt. The lambs cook throughout the night as the heat from the sandstone slowly roasts the meat to a golden brown. At noon the next day, the lambs are transported by pickup truck to the park where a cadre of servers are waiting, knives in hand, to make lamb sandwiches for the hungry crowd.

Lamb Days also functions as an annual homecoming celebration—an excuse for all those who have moved away to return home and enjoy the company of family and renew friendships. Festival organizers in every town understand this, just like they understand the potential of harvest festivals to make community fundraising relatively painless, and many advertise the homecoming aspect of their event. Most importantly, they understand that activities like rodeos, community dances, Dutch-oven cook-offs, and quilt exhibits, plus the opportunity to enjoy the favored local crop, provide the recipe for success. People want to participate in these activities because they embody local culture and traditions, and participating in them reinforces a desired feeling of community.

NEWER AGRICULTURAL FESTIVALS

In recent decades, a number of new food-based harvest and homecoming festivals have been established. Bear Lake's Raspberry Days in Garden City, started in 1984, is one of the most well-known Utah festivals—undoubtedly because hardly anyone can resist

BRIDGERLAND BARBECUED BEEF

"This recipe has been a favorite for city celebrations, church socials, and company parties for many years. For a large group, roasts are often cooked for several hours in a deep pit lined with hot rocks. The meat can also be cooked over a barbeque grill."[18]

1 beef roast (3 to 5 lbs.)
Barbecue sauce
1 to 2 onions, chopped
Salt
Pepper
1 1/2 to 2 tsp. liquid smoke (optional)

Preheat oven to 325 degrees. Place the meat on a sheet of heavy-duty aluminum foil or double layer of regular-weight foil large enough to completely wrap around meat. Pour the sauce freely on all surfaces of the meat. Add onions, salt and pepper, and, if desired, liquid smoke. (Note: Slashes may be cut in the meat to facilitate faster and more uniform penetration of the sauce and other ingredients.) Bring the edges of the foil together and roll them securely so that all the juices will be trapped inside the package. Roast the meat in a shallow pan, and check for doneness by inserting a thermometer into the center of the meat. For a 4-pound roast, cook to about 140 degrees for rare (1 3/4 hours), 160 degrees for medium (2 1/4 hours), or 170 degrees for well done (3 hours).

a raspberry shake! A lesser-known event is Cache Valley's Trout and Berry Days, started in 1990 and held in the very small town of Paradise. As co-chair Gerry Winn explains, "The two biggest industries in town are a trout farm and a berry farm so we decided to name [the festival] after them."[19] In southern Utah's Long Valley along Highway 89, folks in the little town of Glendale established the Apple Cider

Festival in 1998. According to the city website, "The Apple Festival celebrates the production, harvest, and sale of apple products, handicrafts, and games and culminates with a large community banquet dinner at the town park. Glendale is a quaint, historic town, with a vibrant farming community. The Apple Festival is an opportunity to showcase and share the rich heritage of Long Valley."[20]

Two other newer events appeared in the twenty-first century, both designed to honor and celebrate Utah's livestock industry. Kalon Downing, a rancher and the owner of the Black Gold Cattle Company, started what might be a shock to many: the Woodruff Testicle Festival. The event ran from 2000 to 2012, closing down in 2013 with the stated hope of reviving the event in the future. The main activities were an old-time rodeo with "events such as range bull riding and team branding, which are no longer part of modern day competitions"[21] and a benefit concert that raised money for those with special medical needs in the community. Of course, the main draw was the "oyster fries"—bull testicles that have been sliced, battered, and deep fried. They were a draw for the adventurous and for ranch families who grew up working at brandings where eating "Rocky Mountain oysters" or "cowboy caviar" is associated with those rare opportunities for community gathering and sociability.

In 2006, a sixth-generation sheep-ranching family, the Nelsons, decided to honor their family's occupational heritage and their community's century-old history of sheep ranching by creating the Cedar Livestock Heritage Festival. The celebration includes a long list of activities including many that highlight ranching culture such as a sheep wagon exhibit, pulling competitions with draft horses and antique tractors, cowboy poetry and music, and a Dutch-oven cooking contest. Though some of the cook-out contestants are undoubtedly preparing lamb, the most important lamb in this celebration, and the major draw for this event, is still on the hoof. The festival's highlight is the "sheep parade" which involves trailing a thousand head of sheep from Cedar Mountain pastures through the main street of downtown Cedar City—recreating the seasonal movement of sheep that has been part of the town's history since the 1850s.[22]

TODAY AND TOMORROW

In recent years, the number and popularity of out-door public food events in urban Utah has been growing. A neighborhood breakfast or barbecue sponsored by a local organization as a fundraiser, a competitive contest or cook-off designed to showcase specific foods or products, or a commercial event created by local restaurants to introduce their fare to a wider public are all becoming more commonplace. But in rural Utah, there is a long history of folks coming together in an outdoor setting to enjoy each other's company while sharing a very special meal.

There's a reason why these events continue today, why their activities and audiences are expanding, and why small towns continue to put significant resources into producing them. With their parades, displays and competitions, their talent shows, craft exhibits, cowboy poetry recitations, rodeos, fun runs, Dutch-oven cook-offs, and the chance to celebrate together by consuming the fruits of their labor, they honor local history and

they acknowledge the community's shared, and treasured, way of life.

NOTES

1. "Cherry Days History," North Ogden Cherry Days, http://www.northogdencherrydays.com/2013/09/in-1932-group-of-civic-and-church.html.
2. "Peach Days," Brigham Area Chamber of Commerce, accessed January 24, 2016, http://www.brighamchamber.com/peach-days/; "Peach Days," The City of Hurricane, accessed January 24, 2016, http://www.cityofhurricane.com/categories/about/events/peach-days/.
3. "Sauerkraut: A Providence Specialty," *Providence and Her People: A History of Providence, Utah 1857–1974* (Providence, UT: Keith W. Watkins and Sons, 1974).
4. Valerie Phillips, "What Makes Providence Dinner Special? Sauerkraut," *Deseret News* (Salt Lake City, UT), October 24, 2007.
5. "Peach Days," The City of Hurricane.
6. "Richmond's Bovine Beauty Contest," Utah State University Extension, https://extension.usu.edu/cache/files/uploads/Richmond's%20Bovine%20Beauty%20Contest.pdf.
7. "Black & White Days," Richmond, Utah, http://richmond-utah.com/bwdays.html.
8. William Freestone, Harold Thompson, and Floyd Palmer, "Dairy Days," Plain City Utah, http://www.plaincityutah.org/bodily/dairy_days.htm.
9. "Home," Pleasant Grove Strawberry Days, http://www.strawberrydays.org/, and http://plgrove.org/documents/newsletters/newsletter0607.pdf.
10. Payson Historical Society, http://paysonhistoricalsociety.blogspot.com/2015/09/why-payson-celebrates-onion-days.html.
11. Mark Saal, "Hooper Tomato Days Barreling Down on the City Like 900-Pound Concrete Produce," *Standard Examiner*, Aug 31, 2018.
12. "Home," Melon Days, http://melon-days.com.
13. "Wheat and Beet Days 2015," Box Elder County, http://siterepository.s3.amazonaws.com/553/wb_book_2015.pdf.
14. Sarah Jampel, "Food Fest: American Food Festivals

Wonderful and Weird," https://food52.com/blog/7232-food-fest-american-food-festivals-wonderful-and-weird.

15. "Fountain Green," *Utah History Encyclopedia*, http://www.uen.org/utah_history_encyclopedia/f/FOUNTAIN_GREEN.html.

16. Carol Edison, "Roast Beef and Pit-Barbequed Lamb: The Role of Food at Two Utah Homecoming Celebrations," in *"We Gather Together": Food and Festival in American Life*, ed. Theodore C. Humphrey and Lin T. Humphrey (Ann Arbor, MI: UMI Research Press, 1988), 143.

17. Ibid., 144.

18. Paula Julander and Joanne Milner, *Utah State Fare: A Centennial Recipe Collection* (Salt Lake City: Deseret Book, 1995).

19. Mark Havnes, "Annual Food and Fun Festival a Celebration in Paradise," *Salt Lake Tribune* (Salt Lake City, UT), August 29, 1999.

20. Karen Williams, "Glendale Apple Festival October 11–12," *Southern Utah News* (Kanab, UT), September 26, 2013.

21. Kathy Stephenson, "Testicle Festival: At Least It's for Charity," *Salt Lake Tribune*, June 1, 2008.

22. "Home," Cedar Livestock and Heritage Festival, http://www.cedarlivestockfest.com.

PART V FOODWAYS TODAY

62

FOODWAYS TODAY

LYNNE S. MCNEILL

We've come a long way, baby. While much of Utah's past is still active in its present foodways (as evidenced by the continued popularity of Dutch-oven cooking and the preservation of home-grown fruits and vegetables), Utah has been steadily growing out of its foodie-desert reputation and into a hub of good eats.

There's no doubt that the iconic foods of Utah remain familiar identifiers of the state, even if the contexts in which they appear are sometimes quite new. Internet memes abound to show us that even in the age of Web 2.0, Utahns will never shed their connections to their iconic foods.

But there's a pride in the local fare that's evident as well, as it should be; the food and beverage scene in many of Utah's cities has gained national recognition. To outside eyes, it often seems as though Utah's offerings of food and beverages grew rapidly after the 2002 Winter Olympics held in Salt Lake City, but the state's culinary renaissance actually dates back a bit further. Ted Scheffler, editor of *Devour Utah*, a food-themed and foodie-targeting magazine, attributes the biggest recent change to the early 1990s arrival of the restaurant group Gastronomy, Inc. As he explains, "First they opened the New Yorker, followed by Market Street, Baci Trattoria, and other eateries. Baci Trattoria, in particular, was ahead of its time, serving northern Italian fare in a very cosmopolitan setting."[1] Scheffler also credits Bill White's Park City restaurants (an impressive list, including Grappa, Chimayo, Wahso, Windy Ridge, Sushi Blue, Ghidotti's, and Billy Blanco's) with raising the expectations of Utah diners.

Scheffler feels that the best way to describe the current state of Utah dining culture is "eclectic"—there's the familiar bunch of beloved local diners described by Ronda Weaver in this section, not to mention locally

OH YOU'RE FROM UTAH?

TELL ME ABOUT HOW GREAT FRY SAUCE IS

significant fast-food outlets, such as KFC, whose first franchise was opened in Utah, and Café Rio and Costa Vida, two "Fresh-Mex" franchises with a bitter rivalry. But there's also a growing scene that follows larger national trends. Movements like farm-to-table dining, food trucks, backyard chickens, and locavorism are finding a ready-made fit between Utah's rural environments and modern developments. There are currently three farm-to-table establishments operating in Logan, a relatively small town known in recent years for a shortage of fine dining opportunities. As Benjamin Bombard discusses in his contribution, organizations like Local First Utah and numerous CSAs (community-supported agriculture) are aiding these endeavors, as are the farmers markets that Carol Edison describes.

As it always has, food touches on almost every part of life. Utah is growing in population and diversity, and food trends have kept up with the time. Refugee and community gardens, as Adrienne Cachelin describes, are one way that Utahns meet the needs of their changing neighborhoods. As diversity continues to grow, old traditions develop new iterations, like the new holiday of "Pie and Beer Day" as a non-Mormon substitute for the quasi-religious celebration of Pioneer Day. As with many forms of folklore, the flexibility of foodways means that food is adaptable to new situations and scenarios, and the threads of the past remain visible (and edible!) in the present. There are, after all, some foods that Utah just wouldn't be Utah without.

NOTES

1. Ted Scheffler (Editor of *Devour Utah*) in discussion with the author, September 2016.

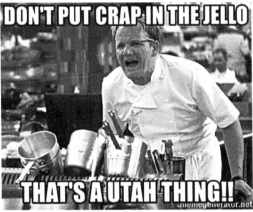

Mrs. Fields employee Caitlyn Billingsley displays a variety of the company's popular cookies. Photo by Carol A. Edison, 2018.

63

MRS. FIELDS LEGENDARY COOKIES

KYLIE SCHROEDER

So the story goes...

There was once a woman who ate a Mrs. Fields cookie and liked it so much that she asked for the recipe. She was told the Utah-based company didn't give the recipe out, but that she could buy it for "two-fifty." The woman thought that $2.50 was a pretty good deal, so she told them to add it to her bill. When she received her credit card statement, she saw that there was a charge of $250 for a "cookie recipe." The woman was so furious that she copied the recipe and shared it with as many people as she could with the following message:

So here it is, and please pass it to someone else or run a few copies....I paid for it; now you can have it for free. Recipe may be halved.

The legend gained so much popularity that Debbi Fields responded to this rumor by posting a sign in her company's stores:

Mrs. Fields recipe has never been sold. There is a rumor circulating that the Mrs. Fields Cookie recipe was sold to a woman at a cost

---

MRS. FIELDS LEGENDARY COOKIES

2 c. butter
4 c. flour
2 tsp. soda
2 c. sugar
5 c. blended oatmeal**
24 oz. chocolate chips
2 c. brown sugar
1 tsp. salt
1 8-oz. Hershey Bar, grated
4 eggs
2 tsp. baking powder
3 c. chopped nuts (your choice)
2 tsp. vanilla

** Measure oatmeal and blend in a blender to a fine powder.

Cream the butter and both sugars. Add eggs and vanilla; mix together with flour, oatmeal, salt, baking powder, and soda. Add chocolate chips, Hershey Bar, and nuts. Roll into balls and place two inches apart on a cookie sheet. Bake for 10 minutes at 375 degrees. Makes 112 cookies.

of $250. A chocolate-chip cookie recipe was attached to the story. I would like to tell all my customers that this story is not true, this is not my recipe, and I have not sold the recipe to anyone. Mrs. Fields recipe is a delicious trade secret.[1]

Snopes.com has outlined the history of this legend, connecting it to companies such as Niemen Marcus and Woolworths, and tracing it as far back as seventy years when the story and recipe for a "25 Dollar Fudge Cake" was published in the 1948 cookbook *Massachusetts Cooking Rules, Old and New.*[2] In the 1960s a similar tale was told about a $350 cake recipe from the Waldorf-Astoria Hotel in New York. The legend was connected to Mrs. Fields Cookies from the 1970s to the 1990s and continues to attach itself to different high-powered companies and, through the sharing, allows the "little guys" a triumph.

NOTES

1. http://jezebel.com/5605541/debunking-the-gazillion-dollar-designer-cookie-recipe.
2. http://www.snopes.com/business/consumer/cookie.asp.

64

OLD-TIME COOKING

RONDA WALKER WEAVER

When my husband, Scott, and I were first dating, I wanted to impress him with my culinary skills. I made shrimp scampi, sweet-and-sour chicken with eggrolls, Massaman curry, and Nopales cactus tacos. Shortly after we were married, Scott came to me with a request: "I love your cooking, but could you make us an old-fashioned dinner once in a while?" I did not have to ask him what he meant. I knew what he wanted.

How is it I knew what an old-fashioned dinner was? My mother cooked the way her mother cooked, good ol' down-home cooking. This was the first kind of food I ate and learned to prepare. In my experience—and Scott's—a traditional, or "Sunday," meal meant meat, potatoes and gravy, yeast bread or rolls, steamed vegetables, and dessert. Key spices? Salt and pepper. Onions and a bit of garlic marked the more adventurous meals. Desserts required copious amounts of sugar.

As the main cook, I understood clearly that the creative meals I prepared for Scott were made up of familiar components—but for him, the variations were disconcerting. It is the differences in preparation and presentation that turn sweet-and-sour chicken into roasted chicken, rice or pasta into potatoes, eggrolls into homemade rolls with homemade jam, and stir-fried vegetables into steamed peas, corn, and carrots. As for dessert, sliced mango over sticky rice covered in coconut milk is often replaced with apple cobbler and vanilla ice cream.

I occasionally do cook down-home traditional foods: roast beef, turkey, chicken, and pork. I make mashed potatoes with gravy; I steam and roast vegetables; and I make stuffing, bread, and plenty of cobblers and chocolate cakes. Yet Scott has taken matters into his own hands and made it his crusade to find the best traditional meal money can buy. When we travel, or even when we go out for dinner, he would rather eat meatloaf, chicken pot pie, or pot roast that tastes like Mom's traditional cooking than a "funky" meal with colors, textures, and tastes unfamiliar to him.

What is it that makes folks go in search of the best home-cooked meal since Sunday dinner at Grandma's? Regardless of one's nationality, the hunt for memories surrounding food seems to be the norm. Here in the Intermountain West, that meal might include the perfect gravy, a great dinner roll, or meatloaf that melts in the mouth. It is the associations that food conjures up at the

Since 1944 Arshel's Cafe in Beaver has been serving hot breakfasts, homemade soup and pies, and old-time favorites with gravy, like pot roast, chicken fried steak, and hot hamburger plates. Photo by Carol Edison, 2004.

forefront of our memory; it is the smells and tastes that can quickly return us to yesteryear when we felt most cared for, most nurtured, most at home.

So, what makes a restaurant a "homestyle" diner? Typically, this is a restaurant that cooks old-time meals, just like mom used to make; that has been in existence for at least fifty years; and that has been owned by the same family continuously. The diner was most likely opened and run by a family, usually a woman who cooked for her own and then went "downstairs" to cook for others, taking the recipes she used for her own meals into the diner's kitchen for others. The meals truly were "just like mom's." Recipes were handed down through the generations, with the cook being someone in the family—not a trained chef, but a family member who had grown up around the grill and walk-in refrigerator. Most of these establishments are remembered and frequented for their basic meals and particular foods such as pies, rolls and breads, jams, and soups—items that have stood the test of time and have not changed.

The persistence of old-time or down-home foods can be attributed to several significant qualities. Old-time cooking has become a symbol for a particular way of life. My grandmother fixed my grandfather and his ranch hands a heavy meal they called "dinner" at the lunch hour and a lighter meal called "supper" in the evening. For the midday meal, she cooked hearty foods to fill a man's stomach, giving him the energy to finish a hard day's work. These meals always included a meat, potato, gravy, vegetable, roll, and either jam or a fruit-based dessert. This meal became known as a "working-man's dinner." If you worked hard, you ate heartily. In my culture, down-home or old-fashioned cooking has become the symbol for an idealized time when men worked hard, tilled the land, and herded the cattle, while the women made bread using the wheat grown in their fields and made jam using the peaches they picked from their orchards.

Often a diner will be searching for a place that can replicate sensations of timelessness and family cohesion: red-checkered tablecloths, ceramic salt and pepper shakers, stoneware plates, and a waitress who calls you "honey" or "boss." Such symbols seem to demonstrate that restaurants value the same things as their customers—family, hard work, a slower and simpler life—and that they can still be experienced at this establishment.[1] The Little Wonder Café in Richfield, Utah, shares this belief with their slogan: "Homestyle Food Away From Home Since 1929." They have a

GRAPE NUT PUDDING
Courtesy Arshel's Café, Beaver

Butter for 2-qt. baking dish
4 c. milk
1 c. Grape Nuts cereal
4 large eggs
1/2 c. sugar
2 1/2 tsp. vanilla extract
1/4 tsp. table salt
1/2 tsp. freshly grated nutmeg

Heat oven to 350 degrees.

Place milk and Grape Nuts into a medium saucepan, simmer, remove from heat, stirring occasionally, and let cool for 15 minutes.

In a bowl mix the other ingredients. Add the Grape Nut mixture to the bowl, stir. Pour into the baking dish, sprinkle top with nutmeg.

Set the baking dish into a deep pan and pour water into this pan until the water reaches about halfway up the sides of the baking dish.

Bake for about 50–60 minutes, until the center jiggles but a knife comes out clean.

Let the pudding sit for about 20 minutes to set and cool.

Serve with whipped cream and sprinkles of Grape Nuts.

picture of a wood-burning cooking stove with steaming, home-cooked foods on the menu, and an interior rich with farmhouse-style décor, including clocks, photos of a bygone era, flowers on the tables, and a staircase to their upstairs banquet area.

In addition to being symbolic of a particular way of life, that way of life is, in turn, deeply emotionally connected to memory. Hearty meals were satisfying to the stomach, and the memories associated with them recall a moment of relaxation after a hard morning's work, a time of rest, and often a time of silence where eating was the dinner-table language. These memories include thoughts of times when life was simpler, less hurried, when people had face-to-face conversations, when a stomach full of tasty food was as fulfilling for the provider as for the consumer. Traditional foods reiterate the *illusion* of these memories, even if they don't always provide the reality. Just driving to a down-home restaurant is enough to take the patron back in time. Being met at the door by the scent of fresh-baked rolls and the sight of flaky crust, fruit-filled pies lining the pie case can feel like a homecoming. Foy's Country Corner Restaurant sits on a corner lot in downtown Panguitch, Utah. The exterior is definitely from the 1950s; they call themselves a "classic hometown diner," and the interior certainly fits this description. One of my favorite country-dining places is Arshel's in Beaver. The menu has a photo of the owner's mother in her youth, and "Great Home Style Cooking for Over 50 Years" printed on the front. The Formica-top tables remind me of my father's restaurants, and the turquoise swivel barstools beg for me to sit down and take a spin! This appears to be a universal theme—we're eager for what we're accustomed to, what we grew up with.

Down-home cooking provides diners with a strong sense of community, too. When was the last time someone cooked a roast-beef dinner for themselves? These are meals meant to be shared. Even after more than ten years of cooking "alternative" meals that have surely become familiar to him, my husband still yearns for a different "familiar," one that includes sharing this meal with others who understand his desire for "good old-fashioned food." Dargavell's Circleville Café in Circleville, Utah, has handwritten messages on

the outside stucco of their building that speak to their community: "Trucks Welcome!" "ATV's Welcome!" "Great Home Cookin'!" They certainly do not want those who recreate in this area to feel like they are not welcome to a home-cooked meal.

As much as these eateries are about community, there is also an us-versus-them mentality that can single out a visitor who isn't familiar with the way that old-time eating works. There have always been social rules to assembling and eating a down-home meal. Meals were typically served family-style with bowls and platters of food placed on the table for everyone to serve themselves. Often a salad came first, meat and potatoes second, and dessert last. Diners waited until everyone at the table had food on their plates, then silence reigned until the meal was finished. Once dessert was served, conversation could begin. If a stranger entered this "conversation" without knowing the rules, there were definitely social faux pas associated with talking with food in your mouth, belching at the table, making a dam with your potatoes and gravy as opposed to a volcano, and so forth. When social norms were violated, the person was either laughed at, talked about, or taught. Food as the object, and eating as the act, resonates with attitudes and emotions related to the individual's understanding and feelings about self, others, and mutual relationships.

When this dynamic moves into a commercial space, the relationship can be more complicated. The home-style diner doesn't want to alienate customers, but they may expect a certain level of familiarity with the customs. If you do not like "smothered in gravy," there may very well be something wrong with you, or you are eating at the wrong establishment!

HONEY BUTTER

Courtesy M. Clyde Walker, Walker Family Restaurant

1 c. butter (2 cubes)
1 c. honey

Soften butter; make sure butter is not melted, but softened.
Add honey, making sure the honey is warm but not hot.
Blend together with a mixer or whip.
Serve in a bowl, with fresh hot rolls.
Can refrigerate.

At Arshel's in Beaver, a group of women walked into the restaurant while my husband and I were there "doing research." They complained to the waitress that the chicken soup recipe had changed, and said they were never going to eat soup at Arshel's again. What was the change? Arshel's was no longer serving their homemade soup over a scoop of mashed potatoes. Nostalgia can certainly be worn with pride in the world of food.

Home-style meals are often served to an older population, those who are in search of a familiar, down-home taste. Perhaps this will change as time wears on, with children taking their parents out to eat at their favorite sushi restaurants, filled with memories. While in today's world, folks go out to eat and then come home and attempt to replicate what they have eaten at a restaurant, old-time restaurant meals do the opposite. My children ate at Idle Isle Restaurant in Brigham City when they were young children, and now as adults they stop at Idle Isle on their way through Brigham City, just to reminisce about their days in the town; to eat the hot, homemade rolls smothered in butter and served with peach jam; and to enjoy the chicken gravy that Mom seldom makes nowadays.

While on a trip to Northern California, I met a couple who, upon hearing where I was from, and that I was a Walker, asked me if I was old enough to remember "Walker's Family Restaurant." When I told them this was my father's café, they closed their eyes, licked their lips, and began telling me stories of the food, service, diners, and events they connected to their meals at the café. It was a treat to hear them reinforce what I have known all along. From the examples of my parents and grandparents, I have learned that sharing food is the ultimate act of service and sacrifice, and that partaking of these foods is the ultimate gift.

Daily special ticket found in an old Walker's Family Restaurant menu in the 1960s:
#1 Roast Tom Turkey
Salad, Soup, Sage Dressing
Snow Whipped Potatoes
Gravy, Cranberry Sauce
Buttered Fresh Frozen Peas
Hot Buttermilk Biscuits with Honey or Bread
Choice of Drink and Dessert
$1.50

Daily Special found on the wipe board at Arshel's Café in 2014:
Turkey Bacon Club
W/ Soup, Salad, Fries
And a House Dessert
Soup: Homemade Chicken Noodle
$7.50

ORIGINALS:

(family-owned and operated for more than one generation)

- Arshel's Café: Chicken-fried steak, Grape Nut dessert, and peanut butter chocolate pie; Beaver, Utah
- JC's Country Diner: Bone-in ham, big portions, good gravy; Tremonton, Utah
- Idle Isle: Idleberry pie, rolls, peach jam; Brigham City, Utah
- Maddox Steakhouse: Turkey steaks, fried chicken; Brigham City, Utah
- Blue Bird: Rolls, raspberry jam, shakes; Logan, Utah
- Ruth's Diner: Mile-high biscuit, raspberry jam; Emigration Canyon, Salt Lake City, Utah
- Lamb's Grill: Fine dining.[2]; Salt Lake City, Utah
- Stockton Miners Café: Pot roast; Tooele (Stockton), Utah
- Little Wonder Café: Filling early bird dinner specials; Richfield, Utah
- Circleville Café: Apple bread pudding; Circleville, Utah
- Foy's Country Corner Restaurant: Great breakfasts; Panguitch, Utah

REPRODUCTIONS:

(local or chain, without the generational history)

- El Bambi Cafe: Fresh-baked rolls, desserts; Beaver, Utah
- Porter's Place: Sourdough bread, steaks; Eureka, Utah
- Chuck-A-Rama: Homestyle cooking, variety; Numerous Utah locations
- Golden Corral: Home-style buffet; Numerous Utah locations
- Leslie's Family Tree: Scones and honey-butter; Santaquin, Utah
- Johanna's Restaurant: Breakfasts, particularly biscuits and gravy; Salt Lake City, Utah
- Cracker Barrel: "Wholesome Fixin's"; National chain with several restaurants in Utah

NOTES

1. Kathy Stephensen, "Oldest Restaurants in Utah Offer History and Charm," *Salt Lake Tribune*, July 14, 2016.
2. Lamb's closed in 2017.

THE CONTEMPORARY FOOD SCENE IN UTAH

BENJAMIN BOMBARD

At the turn of the twenty-first century, I was largely in the dark about the food I ate. I certainly wasn't alone. Like most Americans, I picked items off grocery-store shelves, ordered meals from restaurant menus, and generally ate whatever I desired with hardly a moment's thought about where my food came from or who produced it and how.

In the first decade of this century, a growing number of Utahns, myself included, started to wonder about their food's provenance, for several reasons. As an obesity epidemic swept across the country, we were concerned about our health. As the realities and ramifications of human-caused global climate change became manifest, we were concerned about our future and that of the planet. As our national economy suffered, we were concerned about the financial stability of our local economies. Through all this uncertainty, we began to see how what we eat fits into the wider web of life. Soon enough, wonder became action, and that action was swept up in a movement burgeoning across the country; a renewed focus on our food seemed therapeutic for many of our worries.

With little doubt, the most important development in Utah foodways in the early decades of this century has been the rising popularity of and demand for locally grown and produced food. That trend echoes the growing popularity of local food nationally.

I first began to wonder about my food because I wondered about my books. While working at a local bookshop, I became familiar with the business advocacy organization Local First Utah and its efforts, beginning in 2004, to boost local businesses. In order for the shop I loved to survive the threat of big-box store competitors, it was critical that Utahns understood the value and benefits of buying local. That message soon influenced many of my financial decisions, particularly my food and dining budget.

Local First Utah's efforts are magnified in the state's food system by the Utah Department of Agriculture and Food's Utah's Own branding campaign. Established in 2006, the campaign endeavors to connect consumers with the farmers and companies who grow and make their food.[1] Approximately two hundred companies carry the Utah's Own label,[2] and the bulk of those companies credit the campaign as important to their success.[3] Utah's Own undertook efforts in 2015 to expand its impact across the state's vast rural areas by attending business development events in fifteen counties. They also hold a biannual gathering to connect farmers to food manufacturers. It's like a business-to-business speed-dating event: farmers show off what they grow, food producers explain what they need, and matches are made.[4]

At one time, there were as many places to buy local food in Salt Lake City as there were local bookstores: that is, very few. The Downtown Alliance established a healthy farmers market in 1992, so when interest in local food burgeoned, people knew they could find reputable farmers and tasty goods at Pioneer Park on Saturdays throughout the summer.[5] Home to a hundred food vendors in 2004, the market has blossomed to nearly two hundred vendors almost fifteen years later,[6] with a food-only market on Tuesdays and a market during the winter months that has expanded from a monthly affair to a weekly one. Farmers markets have sprung up across Utah, with forty-four in operation from St. George to Richmond, from Vernal to Moab.[7]

More and more local food has shown up on the shelves at brick-and-mortar grocery stores in Utah. Harmon's, a locally owned market, boasts the widest selection of local products among grocery markets on the Wasatch Front,[8] but chains like Smith's (Kroger), Whole Foods, and even Costco, a warehouse club, now feature local products as well.

Investing in Community Supported Agriculture (CSA) is perhaps the most convenient way for Utahns to get their local-food fix. CSAs facilitate the most direct route from farm to table, providing

Utah towns and cities have led the way in the backyard chicken movement, a growing trend in both rural and urban areas over the past couple of decades. Eggs are regularly shared with neighbors or sold locally, and while the chickens themselves are often treated as pets, they may also be used for meat once they become unproductive. Chicken coops, whether built from repurposed materials, invented anew, or created by following plans downloaded from the internet, are a growing form of vernacular architecture. Here, folklorist Craig Miller holds one of his chickens in front of their coop. Photo by Carol A. Edison, 2018.

consumers with routine deliveries of fruit, vegetables, dairy, meat, honey, and other value-added products, typically on a weekly basis during the growing season. Farm shares are now available from forty-three Utah farms.[9]

With increasing, and increasingly dependable, opportunities to sell their products, Utahns are choosing to become farmers and food producers in greater numbers. There are a handful of

In 2007 Cristiano Creminelli left his family's *salumificio* (salami factory) in Italy to establish Creminelli Fine Meats in Utah. Since then, Creminelli Fine Meats has garnered nine national food awards for its slow-aged artisan salami and deli products. Courtesy Creminelli Fine Meats.

cheese producers in Utah, including national award-winning Beehive Cheese from Weber County.[10] You can buy Amano Artisan Chocolate, which has won top honors at international competitions.[11] You can buy eggs from free-range chickens, butter, grass-fed heritage beef, goat yogurt, heritage pork, raw milk, and authentic Middle Eastern hummus, all grown or produced locally. You can buy table salt mined from the remnants of an inland sea that covered much of Utah during the Jurassic period,[12] and you can buy flour from Central Milling, a Logan-based operation that sources a portion of its grain locally and provides flour to the country's most discriminating bakers.[13]

With the loosening of Utah's liquor laws in recent years, more than a dozen distilleries and thirty-five breweries have popped up locally.[14] Utahns make some of the best whiskey and beer in the country, or indeed the world, and the number of breweries, pubs, and alcohol producers here seems to be growing by the day.[15] To the surprise of many, there's now even a brewery in Utah County, the first since the Rutherford B. Hayes administration.[16]

Utah even attracts international talent. Cristiano Creminelli, a native of Biella, Italy, settled in Utah in 2007. His family has been making Italian salami for hundreds of years. After a cross-country search, he chose to produce salami here because of the ideal climate and the exceptionally high quality of pork in the region—he claims it's superior to the pork his family uses in the Old World. His salami has won national awards, and in 2012 *Bon Appetit* magazine declared Creminelli a "tastemaker...one of the visionaries who are making our lives so delicious."[17]

Locally produced food is the highlight at some of Utah's best and most renowned restaurants, including Hell's Backbone Grill in Boulder, Café Niche and Tin Angel in Salt Lake City, Hearth on 25th in Ogden, and Talisker on Main in Park City. Utah's cuisine has even garnered national attention. Chefs and proprietors Jen Castle and Blake Spalding of Hell's Backbone Grill have been featured prominently in the *New York Times Magazine* and were the subject of a lengthy feature article in the *New Yorker*, as much for their food as for their politics.[18] In 2011, *Food & Wine* magazine recognized chefs Bowman Brown and Viet Pham—of the now-shuttered Salt Lake restaurant Forage—as among the country's best new chefs.[19]

When Pham struck out on other projects—including appearances on the Food Network programs *Extreme Chef* and *Iron Chef*[20]—chef Brown took the reins at Forage and pioneered a dining experience unlike any other in the state, or indeed the country. His elaborate *prix fixe* menu showcased ingredients plucked directly from Utah's lands and waters, including local elk, trout roe, acorns, goose, elm samaras, watercress, cattails, and duck eggs from a neighbor's backyard flock. One early dish on the menu featured locally harvested juniper branches steeped in hot apple cider made from local apples, punched up with a shooter of sorbet made from arugula grown specifically for his restaurant at a farm in Draper. In other words, Brown's menu was uniquely Utah.

My transition from eating conventionally to eating locally was spurred by many factors, the most potent of which was the Eat Local Challenge. Sponsored by several Utah nonprofits dedicated to good, clean, fair, and local food—Wasatch Community Gardens and Slow Food Utah primary among them—the Eat Local Challenge is more or less what it sounds like: a challenge to source your food as locally as possible. Before taking up the challenge in 2012, local foods were more a novelty in my diet than a standby. Seven years later, much of my food comes from our garden, our neighborhood, Utah's

In recent years, food trucks have proliferated in Utah, especially in the Salt Lake Valley. These mobile kitchens operate daily in scheduled locations and prepare food for many special events. They offer a variety that reflects the growing diversity of Utah's culinary heritage. Courtesy Chow Truck.

lakes, streams, and forests, and from the state's farms and food producers.

While Utah has made great progress in building a sustainable and vibrant local food scene, there's still room for improvement. In a recent report, Utah was ranked the forty-fifth-worst state for eating local.[21] It lacks a food hub to centralize local food distribution, has a poor percentage of farms and CSAs relative to its population, and has yet to embrace the cooperative grocery market model that has been so important to local food communities across the United States. The relatively high cost of locally produced food compared to the conventional alternatives also stands as a significant barrier to broader influence of the "locavore" movement, especially in low-income communities and among minority populations.[22] Nevertheless, if Utah's recent past is any indication of its near future, it appears likely that Utahns will continue to build up the state's local food infrastructure and that demand for local food will continue to flourish. I for one won't stop eating locally anytime soon.

NOTES

1. "About Utah's Own," Utah's Own, Utah Department of Agriculture and Food, http://www.utahsown.org/About-Utah-s-Own.
2. Laurie Seron (executive director, Utah's Own) in discussion with the author, 2019.
3. Andrea Smardon, "'Utah's Own' Branding Campaign Expands into Rural Areas," KUER, radio broadcast, May 29, 2014, http://kuer.org/post/utah-s-own-branding-campaign-expands-rural-areas#stream/0.
4. Seron, discussion with author.
5. "History of the Downtown Farmers Market," Downtown Farmers Market, Salt Lake City, http://slcfarmersmarket.org/about/history-of-the-market.
6. "'Yeah! It's market season!': Salt Lake City's Downtown Farmers Market Is Open for Summer," *Salt Lake Tribune*, June 9, 2018.
7. "Utah Farmers Markets," Edible Wasatch, http://www.ediblewasatch.com/resources/farmers-markets.
8. "What's Local in Our Supermarkets," *Be Localicious Utah* (blog), April 2011, http://belocaliciousutah.blogspot.com/p/whats-local-in-our-supermarkets.html.
9. "The Strolling of the Heifers 2018 Locavore Index," Strolling of the Heifers, https://www.strollingoftheheifers.com/locavore/.
10. "Food & Beverage," Utah's Own, Utah Department of Agriculture and Food, http://www.utahsown.org/

Food-Beverage; "Barely Buzzed," Beehive Cheese, http://www.beehivecheese.com.
11. "Amano Artisan Chocolate Awards," Amano Artisan Chocolate, http://www.amanochocolate.com/awards/.
12. "Redmond Salt Mine," Redmond Real Salt, https://realsalt.com/mine/.
13. Benjamin Bombard, "Fine Grain: A look at Central Milling," *Edible Wasatch*, Winter 2014.
14. "Utah Distilleries," Gastronomic: Salt Lake City, https://www.gastronomicslc.com/utah-distilleries/; "Utah Breweries," Utah Ale Trail, https://utahaletrail.com/utah-breweries.
15. "Press Room," High West Distillery, http://www.highwest.com/press/high-west-distillery-wins-best-craft-american-whiskey-jun-3-2010/. Kathy Stephenson, "Utah-made Dandelion Beer wins World Cup Gold," *Salt Lake Tribune*, April 18, 2014; Dawn House, "From Zero to 18, Brewers Flourishing in Utah," *Salt Lake Tribune*, February 4, 2013.
16. "Utah County Has 'Grown Up' and Is Getting Its First Brewery since before Prohibition," *Salt Lake Tribune*, June 22, 2016.
17. "About Us," Creminelli Fine Meats, http://www.creminelli.com/about-us/; "Creminelli Award Winning Salami 4-Pack," Woot!, https://wine.woot.com/offers/creminelli-award-winning-salami-4; "Creminelli Fine Meats Will Whisper Sweet Salami Nothings in Your Ear," *bon appétit*, March 3, 2012.
18. Alexandra Fuller, "Utopia on the Range," *New York Times Magazine*, September 25, 2009; "Why Two Chefs in Small-Town Utah Are Battling President Trump," *New Yorker*, October 1, 2018.
19. "Bowman Brown," *Food & Wine*, http://www.foodandwine.com/contrib.
20. "Viet Pham," Food Network, https://www.foodnetwork.com/profiles/contestants/viet-pham.
21. "Strolling of the Heifers."
22. "How to Bring Farmers Markets to the Urban Poor," *Washington Post*, September 20, 2013.

66

PROVO'S BLACK SHEEP CAFÉ

CAROL A. EDISON

Black Sheep Café co-owner and head chef Mark Mason still enjoys putting on his apron in Provo's first Black Sheep Café. Photo by Carol A. Edison, 2018.

Black Sheep master chef Mark Mason spent part of his youth on the Navajo Reservation and part in Provo, where his folks attended BYU. His parents are both artists—his mom a potter and his dad a silversmith. Today his bicultural childhood and family artistry are evident in the finely crafted dishes he creates for Utah's premier contemporary southwestern Native American restaurant.

Although cooking was never part of his dreams, Mason remembers thinking, even as a child, that this dish or that meal would have been better if something had been added or it had been cooked differently. Today that discerning, unconsciously developed taste helps him blend European forms and techniques with the land- and commodity-based foods of the desert Southwest.

Drawing upon a wide range of culinary traditions gives Mason the freedom to be creative—something Utah's ever-growing foodie culture appreciates. Starting with the ingredients found in Native foods, like fry bread, blue corn tortillas, mutton, cactus, and squash, he makes subtle additions that enhance flavor. New Mexican and Mexican foods, like rice, beans, cotija cheese, and well-seasoned meats and stews, find their way into many of his dishes, with his favorite ingredient, Hatch green chili, taking a prominent place. His formal training in culinary school means that French- and Italian-style roux-based and ragu-style sauces also weigh into the mix.

Everything he cooks continues to be tweaked and modified—except for his mom's fry bread recipe. That bit of perfection remains unchanged. Made from flour, salt, and lard, some see fry bread as an oppressive part of Navajo culture because of its origins in government subsidies.[1] But today fry bread is an iconic part of Navajo foodways, and Mason knows how to feature it.

With attention to details, locally sourced ingredients, small-batch production, and the fusion of different culinary traditions, Mark Mason's Black Sheep Café both honors his own culinary heritage and answers the call of Utah's twenty-first-century culinary zeitgeist.

NOTE

1. Jen Miller, "Frybread: This Seemingly Simple Food Is a Complicated Symbol in Navajo Culture," *Smithsonian Magazine*, July 2008.

67

ARTISAN CHOCOLATE

CAROL A. EDISON

Char and Morgan Coleman, owners of Taste in downtown Provo, produce bean-to-bar artisan chocolate that is sold locally and internationally. Photo by Brandon Hansen, 2018. Courtesy Taste Artisan Chocolate.

It's probably not much of a surprise to Utahns that their love of sweet treats, and especially chocolate, has nurtured one of the most vibrant and innovative artisan chocolate industries in the country. Archaeologists have found traces of cacao in southeastern Utah's Ancestral Puebloan sites dating back to 780 AD, the earliest documented appearance of the bean in the United States.[1] Maybe it's just fate, but whatever the reason, the number and quality of small-batch producers is truly impressive.

Traveling across the planet to procure the finest ingredients directly from independent growers, Utah's artisan chocolatiers produce over four hundred different craft chocolates, one of the largest selections in the country.[2] They call themselves bean-to-bar chocolate makers and their numbers are growing.[3] And it's not only Utahns but chocolate connoisseurs everywhere who have recognized their success, lauding them with an impressive number of national and international awards.

Here is a list of some of Utah's earliest and most celebrated artisan chocolatiers.

- 2001 - Solstice Chocolates, Scott and DeAnn Querry, Salt Lake City[4]
- 2007 - Amano Artisan Chocolate, Art Pollard; Orem[5]
- 2010 - Ritual Chocolate, Robbie Stout and Anna Davies; Park City[6]
- 2010 - Crio Bru, Dr. Eric Durtschi; Lindon[7]
- 2011 - Millcreek Cacao Roasters, Dana Brewster and Mark DelVecchio; Salt Lake City[8]
- 2013 - The Chocolate Conspiracy, A. J. Wentworth; Salt Lake City[9]
- 2014 - Taste, Morgan Coleman, Char Coleman, and Phil Davis; Provo[10]

NOTES

1. David Landsel, "America's Artisan Chocolate Capital Is Probably Not Where You're Thinking," *Food and Wine*, last modified October 25, 2017, http://www.foodandwine.com/travel/americas-artisan-chocolate-capital-probably-not-where-youre-thinking.
2. Amber Gibson, "The Craft Chocolate Capital of America Is…Utah?" *Saveur*, last modified May 23, 2016, https://www.saveur.com/utah-craft-chocolate.
3. Kaitlyn Bancroft, "9 Utah Chocolate Makers Talk about Their Craft," *Deseret News* (Salt Lake City, UT), May 23, 2017.
4. "About Us," Solstice Chocolate, http://www.solsticechocolate.com/about-us/.
5. Amano Chocolate, http://www.amanochocolate.com/.
6. "About Ritual Chocolate," Ritual Chocolate, http://www.ritualchocolate.com/about-1/.
7. "Our Story," Crio Bru, https://www.criobru.com/about-us/.
8. Millcreek Cacao Roasters, http://www.millcreekcacao.com/.
9. The Chocolate Conspiracy, http://www.eatchocolateconspiracy.com/.
10. "Our Story," Taste Artisan Chocolate, https://havetaste.com/pages/our-story.

THE FRESH-MEX SKIRMISHES OF CAFÉ RIO AND COSTA VIDA

JILL TERRY RUDY

My first Café Rio experience was at a downtown Provo, Utah, restaurant now so defunct that the building has even been torn down. This sounds like a contemporary legend, but it's true: My sister's husband's cousins operated *The Roasted Artichoke* near Center Street and 500 West, and we gathered there one April evening to celebrate my sister's birthday. The food, I later learned, was not from that restaurant; it was burritos with rice and black beans all tucked inside a yummy flour tortilla, smothered in an even yummier mild green sauce, surrounded by leafy greens and pico de gallo, and served in a round aluminum pan. What sounds familiar now was completely novel then. My brother-in-law's brother worked for the Stanleys in St. George at the original Café Rio, and he provided the birthday celebration food. I had not eaten such delicious black beans since my LDS mission to Quetzaltenango, Guatemala. Discovering that Provo had its own Café Rio, I especially enjoyed the ritual question, "Black or pinto beans?" in my early years of eating at the first "fast casual" fresh Mexican grill in town.

Soon it was not the only fresh-Mex grill in town—Costa Azul[1] opened in the Fat Cats bowling alley on University Avenue in Provo. Rumors spread about the distinct similarities between the two establishments including menu, serving line, and even aluminum pans. The version I heard involved a former Café Rio employee stealing recipes and other trade secrets; I also heard that the good people my brother-in-law's brother had worked for sold Café Rio. The skirmish went public with the *Daily Herald* in Provo reporting on May 6, 2005, that Café Rio Inc. had sued Costa Azul Holdings LLC for unfair competition.[2] Similar to what I had heard, the lawsuit alleged that a fired Café Rio manager disclosed trade secrets. This fresh-Mex skirmish could be a fascinating case study for law students, historians, business executives, and marketing gurus because it involves court documents, innovative food presentation and business models, and word-of-mouth and social media advertising. Four interrelated areas infused by tradition spark my interest as a folklorist and make this skirmish important to Utah foodways: region, rumor, community, and creativity.

Café Rio and Costa Vida are not the only fresh-Mex grills presenting this eating model; Bajio and Barbacoa are two other chains associated with Utah that have similar food concepts, and the Denver-based Chipotle Mexican Grill and its burritos preceded Café Rio, opening in 1993. Founded in Utah in 1997 and 2003, respectively, Café Rio and Costa Vida remain particularly popular. They point to regions south of the border by their names, online origin stories, décor, and more. The official Café Rio website attributes the inspiration to the founding owners and the Southwest: "The Stanleys used inspired recipes and traditional cooking of Northern Mexico's Rio Grande, Southern Texas, and New Mexico."[3] Costa Vida develops more of an origin story and regional theme, attributing their Baja California décor to an influential vacation: "Following a trip to Cabo San Lucas on the Baja Coast, Costa Vida founders JD and Sarah Gardner were inspired with a vision. While the surf lapped at their feet and they enjoyed the delicious freshly made local cuisine, they brainstormed how they could bring this vibrant lifestyle and incredible cuisine home with them. The result was the first Costa Vida location in Layton, Utah."[4] Given the similarities of the foods and flavors, regionalism is more of a rhetorical framing device to imagine an eating experience than a name to indicate regional cuisines.

These fresh-Mex grills are not to be confused with Mexican restaurants or cooking, and they seldom are. Mostly, they carry Utah associations. A blog post from Orange County, California, questions

A delicious Café Rio copycat sweet pork dish by Favorite Family Recipes. Courtesy Favorite Family Recipes.

the similarities between Café Rio and Costa Vida by highlighting their Utah origins, querying tongue-in-blog, "How many Mexican chains they got over there [in Utah]?"[5] Still, a comment on this blog shows a representative lack of concern over regional authenticity or restaurant distinctions: "MikeHs, Nov 30, 2011, I really don't care how 'authentic' or 'corporate' Café Rio is—I like their food and am happy to eat there. I don't see any problem with their quality, so if Costa Vida is similar, so what?" Other conversations, in person and in cyberspace, take sides and discount the corporatized eating experience of such chain restaurants and their fabricated regionalism. This type of food and these eating establishments, however, remain popular throughout the West, and the continued expansion of stores, including into Canada and on the East Coast, would reward a cultural geographic study. As an imagined vacation or a trip to the local strip mall, some version of the West and Southwest informs Café Rio and Costa Vida, while Utah at the turn of the twenty-first century specifically enables this food.

In addition to regional indicators, narrative drives the intrigue of a shady relationship between Café Rio and Costa Vida, fueled by rumors and backstories. Rumors of corporate theft suggest the worldview and social structures that interest patrons.[6] Intrigue about possibly stolen trade secrets connects especially with issues of loyalty: brand loyalty, employer-employee loyalty, and even family fidelity. Indicating how stories of theft affect brand loyalty, a 2011 online post asserts, "I don't respect that Costa Vida stole EVERYTHING from Café Rio. For that reason alone I'll always support Café Rio."[7] Other online rumors develop a storyline that echoes information mentioned in the lawsuit: "Word on the street? One of the workers from Café Rio got mad at them and stole their recipes and started his own joint. Who knows if it's true, but the pork is suspiciously similar."[8] Rather than attributing this information to a newspaper account or the courts, this blogger suggests the person-to-person transmission of this information, calling it the "word on the street." Although only a sentence long, this version provides something that the newspaper account

didn't—a motive. The worker "got mad at them." Still, the news account gives a reason that could provoke anger: the employee was terminated. In other words, the similarities between Café Rio and Costa Vida practically require a narrative to give explanation, and rumors paired with actual events rise to the challenge.

Other accounts raise the stakes and suggest a worldview of conflicting family and corporate loyalties by making the employees relatives: brothers or spouses. One online post checks the rumor by asking, "Isn't the owner of Costa Vida the ex-wife of the owner of Café Rio?"[9] A post a few minutes later clarifies, "No. JD Gardners brother worked for Rio and left and decided to open up a knock off Rio and his brother (jd) bankrolled it all and is the owner."[10] Although none of the names reported in the lawsuit indicate that the original owners or employees were brothers, this story heightens disloyalty by making them related; the original question works with the interesting fact that both Café Rio and Costa Vida were founded by married couples. It does not take much interpretive license to connect the family-oriented rumor with LDS worldview and lifestyle; married couples and extended family groups are easy to identify as patrons of these establishments. Yet any good storyteller knows that making the antagonists siblings or spouses raises the conflict and suspense. In a measure, this is just great storytelling that happens to confirm the significance of family relationships.

Folklorists will tell you that storytelling affects brand loyalty and community creation. Marketers will tell you this too. A blogger links sibling rivalry and stolen trade secrets with an even more recognizable tradition: family recipe secrets. She writes,

OUR VERSION OF CAFÉ RIO'S CILANTRO-LIME RICE

1 c. uncooked rice (long-grain, white rice)
1 tsp. butter or margarine
2 cloves garlic, minced
1 tsp. freshly squeezed lime juice
1 can (15 oz.) chicken broth
1 c. water
1 Tbsp. freshly squeezed lime juice
2 tsp. sugar
3 Tbsp. fresh chopped cilantro

In a saucepan combine rice, butter, garlic, lime juice, chicken broth, and water. Bring to a boil. Cover and cook on low 15–20 minutes until rice is tender. Remove from heat. In a small bowl, combine remaining lime juice, sugar, and cilantro. Pour over hot cooked rice and mix in as you fluff the rice.[11]

"According to local lore, two brothers opened the restaurant and earned immediate fame with their pulled pork burritos. The pulled pork was so delicious because it was slow cooked in Dr. Pepper. But some family feud drove the two brothers apart, and one of the brothers opened a second, separate restaurant, Costa Vida, with a nearly identical menu, except that the pulled pork is soaked in Mr. Pibb."[12] In this case, the blogger indicates the brand loyalty could go either way: "Is this story true? I have no idea. The details are a little shaky (was Café Rio or Costa Vida the original? I'm not sure.) Regardless, the back story gives the brand some drama, and helps customers both remember and connect with it."[13] This rumor gives both establishments a story that connects with communities. My opening personal experience narrative likewise shows some of my

community affiliations with family, Provo, and Utah figuring prominently. The corporate websites include official origin stories and do not mention lawsuit rumors, to invite readers and patrons to join their conflict-free fresh-Mex communities. Tradition is at work here not only to identify regional cuisines and tell fascinating stories, but to build groups around influential experiences and crucial forms of expression such as eating and storytelling.

The implications of region, rumor, and community converge with the twin laws of folklore and secret recipes. Patrons express variation and repetition when they become do-it-yourselfers and recreate the recipes, often with the guidance of internet connections which are both technological and social. Pinterest pages, blogs, and cookbooks provide copycat recipes for these fresh-Mex chains. In contrast to the rumors and lawsuits over stolen recipes and food concepts, copycat recipes plaster the internet with the possibility of appropriating and remaking the fresh-Mex experience at home. Attribution and branding remain crucial to this creative process, which is what links the conservatism of tradition with its dynamism. The point is to make the recipes at home taste just like those that could be purchased in the eateries. The question becomes "Why go to this creative, possibly controversial effort, when you can go to Café Rio or Costa Vida?" Perhaps the stores are too far away, the cost is prohibitive for the group size, or the challenge of remaking the food is enticing. The blog site Favorite Family Recipes claims to have the first Café Rio pork copycat recipe, and the post about the recipe emphasizes accuracy: "I promise, we are VERY VERY picky about our Café Rio pork and this tasted EXACTLY like it."[14] There is a sense of a challenge successfully met and a mystery solved (this version uses Coke rather than the Dr. Pepper or Mr. Pibb of the rumors). Again, I write from experience. I have made a copycat Café Rio lime cilantro rice from a random website for an extended-family Christmas party. Perhaps in a culinary culture where the Christmas party food might replicate the traditional funeral luncheon, a little fresh-Mex—Utah-style—goes a long way toward linking places, stories, groups, and creativity. Or at least making those gatherings taste better.

NOTES

1. Later renamed Costa Vida because of Costa Azul trademarks out of state; Grace Leong, "Popular Café Rio Sues Rival Costa Azul," *Provo* (UT) *Daily Herald*, May 6, 2005.
2. Ibid. According to a 2013 *Salt Lake Tribune* report, the lawsuit was settled with undisclosed terms in 2007; Dawn House, "Costa Vida Restaurants Are Homegrown in Utah," *Salt Lake Tribune*, July 4, 2013.
3. http://www.caferio.com/our-story.
4. "Our Story," Costa Vida Fresh Mexican Grill, http://www.costavida.com/our-story/.
5. Edwin Goei, "Is Costa Vida Another Café Rio?" *OC Weekly*, November 30, 2011, http://blogs.ocweekly.com/stickaforkinit/2011/11/costa_vida_irvine.php.
6. Jon D. Lee, *An Epidemic of Rumors: How Stories Shape Our Perceptions of Disease* (Logan: Utah State University Press, 2014). Lee discusses differing views of medical experts, journalists, and lay people.
7. ChubbyChaser, "I don't respect that Costa Vida stole EVERYTHING," CougarBoard, Jan 20, 2011, http://www.cougarboard.com/board/message.html?id=6447543. Emphasis in original.
8. Kari, "Café Rio vs Costa Vida," *Gnome Place Like Home* (blog), June 7, 2006, http://shelikesgardengnomes.blogspot.com/2006/06/cafe-rio-vs-costa-vida.html.
9. mulletino, "Isn't the owner of Costa Vida the ex-wife of…," CougarBoard, January 20, 2011, http://www.cougarboard.com/board/message.html?id=6447558.
10. Blue Frog, "No. JD Gardners brother worked for Rio and left," CougarBoard, January 20, 2011, http://www.cougarboard.com/board/message.html?id=6447573.
11. Erica, "Our Version of Café Rio's Cilantro-Lime Rice and Black Beans," *Favorite Family Recipes* (blog), September 29, 2008, http://www.favfamilyrecipes.com/cafe-rio-cilantro-lime-rice-and-black.html.
12. Rikki Rogers, "What Cafe Rio can teach us about marketing," *Rikki writes* (blog), September 12, 2012, http://rikkiwrites.com/2012/09/02/what-cafe-rio-can-teach-the-marketing-world/.
13. Ibid. (But she does prefer Café Rio.)
14. Erica, "The Complete Cafe Rio Sweet Pork Salad Recipe," *Favorite Family Recipes* (blog), November 27, 2007, http://www.favfamilyrecipes.com/2007/11/jare.

69

HOMEMADE COSTA VIDA / CAFÉ RIO PORK

KYLIE SCHROEDER

Café Rio and Costa Vida (formally Costa Azul), Utah-based chains that offer Mexican-inspired fast-food cuisine, were founded in 1997 and 2003, respectively. In 2005, Café Rio "alleged in a 3rd District suit that Costa Vida franchises had wrongfully copied and used its 'trade secrets, menu, layout, food presentation, procedures and processes.'"[1] The lawsuit was settled in 2007, but stories still surrounded the two restaurants.

Some say that a former employee left the company and used trade secrets to open the new restaurant, while others speculate that the first restaurant was owned by a married couple and when they split up, the wife opened her own chain:

> "I had heard that a husband and wife started Café Rio. They divorced and one of them opened Costa Vida. Is this true? Might be why they taste the same to some." (username: jamaklo on PennyPincher)

> "Isn't the owner of Costa Vida the ex-wife of [the owner of Café Rio?]" (username: mulletino on CougarBoard)

CAFÉ RIO-STYLE SWEET BARBACOA PORK

7–8 lbs. boneless pork butt or shoulder (make a 3–4 lb. pork roast if you are just doing your family)
4 c. root beer
5 (8-oz.) cans tomato sauce
4 Tbsp. molasses or honey
3 tsp. minced garlic
1/2 tsp. salt
2–3 c. brown sugar
pepper to taste
4 tsp. cumin

Salt and pepper the pork and cook in crock pot 8 hours or overnight on low in a little water. In the morning remove the roast from the crockpot and pull apart with fork, removing fat. Drain all the water in the crockpot. Don't overshred the pork or it will turn mushy.

Add the rest of the ingredients to the crockpot and add the shredded pork. Stir to combine. Cook another 3–4 hours in crockpot on low. Serve with a slotted spoon.[2]

CAFÉ RIO COPYCAT PORK

Here is one copycat recipe for homemade Café Rio Sweet Pork Barbacoa with some popular variations included.[3]

2 lbs. boneless pork rib meat or pork butt
2–3 cans coke, NOT diet (Other copycat chefs suggest using root beer for the sweet flavor: "Rumor has it that Dr. Pepper or Coke are the preferred pops for Café Rio, but with [Old El Paso roasted garlic sauce], root beer seemed to bring out the best flavor.")
1/2 tsp. garlic salt
1/4 c. water
1 can diced green chilies
3/4 can (10 oz.) red enchilada sauce (if you use root beer instead of coke, consider using one Old El Paso roasted garlic sauce packet)
1 1/2 c. brown sugar

Put the pork in a heavy-duty Ziploc bag to marinate. Add about a can and a half of coke and about 1/4 cup brown sugar. Marinate for a few hours or overnight.

Drain marinade and put pork, 1/2 can of coke, water, and garlic salt in crock pot on high for about 3–4 hours (or until it shreds easily, but don't let it get too dry) or on low for 8 hours. Remove pork from crock pot and drain any liquid left in the pot. Shred pork.

In a food processor or blender, blend 1/2 can coke, chilies, enchilada sauce, and remaining brown sugar (about a cup, you can add a little more or less to taste). If it looks too thick, add more coke little by little.

Put shredded pork and sauce in crockpot and cook on low for 2 hours. That's it!

Both chains now operate nation-wide and each has its own loyal supporters. One menu item, Sweet Barbacoa Pork, is so popular that many people have dedicated time to finding the right mix of ingredients in an attempt to replicate the tasty dish.

NOTES

1. Dawn House, "Costa Vida Restaurants Are Homegrown in Utah," Salt Lake Tribune, July 4, 2013, https://archive.sltrib.com/story.php?ref=/56522679.
2. Christy Denney, "Café Rio's Sweet Pork Barbacoa," last modified October 22, 2008, https://www.thegirl-who-ate-everything.com/missing-cafe-rio/.
3. Recipe adapted from these websites: "Café Rio Sweet Pork Copycat Recipe," Favorite Family Recipes, http:// www.favfamilyrecipes.com/cafe-rio-sweet-pork.html. Jillee, "My Favorite Café Rio Copycat Recipes," One Good Thing by Jillee, last modified May 18, 2013, http://www.onegoodthingbyjillee.com/2013/05/my-favorite-cafe-rio-copycat-recipes.html; Sweet Basil, "Café Rio Sweet Pork," last modified September 11, 2013, http://www.ohsweetbasil.com/cafe-riosweet-pork.html.

70

FARMERS MARKETS

CAROL A. EDISON

The challenge of delivering fresh food to hungry customers is age-old. In nearly every culture from ancient times, market days, market stalls, or centrally located market structures, designating a time or place for farmers to bring their goods to concentrated populations, have provided the infrastructure for food delivery. In modern times, the development of refrigeration, transportation, corporate farms, and large marketing networks has taken over most of that process, especially in the United States. It became common practice for farmers to sell their products to cooperatives or wholesalers who could integrate their products into these supply chains.[1]

But the desire of farmers to deal directly with customers for the benefit of both parties persists. I remember hearing about street vendors, many of whom were Japanese, who sold vegetables in Salt Lake City suburbs in the late 1940s. Though I never witnessed that, I did experience the bounty of the roadside stands those same farm families operated in the 1950s and 1960s. As urban development eliminated more and more farm stands, the Utah Farm Bureau, an advocacy organization for agriculture, developed a new marketing strategy. In 1981, in response to member requests, the bureau established the Murray Farmers Market in the middle of Salt Lake Valley—a weekly summertime opportunity for farmers to sell fresh tomatoes, corn, peaches, and other produce directly to customers. A huge success, the market continues today and is larger than ever.[2]

In the 1990s, another outdoor market was started in Salt Lake's Pioneer Park, sponsored by the Downtown Alliance, an organization devoted to revitalizing the city. This was a time when outdoor markets were popping up in many urban areas across the country to discourage and displace unwanted activity in city centers. The Downtown Farmers Market was an immediate success. Coinciding with growing public awareness of the health and economic benefits of eating locally produced food and the foodie culture in general, it attracted not only conventional farmers and ranchers, but also producers of organic, specialty, and handcrafted foods. Adding vendors with ready-to-eat food, as well as craftspeople, booths for nonprofit organizations, and busking musicians helped create an atmosphere that made the market a communal gathering place and a weekly destination for many.[3] Around three hundred vendors and over two hundred thousand annual visitors make this the largest farm-to-table market in the state; its success also spawned an indoor wintertime market.[4]

Nowadays there are lively farmers markets taking place nearly every day of the week in city suburbs and small towns throughout Utah. Roughly 10 percent of Utah farms now sell freshly picked produce and grass-fed meat directly to consumers.[5] This trend also stimulated many food entrepreneurs to develop a range of small-batch offerings ranging from artisan cheeses and down-home jams to fresh-made pasta. Most importantly, the quality and variety of food consumed in Utah homes has increased because more than thirty seasonal or year-round markets offer consumers the opportunity to meet face-to-face with the producers who feed their families.[6]

NOTES

1. Among the food distribution companies in Utah are Greek-owned Kessimakis Produce and Nicholas & Co.; both have been in business since the 1930s. They help illustrate the surprisingly large role the Greek community plays in all aspects of Utah food culture. See Kessimakis Produce, http://www.kessimakispro.com/. See also Darby Doyle, "Bon Appetit: Celebrating Over a Century of Greek Culture and Cuisine in Utah," *Devour Utah* 2, no. 10 (October 2016): 37–38.
2. Utah Farm Bureau, www.utahfarmbureau.org.
3. Christopher Smart, "Downtown Farmers Market Kicks Off Its 25th Year with a Joyous, Splashy Occasion," *Salt Lake Tribune*, June 14, 2016.

Courtesy Downtown Alliance/Urban Food Connections of Utah.

4. Allison Einerson (market director), telephone conversation with the author, October 2016.
5. "Farmers Market Season Underway," Utah Department of Agriculture and Food, June 8, 2016, available online at https://web.archive.org/web/20161219214544/http://ag.utah.gov/home/blog/605-farmers-market-season-underway.html.
6. "Markets," Utah's Own, http://www.utahsown.org/Markets.

71

ARTISAN BEER AND CHEESE

KATHY STEPHENSON

While many Utah food traditions date back centuries to the American Indians and the Mormon pioneers, new food traditions have emerged in the Beehive State during the past few decades. There are two that might surprise many: beer and cheese.

BEER

Today, there are more than twenty craft breweries in Utah, brewing all kinds of beer styles from lagers and ales to porters and stouts. Some of the larger operations include Epic Brewing, Desert Edge, Red Rock, Shades of Pale, Squatters, and Uinta Brewing in Salt Lake City; Bohemian Brewery and Hoppers in Midvale; Wasatch Brewing in Park City; Rooster's Brewing in Ogden; and Moab Brewery.

"Ice-cold beer is probably not the first thing those outside the state think of when they talk about Utah," says Peter Cole, cofounder with Jeff Polychronis of Squatters Pub Brewery in Salt Lake City. "Not only does it make life a lot more pleasant, the industry employs a lot of people and has a positive effect on our tourism and the perception of the state."

In Utah during 2018, making, distributing, and selling beer provided 12,400-plus jobs, generated more than $227 million in federal, state, and local taxes, and had a total economic impact topping $1.6 billion, according to "Beer Serves America,"[1] a report that offers a snapshot of beer business in the United States.

Utah beer brewers are good at their jobs, as well, regularly winning gold, silver, and bronze medals at national and international competitions including the Great American Beer Festival and the World Beer Cup.

Souvenir pin honoring cheese production, 2002 Salt Lake Winter Olympics. Used by permission, Utah State Historical Society. All rights reserved.

Many times, the names of beer honor Utah's unique landmarks and landscapes, such as Uinta's King's Peak Porter and Epic's Spiral Jetty IPA; other times they celebrate the state's love of outdoor sports like Squatters's Full Suspension Pale Ale. But occasionally—as is the case of Wasatch Brewery's popular Polygamy Porter—they poke fun at Utah's Mormon culture.

As the craft brewing business has grown in Utah, it has sparked an interest in home brewing, which was mostly an underground hobby in Utah until 2009, when the state legislature made it legal. Since then, hobbyists, twenty-one years old or older, who produce less than one hundred gallons of wine or beer in a year for personal or family consumption, are exempt from state licensing requirements.

There are now several brewing clubs in Utah where amateurs meet other beer enthusiasts, learn the craft, and improve their skills. The number of beer supply stores in Utah has increased to handle the demand. There are also two statewide competitions that attract hundreds of home-brewing entries.

Courtesy Beehive Cheese Co.

CHEESE

In the last decade, the number of artisan cheesemakers in Utah has also bloomed. Today, artisan producers make all kinds of award-winning cheeses from cheddar and Gouda to feta and Parmesan.

Some of Utah's most popular makers include Beehive Cheese in Uintah, Drake Family Farms in West Jordan, Gold Creek Farms in Woodland, Heber Valley Artisan Cheese in Midway, Oolite Cheese in Manti, and Rockhill Creamery in Richmond.

These Utah cheesemakers didn't have to go far to learn their craft, as Utah State University's Western Dairy Center in Logan is one of the nation's leading centers for dairy food research. It offers cheese-making courses and educational assistance for these small producers.

Cache Valley, where USU is located, has a long history of cheese making. The Mormon pioneers who settled the valley likely used the milk from their cows to make butter, cream, and cheese. But

A selection of local craft brews, highlighting the diversity of contemporary offerings. Photo by Lynne S. McNeill, 2018.

it became big business in 1941, when Edwin Gossner, a Swiss immigrant, opened Gossner Cheese in Logan. Within five years it had become the largest Swiss cheese–making factory in the world. Every day it produced 120 wheels of cheese weighing two hundred pounds each.

Today, the Utah cheese-making tradition continues. Utah cheesemakers are regular medal winners at the World Cheese Awards and at the annual competition sponsored by the American Cheese Society. Some are farmstead cheesemakers who raise the cows, sheep, and goats that supply the milk for their cheese, while others buy milk from small nearby dairies. Either way, these cheeses have a unique Utah flavor.

Take for instance Beehive Cheese's Aggiano cheese. Named for the Utah State University Aggies, it is made from the milk of the Jersey cows from

Ogden's Wadeland South Dairy. The cows graze near the salty marshes, ponds, and mudflats of the mineral-loaded soil of the Great Salt Lake.

About 150 miles away at Manti's Oolite cheese company, sheep's milk blue cheese is aged on oolite stone that is quarried in the nearby canyons. It is the same stone that the pioneers used to build Manti's Mormon temple and many local homes.

And in Richmond, the Rockhill Creamery sits on a farm that dates back to 1895. The owners, Pete Schropp and Jennifer Hines, have received national recognition for preserving the historical buildings where they now make several varieties of aged cows' milk cheeses—about two hundred pounds a week. The farm is also the site of a weekly summer farmers market.

NOTE

1. "State & Congressional District Data," Beer Serves America, http://beerservesamerica.org/.

72

SODA POP WARS

BRANT ELLSWORTH

In 2010, entrepreneur Nicole Tanner opened a small, drive-through drink shop near Dixie State University in St. George, Utah. Her store, Swig, sold ice cream, snow cones, sugar cookies, and flavor-infused fountain drinks Tanner called "dirty" soda. This borrowed terminology, evoking both espresso drinks and cocktails, offers Utah Mormons the opportunity to partake in their own version of mixology. These dirty sodas, such as "Dirty Diet Coke" and "Dirty Dr. Pepper" (made by mixing fruit syrups and half-and-half into fountain drinks), caught on, inspiring a new business model across the region. These drinks rapidly became a statewide obsession in a heavily Mormon state where alcohol and coffee consumption is eschewed and sugar is the vice of choice.

The rise in popularity of "dirty" sodas in Utah coincided with a 2012 announcement made by the LDS Church clarifying its stance on the Word of Wisdom and the consumption of caffeinated beverages. In many Mormon circles, drinking caffeinated sodas had been seen as taboo. However, after photographs surfaced of Republican presidential nominee and well-known Mormon Mitt Romney celebrating his sixty-sixth birthday with a Diet Coke in hand, the LDS Church clarified its position with an online statement: "The Church does not prohibit the use of caffeine." This announcement led many Latter-day Saints to conclude the consumption of caffeinated beverages was no longer taboo.

In 2013, Sodalicious, Swig's major competitor in the Provo/Orem region, opened, offering drink options whose names reflect Utah Mormon culture, especially Mormon dating, courtship, and marriage culture. Sodalicious offers the "Second Wife," a drink blending Mountain Dew, blood orange syrup, and mango syrup, a gentle dig at Mormons' contentious history with plural marriage; the "Eternal Companion," a mix of 7-Up, blue curacao syrup, and peach syrup, referencing a common phrase in Mormonism that derives from the belief in eternal marriages; and the "NCMO" (pronounced "nick-mow"), a mix of Code Red Mountain Dew, red raspberry syrup, and pineapple syrup, whose name is a colloquial acronym for "non-committal make-out," the Mormon version of "hooking-up."

In April 2014, as the competition increased and prospered (in addition to Sodalicious's three

DIRTY DIET COKE
(MAKES 1 SERVING)

2 Tbsp. coconut syrup
Crushed ice
1/2 lime (cut into quarters)
12 oz. Diet Coke
1 1/2 Tbsp. half-and-half

Pour coconut syrup into a 24-ounce glass. Fill it about halfway with crushed ice. Squeeze the lime quarters over the ice and drop them into the glass. Pour the Diet Coke over the limes. Stir in half-and-half. Enjoy!

Courtesy Sodalicious.

locations, Utah now includes start-ups like Bev's, Chugz, Fitz, Fryz, Pop Shop, Sip-It, Sip-N, The Slurp, Slurps' Up, Soda Pop Culture, and Straws), Swig took legal action against Sodalicious, claiming that they use the copyrighted term "dirty" and took other aspects of Swig's business concept. Sodalicious maintains that "dirty" drinks predate Swig's copyright, citing the dirty martini as an example of a traditional drink that existed long before the commercial success of the "Dirty Diet Coke." While the courts may ultimately decide the outcome of the "dirty" legal battle between the two companies, Swig's legal action has sparked passionate reactions from both brands' loyal customers, inspiring many to take to social media to support their favorite and criticize the other. Many Utahns, however, ignore the fight and continue to line up with punch cards in hand to get their next caffeine and sugar fix.[1]

NOTES
1. For further reading, please see the following:
    Amy McDonald, "Playing 'Dirty': Inside the Fizzy, Sugary Rise of Soda Shops in Utah," *Salt Lake Tribune*, September 14, 2015; Amy McDonald, "Utah Soda Drinkers Lash Out at Swig on Social Media After Hearing About Suit Against Sodalicious," *Salt Lake Tribune*, September 15, 2015; Julie Turkewitz, "In Utah Feud Over 'Dirty' Sodas, Flavored Darts Are Fixed," *New York Times*, November 29, 2015; Peggy Fletcher Stack, "OK, Mormons, Drink Up—Coke and Pepsi Are OK," *Salt Lake Tribune*, September 5, 2012.

73

PIE AND BEER DAY

LYNNE S. MCNEILL

Some of the entries in Joanna Zatterio's 2016 Pie and Beer Day pie baking contest.
Courtesy Lynne S. McNeill.

On July 24 every year, Utah Mormons commemorate the 1847 arrival of the first Mormon pioneers into the Salt Lake Valley with a celebration, Pioneer Day, that rivals typical Fourth of July festivities in other parts of the country. On the same day, many Utah non-Mormons celebrate "Pie and Beer Day,"[1] a gently parodic holiday that pairs local brews with pies (and sometimes pizza pies). Pie and Beer Day's origins are appropriately shrouded in mystery; most believe that the custom began in the early or mid-2000s. The Utah Beer Blog explains that the holiday's origins were rooted in inclusiveness, giving non-Mormon Utahns a sense of regional connection to an otherwise religion-specific celebration. As blogger Mikey explains, non-LDS folks "may understand why some find [July 24] important, but for the most part it feels like a waste of a free day. Pie and Beer Day was created as a counter culture alternative for the people that don't fit into the established green jello and handcart mold that has been around for generations."[2]

On a small scale, family and friend groups plan their own celebrations, some with competitions for the best pie and beer pairing. Local breweries and bars have begun to get in on the action, too, holding events and fundraisers that build on the grassroots enthusiasm for the new festival. KRCL, a local radio station in Salt Lake City, managed to raise $8,000 with its 2014 Pie 'n' Beer Day event, where bakers donated

Utah is the second-largest producer of tart cherries in the nation. Before dried cherries became popular, almost all of the crop was turned into pie filling. Cherry pie souvenir pin, 2002 Salt Lake Winter Olympics. Used by permission, Utah State Historical Society. All rights reserved.

pies to be served at a local beer bar.

JOIN US FOR A
PIE BAKING CONTEST
In Observance of Pie and Beer Day 2016
HOSTED BY THE NATIONAL BAKED PIE HOLES COUNCIL

Sunday, July 24 from 6:00 to 8:00 pm. Pie judging begins at 6:30 pm, prizes awarded at 7:00 pm. Pie eating to follow.

TO ENTER YOUR PIE:
Contact Joanna at 509-531-4222 or joanna.zattiero@gmail.com
RSVP by July 20 to Joanna so that you can reserve your spot as a baker, judge, pie eater, or beer drinker!

Photo by Lynne S. McNeill, 2016.

NOTES

1. Sometimes written as "Pie 'n' Beer Day" to emphasize the similarity in sound to "Pioneer Day."
2. Ric Wayman, "'Pie and Beer Day'? A Made Up Holiday for the Rest of Utah," *St. George News*, July 24, 2017.

74

REFUGEE FOODWAYS

Nourishing a Sense of Place

ADRIENNE CACHELIN

"Eating is nothing but sharing cultures."[1]

These are the words of a Palestinian refugee and active participant in a community kitchen in Salt Lake City's Glendale neighborhood. Haytham Ibrahim understands that food nourishes more than our physical bodies.

While we don't often think about it, our choices and traditions around food tell the story of who we are and where we've been. Cooking and sharing food are critical parts of our identity, describing a set of social and ecological relationships that are often geographically based. In a world with increasing displacement, and at a time when the number of people forced from their homes because of political, economic, and environmental collapse has never been higher, food practices take on new significance.[2] Worldwide, one of every 122 of us is now a refugee, internally displaced, or seeking asylum, and these numbers are predicted to increase.[3]

In many ways, refugees are the face of the new West. In Utah alone, sixty thousand refugees have been resettled at a rate of about a thousand individuals per year.[4] While this influx infuses and enhances Utah's foodscape with an abundance of exotic foods and cultural practices around food, there is the very real threat that refugees' foodways will be crushed under the weight of acculturation and the financial realities of resettlement.

Ninety percent of Utah refugees settle in the Salt Lake Valley, and most often in places where access to healthy food is compromised[5]—places the U.S. Department of Agriculture calls food deserts. We know that healthful diets often deteriorate as acculturation progresses.[6] This interruption of foodways, combined with both a Western narrative of eating subsidized "nutrients" and junk-food marketing that targets minority communities, may be the largest threat to traditional food practice.[7] So how can we hold onto the magic of diverse foodways and ensure refugee nourishment in the broadest sense of the word?

Community kitchens, incubator kitchens, and community gardens are just some of the successful strategies in place in Utah. These efforts are incredibly important to healthy resettlement when we recognize that foodways signify cultural continuity,[8] serve as a way to exert control during times when individuals lack control, and provide psychological comfort.[9]

Amazing things are happening at the Glendale Community Learning Center Kitchen in Salt Lake City, for example. In this community space, "diverse individuals…connect, and relish the importance of sharing food despite living in a neighborhood with a broken food system."[10] The stories told there are as rich and diverse as the food itself. Kitchen users describe the ways their direct dependence on the physical landscape—growing what was needed—has changed; they describe cooking and eating as group activities from which no one was excluded at home, and note how sharing the flavors of their home with new neighbors and coworkers has served to create and strengthen relationships.[11] In this kitchen, in dialogue with its users, we see how food confers a sense of place no longer fully dependent on immediate geographies.

Both the International Rescue Committee's (IRC) New Roots Program and the Wasatch Community Gardens celebrate the wisdom and talents

Two Karen refugees, originally from Burma, tending to their peas in the refugee garden organized by the Cache Refugee and Immigrant Connection (CRIC) in Logan, Utah. CRIC now has over twenty families, mainly people from the different ethnic groups of Burma, working in the garden, which officially began in 2015. Photo by Nelda Ault, 2016.

A program for refugees in the Glendale area of Salt Lake City resulted in the 2015 publication of this "cookbook." It features twelve cooks from countries as far-flung as Nepal, Tonga, Brazil, Thailand, and Palestine and is more about the cooks and their stories than it is about the recipes. Courtesy Adrienne Cachelin.

LU PULU

(SERVES 8-12)

"A savory spinach, onion, and corned beef casserole served with baked plantains and a coconut milk drizzle." This recipe makes two versions of Lu Pulu—you can make one or both.

2 bunches of fresh spinach
2 bunches of frozen spinach
1 large can New Zealand corned beef, broken up into small pieces
2 onions, finely chopped
1 can coconut milk
1/2 c. shredded cheese (any semihard cheese that melts well), optional
6 plantains, halved

Preheat oven to 400 degrees F.

In a 9-by-13-inch baking dish, layer 1 bundle of fresh spinach, 1/4 onion, 1/2 can of corned beef, and 1/2 can of coconut milk.

Add another bundle of spinach, 1/4 onion, and 1/2 can milk.

Use another 9-by-13-inch baking dish to make a similar Lu Pulu dish, only this time you'll use the frozen spinach. (This dish is best utilized when fresh ingredients are unavailable.)

Layer 1 bundle of frozen spinach, the rest of the corned beef, and 1/4 onion.

Add the remaining frozen spinach and onions on top. You may sprinkle the cheese on top if desired.

Bake for 1 1/2 hours at 400 degrees F.

Boil plantains for 30–40 minutes, or until cooked. Drain the water and set aside.

Once the baking dishes are cooked, remove and let cool. Serve with plantain drizzled with the remaining coconut milk.[12]

program as one that is "about healthy families, secure communities and a more sustainable future. It's about dignity, determination and the boundless possibility of human connection."[13] The Spice incubator kitchen goes one step further, providing access to a commercial kitchen and business training, thus removing many of the financial barriers that exist for budding refugee food entrepreneurs.

Because food provides a unique and powerful point of entry into building community, these kitchens and gardens play a pivotal role in maintaining comprehensive health. They provide space for developing a collective consciousness, for respecting and understanding other cultures, and for nurturing a different way of being in the world. Cooking can be an act of resistance: resistance against placelessness, against isolation, and against the cheap and unhealthy calories wrought by the corporatization of food. Maintaining foodways, even those shaped by displacement and colonization, is a basic element of justice, one that nourishes the placemaking that is so essential for revitalizing our communities and ourselves.

NOTES

1. Haytham Ibrahim, *Savor: Stories of Community, Culture, & Food*, ed. A. Cachelin (Salt Lake City: Salt Lake Education Foundation, 2015), 19.
2. Tim Gaynor, "2015 Likely to Break Records for Forced Displacement—Study," United Nations High Commissioner for Refugees, December 18, 2015, http://www.unhcr.org/5672c2576.html.
3. Ibid.
4. Paige Keiter, producer, *Finding Home: Utah's Refugee Story*, PBS video, 27:47, http://www.kued.org/whatson/kued-local-productions/finding-home-utahs-refugee-story.
5. SLCGreen, "Salt Lake City Community Food

of refugees as well, providing spaces for growing, cooking, and sharing food. The IRC describes their

Assessment," 2010, http://www.slcdocs.com/slcgreen/CommunityFoodAssessment.pdf.

6. G. X. Ayala et al., "A Systematic Review of the Relationship between Acculturation and Diet among Latinos in the United States: Implications for Future Research," *Journal of the American Dietetic Association* 108, no. 8 (2008): 1330–44.

7. A. Freeman, "Fast Food: Oppression through Poor Nutrition," *California Law Review* 95, no. 6 (2007): 2221–60.

8. G. Sabar and R. Posner, "Remembering the Past and Constructing the Future over a Communal Plate," *Food, Culture, & Society: An International Journal of Multidisciplinary Research* 16, no. 2 (2013): 197–222.

9. A. Locher et al., "Comfort Foods: An Exploratory Journey into the Social and Emotional Significance of Food," *Food and Foodways: Explorations in the History and Culture of Human Nourishment* 13, no. 4 (2005): 273–97.

10. K. Harrington and M. McIntyre, *Savor: Stories of Community, Culture, & Food*, ed. A. Cachelin (Salt Lake City: Salt Lake Education Foundation, 2015).

11. Ibrahim, *Savor.*

12. From Harrington and McIntyre, *Savor.*

13. International Rescue Committee, Overview of New Roots Program, http://www.rescue.org/us-program/us-salt-lake-city-ut/new-roo.

INDEX OF RECIPES

CONTRIBUTORS

David A. Allred is professor of English and philosophy at Snow College, where he serves as department chair and teaches composition, literature, and folklore. He is a former board chair of Utah Humanities and a past director of the Snow College Honors Program. He earned a PhD from the University of Missouri, specializing in folklore and English.

Elizabeth Archuleta, associate chair of Ethnic Studies in the School of Cultural and Social Transformation at the University of Utah, has published on American Indian literature in scholarly journals and edited collections. In her down time, she's a fan of science fiction and fantasy novels and Marvel television and movies.

Curtis Ashton was born in Salt Lake City and grew up in Utah County. He studied folklore and library science at Indiana University. He is a curator for historic sites of the Church of Jesus Christ of Latter-day Saints and teaches humanities classes at Utah Valley University.

Nelda R. Ault-Dyslin, who considers herself a "stealth folklorist," works at Utah State University, guiding students to engage with the Cache Valley community through service. She is also a founding member of the Cache Refugee and Immigrant Connection, a nonprofit that assists northern Utah's newest residents.

Roger G. Baker was associate professor of English at Brigham Young University and emeritus professor at Snow College. Having earned a doctorate in educational psychology, he taught Bible as literature and a variety of other composition, literature, and education classes. He spent his adult life in Sanpete County and passed away in 2017.

Elaine Bapis is a lifetime educator with a master's degree in English and a PhD in American history. In her article, she combines her background in cultural history with her culinary skills, learned in a household where hospitality and the family meal were a way of life.

Kristi A. Bell is the retired curator of the William A. Wilson Folklore Archive at the L. Tom Perry Special Collections in the Harold B. Lee Library at Brigham Young University. She holds a BA and MA in English from BYU.

Benjamin Bombard is a writer and a producer of RadioWest on KUER 90.1. A self-trained chef, he cooked his first full Thanksgiving dinner when he was sixteen years old and has since worked at restaurants and cafes across the country. He and his wife live in Salt Lake City, mere blocks from where they both grew up. The kitchen is the heart of their home.

Erica VanAmen Brown serves as the chief marketing officer at Thanksgiving Point, a 501(c)3 nonprofit farm, garden, and museum complex located in Lehi, Utah. In 2014, she helped found the Utah Foods Cook-Off, an annual cooking competition held around Pioneer Day.

Adrienne Cachelin is a faculty member with the Environmental and Sustainability Studies program at the University of Utah. She also serves as the university's director of Sustainability Education and the Bennion Center's Community Engaged Faculty Fellow. Adrienne is committed to community-engaged research in the areas of environmental and food justice.

Brock Cheney (MA American Studies, Utah State University) is the author of *Plain but Wholesome: Foodways of the Mormon Pioneers* (University of Utah, 2012). He teaches writing and literature at Box Elder High School in Brigham City, Utah, and has worked at several living history museums. He lives in Willard, Utah, where he tends a vegetable garden, tests historical recipes, and bakes bread in a wood-fired brick oven.

Danille Elise Christensen holds a PhD in folklore from Indiana University and is assistant professor in the Department of Religion and Culture at Virginia Tech, where she is faculty in the Material Culture and Public Humanities graduate program. Her

work explores the rhetorical positioning of vernacular knowledge, skills, and creativity.

Michael Christensen grew up in Logan, Utah, where he attended Utah State University, sadly never becoming a True Aggie. After a few years of teaching he joined the Utah Cultural Celebration Center where he is a folklorist disguised as the Visual and Performing Arts manager for West Valley City's Division of Arts and Culture.

Frank Christianson is a professor of English at Brigham Young University where he has taught since 2002. His research and teaching interests include Transatlantic Literary History and the literature of the American West. He began working for Apple Beer in 1997 as a graduate student. He continues to manage production and distribution for the company.

Elaine Clark is a radio and documentary film producer for RadioWest on KUER, NPR Utah. She studied folklore and Germanic studies at Indiana University and earned a master's degree in Middle East studies from the University of Utah. She lives in Salt Lake City.

Christine Cooper-Rompato is an associate professor of English at Utah State University where she teaches medieval literature. Her research interests include medieval religious literature (specifically sermons and saints' lives), the history of mathematics and technology, and nineteenth-century U.S. history. She coedits the *Journal of Medieval Religious Cultures*.

Melissa Coy is an archivist and historian in Salt Lake City and has been a curator with the Utah Division of State History since 2004. Despite an interest in the history of food and the body, Melissa does not like to cook.

Dennis Cutchins is a professor of English at Brigham Young University. In 2018 he coedited the *Routledge Companion to Adaptation* and *Adapting Frankenstein: The Monster's Eternal Lives in Popular Culture* (Manchester University Press, 2018). He is currently working on ways to apply cognitive brain research to adaptation studies.

Lisa Duskin-Goede received a master of science in American Studies and Public Folklore at Utah State University in 2004. She is an avid fieldworker, traveling throughout the Intermountain West to document cultural heritage and the people who shape it. Currently, she coordinates the programs of the Bear River Heritage Area in Logan, Utah, where her research has been used in the development of heritage tourism, and educational programs and publications.

Carol A. Edison retired as director of the Folk Arts Program of the Utah Arts Council in 2011. For thirty-three years she conducted field work in Utah's Native American, rural, occupational, and ethnic communities, producing exhibits, concerts, festivals, audiovisual productions, and publications, including *Cowboy Poetry from Utah: An Anthology* (Utah Folklife Center, 1985) and *Willow Stories: Utah Navajo Baskets* (Utah Arts Council, 1996). Edison is a recipient of the American Folklore Society's Benjamin A. Botkin Prize for lifetime achievement in public folklore.

Eric A. Eliason is a professor of folklore at Brigham Young University and former chaplain for the 1st Battalion, 19th Special Forces Group (Airborne). His books include *The J. Golden Kimball Stories* (University of Illinois Press, 2007); *Latter-day Lore: Mormon Folklore Studies* (with Tom Mould, University of Utah Press, 2013); *The Island of Lace: Drawn Threadwork on Saba in the Dutch Caribbean* (with Scott Squire, University Press of Mississippi, 2019), and *Hammerhead Six: How Green Berets Waged an Unconventional War Against the Taliban to Win in Afghanistan's Pech Valley* (with Tad Tuleja and Ronald Fry, Hachette, 2016).

Brant Ellsworth is an assistant professor of humanities at Central Penn College in Summerdale, Pennsylvania. He is the editor of the *Children's Folklore Review* and president of the Eastern American Studies Association. He remains skeptical of Jell-O molds.

Spencer Green is a teaching professor at Pennsylvania State University–Harrisburg. His research examines the folklore of Latter-day Saint adolescents as well as Americans' experience with and conception of nature.

Lyman Hafen is the author of a dozen books intent on connecting landscape and story in the American Southwest. He is executive director of the Zion National Park Forever Project and is past president of the national Public Lands Alliance. He's been writing and publishing for more than thirty-five years and was founding editor of *St. George Magazine*.

He's won literary awards from the Utah Arts Council, as well as the Wrangler Award from the National Cowboy and Western Heritage Museum. He lives in Santa Clara, Utah, with his wife, Debbie.

Jean Tokuda Irwin was born in Yokohama, Japan. The family's beloved housekeeper, Onishisan, taught her to cook and to feed the eye, soul, and body. She is a board member of the Salt Lake City Nikkei Center that serves a monthly luncheon to Japanese seniors. On Christmas Eve she always leaves Santa three or five inarizushi, never four.

Robert King is on the English and American Studies faculty for Utah State University. His current research emphasis is on religious experience in American modernity, thus his studious engagement with Dutch-oven cooking and other foodway forms of communion.

Jean Little has an MA in English from Brigham Young University (2016) and is currently a PhD student at the University of California–Irvine, specializing in history of math and science, aestheticism, and theory of the novel. Her current project focuses on portrayals of the infinite in eighteenth- and nineteenth-century literature.

Barbara Lloyd, a native Utahn, lived in Salt Lake throughout her girlhood and in Cache Valley for nearly three decades. Her professional career as a folklorist includes editing, archiving, writing, teaching, and database management. During leisure time, she enjoys long walks and dabbling in fiber arts. She lives in Ohio.

Kathryn L. MacKay earned her PhD from the University of Utah and is currently a professor of history and the director of the public history program at Weber State University. She serves on the Ogden City Landmarks Commission and on the boards of Brigham City Art and History Museum and the Weber County Heritage Foundation.

Kimberly Jenkins Marshall is associate professor of anthropology at the University of Oklahoma. She researches the poetics and politics of expressive culture and religious shift in Native North America. Her book *Upward, Not Sunwise: Resonant Rupture in Navajo Neo-Pentecostalism* was published in 2016 by the University of Nebraska Press. Beverly and Elaine Joe (both Navajo) live in a rural community in the northern part of the Navajo Nation near Shiprock, New Mexico, where they are active participants in the Oodláni (Believers) religious movement. Their mutton stew is excellent.

Amy Maxwell-Howard received a BA in anthropology from Brigham Young University in 2009 and an MA in American studies and folklore from Utah State University in 2014. Over the last five years, she has worked on multiple folklife documentation projects in Utah, Idaho, and Oregon in addition to teaching at Idaho State University. She and her family currently live in Atlanta, Georgia.

Heather May is an award-winning freelance writer based in Salt Lake City with twenty years of experience, including fifteen years covering education, politics, health, and food at the *Salt Lake Tribune*.

She is a graduate of the University of Utah in mass communication.

Ted McDonough, a Utah native, was a newspaper reporter at the *Salt Lake City Weekly*, where his contribution to this book originally appeared as "Greeks Bearing Burgers."

Lynne S. McNeill holds a PhD in folklore from Memorial University of Newfoundland and serves as chair of the Folklore Program in the English Department at Utah State University. Her research interests include legend, belief, fandom, and digital culture. She serves on the boards of the Western States Folklore Society and the International Society for Contemporary Legend Research and is reviews editor for the journal *Contemporary Legend*. She has made several appearances on national television and radio programs, and she is the author of the popular textbook *Folklore Rules*, published by USU Press in 2013.

Edith Mitko, an educator from both higher education (Salt Lake Community College and director of student services at Utah System of Higher Education) and public education (special-education teacher for seventh, eighth, and ninth grades), was appointed by Governor Leavitt to serve in Utah's Ethnic Affairs Office as the director of Asian Affairs. She is now enjoying retirement via travel with her grandchildren.

Dean G. Morris grew from generations of plant farmers and foragers and was certified a Master Herbalist in 1997 and granted full practicing privileges in the Center for Alternative Medicine at a Columbia Hospital in Miami Beach, Florida. He directed product research and development for Schwabe North America Phytopharmaceuticals. He continues to train foraging and herb usage worldwide with Nebo Health in Springville, Utah.

Eruera "Ed" Bryers Arena-Napia is from the Te Whiu, Te Honihoni, and Te Popoto Hapu (sub-tribes) of the Ngapuhi Iwi (tribe) from Aotearoa–New Zealand. Eruera has lived in Los Angeles, Utah, and Hawaii where he worked at the Polynesian Cultural Center. Currently he works in Utah in health promotion and disease prevention and is a clay artist.

Valerie Phillips has spent over twenty-five years exploring Utah's culinary scene, as a former food editor for both the *Deseret News* and the *Ogden Standard-Examiner*, and now as a popular blogger at Chewandchat.com. She authored the cookbooks *Soup's On! 100 Savory Soups, Stews and Chilis Made Easy* (Covenant Communications, 2012) and *Dining by the Decades: Foods that Defined the 20th Century* (*Ogden Standard-Examiner*, 2000), and her freelance work has appeared in the *New York Times*, *Utah Life*, *Wasatch View*, *Devour*, and *Food Network Magazine*. She holds a bachelor's degree from Utah State University.

Sally Haueter Rampe is a descendant of Utah pioneers and a graduate of USU's Folklore Program. Inspired by her family history, she has collected oral histories in Utah's Wasatch County and the Bear River Heritage Area. Former program coordinator for the National Council for the Traditional Arts, program manager for the Western Folklife Center, and artistic director for the American West Heritage Center, she currently lives with her family in Woodland Park, Colorado, where she enjoys volunteering her time teaching folklore to elementary school kids.

Jill Terry Rudy, associate professor of English at Brigham Young University, edited *The Marrow of Human Experience: Essays on Folklore* by William A. Wilson (Utah State University Press, 2006) and coedited *Channeling Wonder* with Pauline Greenhill (Wayne State University Press, 2014). *The Routledge Companion to Media and Fairy-Tale Cultures*, coedited with Greenhill, Naomi Hamer, and Lauren Bosc, was published in 2018.

Kylie Schroeder received her MA in folklore from Utah State University's English Department in 2018. Originally from Wisconsin, she completed her undergraduate degrees in anthropology, folklore, Celtic studies, and religious studies from the University of Wisconsin–Madison in 2014. Past research has focused on variations of cultural heritage tourism.

Steve Siporin is a retired professor of folklore with a special interest in Italian and Jewish folklore and culture. He taught at Utah State University for thirty years.

Kathy Stephenson is a Utah native and University of Utah graduate. She has been a reporter at the *Salt Lake Tribune* for more than thirty years. She writes about food, dining, alcohol policy, and other topics. For fun, she reads, hikes, gardens, attempts yoga, and cooks recipes that celebrate her Greek heritage.

Elaine Thatcher, who has an MA from Utah State University, has worked closely with many ethnic, occupational, and geographic communities of the West. She was the 2006 recipient of the Benjamin A. Botkin Prize given by the American Folklore Society for outstanding achievement in public folklore.

Linda Thatcher is a historian, and retired from the Utah Division of State History as the collections manager. Her publications include *Differing Visions: Dissenters in Mormon History* (with Roger D. Launius, University of Illinois Press, 1994) and *Women in Utah History: Paradigm or Paradox?* (with Patricia Lyn Scott, Utah State University Press, 2005).

Rosa Thornley completed her master's degree in American Studies and Folklore at Utah State University where she teaches The Farm in Literature and Culture. Her research interests are marriage rites in shivaree and quilt communities on social media. She is also a consultant for a Utah-based transportation company in the food industry.

Jacqueline S. Thursby (PhD) was a folklore, cultural studies, and secondary education faculty member in the BYU English Department for twenty years. Now retired, she lives in Provo with her husband and enjoys many interests including sixteen grandchildren, cooking, gardening, reading, writing, artwork, travel, volunteer work, and family history.

Patty Timbimboo-Madsen, born in Ogden, Utah, to Frank and Helen (Pubigee) Timbimboo, is a member of the Northwestern Band of Shoshone. Patty has spent the last twenty-one years as the Cultural/Natural Resource Manager for the tribe and is a passionate advocate for the culture of her tribe to help maintain, preserve, and educate members and others.

Ronda Walker Weaver was raised in rural Idaho. Her parents owned family-style restaurants, and her father was a Mormon bishop; food and service were always entwined. Ronda and her husband seldom pass up an opportunity to keep this legacy alive. Ronda teaches composition and works as a healthcare chaplain in Utah Valley.

Randy Williams is emerita faculty at Utah State University, where she served as the Fife Folklore Archives curator. She directed Northern Utah Speaks, a bold, collaborative oral history initiative focused on gathering, preserving, and presenting the voices of the people and heritage of the Intermountain West, especially the historically excluded. She is currently the chair of Utah Humanities.

Nora Zambreno put her folklore studies and field work in foodways and rural culture to work at Utah Public Radio where she helped organize special events and provide community outreach for seventeen years. Among her favorite projects is a cookbook comprised of recipes from station members across Utah.